Revolution and Its Alternatives

Studies in Critical Social Sciences Book Series

Haymarket Books is proud to be working with Brill Academic Publishers (www.brill.nl) to republish the *Studies in Critical Social Sciences* book series in paperback editions. This peer-reviewed book series offers insights into our current reality by exploring the content and consequences of power relationships under capitalism, and by considering the spaces of opposition and resistance to these changes that have been defining our new age. Our full catalog of *SCSS* volumes can be viewed at https://www.haymarketbooks.org/series_collections/4-studies-in-critical-social-sciences.

Series Editor
David Fasenfest (SOAS University of London)

Editorial Board
Eduardo Bonilla-Silva (Duke University)
Chris Chase-Dunn (University of California–Riverside)
William Carroll (University of Victoria)
Raewyn Connell (University of Sydney)
Kimberlé W. Crenshaw (University of California–LA and Columbia University)
Heidi Gottfried (Wayne State University)
Karin Gottschall (University of Bremen)
Alfredo Saad Filho (King's College London)
Chizuko Ueno (University of Tokyo)
Sylvia Walby (Lancaster University)
Raju Das (York University)

Revolution and Its Alternatives

Other Marxisms, Other Empowerments, Other Priorities

Tom Brass

Haymarket Books
Chicago, IL

First published in 2018 by Brill Academic Publishers, The Netherlands.
© 2018 Koninklijke Brill NV, Leiden, The Netherlands

Published in paperback in 2020 by
Haymarket Books
P.O. Box 180165
Chicago, IL 60618
773-583-7884
www.haymarketbooks.org

ISBN: 978-1-64259-071-5

Distributed to the trade in the US through Consortium Book Sales and Distribution (www.cbsd.com) and internationally through Ingram Publisher Services International (www.ingramcontent.com).

This book was published with the generous support of Lannan Foundation and Wallace Action Fund.

Special discounts are available for bulk purchases by organizations and institutions. Please call 773-583-7884 or email info@haymarketbooks.org for more information.

Cover design by Jamie Kerry and Ragina Johnson.

Printed in United States.

10 9 8 7 6 5 4 3 2 1

Library of Congress Cataloging-in-Publication Data is available.

*For Amanda, Anna, Ned, and Miles;
and in memory of my parents*

Contents

Acknowledgements   XI

Introduction: The Best of Times, the Worst of Times?   1
1. The Vanishing   3
2. The Banishment   7
3. Making a Difference?   8
4. The Shrewd Scholar?   11
5. Something They Have Forgotten?   13
6. Themes   15

PART 1
Revolutionary/Counter-revolutionary Practice/Theory

1. **Revolution in Practice**   23
   1. Introduction: Revolution, or Reform (and Counter-revolution)   23
   2. Educate them to Revolt   25
   3. The Greatest of All Proprietors   28
   4. Desperation and Vengeance   31
   5. As the Part to the Whole   34
   6. Conclusion   38

2. **Revolution in Theory**   40
   1. Revolution and/as Modernity   42
   2. To the Barricades?   47
   3. Half the Voters Plus One?   49
   4. Confused Chatter and Legislative Obstruction   54
   5. Modernity and/as Bourgeois Democracy   57
   6. Conclusion   62

3. **Refusing Revolution, Empowering Counter-revolution**   65
   1. Introduction: To the Barricades?   65
   2. What History Taught Us   66
   3. The Nation's Great Concerns   72
   4. The Balance of Class Power?   75
   5. To the Barricades   78

	6	The World We/(They) Have Lost 83
	7	A (Marxist) Warning from History 87
	8	Conclusion 89

PART 2
Other Marxisms, Other Priorities/Identities

4	The (Revolutionary) Path Not Taken 95
	1 Introduction: Promoting Capitalism, Not Socialism 95
	2 *Laissez-faire* Discourse-for 101
	3 In the Footsteps of *Laissez-faire* 105
	4 Capitalism – or Socialism? 109
	5 The Path Not Taken 111
	6 Conclusion 113

5	Avoiding Revolution: A Return to Patronage 116
	1 Introduction: From Periphery to the (Academic) Core 116
	2 Empiricism, Patronage and Subsistence 119
	3 Personal Tie of Affection? 122
	4 Two Concepts, or One? 125
	5 A Caring State… 127
	6 …or Permanent Revolution 130
	7 Conclusion 131

6	Misunderstanding Revolution: (Re-)Defining Labour Coercion? 133
	1 Introduction: A Necessary Journey? 133
	2 The Debate 135
	3 The Debate Transcended? 139
	4 Problems with Theory 143
	5 Butterfly Collecting 149
	6 Conclusion 151

7	Other Priorities, Other Identities: Unmasking the Subaltern 153
	1 Introduction: (Armchair) Generals Go to War 153
	2 Subaltern Conquests 156
	3 Nationalist Appropriation I: Cambridge and England 158
	4 Nationalist Appropriation II: Delhi and India 161
	5 Critique of a Critique 164
	6 Difference and Sameness 167

7 'A Reiteration of the Already Said'   170
8 Conclusion   175

PART 3
Alternatives to Revolution?

8 **Betraying Revolution (Again)**   181
   1 Introduction: Revolutionary Socialism as the Fifth Horseman   181
   2 Peasants, Left and Right   184
   3 A Plan of Campaign?   186
   4 Power Wanting, But Wanting Power?   194
   5 Resistance, Not Revolution   198
   6 Conclusion   201

9 ***Viva La Revolución?*** **Eric Hobsbawm on Peasants**   203
   1 Introduction: A Time There Was …   203
   2 Big in Brazil   205
   3 Hobsbawm and Feudalism   208
   4 Hobsbawm and the *Hacienda* System   211
   5 Hobsbawm and Capitalism   215
   6 Hobsbawm and Marxism   217
   7 Outside Latin America   219
   8 Conclusion   222

10 **Marxism, or Postmodern Precursor? John Berger on Peasants**   224
   1 Introduction: Holy Humble Peasants?   224
   2 No Country for Old Peasants   228
   3 Migrants, Gender, Money   231
   4 Different Stories, Same Themes   235
   5 Looking, But Seeing?   239
   6 Too Much History, Too Many Lives   244
   7 Conclusion   249

Conclusion   250

Bibliography   265
Author Index   284
Subject Index   289

Acknowledgements

Two inescapable features of the global capitalist system currently are an unwillingness to challenge the growing incidence of inequality, coupled with a seeming inability to increase taxation in order to redistribute income. Historically, such a combination has invariably generated 'from below' opposition that in particular instances took the form of revolutionary agency. Now, however, the latter kind of direct action has all but vanished from the political agenda of the left, replaced at best with an embarrassingly grateful acceptance of nothing more than crumbs-from-the-table granted the rest of us by the rich generally and CEOs of multinational corporations, hedge funds, and banks that have profited from neoliberal capitalism. This has been accompanied by outsourcing/downsizing/relocation of employment, resulting in a situation where those who still have or might expect to have had a well-paid job find themselves competing in labour markets with a globally expanding industrial reserve army. In many ways, this situation mimics the one faced at the end of the nineteenth century and beginning of the twentieth by Austro-Marxists, whose tepid parliamentarian approach and political reformism paved the way for the rise of the far right.

Marx, we are now told (even by some commentators in the conservative press), is back on the agenda of political economy as this applies to metropolitan capitalist nations. Yet it is necessary to ask what kind of Marxism this is, given that in most instances it is presented as a theory which is devoid of concepts such as revolution and a socialist transition, both at home and abroad. If not revolution and socialism, then what sort of systemic outcome remains on the agenda? Many on the left seem to think that among the alternatives are protecting/reinstating peasant economy and (more broadly) the pursuit of bourgeois democracy and a 'pure' form of capitalism, in the (vain) hope that such objectives entail a return to or the realization of a benign form of accumulation. However, without Marxist concepts like revolution and socialism, not only is there little or no prospect either of 'from below' progress or of eradicating unfree production relations, but opposition to capitalism is reduced to appeals to the patronage of its state, invoking in the process a (non-existent) neoliberal moral order. Currently and historically, evidence suggests that in these circumstances a radical politics remains on the agenda, but with the difference that working-class support can be – and is – transferred instead to rightwing populist movements offering empowerment on the basis of non-class identities (nationalism, ethnicity).

Accordingly, these days Marxism generally has to find its own space among a number of competing theories privileging these other (non-class) identities and other (ideological) priorities. Among the latter is the 'new' populist postmodernism which, because it deals principally in ethnic/national identity, tends especially in its post-colonial guise to attack not the rich and powerful – owners/controllers of the means of production, distribution, and exchange – but rather all those belonging to an erstwhile colonial/imperial power. In the recent past and continuing into the present, therefore, the 'new' populist postmodernism tends to make no distinction between the ruling class and its plebeian component, let alone the weak and poor, in what were once colonizing nations. Consequently, struggle as interpreted by this kind of epistemology is mainly or only about national empowerment on the part of countries and/or populations that are or were once colonies. As such, the 'new' populist postmodernism is a political approach that is largely unconnected with the formation/consciousness/agency of those whose identity is based on class; namely, revolutionary struggle undertaken by workers to realize a socialist transition, a process that constitutes a form of 'from below' mobilization which necessarily transects national/ethnic boundaries.

The political influence of postmodernism can be gauged from the impact of aporia, the unfixing of meaning consequent upon a decoupling of language and material conditions. It is perhaps no more than a commentary on the baleful state of the present that bourgeois politicians in capitalist nations – non-western as well as western – now routinely use language devoid of meaning: words that promise to address and rectify specific economic and/or social problems are known to be insincere even as they are uttered. A case in point is the word 'reform', which used to mean 'to make better' (land reform, income redistribution, public spending), now denotes 'to make worse' (labour process restructuring, cutting public spending and welfare provision, union busting, deregulation, privatisation) when invoked by supporters of austerity. Emptied of positive content, to the degree that what replaces it actually denotes the opposite of the historical meaning found in the lexicon of the left, this epistemological shift ought to create a space for the conceptual readmission of revolution and socialism to the Marxist theoretical pantheon. Clearly, this has not happened to the extent that it should: rather like creatures transfixed in the headlights of an oncoming vehicle, many on the left have instead focused on a search for positive elements within bourgeois ideology, thought by them to be 'empowering' or 'progressive'.

This contradiction has as one of its more important effects the leftist academic who these days insists s/he still adheres to Marxist theory but eschews conceptually what this commits one to in terms of practice. At best, it is the position accurately captured by Saint Augustine in his dictum justifying procrastination ('Lord make me chaste, but not yet'); at worst, it amounts to no more than an academic version of the 'neck verse' (a biblical text learned by those in court so as to avoid capital punishment, by demonstrating to the judge and jury that they were literate). Since revolution is not a tea party (as Mao once observed), this indisputable fact would of itself account for the understandable reluctance of many to advocate this kind of direct action. What is less comprehensible, and certainly less forgivable, is the ease with which revolution aimed at replacing capitalism with socialism has been discarded conceptually by the majority of those who continue to regard themselves as Marxists. Nowhere is this more evident than in academia, where a veritable publishing industry is currently devoted to analyses proclaiming the impossibility, the undesirability, or the lack any longer for the necessity of revolutionary agency. When produced by a non- or anti-Marxist, such arguments do not surprise; however, as many of them are composed not by conservatives but by those claiming to be leftists of one kind or another, an explanation is required, and the latter is what this volume seeks to provide.

Special thanks are due to the following people. To Professor David Fasenfest, the Series Editor, for encouragement; to Rosanna Woensdregt, Jennifer Obdam, and Judy Pereira of Brill publishers, who guided the book through production; and to my daughter Anna Luisa Brass, who designed and drew the cover illustration. She drew the cover for four of my previous books – *New Farmers' Movements in India* (1995), *Labour Regime Change in the Twenty-First Century* (2011), *Class, Culture and the Agrarian Myth* (2014), and *Labour Markets, Identities, and Controversies* (2017) – as well as the drawings which have appeared at the start of each section in past volumes, and do so also in the present one. Here the front cover (drawing title: *citta*) depicts the continuing attempts by Marxists to build socialism, a task symbolized in the illustration of a city steered into its historical place by wheelbarrow. Why at times this seems like a Sisyphean task is hinted at in the drawings which precede each of the three sections in the book.

A number of chapters draw on materials which have appeared previously in *Critical Sociology, Science and Society, Critique of Anthropology, Capital and Class, The Journal of Peasant Studies*, and *The Journal of Contemporary Asia*. Other chapters have not been published before and appear here in print for the first time. Like all my previous monographs, this one is dedicated to two sets of kin. To my family: Amanda, and Anna, Ned and Miles. Also, to the memory of my parents: my father, Denis Brass (1913–2006), and my mother, Gloria Brass (1916–2012).

Richmond-upon-Thames
April 2018

Introduction: The Best of Times, the Worst of Times?

> 'My purpose is to tell of bodies which have been transformed into shapes of a different kind'.
> The opening sentence of Book I of *The Metamorphoses* by OVID.[1]

∴

Like so much else, what constitutes revolutionary agency, and how it is to be interpreted politically, is to some degree still governed by film images circulating in the domain of popular culture which depict crowds moving with intent towards a place or person embodying ruling class and/or state power. Whether such movement is in the end successful, and its object is captured, or unsuccessful, as its subjects are fired upon and dispersed, is bound up with the wider issue of the way revolution is portrayed as either benign or malign. What is clear, however, is that the image of a crowd-in-motion soon becomes the 'mob-in-the-streets' in films which are politically unsympathetic to revolution as a form of agency.

Where the 1917 Russian revolution is concerned, therefore, the spectrum extends from *October* (1927), directed by Sergei Eisenstein, at the benign end of the scale, to the less supportive narratives which inform films like *Knight Without Armour* (1937), directed by Jacques Feyder, *Doctor Zhivago* (1965), directed by David Lean, and *Nicholas and Alexandra* (1971), directed by Franklin Schaffner.[2] Ironically, an aspect of counter-revolutionary agency also possesses a filmic

---

1 Ovid (1955: 31).
2 The contrast between the positive/negative way a crowd-in-motion can be shown in film emerges from a comparison of *October* and *Knight Without Armour*. Whereas in *October* the crowd is moving away from the camera and towards the Winter Palace, in *Knight Without Armour*, by contrast, the crowd moves towards the camera. In the latter film, about the rescue from the Bolsheviks of a Russian countess by a British agent, the entrance of the revolutionaries takes the form of an armed and hostile crowd which crests a hill and descends onto the estate, threatening its owner the countess. In the case of *October*, therefore, the ordering of the action places the film audience behind the crowd-in-motion, licensing a perception as part of the crowd itself, and thus to sympathize with its agency and objectives. In the *Knight Without Armour*, however, the ordering means the crowd is advancing towards the camera – much like Eisenstein's *The Battleship Potemkin* (1925) where soldiers descending the Odessa steps similarly advance menacingly toward the camera – and as such is much rather perceived as a double threat, both to the countess who has her back to the camera, and the audience watching the film.

presence, albeit an unexpected one. In *The Fall of the Roman Empire* (1964), directed by Anthony Mann, as the hero – a successful Roman general – walks away after having killed the tyrannical emperor Commodus in a duel, he is approached individually by a series of wealthy senators, each of whom in turn offers him an ever larger sum of money if nominated as the next emperor. Underlined thereby is the fact that, historically (and currently), it always remains possible for those with power and wealth to subvert – or reverse – even the smallest of progressive steps taken forwards.³

Broadly speaking, revolutionary agency entails a mass uprising, and as such leads to and simultaneously consists of the most radical form of overturning, a transcendence of a previously existing system. In Marxist terms, it is – and can only ever be – the way in which class struggle is waged successfully, first by capitalists against a feudal system, and then by workers against capital and its State. Unlike the 'everyday-resistance-to the State' which underwrites postmodern agency, a form of practice indistinguishable from neoliberal State-shrinking that informs conservative *laissez faire* ideology, Marxism has always advocated seizing control of (and ruling through) the State. Having captured the capitalist State, workers as a class gain power and take into common ownership the means of production, distribution and exchange.

In economic terms, the anarchy of the market gives way to central planning, and profit to need as the criterion of production. Ideologically, ethnic identity and national 'belonging' are replaced by consciousness of class, solidarity of which extends beyond ethnic/national boundaries. Politically, therefore, a socialist transition cannot be confined to a particular nation, let alone a region within this unit: it must necessarily be international in scope, so that alliances are established and reproduced along horizontal lines (intra-class), in order to prevent/challenge/pre-empt vertical ones (inter-class).⁴ Rather than such a

---

3   That any gains made in the course of a revolution can be reversed by counter-revolutionary action is self-evident, and a possible outcome that has long been acknowledged as such. In the case of Russia during 1917, this is clear from the content and warning tone of a letter sent by a landlord of Tula to peasants who had taken over and redistributed his property (Rhys Williams, 1929: 185): "'Brother Mujiks: Go on as you have begun. Divide all the furnishings of my manor-house. Take my cattle and the hay to feed them with. One thing I ask of you! Don't chop down my lime trees. These I will need to hang you on when I return...'".

4   That internationalism has to be a central aspect of any socialist theory was a self-evident to all Bolsheviks. Indeed, the 'from above' interconnectedness of global capital and landownership in particular national contexts, even at the start of the twentieth century, made a corresponding 'from below' unity across frontiers a necessity. Thus in his classic account of the 1917 revolution, John Reed (1926: 272) reports Lenin saying that '[a]t this moment we are not only trying to solve the Land question, but the question of Social Revolution – not only here in Russia, but all over the world. The Land question cannot be solved independently of the other problems of Social Revolution...For example, the confiscation of the landed estates

view, there are now a plethora of what claim to be theories not so much about the future shape of socialism as new political versions of it.[5] The latter invariably turn out to have very little to do with socialism or revolution, which raises a central question: why is revolutionary agency, a crucial element of Marxist theory, no longer on the political agenda of the left.

Accordingly, the main question examined here – why is revolution no longer conceptually part of a leftist political agenda – means examining the way the presence or absence of revolutionary agency is in turn bound up with a number of other issues: the systemic object of struggle (restoration of a 'nicer' capitalism, or a transition to socialism), its subject (the proletariat; workers and peasants; or simply the peasantry), its form (capture of state power or resistance at village level), its political discourse (about class, or non-class identities such as religion, sectoral or rural-not-urban, regional, ethnicity and the national question), and the mobilizing role in all this of categories/strata outside the working class (petty bourgeoisie, academics, intellectuals).

At times, it seems that leftist academics would do almost anything rather than endorse activity in furtherance of revolutionary socialism.[6] This has entailed what is now a never-ending search for alternatives, in the form of other variants of Marxism, of other kinds of empowerment, and politically other sorts of priorities. None of the latter have a place for radical agency by the working class designed to capture and exercise power through the state. Why this is so, and how such a position has come about, is the focus of this book.

1   The Vanishing

That a fear of revolution is in an important sense always present at the back of the bourgeois mind is clear, a concern that extends from the capitalist workplace itself all the way to the state apparatus. Hence opposition to the political empowerment of workers as a class stemmed in part from an apprehension that a class-in-itself would become a class-for-itself, a shift that contained within it a dynamic culminating in potential revolutionary action

---

will provoke the resistance not only of Russian landowners, but also of foreign capital – with whom the great landed properties are connected through the intermediary of the banks...'

5   Recent examples include Bensaïd (2002), Ginsborg (2008), Badiou (2010), Žižek (2010), Wright (2010), and many of the contributions to the volume edited by Panitch and Albo (2016).
6   In making a distinction between 'learned expert' and 'professional revolutionary', Kautsky (see Chapter 1 below) delineated accurately the position criticized by the Bolsheviks: namely, subscribing to the theory of revolution, but not its practice. It was, in short, the divide separating advocates of revolutionary socialism (='professional revolutionary') from *katheder-socialism* (='learned expert').

aimed ultimately at transforming property relations themselves. Such misgivings about the implications of generating a potentially revolutionary 'urban mob' applied in the case of the antebellum American South, for example, where the debates on slavery taking place during the 1840s were structured by an underlying fear of a threat to property relations.[7] Concerned lest an emergent rural proletariat would ultimately demand the expropriation of the Southern landowning class, therefore, anti-abolitionists advocated ruling class unity between Northern property owners and Southern planters in defence of slavery in order to counter a potential working class challenge to existing property rights.

An analogous disquiet about revolutionary action leading to expropriation of large estates, land reform, collectivization/planning, processes to be accompanied more generally by confiscation/redistribution of wealth and property, informed hostile bourgeois reaction to worker mobilization in contexts as different as Spain during the early 1930s and Chile in the early 1970s. In the case of Spain, revolutionary agency increased following the resignation of the dictator Primo de Rivera during 1930, the replacement of the monarchy with a republic in 1931, and subsequent electoral gains by the left.[8] Much the same happened in Chile, where following electoral success in 1970 a leftist government embarked on a broadly socialist programme of agrarian reform and nationalisation of foreign-owned mineral resources in the country. In both these contexts, bourgeois reaction again followed a similar pattern (civil war, military coup, dictatorship, widespread oppression, 'disappearances') designed to prevent democracy 'growing over' into a socialist revolution: that is, not just to avoid further 'from below' challenges to property rights, but also to roll back any political and economic gains made hitherto by workers and poor peasants in the course of previous radical mobilization/programmes.[9]

Claims to the effect that revolution is neither feasible nor desirable exhibit distinct trajectories and forms, which nevertheless crop up periodically

---

7 On this point, see Dew (1966) and Kaufman (1982:121ff.).

8 Writing about Spain, where later he observed that fascism 'is not feudal but bourgeois reaction', Trotsky (1973b:105–6, 307) commended the following action in 1931, at the outset of the republic: 'The communists must immediately work out a revolutionary agrarian programme. Its basis must be the confiscation of the lands of the privileged and rich classes, of the exploiters, beginning with the monarchy and the church, for the benefit of the poor peasants and the soldiers... [The left] will win the confidence of the proletariat and the great majority of the poor peasants. They will take power [and] will open up the era of the socialist revolution'.

9 Democracy 'growing over' into a socialist revolution was the way Trotsky (1973b: 122–23) – and Lenin – described the process of permanent revolution.

throughout the nineteenth and twentieth centuries. Some of these surface within Marxist theory itself, and take their cue from revisionist/reformist positions in the late nineteenth century (Eduard Bernstein, Werner Sombart, Georg von Vollmar, and Eduard David) arguing that revolution is no longer necessary because the kind of class formation which led to this kind of 'from below' agency has not materialised.[10] Consequently, the class struggle lacks both its main components: the depeasantized smallholder separated from his/her means of labour, and an immiserized working class. After the 1917 Russian revolution, opposition from within Marxism (Karl Kautsky) adopted a different position, maintaining that this kind of radical agency was no different from civil war, and as such was politically and economically undesirable: the dictatorship of the proletariat which emerged from revolution was anyway undemocratic.

After the end of the 1939–45 war, the debate within Marxist theory about revolutionary action took a somewhat different form. In a variation of late nineteenth century revisionist/reformist views, during the 1960s Herbert Marcuse argued that, by co-opting the working class ('The integrated man lives in a society without opposition'), capitalism had succeeded in avoiding struggle designed to transcend it as a system, and that consequently neither bourgeoisie nor proletariat were any longer historical agents of transformation.[11] This capitalism was able to do because at that conjuncture there appeared to be no limits to its capacity for economic growth. Instead of Marxist theory having underestimated the survival capacity of peasant economy, and thus not generating class divisions in rural society, as Eduard Bernstein and Werner Sombart maintained, therefore, the critique levelled at Marxism by Marcuse now concerned the absence of conflict waged by an already-formed working class in metropolitan industrial capitalism. In short, the debate shifted from the formation of class (class-in-itself) to one about its practice (class-for-itself).

For Marcuse, therefore, the absence of class struggle and with it revolutionary agency stemmed from what he perceived as the ability of capital actually/potentially to produce abundance, thereby providing workers with full employment and higher living standards.[12] At that same conjuncture, moreover,

---

10 Details about these revisionist/reformist arguments are outlined below, in Part 1 of this volume.
11 About the pessimism of Marcuse, Mattick (1967: 377) comments that 'hope for a socialist working class revolution is given up in the expectation that social problems are solvable by way of reforms within the confines of capitalism. In this view, revolution has become not only highly improbable but entirely unnecessary'.
12 However, others recognized that full employment was never going to be acceptable to capitalists. Thus, for example, in a lecture at Cambridge during 1942, entitled 'Political Aspects of Full Employment', the economist Michael Kalecki noted: 'We have considered

Paul Mattick pointed out that Marcuse had overlooked the dynamic that Marx attributed to capitalism: namely, that the object of the accumulation process was an abundance not of produce but of profits, and that the latter would decline relatively as capitalism spread.[13] What Marcuse had overlooked, therefore, was that accumulation depended on profits, which in turn led to capitalist enterprises having to outcompete one another by lowering wages/conditions of their workforce, thereby creating the struggle that culminates in revolutionary action.

Within Marxism, another kind of hostility towards revolution takes the form of a what-we-have-now-is-not-proper-capitalism argument, exponents of which currently extend from advocates of the semi- feudal thesis (Byres, Patnaik) to those who argue for the presence of 'financialisation' (Harvey, Hardt, Negri, Graeber).[14] Since unfree labour is interpreted by the semi-feudal thesis as a 'pre-capitalist' relation, its presence signals that any transition is to be to yet more efficient capitalism, not socialism. In keeping with this, the concept 'financialisation' is based on the premiss that what exists now is no longer capitalism in the sense understood by Marxism but rather some form of control by market forces, largely or wholly unconnected with accumulation in industrial economies. Common to each approach is the view that a 'fully functioning' accumulation process is either absent, has yet to be realized, or is not yet sufficiently in place. In effect, revolutionary agency by the working class anywhere is postponed *sine die*. While the semi-feudal thesis ignores the acceptability to capitalist enterprises of production relations that are unfree, therefore, 'financialisation' overlooks the international link connecting funding and manufacturing. The latter are certainly spatially distinct and distant,

---

the political reasons for the opposition to the policy of creating employment by government spending. But even if this opposition were overcome – as it may well be under the pressure of the masses – the maintenance of full employment would cause social and political changes which would give new impetus to the opposition of business leaders. Indeed, under a regime of permanent full employment, the "sack" would cease to play its role as a disciplinary measure. The social position of the boss would be undermined, and the self-assurance and class-consciousness of the working class would grow. Strikes for wage increases and improvements in conditions of work would create political tension... [The] class instinct [of business leaders] tells them that lasting full employment is unsound from their point of view, and that unemployment is an integral part of the "normal" capitalist system'.

13 'It is true, nonetheless', argued Mattick (1967: 378) against Marcuse, 'that the absence of any effective opposition to the capitalist system presupposes the system's ability to improve steadily the living conditions of the labouring population'.

14 Further aspects of what-we-have-now-is-not-proper-capitalism argument are considered below in Chapter 4.

but not economically separate: thus manufacturing has not so much vanished from industrial countries as been outsourced/decentralized/downsized, so that production takes place in smallscale units – at home and abroad – that have replaced largescale factories.

2   The Banishment

Other forms of hostility to revolutionary agency circulated outside Marxism, emerging in a large part from political opposition to the 1789 French Revolution. In response to the latter, and more broadly Enlightenment discourse, antagonism expressed by German Romanticism (Möser, Herder) took the form of support for pre-revolutionary traditional forms/institutions and both the specificity and innateness of cultural/ethnic/national identity. At the centre of this discourse was an essentialist concept of an homogenous smallholding peasant, whose pristine cultural 'otherness' was said to embody both Nature and nationhood. The same identity was present not only in Russian populist/neo-populist ideology at the end of the nineteenth century and the beginning of the twentieth, but also in Italian fascism and German Nazism. After the defeat of the latter, and in order to pre-empt/prevent peasant rebellions which might threaten property relations beyond the rural and initiate revolution, 1960s bourgeois modernisation theory promoted agrarian reform programmes so as to improve the economic and political lot of smallholders within the capitalist system. Exponents of this approach (Rogers, Weiner, Rostow) argued that additionally a combination of individual proprietorship, land and income redistributive policies, would encourage capital investment and thus generate development.

From the 1980s onwards, however, outside Marxism the focus of debate about rural grassroots empowerment shifted once again, from the economic sphere of modernization theory back to the domain of culture, privileged now by the then-emerging 'new' populist postmodernism. Invoking non-class identities (among them 'subaltern' and 'multitude'), this approach maintained that the most significant kind of rural grassroots agency undertaken by petty commodity producers was not revolution but resistance. It replaced thereby mobilisation the object of which was capturing the state and systemic transcendence with quotidian struggle designed to achieve nothing more than a localised defence of the status quo within a wider capitalism. Oppression was no longer confined to that of worker and class identity, and struggle was regarded by many as no more than the attempt by the oppressed to improve their position within capitalism.

This approach informs the analysis by 'new' populist postmodern discourse of emancipatory struggles by many rural grassroots movements composed of non-class yet alienated 'others': that is, by a wide variety of social groups and NGOs for human rights, democracy and/or civil society; by indigenous people for land and the recognition of their cultural identity; and by women and gays against gender and/or sexual oppression. For the 'new' populist postmodernism, therefore, a 'commonsense' ethnocentrism is both inevitable and at the centre of its own discourse. Since what it defends/endorses is a socially non-specific notion of 'democracy', the locus of which is an equally unspecific 'society', these concepts are theoretically interchangeable with 'nationhood'. Non-revolutionary (and in some instances counter-revolutionary) in theory and practice, these mobilizations underline the vast gulf between the oppositional discourse of the 'new' populist postmodernism and the teachings of classical Marxism about the necessity of and revolutionary struggle for socialism.[15]

3   Making a Difference?

What currently passes for development theory in the social sciences oscillates uneasily between two antithetical positions. On the one hand, therefore, it involves never-ending searches – mainly by bourgeois economics – for more effective forms of production, a quest for yet more efficient methods of accumulation; epistemologically, this informs the view that a 'true' kind of capitalism is not yet present, or that what exists is not capitalist enough.[16] In part, this overlaps conceptually with economic 'trickle down', or the view that accumulation will not only benefit labour as well as capital, but also that this process will itself be based on a proletariat enjoying well-paid permanent employment. On the other are non-economic approaches which claim that specific non-class categories/identities of 'those below' (subalterns, multitudes) are engaged in struggle designed to realize only cultural empowerment (recognition, dignity), nothing more. Notwithstanding the apparent difference, both these positions correspond to a pro-capitalist and anti-capitalist discourse each of which is conservative.

Nowhere is this more evident than in 'new' populist postmodernist approaches to development theory which have altered the political narrative

---

15   Ways in which the 'new' populist postmodernism and Marxism diverge theoretically and politically are examined below in Chapters 7 and 10.
16   As will be seen below, especially in Chapter 4 with reference to the semi-feudal thesis, this is the reason for the existence of an overlap between bourgeois economics and Marxist variants of the what-we-have-now-is-not-proper-capitalism approach.

by reconceptualising the element of victimhood, shifting this from class to non-class identities, and privileging the empowerment of the latter in any/every struggle taking place. Such as it was, struggles undertaken by non-class categories would take the form not of revolution but of 'resistance': the latter would henceforth be exercised only at village level, thereby eschewing the necessity of capturing the state.[17] Associated with the ubiquitous 'everyday forms of resistance' theory popularised by James Scott, such arguments incorrectly conflate agency with empowerment, the somewhat patronizing assumption being that any manifestation of whatever kind of 'from below' worker mobilization is automatically and necessarily to their advantage and hence to the disadvantage of employers.[18]

Apart from the rather obvious difficulty such a view has with categorizing the many successful attempts by employers to divide and conquer workforce solidarity by introducing segmentation along ethnic lines (which gives rise to racism) as a form of worker empowerment, one sub-text to the framework in which worker agency = empowerment is that labour is doing well, and that accordingly there is not much need for change. Moreover, in the absence of socialist ideas/practice, and as capitalism spreads across the globe, this form of postmodern discourse can also be deployed effectively by populists who claim it is the only way to safeguard/retain workers' jobs and living standards.[19]

---

17   'There can be no return from class struggle to the unity of the bourgeois nation' wrote Trotsky (1972a: 55–56), adding: 'The "lack of results" of the [1905] Russian revolution is only a temporary reflection of its profound social character. In this bourgeois revolution without a revolutionary bourgeois, the proletariat is driven, by the internal progress of events, towards hegemony over the peasantry and to struggle for state power. The first wave of the Russian revolution was smashed by the dull-wittedness of the *muzhik*, who, at home in his village, hoping to seize a bit of land, fought the squire, but who, having donned a soldier's uniform, fired upon the worker. All the events of 1905 can be viewed as a series of ruthless object lessons by means of which history drums into the peasants' skull a consciousness of his local land hunger and the central problem of state power'.

18   Lenin (1961a: 349ff.), for example, warned against the opportunistic espousal/endorsement of spontaneous conflict 'from below' simply because this happened to be taking place, and emphasized instead the importance of party organization structured by a specifically *political* input into the formation of what would eventually become a consciousness of class. Although it was aimed at the politically limited objectives inherent in trade union consciousness, the warning applies with equal force to those who frame their support of 'the oppressed' against imperialism and international capitalism in terms of ethnic/national identity and not class. In short, against the politically insidious proposition that any oppositional idiom (= 'the-voice-from-below') is always necessarily politically progressive.

19   Thus, for example, to the postmodern argument emphasizing the cultural identity of the migrant-as-'other'-nationality, the far right populist counterposes an argument similarly emphasizing cultural identity, only this time the nationality of the non-migrant worker. By deploying non-class identities in this manner, the capacity to build solidarity along

Ominously, therefore, just as many on the left of the political spectrum moved rightwards, abandoning core beliefs (socialism, class, revolution) and espousing postmodern notions of non-class identity as innate/empowering, so the far right has in turn moved onto the political ground they vacated, incorporating class identity into its own ideology.

In opposing the necessity of revolutionary agency as a means of transcending capitalism, therefore, both reformist/revisionist Marxism and non- or anti-Marxism failed to consider two potential occurrences. On the one hand, both the fact and implications of the return to the centre of development theory of the industrial reserve army, together with its crucial role in transforming the global capitalist system; and on the other, the resulting emergence and consolidation of political parties on the far right of the spectrum. Together with some forms of non-Marxist theory, Marxists of the reformist/revisionist kinds underestimated the ability of capital to reproduce itself through access to hitherto untapped sources of cheap workers drawn from what has become a global industrial reserve army of labour. The latter has expanded principally as a result of two developments: rural populations driven off the land in so-called Third World contexts, and the incorporation of ex-socialist counties into the international division of labour.

During the 1960s, therefore, the failure of modernization theorists such as Rostow and Marxists like Marcuse to consider this possibility stemmed from a mistaken belief that, as Keynesianism had solved the unemployment problem, and consequently an over-supply of the labour market leading to declining wage levels would cease to be a feature of the accumulation process.[20] By contrast, a concern expressed by much current non-Marxist development theory, particularly those who deploy the concept 'precariat', is how will labour-power that is temporary and poorly paid reproduce itself in future, whereas as long as capital can draw on unlimited supplies of labour from what is now a global industrial reserve army, this concern does – and will – not arise. Given the latter, a moral concern for the well-being of its workers – which in the past gave rise to Victorian employer philanthropy and the post-1945 welfare state – is something that nowadays capital simply no longer has to worry about.[21]

---

class lines as workers diminishes. The concept of 'difference' ceases its attachment to class, and is affixed instead to non-class identities.

20 Presciently, Mattick (1967: 381) warned that: 'Notwithstanding the long duration of rather "prosperous" conditions in the industrially advanced countries, there is no ground for the assumption that capitalist production has overcome its inherent contradictions through State interventions in the economy'.

21 On the expansion and role of the industrial reserve, see Glyn (2006a, 2006b) and Brass (2017b: Chapter 19), and also Chapter 3 below. Among those who emphasized its centrality to Marxist theory was Trotsky. Writing in the late 1930s, he observed (Trotsky, 1940: 17–18):

4   The Shrewd Scholar?

Having discarded the twin concepts of socialism and revolution, and endorsed instead the non-class forms of mobilization/empowerment associated with the 'new' populist postmodernism, erstwhile leftist academics who continued to participate in debate crucially found themselves high and dry in intellectual terms, outflanked theoretically and wrongfooted politically by those who remained Marxists. A not uncommon response to this dilemma on the part of those who faced it has been surreptitiously to incorporate the more radical views, and then claim implausibly that they had always subscribed to them.[22] This in turn has given rise to two interrelated phenomena: on the one hand a shift of radical views from the intellectual/political margins (inhabited by those who remained Marxists) into the academic mainstream (inhabited by those who were no longer or never had been Marxists), in the course of which they metamorphose into positions that are more acceptable to bourgeois discourse; on the other to patterns of intellectual inconsistency as mainstream views are subject to constant change.[23]

For this reason, radical arguments formulated on the margins of academia tend to reappear in the mainstream subsequently, albeit with different political conclusions.[24] An illustration of the way a radical argument formulated

---

'The industrial reserve army makes up an indispensable component part of the social mechanics of capitalism, as much as a supply of machines and raw materials in factory warehouses or of finished products in stores. Neither the general expansion of production nor the adaptation of capital to the periodic ebb and flow of the industrial cycle would be possible without a reserve of labour-power... [d]isintegrating capitalism has brought up a whole generation of young people who have never had a job and have no hope of getting one. This new sub-class between the proletariat and the semi-proletariat is forced to live at the expense of society.'

22   Some, of course, continued to argue that Marxist theory generally was mistaken and/or no longer relevant to an interpretation of the present conjuncture.

23   Given that in academia it is always safer to criticize the views of those long dead, to draw attention to the intellectual inconsistency of those who are both senior and very much alive carries predictable risks. Clearly, to do so on occasion is even more risky, as described by Clover (2016: 117): 'Academic disputes in Russia are notoriously prone to getting out of control. Scholars have always been very passionate about their subject and take disagreement very personally, tending to emotional and no-holds-barred polemics. Colleagues tend to pursue each other not just in the pages of specialist journals and conference papers...in the Soviet period, disagreements between academics could still be a matter of life and death'.

24   A case in point is the transfer of critiques of the 'new' populist postmodernism from the margins of academic discourse to its mainstream. Hence the belated recognition by exponents of 'new' populist postmodernism who colonized development studies and the debate about the peasantry that 'something was wrong'. It is adherents of this ideological tendency which, having taken over the editorial of the *Journal of Peasant Studies* and

on margins undergoes a political metamorphosis when it reappears – unacknowledged – in the mainstream involves the concept deproletarianisation, or the view that because of cost/discipline/profit considerations unfree production relations are acceptable to capitalists who use them in preference to free labour. The issue concerns not so much a change of interpretation, therefore, as the reason for this, plus the attempt to deny that such a change has taken place, and also what the Marxist deproletarianization framework is then said to presage systemically.

To begin with, the Marxist view adopted had not only been condemned earlier as wrong by those in the mainstream, but was then used by the latter so as to argue that the existing (= neoliberal) state apparatus should restore a more benign ('kinder'/'caring') capitalism. Whereas the object of the original Marxist framework as formulated on the margins was to show the connection between deproletarianization and a transition to socialism, mainstream arguments which incorporated the same approach by contrast maintain that it leads simply to a 'nicer' capitalism. Having originally formulated the Marxist deproletarianization framework, therefore, it was necessary to point out the politically mistaken use to which this framework has been put subsequently.[25]

Thus a new interpretation, one that surfaces on the margins of academia and challenges previous arguments circulating within the mainstream, is frequently the subject of an attack by those in the latter context not because it is wrong, but much rather because it is correct.[26] Amongst other things, this

---

turned it into a platform for populism (on which see Brass 2015), are in the process of recognizing their error, and trying to compensate by being critical of what they term 'authoritarian populism'. However, this attempt to rectify the situation has not been successful, since there is still a failure on their part to realize that over a whole series of economic and political issues there is actually no distinction between 'authoritarian populism' and their own 'new' populist postmodernism.

25   Issues/contradictions arising from such attempts to redefine the meaning and political outcome of class struggle in which employers use unfree labour in preference to free equivalents are covered by me elsewhere (Brass, 2011: Chapter 3; Brass, 2017b: Chapters 16 and 17) as well as in Part 2 of this volume. In contrast to Marxism, much bourgeois economic theory interprets unfree labour relations as based on incentives, and from the viewpoint of labourers constitute a desirable arrangement which amounts to a form of 'subsistence guarantee'. The argument that unfree labour benefits employers and workers alike reproduces the neo-classical economic stereotype of the agricultural worker as a risk-averse choice-making individual who exercises subjective preferences in a benign/tension-free context, and who is to all intents and purposes a free agent (= free labour).

26   As the following description confirms, this kind of shape-shifting long precedes its academic variant. In the introduction to an historical account of German imperial expansion written a century ago by Friedrich Naumann, therefore, one is informed that (Naumann, 1916: vii) 'the economic philosophy of his earlier books was rapidly overthrown. Rapidly and almost silently [there was] what is in fact a pretty complete change in mental attitude. Naumann is one of those men who are peculiarly sensitive to the movement of

enables a subsequent claim to be made on the case advanced prior to transforming it politically, on the grounds that because the original was in some sense flawed what is now being presented as an alternative is a version that is entirely 'new'.[27] Lest this interpretation be thought too cynical, much the same view was expressed some four decades ago by a scion of academic liberalism, who observed '[t]he shrewd scholar always waits until the parade is passing his door and then steps bravely out in front of the band'.[28]

5   Something They Have Forgotten?

It is clear, moreover, that such unacknowledged intellectual about turns are by no means confined to economics. A result of this kind of epistemological combination – initial mistake rectified by subsequent 'adjustment', not just making a 'new' version that leaves the accumulation process intact, but also conveying thereby the erroneous impression that such a view has been reached uninfluenced – is that consequently no one can ever be thought to have been wrong.[29] Ironically, this situation generates one of the central dilemmas of capitalism itself: competition and its attendant contradictions. While it is not possible to reproduce exactly the radical theoretical formulations which surface on the margins, it is nevertheless impossible to ignore them entirely

---

contemporary feeling, and easily convinced of the wisdom of every cause they advocate, without being restrained by any very strong craving for intellectual consistency'.

27   Such procedures rarely escape notice, and on occasion can invite an amusingly waspish retort. Thus, for example, in the second volume of his trilogy about the German peasant war of 1525, Bax (1899: vi–viii) comments as follows: 'A former volume, dealing with German Society in Reformation times, received favourable recognition, I believe, in every quarter save one. The one hostile review appeared anonymously in a literary journal… Internal evidence identified the critic as a gentleman who has been believed, rightly or wrongly, to have been for some years preparing material for a work on German Reformation History. Of the somewhat laboured attempts in the article in question to prove the inadequacy of my book…the reviewer stigmatised it as… "an obsolete method of writing history"…I can only say that if such writing be obsolete, the sooner it be revived the better'.

28   For these views, see Galbraith (1977: 203, 207, 220, 222), who writes: 'The curse of the public man is that he first accommodates his tongue and eventually his thoughts to his public positions. Presently saying nothing but saying it nicely becomes a habit… when the men of great reputation are wrong, it is the worst of personal tactics to be right…The shrewd scholar always waits until the parade is passing his door and then steps bravely out in front of the band…In economics it is a far, far wiser thing to be right than to be consistent'.

29   This sort of unacknowledged *volte face* was highlighted neatly and tellingly in the film *Inside Job* (2010), when one economist was shown to have altered the title of an article in his cv, indicating that – rather than having failed to predict the 2008 capitalist crisis – he had, after all, foreseen the instability of neoliberalism.

(one has to be right), with the result that such views have to be tailored to the needs of the bourgeois university.

The connection between such about turns and the departure from the intellectual agenda of revolution and socialism is not difficult to discern. Hence the consequent need always to be right as an important condition of employment/reputation in the academic mainstream is but one form of a broad range of what might be termed survival strategies. Chief amongst these is never being seen to be too far out of step with prevailing intellectual orthodoxy, an approach which entails not so much anticipating as following a (marginal) position once established.[30] This shape-shifting is in an important sense one outcome of the abandonment of revolution as a form of agency and socialism as a politically desirable/feasible objective. However, it would of course be an exaggeration to suggest that a description by Machiavelli of the way rulers exercise power accurately conveys the same kind of process at work in academia, and consequently accounts for every case in which an erstwhile radical politics vanishes from the intellectual agenda.[31]

Insofar as the left has become part of academia, therefore, it has ceased to contribute to the formation of cutting edge radical theory; when the latter is formulated elsewhere – on the margins – such heterodoxy therefore tends to be assimilated and reproduced in a 'new' form.[32] This requires that radical

---

30   Although non-fictional accounts by academics of this kind of thing are for obvious reasons lacking, this is not the case where fiction is concerned. An example of the latter, written by a liberal academic (McCarthy, 1953) in the United States during the 1950s, when leftist university lecturers were the object of witch-hunts conducted by the HUAC, addresses in fictional form the political dilemmas raised by this process for those teaching at bourgeois institutions of higher education.

31   See Machiavelli (1938: 134–5), who observes: 'Upon this question arises: whether it be better to be loved than feared or feared than loved? It may be answered that one should wish to be both, but, because it is difficult to unite them in one person, it is much safer to be feared than loved, when, of the two, either must be dispensed with. Because this is to be asserted in general of men, that they are ungrateful, fickle, false, cowards, covetous, and as long as you succeed they are yours entirely; they will offer you their blood, property, life, and children...when the need is far distant; but when it approaches they turn against you. And that prince who, relying entirely on their promises, has neglected other precautions, is ruined; because friendships that are obtained by payments, and not by greatness or nobility of mind, may indeed be earned, but they are not secured, and in time of need cannot be relied upon; and men have less scruple in offending one who is beloved than one who is feared, for love is preserved by the link of obligation which, owing to the baseness of men, is broken at every opportunity for their advantage; but fear preserves you by a dread of punishment which never fails'.

32   Drawing attention to these kinds of transfer from the Marxist margins to the bourgeois mainstream carries risks, of course, a problem recognized as long ago as the mid-seventeenth century by the Spanish Jesuit, Baltasar Gracián (1953: 54–55, original

views are not only unacknowledged but also remade in a form acceptable to the continuation of the accumulation process. It was precisely just such a transfer from the radical (Marxist) margins to the reformist ('Marxist') academic mainstream that lay behind the antagonism exhibited historically by Bolsheviks towards Austro-Marxist *katheder*-socialism. Having taken unto themselves the role of interpreting what Marxism really meant, Austro-Marxist academics then proceeded to depoliticized it, embarking on a revision of Marxist theory in order to make it acceptable to the bourgeoisie.[33]

In the recent past, this has taken an ideological form that corresponded to the widespread intellectual rejection of progress as either a desirable or a feasible object and outcome of socio-economic development. As noted above, and in the chapters to follow, the main culprit in this regard has been the rise from the 1980s onwards of postmodern theory, a conservative but fashionable and influential anti-Marxist discourse.[34] Now, however, there is a discernible rejection of that discursive trend by many who originally espoused it uncritically: among the issues raised by the resulting attempt to recuperate some kind of Marxism – albeit as a theory shorn of its revolutionary agency – is precisely that of practice, or how are the objectives of any grassroots movement to be achieved.

6   Themes

This book is divided into three parts, the first of which (Chapters 1–3) considers how and why the concept of revolution has vanished from the leftist political agenda, plus what kind of politics have benefitted from the resulting lacuna. The effects of this absence are considered in the second part (Chapters 4–7), among them the epistemological difficulty confronting those mainly

---

emphasis), who – cynically, but accurately – described the issue faced thus: '*Avoid victories over your superior*. Every triumph is odious and if it is over your superior it is either foolish or disastrous. Superiority is invariably disliked, more especially by those who are themselves in high positions... You may well find some people who may be willing to grant you pride of place [but] least of all a ruler: this attribute is kingly, and it follows that any offence against it ranks as *lèse-majesté*. Sovereigns are sovereigns, and like to be so in respect of the most regal of qualities. Rulers like to be assisted but not to be outshone, and they prefer that advice should appear to be rather a reminder of something they have forgotten than a light upon something that is beyond their understanding'.

33 Details about this are contained in Part 1 of this volume.
34 Unsurprisingly, those who historically have condemned the tendency to follow fashion include Lenin (1961a: 395–96): 'How much better it would be to repeat the elements and, without "imposing" anything upon anybody, swing with every "turn"'. It is difficult not to conclude that these words apply equally to all those who uncritically jumped on the 'new' populist postmodern bandwagon.

academics who continue to analyse contemporary social movements at the rural grassroots and account for their political success/failure. The third part (Chapter 8) begins by examining the way in which the centenary of the 1917 Russian Revolution has been marked – not celebrated – in popular culture. Then two particular examples of popular culture are scrutinized (Chapters 9 and 10), involving non-fictional and fictional depictions by an historian and a novelist who have exercised a broad influence in the domain of popular culture (transcending academia, in other words) over conceptions of what the peasantry in Latin America and Europe are, do, and want. Whereas the views examined in the second part are restricted largely to academia, those in the third circulate beyond the university, and on account of this have had an impact outside this institutional context.

The case studies covered, which include rural contexts in Asia, Africa, Latin America, and Europe, are rather obviously not meant to range over every aspect of revolutionary agency. Much rather, the object is to illustrate the contrasting ways in which direct 'from below' agency can be approached in terms of theory and practice. Unlike some of the non-Marxist theory considered mainly in Part 1, which endorsed the idea of progress as a feasible/desirable project, albeit from a bourgeois view which perceived capitalist development as unproblematically beneficial to employers and workers alike, other non-Marxist theory examined elsewhere in the book constitutes an intellectual rejection of development-as-progress, either as a desirable or as a feasible object/outcome of socio-economic change.

Chapter 1 looks at the different forms taken by revolutionary practice, together with their distinct objectives, as pursued by the populist Will of the People and the Bolsheviks in late nineteenth and early twentieth century Russia. Populist agency was individual, and such action appeared to be an end in itself ('propaganda by the deed'). The target was the apparatus of Tsarist autocracy at the rural grassroots, and agency was designed to achieve nothing more specific than 'popular sovereignty' by empowering peasant smallholders on the basis of unmediated 'needs'/'wants' as these already existed at village level. By contrast, what Marxism advocated was extensive politicization followed by collective organization. Unlike populists, Bolsheviks sought to mobilize workers, agricultural labour, and poor peasants, so as to capture the state and effect a socialist transition. Again unlike populists, Bolsheviks argued that consciousness of class had to come from the outside, since workers by themselves arrived only at trade union consciousness, aimed at improvements in wages/conditions, not challenging the subjugation of labour to capital. For all these reasons, Bolsheviks opposed both 'spontaneity' and attempts to ameliorate capitalism ('economism').

The theory informing these – and other – kinds of 'from below' agency is examined in Chapter 2. Although populism and Bolshevism concurred as to the necessity of direct action, their reasons for doing so diverged substantially. Revolution was seen by the Bolsheviks both as a necessary outcome of modernity and simultaneously as a way of realizing this objective, in that it was the method whereby capitalism supplanted feudalism, and socialism then displaced capitalism. Central to this dynamic was the class formation/struggle that resulted as accumulation penetrated the countryside, and peasants were differentiated into rich, middle, and poor strata. Populists, however, rejected the occurrence both of differentiation and of depeasantisation, arguing instead that the peasant family farm was a pan-historical category the reproduction of which was endogenous, based on the 'consumer'/'producer' balance within the domestic unit.

Much the same case was made by revisionist theory within Marxism itself, which maintained that no peasant differentiation was taking place, depeasantisation which gave rise to class formation/struggle was lacking, and with it the historical subject on which both revolution and socialism depended. Consequently, reformist ends pursued via the existing parliamentary system were the only viable path, a theory championed by Austro-Marxism. Electoral success therefore required peasant support. Each side to this argument was represented in the 1920s debate as to the efficacy of democratic reform or revolution. During the 1960s, bourgeois modernisation theory advocated the same reformist path as a means of realizing economic development within the capitalist system. Banishing class struggle and economic crisis from capitalist reproduction, modernity was now equated by this later variant of reformism simply with bourgeois democracy. Progress required no more than the political incorporation by the democratic process of peasant economy, a strategy that left intact traditional rural culture that the 'new' populist postmodernism would later mobilize against the capitalist state.

Chapter 3 follows the trajectory from on the one hand a refusal of revolution, by restricting an increasingly acute form of working class struggle within the bounds of parliamentary reformism, to on the other the empowerment of counter-revolutionary discourse and mobilization. Hence class solidarity in late nineteenth and early twentieth century Austria was undermined by an expanding industrial reserve army, a development that accentuated rivalry between workers differentiated along ethnic/national lines. Class struggle gave way to ethnic/national conflict, and the search for protection from market competition by cheap migrants replaced collective bargaining with employers. The political timidity of the way in which Austro-Marxism addressed inter-ethnic rivalry in the labour market, an outcome of its espousal of parliamentary reformism, led to Social Democracy being outflanked in terms of practice by the populist far right offering a more radical form of non-parliamentary action. Much the same kind of populist ideology has now resurfaced in Europe, generating similar 'from below' support for counter-revolutionary mobilization.

Part 2 looks critically at the problems faced by mainstream analyses in the social sciences as a consequence of having discarded the twin Marxist concepts of revolution and socialism and attempted to replace them with variants of a 'new' populist postmodern framework privileging non-class forms of 'selfhood' and resistance as empowering 'from below' identity and agency.

Traced in Chapter 4, therefore, are the historical roots of the vanishing process, located further back in the way following the 1789 French Revolution the concept of a radical overturning has been conceptually disinherited and dismembered, both economically and politically. The late eighteenth and nineteenth century marked the theoretical and political emergence of a liberal political economy corresponding to a *laissez-faire* project in defence of 'pure' capitalism, leading to neo-classical economic theory, and culminating in present-day neo-liberalism. An examination of what this *laissez-faire* ideology approved/disapproved of, in terms of landownership, free/unfree labour-power, class formation and struggle, industrial production, and the state, reveals a surprising adherent. It is argued that much of this discourse is shared by a variant of Marxism, the semi-feudal thesis, an influential participant in Third World development debates from the 1960s onwards. Currently, however, another variant of Marxist theory departs from the way both *laissez-faire* and the semi-feudal thesis interpret the role of free/unfree labour-power in the course of class struggle.

Examined in Chapter 5 is another example of the difficulties stemming from development theory being behind the political curve, a result of having ceased to argue for revolutionary socialism. In epistemological terms this, too, involves misinterpreting the current role played by unfree labour-power in the class struggle. The result is that an initial interpretation of bonded labour as a benign form of 'subsistence guarantee' and landlord 'patronage', whereby workers struggled to retain such unfree production relations, has had to be replaced with a more radical Marxist interpretation – the class struggle argument – formulated on the margins. Although a comparison of late and early interpretations structuring the analysis in question reveals a change of mind, the epistemological approach nevertheless retains its initial premise: that a 'benign' capitalist state will in the end be prevailed upon to abolish unfree production relations that are central to the success of the accumulation process. In one crucial respect, therefore, this view has not really changed, merely substituting the patronage of the capitalist state for that of the landlord.

Chapter 6 considers a different approach to the same problem of being behind the curve: the resort to empiricism. This takes the form of compiling taxonomies of what are presented as distinct variants of unfreedom, an empiricist categorization of production relations which ends up conceding what it starts out by denying. Namely, that what structures both the definition and effects of all the variants identified is the simple polarity entry-into/exit-from the work arrangements concerned, a dichotomy which in turn informs the difference between labour-power that is free and that which is unfree. Consequently, all attempts to define production relations in terms of multiple variants and causes in the end prove fruitless, and epistemologically fail to advance the debate about systemic change.

The Subaltern Studies project constitutes yet another example both of the outcome of discarding Marxism/socialism and replacing the latter with the 'new' populist postmodernism, and also of the subsequent transfer of radical theory from the academic margins to the mainstream. Scrutinized in Chapter 7, therefore, are claims made either by or on behalf of three historiographical groups involved in the critical reaction to the Subaltern Studies series. These suggest that attempts at a nationalist appropriation of this critique are underway. Dismissing or disregarding its rivals, each claim asserts that credit for unmasking the complicity between the postmodern epistemology of the project and the discourse of nationalism, populism and conservatism was due mainly to those either outside India or inside India. By contrast, it is argued that the critique was both cumulative and international, and further that, although the timing of each critical reaction was important, the presence/absence of a politics was paramount in understanding what each group succeeded in theorizing or failed to problematize.

The focus of Part 3 is on the same kind of discourse from which radical notions of revolution and socialism have been excluded, but with the difference that the influence of each of the analyses involved – the way popular culture has marked the centenary of the 1917 Russian Revolution, plus interpretations of peasantry by Eric Hobsbawm and John Berger – is not confined to academia. That both the latter are regarded by many on the political left – and, indeed, regard themselves – as Marxists compounds the problem of misinterpreted theory and practice.

Chapter 8 considers how the 1917 Russian Revolution is seen from 2017, and in particular the negative manner in which popular culture marked the centenary. One hundred years on, the way the revolution is being commemorated – not celebrated – in western capitalism has given rise to what can only be described as a carnival of reaction. The sole legacy of value is deemed to be aesthetic: it is the culture generated by the 1917 Russian Revolution – film, music, art – not its politics, which is depicted as worthwhile. That the anniversary has been the occasion for anti-Marxists to condemn both revolutionary agency and socialism is unsurprising; rather more surprising, however, is that much the same kind of criticism has also been voiced by many of those who perceive themselves as belonging to the left. The reasons for the latter are traced in part to a shift of Marxism from the street to academia, and the consequent rise of the 'new' populist postmodernism, an effect of the transfer of radical theory at the margins and its depoliticization by the mainstream. At both ends of the political spectrum, therefore, revolution as a concept has vanished from the political agenda.

Chapter 9 considers another form of banishing revolutionary agency, which is to claim that the conditions necessitating such action are still not in place, since the accumulation process has not yet run its course. This is the approach of those Marxists who adhere to the semi-feudal thesis. Examined critically, therefore, are the writings by Hobsbawm on peasants in Latin America. Eschewing participant/observation, his analyses missed crucial aspects of rural society in Peru during the pre-reform era, a consequence being the mistaken belief that production relations on *latifundia* were obstacles to economic growth and would therefore vanish once landlords were expropriated. Because they are compatible with capitalist development, however, these same unfree work arrangements continued into the post-reform era, but used now by rich peasant beneficiaries of the agrarian reform programmes carried out by the state.

Finally, Chapter 10 looks at the way peasant society is interpreted by John Berger, an influential cultural critic. Eschewing both Marxist and bourgeois theory about the desirability in village communities of development/progress/modernity, he endorsed instead a view deployed by populists and/or ethnographers of undifferentiated peasant family farmers engaged in subsistence cultivation. Breaking with Marxism which saw the fragmentation of the peasantry along class lines as capitalism penetrated the countryside as a necessary prelude to socialist transition, Berger maintained by contrast that the erosion of what he perceived as an homogenous peasantry was undesirable as a solution to the plight faced by French rural society. Like populists, therefore, he lamented the process of depeasantisation linked to development-as-modernization, and – unlike Marxism – seemingly wishes to reverse this by defending subsistence-oriented peasant cultivation on the family farm. This same view resurfaced subsequently as the 'cultural turn', which similarly championed rural petty commodity producers as 'eternal'/'authentic'/'natural' subaltern identities, in the process abandoning not just class and socialism but also notions of development/progress/modernity. For this reason it is argued that, where interpretations of peasant society are concerned, Berger can be regarded as a precursor of the 'new' populist postmodernism.

PART 1

*Revolutionary/Counter-revolutionary Practice/
Theory*

© ANNA LUISA BRASS

CHAPTER 1

Revolution in Practice

'In order to bring about the [1789] French Revolution, it was necessary to overthrow religion, outrage morality, violate every propriety, and commit every crime. This diabolical work required the employment of such a number of vicious men that perhaps never before had so many vices acted together to accomplish any evil whatsoever.'
   Revolution as perceived in 1797 by JOSEPH DE MAISTRE, one of its most vehement rightwing critics.[1]

•••

'A story is being circulated in Germany that the prison chaplain visited Pastor Niemoeller and said to him: "Why are you in prison, brother?" "Why are you *not* in prison, brother?" replied the leader of the Protestant clergy' (original emphasis).
   An observation BY STEPHEN KING-HALL in 1938.[2]

•
• •

1   Introduction: Revolution, or Reform (and Counter-revolution)

Although scrutinizing forms taken by political action necessarily raises the question both of the ideology and the aims guiding this, the object of this chapter is simply to consider different kinds of agency.[3] Broadly speaking, the forms themselves divide between on the one hand adherence to the legalism defined by a parliamentary system, in which only reformist ends are permitted, and on the other illegal and thus proscribed activity outside the parliamentary system designed both to challenge its political legitimacy and then to replace it as a ruling institution. In political terms these two forms – revolutionary (or counter-revolutionary) and reformist – are rather obviously not mutually

---

1   de Maistre (1974: 140).
2   King-Hall (1938: Newsletter Supplement 86).
3   The theory informing agency, and the debates which give rise to this, are the subject of the next chapter.

exclusive, since leftist and far-right political movements can be found in either. Into the revolutionary category, therefore, come populists (the Will of the People) and socialists (Bolsheviks) in Russia, and fascists in Germany and Austria (National Socialists), whilst in the latter context those adhering to reformist agency similarly include both socialists (Austro-Marxism) and the far-right (Pan-Germanism).

Since the focus in Part 1 of this volume is on what might be termed direct forms of political agency (counter-revolutionary as well as revolutionary), examined in Chapters 1–3 are movements in Russia such as the Will of the People and the Bolsheviks, and Austrian mobilizations such as Pan-Germanism.[4] These are considered in terms of the views expressed by, respectively, Vera Figner (1852–1942), V.I. Lenin (1870–1924), and Georg Ritter von Schönerer (1842–1921), all of whom were important participants in the events to which they refer. Each of them spent time in prison on account of political beliefs held, which if nothing else underlines both the radical nature of their agency and the extent of their commitment. Despite the fact that the three approaches considered here not only originated at different ends of the political spectrum, but also and consequently pursued very different ends, plus the fact that all emerged and held sway around the end of the nineteenth century and the beginning of the twentieth, the lessons each of them taught in terms of radical practice are, it is argued here, still relevant today.

After the emancipation of the serfs in 1861, among those who sought to organize the peasantry were populist groups such as Land and Freedom and *Narodnya Volya*, the object being 'to throw its own forces without delay into a ruthless battle with the Autocracy, directing its blows against the head of state...[a] battle by means of violence against violence' culminating in the assassination of Emperor Alexander II in 1881.[5] Until 1876, revolutionary

---

4 Clearly, it will be necessary to compare these revolutionary/counter-revolutionary/reformist movements of both left and right with other equivalents, also of the left and right, so as to gauge their political efficacy.

5 See Figner (1927: 9), whose seminal account of the agency and its trajectory undertaken by non-Marxist revolutionary groups in late nineteenth century Russia informs much of what follows. From a 'family of prosperous noblemen', she (Figner, 1927: 23, 36) evinced the concern expressed by 'repentant noblemen' about the lives and work conditions of rural subordinates on the estates, confessing that before joining the ranks of the revolutionary groups 'I had never heard of the system of forced labour by the peasants, never witnessed any acts of oppression, or heard any complaints. No relations of any kind between the proprietor and his serfs were in my field of vision. The only serfs that I knew were our house servants. Mother was always kind and indulgent towards them'. Her father, a substantial landowner possessing 17,000 acres, told her (Figner, 1927: 9, 25) '[i]f the serfs had not been freed, I should have led their rebellion': yet he condemned as 'mischief-makers' attempts by militants to ques-

groups in Russia were divided between propagandists and insurrectionists. Descended politically from populism (*narodniki*), the former group coalesced around the Land and Freedom movement (*Zemlya i Volya*), while the latter one consisted of adherents belonging to the Will of the People faction (*Narodnya Volya*). Although both revolutionary tendencies operated at the rural grassroots, their methods and objectives were distinct.[6]

2 Educate them to Revolt

Whereas propagandists sought to inform villagers about politics, and then formulate consciousness so as to build and organize on this basis, insurrectionists by contrast viewed peasants as innately socialist, who required no political instruction, lacking only a single event to generate a mass uprising.[7] In ideological terms, therefore, the programme of the *Narodnya Volya* was based on the consciousness as this already existed and was reproduced at the level of the rural grassroots, the justification for this being that popular perceptions (= long established views) were anyway difficult to change. It was from this 'given' ideological base that any revolutionary activity must of necessity commence, from the discourse – whatever its politics – as encountered by the *Narodnya*

---

 tion the benign objective of the 1861 emancipation, fearing that 'another freedom will come, when all the land of the proprietors would pass on to the peasantry gratis. These rumours, so father said, injured the essential interests of the peasantry, by disturbing their friendly relations with the proprietors'. According to Figner (1927: 41), such antithetical views were not uncommon: a student from a landlord family who protested at the shooting down of estate tenants elsewhere protesting about their situation 'was himself oppressing the peasants, imposing exorbitant penalties for damage done to grain on his estate'. What this contradictory discourse reflected was the underlying – and in terms of its assumptions, consistent – self-perception of the landlord class as benign proprietors, along the lines of 'my tenants have nothing to complain about, but if they want to protest about things in general, it is my duty as the person responsible for their well-being to take charge of this'.

6 Trained as a doctor, it was at village level that Figner (1927: 54–55, 60) encountered poverty, illness and destitution at first hand. It could be argued that for young women from her kind of background, being 'useful' in this manner was a break with the gender expectations imposed on them by their landowning families, and thus to some degree becoming 'repentant noblemen' was an emancipation as much of the self as of the 'other'. This is implied in her memories of what it was like to be not just a militant but also 'useful': 'This life of ours [in the village], and the relations between us and these simple folk, who felt that light was near at hand, possessed such a bewitching charm, that even now it is pleasant for me to recall it; every moment we felt that we were needed, that we were not superfluous. It was this consciousness of one's usefulness that was the magnetic force which drew our Russian youth into the village'.

7 See Figner (1927: 50ff.). These distinctions in approach are set out in the following Table:

Volya in the villages. Unsurprisingly, 'the ideals already ripe in the consciousness of the people' included proprietorship by individual smallholders.[8]

In the course of carrying out work among peasants in the village, however, those belonging to the *Narodnya Volya* perceived that the only feasible programme was direct action (= 'violence to protect justice'). Grassroots organization *per se* was pointless, since a ruling class which operated and exercised power at all levels of society as a result possessed the capacity to prevent/pre-empt – and thus frustrate – any forms of politicization and all consequent attempts at agrarian mobilization. The only alternative was 'propaganda by the deed', a tactic aimed at those in authority, whether at village or national level.[9] Accordingly, the method of 'going to the people' had a threefold purpose. First,

	Propagandists	**Insurrectionists**
Location	Northern Russia	Southern Russia
Influences	Lavrov's *Forward*	Bakunin
Constituency sought	Common people	Common people
Agency	People = blank sheet of paper upon which to inscribe socialism. Therefore political instruction and organization paramount. Reasons for and form taken by grassroots action had to be formulated and constructed.	No need to teach people about politics, since their situation made them instinctively socialist. Therefore no instruction or organization needed.

---

8   The programme of *Narodnya Volya* maintained that (Figner, 1927: 52) 'as in the case of every other nation at a certain stage of its historical development, the Russian people have an outlook of their own, corresponding to the level of their moral and mental conceptions that have been formed under given environmental conditions. As part of this outlook one must regard popular attitudes toward political and economic questions. Under ordinary conditions it is extremely difficult to transform these established views, before changing the dominating institutions. Hence it is necessary to make an attempt in the revolutionary activity to use as a starting point the attitudes, aspirations, and desires prevalent among the people at the given moment, and inscribing on the revolutionary banner the ideals already ripe in the consciousness of the people. Such an ideal in the economic field was the possession of land by those who till it and only for as long as they till it'.

9   Whilst studying medicine at Zurich University in the 1870s, Figner (1927: 44) came to the conclusion that 'the only way to cure these [economic and social] evils was to change this order through active warfare, with the purpose of overthrowing the tyrannical and privileged classes'. Thus, she 'planned to impart [socialist] doctrines to the people directly, to live and work with them, gradually educate them to revolt'.

to contribute materially to the well-being of rural inhabitants, so as to become acquainted with their working/living conditions and thus be able to build a programme based on eliminating oppressive/exploitative aspects of rural society. Second, to do this because village inhabitants were 'crushed by poverty', and did not have the strength to undertake this process themselves. And third, the need to attract 'revolutionary youth' to the cause, who – although deterred by the limited prospect of change effected through work amongst peasants – might respond to demonstrations of more direct forms of action designed to achieve the same end.

To some degree, the latter consideration also informed the methods of populists in the *Zemlya i Volya* movement, who maintained that its city membership was avoiding conflict with the urban ruling class, thereby diverting young revolutionaries from what was the main task. The latter, argued populists, was 'agrarian terror in the villages', aimed not at an urban but at a rural authority structure.[10] However, direct action carried out in rural areas had little impact beyond the village where it occurred; comparatively speaking, therefore, propaganda by the deed was more effective when carried out it cities than in the far more remote countryside. Whether or not terror should be used was for the *Zemlya i Volya* movement simply a matter of pragmatism: the focus of concern was would the actions undertaken make an impression on the largest number of people, not what political and ideological meanings such actions might convey; that is to say, its form not its political content.

It was because of this change of direction on the part of *Zemlya i Volya* that Georgi Plekhanov shifted his allegiance from populism to Marxism. His opposition to 'terroristic activity' in rural areas stemmed from a number of reasons: it resulted in losses for the party, attracted further government repression, and 'lured youth from its constructive, legitimate work among the people, whose support was so indispensible to the party'.[11] When *Zemlya i Volya* split, therefore, the divergent paths reflected the same kind of concern: between on the one hand those who – like Plekhanov – wanted to focus on the agrarian question and the economic interests of smallholders, and on the other advocates of propaganda by the deed aimed at the overthrow of autocracy.[12] For the latter – the *Narodnya Volya* – the main enemy now became the state itself, because it had converted the Russian population into a 'tax-paying class'; after 1861 this levy was imposed on the peasantry in order to fund the armed forces and meet the foreign debt.[13] In the discourse of *Narodnya Volya*, therefore, this

10 Figner (1927: 68).
11 Figner (1927: 69).
12 Figner (1927: 74).
13 See Figner (1927: 74–78) for details about the *Narodovoltsy* (= the Will of the People).

appropriation by the state 'demonstrated perfectly the principle that the people existed for the government, and not the government for the people'.

3 The Greatest of All Proprietors

Throughout the 1860–80 period, the state encouraged accumulation, 'striving to create a bourgeoisie', supporting capital by means of fiscal and other policies (subsidies, tariffs). According to *Narodnya Volya*, whereas in the West the state served those *already* wealthy, in Russia at this conjuncture it was a means to obtain wealth: hence the view that the state itself was responsible for the creation of the exploiting classes.[14] On the basis of this economic role *Narodnya Volya* not only described the state as 'the greatest of all proprietors', but also justified its practice of propaganda by the deed.[15] Whatever the sort of leftist politics to which one adheres, and regardless of political disagreements with this kind of practice, there can be no doubting the element of self-sacrifice, dedication, and personal courage of members belonging to *Narodnya Volya* who were active at this period of Russian history.[16] It scarcely needs

14 Something akin to the same interpretation of the state – distinguishing between European nations where historically it was set up by those who had previously amassed wealth as a political instrument representing their interests, and other countries where the state apparatus which already existed then became the means for generating wealth – was advanced in the course of the 1960s development debate by Hamza Alavi (on which see Brass, 2014b: 127–30). What he characterized as the post-colonial state in Third World nations was a view based on the theory that, unlike Europe where the bourgeoisie had economic power that needed representation at state level, in decolonized nations the state had already been shaped by a foreign bourgeoisie. For this reason, the state in Third World countries became the object of competing attempts to wrest control of its resources. It could be argued, however, that following the implementation from the 1980s onwards of a *laissez faire* project in metropolitan capitalist nations, whereby state-owned assets have been privatized, the struggle to wrest control of the state and its resources is no longer confined to Third World countries.

15 'All the stranger was the title of terrorist organization which [the *Narodnya Volya*] later acquired', writes Figner (1927: 79), adding: 'The public gave it that name because of the external aspect of its activity, the one characteristic which caught their attention. Terror for its own sake was never the aim of the party. It was a weapon of protection, of self-defence, regarded as a powerful instrument for agitation, and employed only for the purpose of attaining the ends for which the organization was working… The work of propaganda and organization always went hand in hand with that of destruction; it was less evident, but was nevertheless destined to bear its fruits'.

16 According to Figner (1927: 80, 95), membership entailed 'the promise to devote all one's mental and spiritual strength to the revolutionary work, to forget for its sake all ties of kinship, and all personal sympathies, love and friendships;…to give one's life also, if

highlighting the extent of the contrast between such commitment and the kinds of political engagement undertaken currently by most – if not all – of those who still belong to the political left.[17]

For *Narodnya Volya*, the main problem in the late nineteenth century Russian countryside was 'the lack of political freedom', which constituted an obstacle to 'the needs of the people', a non-economic objective that might in theory be achieved without having to transcend an existing and as yet nascent capitalism.[18] Once the autocracy of the Tsar had been eradicated, replaced politically by a non-specific notion of popular sovereignty, therefore, accumulation itself might proceed unchallenged. Insofar as the main programmatic aim of *Narodnya Volya* was the realization of nothing more than political freedom itself, therefore, it is necessary to ask what else its project envisaged. Defining itself as 'populists-socialists', *Narodnya Volya* maintained that political freedom was not an end but a means to an end: 'breaking our way through to the people; by adding the term 'socialist' to 'populist', *Narodnya Volya* signalled an intent to meet the 'conscious needs and wants of the people', rather than 'the abstract, ultimate aims of socialist teaching'.

Where revolutionary agency and objectives are concerned, the politically uneasy juxtaposition at the centre of this discourse highlights the presence of a contradiction. Notwithstanding the apparent equilibrium projected in its 'populists-socialists' definition, of greater interest to *Narodnya Volya* were ideas of unmediated 'needs'/'wants' already held by the people (= populism) than in the 'ultimate aims' of theory (= socialist objectives, such as central planning, common ownership of the means of production/distribution/exchange). In terms of its revolutionary practice, therefore, *Narodnya Volya* accepted that

---

necessary, taking no thought of anything else, and sparing no one and nothing;...to have no personal property, nothing of one's own'. Among those who recognized the courage and dedication this required was Karl Marx.

17   Together with the privations experienced by those like Victor Serge (2012), the grassroots commitment of *Narodnya Volya* underlines the vast gulf separating what one might term 'authentic' revolutionary engagement from what nowadays passes for this, as evidenced by the sauntering out to the occasional demonstration on the part of present-day equivalents of *katheder*-socialists.

18   See Figner (1927, 63), who elaborates: 'This absence of political freedom might be disguised, might not be keenly felt, were the despotic power to serve some way...the aspirations of society. But if instead, it goes its own way, ignoring...these factors; if it is deaf to the lamentations of the people, and to the demands of the...worker, and to the voice of the publicist; if it is indifferent to the serious investigations of the scholar, and to the figures of the statistician; if not one single group of its subjects has any means of influencing the course of social life; if all the expedients are useless, all paths forbidden, and the younger, more ardent part of society, finds no sphere for its activity...then the situation becomes unendurable'.

socialist 'ultimate aims' would be postponed until 'the more or less remote future', a recognition perhaps that unmediated 'needs'/'wants' as expressed by petty commodity producers at the rural grassroots may after all be incompatible with the 'ultimate aims' of socialist theory applied to the wider society. Simply put, this discourse was informed by a concept of an ever-present and pristine Nature, the restoration of which to its rightful owners – smallscale peasant farmers engaged in subsistence production within the context of the village economy – underwrote the agrarian myth narrative of populism.[19]

The extent of this irreconcilability is underlined by the fact that *Narodnya Volya* 'placed as its nearest goal in the economic field' giving land ('the chief instrument of production') to peasants, and its political objective as replacing autocracy with popular sovereignty.[20] Its programme amounted, in essence, to a combination of two elements: individual peasant proprietorship + abolition of monarchy. The difficulty facing these objectives is simply stated. Once smallholders owned land they had cultivated as serfs, sharecroppers, or tenants, it was unlikely that there would be any support by them for collectivization, which – for the purposes of planning – transferred the title to all land from individual proprietors to the state, not least because the latter institution was regarded by *Narodnya Volya* as the main enemy.[21] Similarly, abolition of the monarchy (= autocracy) as an end in itself fails to address the character of the socio-economic system which emerges as a result: that is, whether (or not)

---

19 In their 1850 critique of Thomas Carlyle, Marx and Engels (1978: 306) expressed disapproval of his approach in a way that applies equally to agrarian myth ideology espoused by populism: 'The whole process of history is determined not by the development of the living masses themselves, naturally dependent on specific but in turn historically created changing conditions, it is determined by an eternal law of nature, unalterable for all time, from which it departs today and to which it returns tomorrow, and on the correct apprehension of which everything depends. This correct apprehension of the eternal law of nature is the eternal truth, everything else is false. With this mode of thinking, the real class conflicts, for all their variety at various periods, are completely resolved into the one great and eternal conflict, between those who have fathomed the eternal law of nature and act in keeping with it, the wise and noble, and those who misunderstand it, distort it and work against it, the fools and the rogues'. This same distinction between Marxism and populism went on to inform the critiques not just by Lenin and Trotsky but also those aimed currently at the anti-capitalist discourse of the 'new' populist postmodernism.

20 See Figner (1927: 78).

21 It is important to note the presence of a distinction between opposition to the state by anarchist groups, and current anti-state discourse associated with the everyday-forms-of-resistance framework. Although exponents of the latter maintain that their approach is consistent with anarchism, and should accordingly be seen as progressive in political terms, another interpretation of such populist historiography (Brass, 2012; Brass, 2017b: Chapter 12) indicates that the anti-state discourse of the everyday-forms-of-resistance framework is more accurately viewed as that of neoliberal economics and *laissez faire* theory.

the accumulation process would continue, under what kind of direction, and to what purpose. Despite *Narodnya Volya* retaining the seizure of state power by revolutionary action as its preferred means, therefore, all that this radical practice sought to achieve was an order reflecting 'the freely expressed popular will'.

In many ways, the 'other' of the kind of revolutionary agency pursued by *Narodnya Volya*, together with the reasons for this, was that advocated by Lenin, as set out in his seminal 1902 text *What Is To Be Done?*, on which the Bolshevik strategy for the 1905 and 1917 revolutions was based. It shared with *Narodnya Volya* the view that anything short of a radical overturning of the existing system represented failure, and that consequently the aim of direct action was – and could only ever be – to capture the state. The differences between them, however, were as fundamental: whereas the propaganda by the deed of *Narodnya Volya* was agency that was both immediate and individual in design and execution, that of the Bolsheviks required extensive politicization and was based on collective organization. Although notionally committed to a 'populist-socialist' project, *Narodnya Volya* relegated the 'ultimate aims' of socialism to the status of an aspiration which might be realized – if at all – at some unspecified future conjuncture.

4 Desperation and Vengeance

For *Narodnya Volya*, a radical grassroots political consciousness encountered at village level and incorporating all its inhabitants already existed, needing only direct action undertaken by militants to set the revolutionary process in train. Bolsheviks, by contrast, sought to build an entirely new form of political awareness: this was to be achieved by, first, formulating and then consolidating a political consciousness of class – an identity that necessarily excluded the better-off elements at village level – which could only be brought to rural areas from the outside. Accordingly, both the historical subject and thus the object of mobilization were in each case different: revolutionary action of *Narodnya Volya* was designed to empower rural smallholders, who would as a result become individual peasant proprietors engaged largely or only in subsistence farming. The goal of agency undertaken by the Bolsheviks, however, was to empower workers, a category which included the landless agricultural labourers and/or poor peasants with insufficient holdings for them and their family members to cultivate. Unlike *Narodnya Volya*, the tenure pattern arising from this kind of empowerment would be the collective farm, a centralized and surplus-generating production unit owned and administered by the workers' state.

These differences structured the consciousness/spontaneity dichotomy informing the theoretical analysis by Lenin of revolutionary agency and its political objectives. Ostensibly, the target of his critique was what he termed a 'new trend' devoted to criticizing 'dogmatic Marxism', the principal exponent of which was the revisionist Eduard Bernstein.[22] Because there is no increasing impoverishment, no proletarianisation, and no intensification of capitalist contradiction, advocates of this 'new trend' maintained that 'Social Democracy must change from a party of social revolution into a democratic party of social reforms'.[23] The 'ultimate aim' of a revolutionary transition to socialism, as advocated by the Bolsheviks, was thereby declared unsound, and the dictatorship of the proletariat 'completely rejected'. According to this 'new trend', therefore, the role of workers was simply to undertake economic struggle (for a reformed capitalism), while Marxist intellectuals merged with liberals pursuing the political struggle (for a reformed capitalism).[24] It was in the course of making this critique that Bolshevism located a weakness shared by revisionists and – ironically – *Narodnya Volya*: that is, an adherence to 'spontaneity', or a desire to do no more that represent and/or mobilize on the basis of grassroots ideology as they find it.[25]

This approach was criticized by Lenin, since agency undertaken by those who 'worship spontaneity, i.e. of that which exists "at the present moment"' merely sought to empower long-standing village ideology, regardless of what it advocated economically and attempted to achieve politically.[26] Against this, the Bolsheviks maintained that working class consciousness had to come from the outside, the necessity for which derived from the fact that all a workers' movement was able to accomplish on its own was to 'develop only trade

---

22 See Lenin (1961a: 353), whose differences with Austro-Marxism and *katheder*-socialists are examined in the next chapter.
23 Lenin (1961a: 353).
24 Complaining 'how English liberalism had eroded Bernstein's socialist ideals', Wilhelm Liebknecht (Dominick, 1982: 398) observed in the late 1890s that 'I no longer read what he [Bernstein] writes: I have always already read it in the *Daily Chronicle* [a liberal English newspaper]'.
25 The element of irony derives from the very different kinds of agency espoused: propaganda by the deed in the case of *Narodnya Volya*, and parliamentary democracy in the case of revisionism.
26 See Lenin (1961a: 367, 374–75 original emphasis), who explains that 'the "spontaneous element", in essence, represents nothing more nor less than consciousness in an *embryonic form*. Even the primitive revolts expressed the awakening of consciousness to a certain extent', but agency that resulted was 'more in the nature of outbursts of desperation and vengeance than of *struggle*'.

union consciousness'.²⁷ The latter aimed to do no more than put pressure on an existing government to pass and implement labour legislation.²⁸ For this reason, therefore, those populist groups which in late 1890s Russia mobilized along 'spontaneous' lines were dismissed by Lenin on the grounds that 'what was only part misfortune became full misfortune when this consciousness began to grow dim...when there appeared people...that were prepared to regard shortcomings as virtues, that even tried to invent a *theoretical* basis for their *slavish cringing before spontaneity*'.²⁹

Among the reasons advanced by Lenin for opposing 'spontaneity' in this manner was the ability of those who own/control the means of communication – 'more fully developed' which 'has at its disposal *immeasurably* more means of dissemination ' – to formulate and reproduce the kinds of concepts and ideology circulating at rural grassroots level.³⁰ Despite being accused of underestimating the power of control exercised over the means of communication, its impact on what through time became entrenched forms of discourse at the rural grassroots, and thus misrecognizing the extent of village opposition to their programme, therefore, the Bolsheviks were fully aware of the need constantly to challenge already existing rural traditions and institutional structures. In a way that anticipates the difficulty which the present-day capitalist monopoly over the electronic and print media poses for leftist views, the link

---

27 About this, Lenin (1961a: 375) argued that 'there could not have been Social-Democratic consciousness among the workers [and therefore it] would have to be brought to them from without. The history of all countries shows that the working class, exclusively by its own effort, is able to develop only trade-union consciousness, i.e. the conviction that it is necessary to combine in unions, fight employers, and strive to compel the government to pass necessary labour legislation, etc'.
28 As will be seen below in Chapter 5, notwithstanding its obvious political weakness, this kind of approach is still deployed currently with regard to workers in India, by those who mistakenly perceive themselves to be leftists of one kind or other.
29 Again, it goes without saying that the same critique applies with equal force to current exponents of resistance theory, itself part of the 'new' populist postmodern approach to analysing contemporary rural social movements. 'Since there can be no talk of an independent ideology formulated by the working masses themselves in the process of their movement', noted Lenin (1961a: 384, original emphasis), 'the *only* choice is – either bourgeois or socialist ideology. There is no middle course...' Lest this be misinterpreted as excluding a plebeian voice, he immediately added that '[t]his does not mean, of course, that the workers have no part in creating such an ideology...'.
30 This point is underlined (Lenin 1961a: 386, original emphasis) thus: 'But why...does the spontaneous movement, the movement along the line of least resistance, lead to the domination of bourgeois ideology? For the simple reason that bourgeois ideology is far older in origin than socialist ideology, that it is more fully developed and that it has at its disposal *immeasurably* more means of dissemination'.

between on the one hand successful revolutionary action and a socialist programme, and on the other effective politicization/organization conducted at the rural grassroots was a connection stressed by Lenin himself (along the lines of 'we must strive continuously to get our own political interpretation across').

5   As the Part to the Whole

Why the Bolshevik concerns about the politically debilitating impact on grassroots movements in the countryside of 'spontaneity' – building what is intended to be a radical political mobilization simply on the basis of long-standing rural traditions/customs/institutions that already exist – continue to be relevant is not difficult to discern.[31] Currently, a variant of 'spontaneity' informs the approach – examined below in Chapter 5 – of those who continue to look to the capitalist state for solutions to poverty, exploitation and oppression, in the process labelling government 'uncaring' when it fails to meet what are wrongly perceived to be its obligations in this regard.[32] In an important sense, this sort of plea – an entreaty by a supplicant on behalf of those below – grows directly out of agency the focus of which is to seek improvements to wages/conditions (='spontaneity'), nothing more; that is, as Lenin argued, all political approaches 'which do not remove the subjection of labour to capital'.[33]

---

31   Identifying populism as a 'new trend' the practice of which failed to challenge – let alone displace – existing grassroots consciousness, traditions, and institutions, the Bolsheviks (Lenin, 1961a: 396, 564 note 166) maintained that 'we have become convinced that the fundamental error committed by the "new trend" [in Russian Social Democracy] is its bowing to spontaneity and its failure to understand that the spontaneity of the masses demands a high degree of consciousness from us Social-Democrats [= Bolsheviks]'. A century on, the problem hasn't changed that much; its main protagonists are still populists of one sort or another, and Marxism.

32   The weakness of this approach, conducted nowadays by NGOs and similar organizations concerned with upholding legislative ordinances relating to human rights, is evident from numerous instances where, having been 'exposed' for contravening national or international laws protecting workers, corporations quickly declare that conditions will soon change for the better. Despite such commitment to meet desired standards, eliminate 'abuses', increase wages to the required level, therefore, subsequent investigations merely confirm that nothing has in fact changed.

33   The crucial distinction between on the one hand agency designed to do no more than make a moral appeal to the capitalist state based on concern for its workforce, thereby leaving in the hands of those who oppressed/exploited labourers solutions to this very oppression/exploitation, and on the other action the object of which is to convert the state into a workers' government that could be relied on to effect the necessary change, was underlined by Lenin (1961a: 387): 'The economic struggle of the workers is very often connected (although not inseparably) with bourgeois politics, clerical politics, etc....if by politics is meant trade-union politics, viz., the common striving of all workers to secure

While voicing criticisms of 'spontaneity', however, Lenin nevertheless recognized both the political value to Marxist theory/practice and the contribution to revolutionary agency made by what was termed 'exposure literature'.[34] The latter consisted in the main of leaflets revealing the conditions in factories and workshops, as these affected workers and as seen from their point of view. Evidence provided by workers themselves confirmed the 'unbearably hard toil', the 'lack of rights', and the 'miserable existence' of those employed in these contexts: the accounts publicized by this 'exposure literature' had a big impact, and 'stirred everyone'.[35] Yet the Bolsheviks were also fully aware of the limits posed by reliance solely on this kind of publicity as a guide to revolutionary action: these leaflets, Lenin noted, 'acquired the significance of a strong moral influence', adding that 'Social-Democracy leads the struggle of the working class, not only for better terms for the sale of labour-power but for the abolition of the social system that compels the propertyless to sell themselves to the rich'.[36]

For the Bolsheviks, therefore, reforms were merely a step along the revolutionary path leading to socialism, not an end in themselves.[37] Along with

from the government measures for alleviating the distress to which their condition gives rise, but which does not abolish that condition, i.e., which do not remove the subjection of labour to capital. That striving is common to the English trade-unionists, who are hostile to socialism, to the catholic workers...'.

34   On the 'exposure literature' and its useful but limited political role, see Lenin (1961a: 398), who also notes that Engels described this genre as a form of 'resistance to capitalists' – a variant which is replicated currently in what Scott proclaims as 'everyday-forms-of-resistance', or the agency of the 'new' populist postmodernism.

35   'Everyone knows that the economic struggle of the Russian workers underwent widespread development and consolidation simultaneously with the production of "literature" exposing economic (factory and occupational) conditions', reported Lenin: 'The "leaflets" were devoted mainly to the exposure of the factory system, and very soon a veritable passion for exposures was roused among the workers. As soon as the workers realized that the Social-Democratic study circles desired to, and could, supply them with a new kind of leaflet that told the truth about their miserable existence, about their unbearably hard toil, and their lack of rights, they began to send in, actually flood us with, correspondence from the factories and workshops. This "exposure literature" created a tremendous sensation...the "truth about the life of the workers" stirred everyone'.

36   Critical of 'exposure literature' viewed as an end in itself, Lenin (1961a: 399–400, original emphasis) outlined his reasons for thinking this: 'The overwhelming majority of Russian Social-Democrats have of late been almost entirely absorbed by this work of organizing the exposure of factory conditions. Suffice it to recall...that they have lost sight of the fact that this, *taken by itself,* is in essence still not Social-Democratic work, but merely trade-union work...Social-Democracy leads the struggle of the working class, not only for better terms for the sale of labour-power, but for the abolition of the social system that compels the propertyless to sell themselves to the rich'.

37   'Revolutionary Social-Democracy has always included the struggle for reforms as part of its activities', argued Lenin (1961a: 405–6, original emphasis), since 'it considers it its duty

appeals to a non-existent capitalist morality (= a 'caring' attitude towards its workforce), reforms in the shape of concessions that do not threaten profitability or licence a challenge to property relations in the long term are seen by employers as allowable, in that compromises of this sort – modifications consistent with the continued functioning of the accumulation process – will not lead to socialism as long as workers perceive them as ends in themselves. Contrary to many on the contemporary left who interpret economic concessions made by capitalism and its state as evidence for the effectiveness of the struggle waged by 'those below', therefore, Lenin viewed them as methods which were supportive of struggles waged by 'those above': that is, 'pseudo-concessions' aimed at winning 'the confidence of the masses'.[38]

Not the least significant impact of such economic concessions (or 'pseudo-concessions') was that on the formation and/or consolidation of a consciousness specifically of class, an important aspect of any revolutionary struggle to bring about a socialist transition. Once again, in contrast to the primacy currently allocated to micro-level quotidian agency (= 'everyday-forms-of-resistance'), the focus of which is confined largely to 'from below' forms of struggle as these operate in a particular locality, the Bolsheviks insisted that struggle based on class necessarily required political knowledge that in socio-economic terms is total. It calls for an understanding which extends to cover *all* elements and strata in society, in order that a worker is able to situate him/herself within an entire socio-economic context the functioning of which s/he understands, the latter in turn informing any political action embarked upon subsequently.[39]

---

to present this demand [that government cease to be autocratic] not of the economic struggle *alone*, but of all manifestations in general of public and political life. In a word, it subordinates the struggle for reforms, as the part to the whole, to the revolutionary struggle for freedom and socialism'.

38 According to Lenin (1961a: 406), therefore, '"Economic" concessions (or pseudo-concessions) are, of course, the cheapest and most advantageous from the government's point of view, because by these means it hopes to win the confidence of the working masses'.

39 Hence the view (Lenin, 1961a: 412–13, original emphasis): 'The consciousness of the working masses cannot be genuine class-consciousness, unless the workers learn, from the concrete, and above all from topical, political facts and events to observe *every* other social class in *all* the manifestations of its intellectual, ethical, and political life... Those who concentrate the attention, observation, and consciousness of the working class exclusively, or even mainly, upon itself alone are not Social-Democrats; for the self-knowledge of the working class is indissolubly bound up, not solely with a fully clear theoretical understanding...of the relationships between *all* the various classes of modern society... In order to become a Social-Democrat, the worker must have a clear picture in his mind of the economic nature and the social and political features of the landlord and the priest, the high state official and the peasant, the student and the vagabond...'.

Outlining the form to be taken by consciousness of class led the Bolsheviks to a consideration of 'the question of education for revolutionary activity', on which basis Lenin drew what initially appears a surprising parallel between two radically distinct forms of agency and objectives: 'Economists' (those whose agency is designed to ameliorate capitalism) and 'terrorists' (whose aim is to destroy this system). He accepts this conflation appears as a 'paradox', given that 'Economists' adhere to the 'drab everyday struggle' (= 'everyday-forms-of-resistance'), whereas 'terrorists' favour its antithesis – propaganda of the deed. Notwithstanding this difference between 'Economists' and 'terrorists' in terms of their respective forms of revolutionary action, however, his view was that when considered in the light of a shared 'subservience to spontaneity', this distinctiveness vanished.[40] Accordingly, 'Economists' follow a variant of spontaneity governed by an inability to go beyond the immediacy of the labour movement, while 'terrorists' adhere to a form of spontaneity (= immediacy of instinctive action) arising from an inability to connect with the working class movement. Hence the 'passionate indignation' of those who object to the status quo, but have little idea of how to change this, apart from pointless acts of outrage (= self-sacrifice).[41]

The kind of agency Lenin criticizes, therefore, is one which 'desires to substitute terror for agitation', whereas his view is that 'the pressing needs of the working class [are] for political knowledge and political training'.[42] That the Economists cannot provide this is for him not just the crux of the issue surrounding the question of revolutionary agency, but also the reason why an external consciousness of class has to be brought into the labour movement from the outside.[43] It was a critique he aimed both at populists (whose agency

---

[40] 'The Economists and the present-day terrorists have one common root', observed Lenin (1961a: 418, original emphasis), 'namely, *subservience to spontaneity*... At first sight, our assertion may appear paradoxical, so great is the difference between those who stress the "drab everyday struggle" and those who call for the most self-sacrificing struggle of individuals. The Economists and the terrorists merely bow to different poles of spontaneity; the Economists bow to the spontaneity of "the labour movement pure and simple", while the terrorists bow to the spontaneity of the passionate indignation of intellectuals, who lack the ability or opportunity to connect the revolutionary struggle and the working class movement into an integral whole... Thus, both forms of subservience to spontaneity [proclaim]: Let the workers wage their "economic struggle against the employers and the government"...and let the intellectuals conduct the political struggle by their own efforts – with the aid of terror, of course!'.

[41] Discarding the latter aspect (self-sacrifice), the term 'passionate indignation' describes rather well the approach of those such as Breman (see Chapter 5 below).

[42] Lenin (1961a: 420–21).

[43] The reason why Economists are unable to supply the required political knowledge and training is (Lenin, 1961a: 421–22, original emphasis) 'their conviction that it is possible to develop the class political consciousness of the workers *from within*, so to speak, from

stemmed from whatever existed at the rural grassroots) and at other kinds of Marxists (whose agency similarly failed to transcend narrowly trade-union demands). Hence the questioning by Lenin of the extent to which it is ever possible for workers – by themselves and on the basis of their own experiences and locality – to formulate simply from within the labour movement a wider consciousness of class, and thus to undertake radical action in furtherance of this particular identity.[44] Qualifying the identity of the subject in this manner – an identity based only on class – raises immediately the question of agency derived from other, non-class forms of selfhood, and it is this issue that will be examined below, in Chapter 3.

6   Conclusion

In a number of crucial ways, late nineteenth century populism differs both from Marxism at that same conjuncture and from its own subsequent variants. The main distinction entails the subject of history, and thus also the progenitor of agency consequent upon this. For populism, therefore, it is the peasant smallholder who is the object of mobilization, a process confined largely to the village, and designed to realize no more than an agrarian regime of independent proprietorship. By contrast, Marxism allocated the same historical role not to peasants but to workers, mainly (but not only) in urban contexts, an identity the solidarity of which transcended national boundaries. Late nineteenth century populism also differed from its current variant – the 'new' populist postmodernism – in terms of agency; whereas both *Zemlya i Volya* and *Narodnya Volya* espoused radical forms of direct action, the preferred agency of 'new' populist postmodernists who privilege everyday-forms-of-resistance at the level of the village leave intact not just the urban class structure and its accumulation project but also the wider capitalist system.

---

their economic struggle, i.e., by making this struggle the exclusive (or, at least, the main) starting point... Such a view is radically wrong... Class political consciousness can be brought to the workers *only from without*, that is, only from outside the economic struggle, from outside the sphere of relations between workers and employers. The sphere from which alone it is possible to obtain this knowledge is the sphere of relationships of *all* classes and strata to the state and the government, the sphere of the interrelations between *all* classes'.

44   On this point, Lenin (1961a: 426, 428 original emphasis) insisted that '[t]rade unionist politics of the working class is precisely *bourgeois politics* of the working class', a situation which in turn generates the need 'to direct the thoughts of those who are dissatisfied...to the idea that the entire political system is worthless'.

Central to the way the Bolsheviks conceptualized revolutionary agency was the view that, as socialism as a political and economic idea was formulated by the intelligentsia in Europe, so too in Russia it was a practice the theory of which would emerge from outside the working class movement. The corollary was that, on its own 'from below' mobilization and agency was unable to proceed beyond trade union consciousness (= 'spontaneity'). This applied equally to rural components, consisting of agricultural labourers and poor peasants. For this reason, argued Bolshevism, revolutionary socialism was an externally derived objective that did not – and could not – arise from any spontaneous grassroots resistance and organization. This is the opposite of what populists and *Narodnya Volya* maintained was the case historically, and – as will be seen in the chapters which follow – what is now argued is the case by the 'new' populist postmodernism: namely, that any agency and organizational impetus should merely reflect what already exists at the rural grassroots, no matter what ideological form this takes.

Most emphatically, holders of this view insist that this is because any 'outside' concepts/theory accompanying an intelligentsia are by their very nature 'foreign' (= 'foundational', 'Eurocentric'), and consequently do not – and cannot – reflect a mainly cultural reality that is 'authentic' because it is rooted in a particular locality, in a particular time, and in a particular identity, all of which are contextually specific. An inevitable theoretical corollary of such an approach is that if peasants wish to remain petty commodity producers, cultivating subsistence crops or mobilize on the basis of non-class (ethnic/national/sectoral) forms of selfhood, as interpreted by the Subaltern Studies project (see Chapter 7), then so be it. Significantly, perhaps, the feeling of usefulness, and thus not being superfluous, which members of *Narodnya Volya* experienced when 'going to the people' in the countryside of 1880s Russia, was also shared by the novelist and art critic John Berger, when a century later he settled in a French village to chronicle the lives of its peasant smallholders (see Chapter 10 below).

CHAPTER 2

Revolution in Theory

"Revolution appears to a conservative as collective madness only because it raises the "normal" insanity of social contradictions to the highest possible tension... Revolution appears as utter madness only to those whom it sweeps aside and overthrows. To us [Bolsheviks] it was very different'.
> An observation by LEON TROTSKY.[1]

∴

'To throw some light on discussions about the "people" and the "popular", one need only bear in mind that the "people" or the "popular" ("popular art", "popular religion", "popular medicine", etc.) is first of all one of the things at stake in the struggle between intellectuals. The fact of being or feeling authorized to speak about the "people" or of speaking for (in both senses of the word) the "people" may constitute, in itself, a force in the struggles within different fields..'.
> An observation by PIERRE BOURDIEU in 1982, coinciding with the emergence of the 'new' populist postmodernism.[2]

∴

Turning from a consideration of revolution in practice to the theory informing the latter process, it quickly becomes clear that there are divisions between advocates and opponents of such action. Although both the Bolsheviks and the Russian populists championed direct action, each associated this within a different historical subject: for the Bolsheviks, therefore, revolution entailed the organization/mobilization of workers and poor peasants, whereas for populists the same was true of the peasantry as a whole. This distinction in turn foregrounds a number of other issues, among them the kind of class formation/consciousness and struggle occurring in the countryside, and the presence there of unfree relations of production. Linked to this is the disappearance/persistence of the peasantry itself, and whether or not the agrarian economy is differentiated

---

1 Trotsky (1930: 156).
2 Bourdieu (1990: 150).

into rich/middle/poor peasant strata. For Marxism, consequently, these issues of theory raise the question of how to respond politically, by supporting either depeasantization or repeasantization in a system that remains capitalist, and either individual or collective tenure in the course of a transition to socialism.

Not the least important aspect of this long-standing debate between Marxism and populism, therefore, derives from the fact that the dispute centres on an issue – peasant disappearance or persistence – which is at the centre of the revisionist case (historically and currently) against Marxist theory. It is precisely the seeming historical durability of the peasantry, and the reasons for this, therefore, which revisionism invokes when disagreeing with Marxism, and in particular when opposing those who insist on conceptualizing the necessity of revolutionary agency in order to effect a socialist transition. This issue surfaces in most, but not all, the political theories hostile to Marxist advocacy of direct action, both internal to Marxism itself and also external to leftist ideas generally.

Accordingly, the alternatives to the pursuit by Marxism of revolutionary agency aimed at overturning capitalist system and capturing the state in furtherance of a socialist transition have taken four specific forms. Historically, revisionists from within the ranks of the left itself have in political terms espoused reform within the existing parliamentary democratic system, while in economic terms supporting peasant family farming and expropriating only inefficient landlords. In many respects, such an approach is indistinguishable from that advocated subsequently by bourgeois models similarly opposed both to Marxism and to its revolutionary agency. Modernization theorists, who in order to avoid a revolutionary challenge to capitalism (= the threat 'from below'), sought via land reform programmes to incorporate smallholders within capitalism as individual proprietors, while analytically the 'new' populist postmodernism replaced direct mass action with smallscale quotidian 'resistance' by petty commodity producers engaged in subsistence cultivation outside the logic of accumulation. Significantly, the single alternative to Marxism and populism which nevertheless shares their ideas about the necessity of direct action aimed at the state is located on the far right of the political spectrum. However, and as will be seen in the next chapter, what it puts on the agenda is not revolution but counter-revolution.

This chapter consists of four sections, the first of which examines the different ways peasants feature in debates between Marxist, revisionist, and populist theory about systemic transcendence. Of importance in this regard are the views of Austro-Marxists, whose adherence to parliamentary reformism laid the ground for the populist far right, a process considered in the second section. The third outlines how radically distinct paths to socialism, that of parliamentary democracy and permanent revolution, were depicted in the 1920s debate between Kautsky and Trotsky, while the fourth looks at how the mistaken assumptions about the tension-free way capitalism would develop underwrote 1960s bourgeois modernization theory.

Central to any discussion about the desirability or otherwise of revolutionary transformation has been (and, as will be seen below, remains) the role of peasant economy. Whether and why it should be maintained became a more acute issue towards the end of the nineteenth century, when industrialization spread to new areas (Russia, America). Crucially about the transformation of social relations in the countryside and the resulting impact on economic growth, from the 1860s onwards Russian populists (Engel'gardt, Uspenskii, Vorontsov, Chayanov) strongly opposed the Marxist conceptualization of rural community as differentiated internally along socio-economic lines. This debate surfaced with a vengeance before, during, and after the 1917 Russian revolution, when the Bolsheviks took issue with agrarian populists over the role of peasants under socialism.[3]

1   Revolution and/as Modernity

Populists maintained both that undifferentiated peasant economy was an innate organizational form, and that it would continue to exist despite 'external' systemic transformations (from feudalism to capitalism, and from the latter to socialism). In the case of Russia, they argued that an homogenous peasantry composed of self-sufficient petty commodity producers constituted a pan-historical socio-economic category which, in theoretical and political terms, was the mirror image of the classical Marxist view. Denying that capitalist penetration of agriculture entailed 'depeasantization', populists such as Chayanov maintained instead that the economic reproduction of each individual peasant family farm was determined endogenously, by its demographic cycle.

Hence the basic aspects of rural social organization, such as landholding size, food output, and work motivation ('self-exploitation') by sociologically undifferentiated petty commodity producers were governed by a specific combination of factors. These were the size of the peasant family itself, the ratio of working to non-working household members('labour-consumer balance'), and the necessity of having to provide all the latter with their subsistence requirements ('drudgery of labour'). According to populists, therefore, not only

---

3   The basic difference in the approach to the peasantry on the part of populism and Marxism is summed up by Trotsky (1969: 113) thus: 'Populists regarded all workers and peasants simply as "toilers" and exploited ones...while to Marxists a peasant was a petty-bourgeois, capable of becoming a socialist only to the extent that he either materially or spiritually ceased being a peasant...[a]long that line was fought for two generations the principal battle between the revolutionary tendencies of Russia'.

was an egalitarian and innately virtuous smallholding agriculture unaffected by capitalism, but peasant economy was bolstered by and in turn reproduced a local version of 'civil society' – based on subsistence cultivation by the peasant family and household – they thought was already present in the village (*mir*).

Bolsheviks, by contrast, insisted that the peasantry was differentiated along class lines in the course of capitalist development, its top stratum (= rich peasants) consolidating means of production and becoming small capitalists, while its increasingly landless bottom stratum (= poor peasants) joined the ranks of the proletariat.[4] Underlying this approach was the fact that agricultural workers saw better-off peasants simply as employers, with whom they shared few – if any – economic and political interests; much rather, the relationship between them tended to be one based on antagonism, a situation that would anyway surface in policies effected by a workers' government.[5] Trotsky argued that since peasants did not constitute a class, they should be seen as a revolutionary force only insofar as they ceased to be peasants, and – like Preobrazhensky – warned that because one of the first acts of a revolutionary government headed by workers would be to expropriate all private property, the peasant proprietor should be regarded not as passively conservative but rather as actively counter-revolutionary.[6]

---

4   See Lenin (1964a) and also Trotsky (1934: 67, 68), who notes: 'At that time when the more backward landlords and small peasants were selling on a large scale – the former their estates, the latter their bits of land – there emerged in the capacity of principal purchaser a new peasant bourgeoisie. Agriculture entered upon a state of indubitable capitalist boom. The export of agricultural products from Russia rose between 1908 and 1912 from 1 billion roubles to 1½ billion'.

5   'In politics it is impossible to operate with imaginary or hypothetical quantities', maintained Trotsky (1973a: 308) in 1931, adding: 'When we speak of a workers' government then we can explain to a farm labourer that we are referring to that kind of government which will protect him against exploiters even if they are peasants. When we speak of a workers' and peasants' government then we confuse the farm labourer, the agricultural worker, who...is a thousand times more important to us than the abstract "peasant" or the "middle peasant" who is hostile to us'.

6   See Trotsky (1962) and Preobrazhensky (1980). Just how petty commodity producers would be drawn into the political net of the counter-revolution is a point to which Trotsky (1956: 38, 39, 72, 91, original emphasis) continuously returned, and constantly warned against, describing the problem thus: 'In case private capital succeed, little by little, slowly, in dominating state capital, the political process would assume in the main the character of the degeneration of the state apparatus in a bourgeois direction, with the consequences that this would involve for the party. If private capital increased rapidly and succeeded in fusing with the peasantry, the active counter-revolutionary tendencies directed against the Communist Party would then probably prevail. [...] The counter-revolutionary tendencies can find a support among the kulaks, the middlemen, the retailers, the concessionaries, in a word, among elements much more capable of surrounding the state apparatus than the party itself. [...]

Much the same point was made by Rosa Luxemburg, who opposed land seizures by peasants, since this created a new and powerful stratum of proprietors in the countryside who would – with greater success than a small group of landlords – block further attempts to socialize the ownership of agricultural land.[7] Instead of private property – the individualist smallholding economy – supported/advocated by populists, the Bolshevik programme of agrarian reform was based on collective agriculture, where rural property was owned/controlled by the State. Among the reasons for this was that the latter approach facilitated central planning.

From the end of the nineteenth century onwards the debate took a different turn, as revisionists on the political left – among them not just Austro-Marxists such as Bauer (see Chapter 3) but also Eduard Bernstein, Werner Sombart, Georg von Vollmar, and Eduard David – maintained that socialists should seek to recruit a following among small property owners in rural areas.[8] Because peasants corresponded to the 'middle strata' eroded by capitalism, yet de-peasantization appeared not to be happening, in the opinion of Bernstein and Sombart the decline of the middle strata would no longer result in a crisis of capitalism. If de-peasantization was not occurring, concluded revisionist theory, then this opened the way to include within the ranks of leftist parties all those rural categories hitherto discounted politically by Marxism: petty commodity producers, smallholding proprietors, and peasant farmers

---

In the struggle of state industry for the domination of the market, planned economy is our principal weapon. Without it, nationalisation itself would become an obstacle to economic development, and private capital would inevitably undermine the foundations of socialism. By state economy we mean of course transportation, foreign and domestic trade and finance, in addition to industry. This whole "combine" – in its totality as well as in its parts – adapts itself to the peasant market and to the individual peasant as a taxpayer. But this adaptation has as its fundamental aim to raise, to consolidate and develop *state industry as the keystone of the dictatorship of the proletariat and the basis of socialism...* It is precisely the kulak, the retailer, the new merchant...who seek a market link with the peasant producer of grain...and the endeavour to crowd the Soviet state out of this union. It is precisely on this field that the main battle is now developing. Here, too, politics serves economic interests. Seeking to forge a link with the peasant and to gain his confidence, the private middleman obviously readily welcomes and spreads the old falsehoods of the landlords...'.

7 Luxemburg (1961).
8 For this debate, see Salvadori (1979) and Hussain and Tribe (1984). As will be seen in the chapters which follow, this revisionist trend is closely linked to the way in which Marxist theory is depoliticized once the definition of its meaning becomes the sole preserve of bourgeois academia. This was the view of Lenin (1961a: 357), who noted that 'it is precisely the extensive participation of an "academic" stratum in the socialist movement in recent years that has promoted such a rapid spread of Bernsteinism'.

generally should henceforth be recruited by socialism to form a united anti-capitalist front.

Bernstein's view that the economy of smallholding peasant proprietors had not merely survived but was thriving led him to challenge the main tenet of Marxism.[9] Namely, that class formation – arising from on the one hand the disintegration of the peasant family farm and on the other the consolidation of large agribusiness holdings – would generate a capitalist crisis that would in turn lead to revolutionary agency which would bring about a socialist transition. Instead, Bernstein saw in the agrarian co-operative an institution within the capitalist system that would halt the process of class differentiation, landlessness and impoverishment as these affected the peasantry.[10]

The revisionism of Sombart, like that of Bernstein, amounted in effect to a similar negation of Marxism; his 'defence' of the latter entailed an abandonment of virtually every single theoretical claim made by historical materialism.[11] Not only did he claim that systemic change was evolutionary, not revolutionary, but he also denied the existence of a trend either towards the concentration of capitalist enterprises (particularly in agriculture), towards monopoly capital, or towards working class immizeration. Given the absence of pauperization, working class struggle was in his opinion non-material in origin, and prompted by envy. Most significantly, this benign view of capitalism led Sombart to question whether the seeds of socialism were indeed to be

---

9   Writing in 1899, Bernstein (1961: 71) insisted that 'there can be no doubt that in the whole of Western Europe, as also in the Eastern States of the United States, the small and medium agricultural holding is increasing everywhere, and the large and very large holding is decreasing...[t]he concentration of enterprises is not accomplished here in the form of annexing an ever greater portion of land to the farm, as Marx saw in his time...'. This, as Gay (1952: 194) points out, was the crux of the matter: 'Here, if anywhere, the difference between orthodox and Revisionist agrarian theory must be sought'.

10 See Bernstein (1961: 109ff., 185). However, as many different case studies confirm, in a capitalist system the agrarian co-operative does not slow but much rather accelerates peasant socio-economic differentiation. Noting that in Russia as early as 1906 capitalist farmers emerged from the peasantry as a result of purchasing or leasing holdings from landlords, Trotsky (1934: 68) added that '[r]eal power in the co-operatives belonged...only to rich peasants, whose interests in the last analysis they served'. He continued: 'The Narodnik [= populist] intelligentsia, by concentrating its chief forces in peasant co-operation, finally succeeded in shifting its love for the people on to good solid bourgeois rails. In this way was prepared, partially at least, the political bloc of the "anti-capitalist" party of the Social Revolutionaries with the Kadets, the capitalist party *par excellence*'. Decades later much the same turned out to be true of cooperatives in India (Thorner, 1964) and Latin America (Brass, 2007). This was because such units enable rich peasants to expand and/or consolidate landownership, to expel poor peasants from co-operative membership, and then to re-employ them as workers.

11 Sombart (1909).

found in capitalism, thereby aligning himself with those anti-Marxists who argued against either the need for or the possibility of a transcendence of capitalist production. This was a view to which the Austro-Marxist theoretician Otto Bauer also subscribed.

In a break with all previous Marxist theory about agrarian transformation, Bauer maintained that under socialism not only would private ownership of land continue but that the State would ensure the reproduction of peasant economy in a number of crucial ways.[12] Input and output prices for those commodities purchased and sold by peasants would be fixed at a level that guaranteed their subsistence, they would be protected from the impact of lower world market prices for agricultural commodities, a system of marketing cooperatives would be set up, and proprietors would receive debt relief.[13] Bauer equated capitalism simply with finance capital, and that those categorized by him uniformly as 'peasants' might contain rich peasants and/or commercial farmers – potential/actual agrarian capitalists, in other words – was not a possibility the political effects of which that he considered. In essence, this 'socialist' economic programme he drafted for the Austrian Social Democrats in the mid-1920s was no different from that advocated by the neo-populist theorist Chayanov in Russia at that same conjuncture.[14]

---

12 See Bauer (1919: 78–88) and also Pollock (1984: 163ff.). According to the latter source, in his 1925 Austrian Social Democratic agrarian programme Bauer 'takes over the doctrine of the 'eternal peasant', previously rejected bluntly by [Marxist] theory...' Of this Pollock (1984: 168) asks the following two pertinent questions: '[H]ow can one possibly incorporate an explicitly anti-collectivist stratum of the population, which is attached to private property, into a classless society? Is not [the] conception of the small peasantry as an important stratum of the classless socialist society itself a contradiction?'

13 In keeping with his fear lest a move against bourgeois property rights elicited a backlash from foreign investors and more generally imperialism, Bauer (Blum and Smaldone, 2016: 351) maintained that to 'want the Communist perspective, to will expropriation without compensation, is completely wrong...one must still consider that a country that relies on its international connections will suffer great resistance from these relationships if it expropriates without compensation', adding: 'One must attend to this consequence. Expropriating without compensation can only be considered in a country that cannot be affected by foreign powers'. Because the 'socialist' programme of Bauer was based only on the taxation of existing wealth, and not on the confiscation of property belonging to industrialists and landowners, it was dismissed by Lenin (1965: 361) in the following terms: '...he [Bauer] grew frightened and *began to pour* the oil of *reformist phrase-mongering on the troubled waters of the revolution*'. (original emphasis) For the same kind of criticisms levelled at Austrian social democrats, see Trotsky (1934: 910ff.).

14 According to Bauer, therefore, '[t]he peasant was there before feudal society. He lived through feudal society as well. And in the framework of socialist society too, peasants will live on their own patch of land as a free proprietor' (cited in Pollock, 1984: 165). It was precisely for this reason that he approved of the New Economic Policy in the Soviet Union, described by him as 'a capitulation to capitalism', an endorsement that

2   To the Barricades?

In a sense this is unsurprising, since the principal object of the 1925 agrarian programme of Austrian Social Democracy was to gain peasant support.[15] To this end, the agrarian programme undertook to encourage the economic reproduction of individual peasant family farms, and ensure they were protected by legislation, not least because they provided large enterprises with the labour-power that was needed. Consequently, argued Bauer, rural smallholders had nothing to fear from the establishment in Austria of socialism, since it guaranteed the survival of what would become a thriving peasant economy.[16] This was in keeping with the project of Austrian Social Democracy, he explained, which was to increase labour productivity by among other things transferring land to rural communities, cooperatives, or 'hardworking landowners'.

Accordingly, large landowners who managed their property efficiently would not just avoid expropriation but actually become beneficiaries of the land redistribution. For economic reasons, only land at the margins of large estates – not the estate itself – would face expropriation. Furthermore, as large landed estates were necessary for technical progress in agriculture, this required that only 'able farmers' be in charge of cultivation. Dismissing the likelihood of collective farming, therefore, Bauer maintained instead that 'large enterprises should be leased to the most competent farmers'; given that the latter would be producers either owning or with access to technology and other inputs, such beneficiaries of the Social Democratic agrarian programme could only have been rich peasants and commercial producers.

Despite conveying the impression that the Austrian peasantry was undifferentiated socio-economically, Bauer nevertheless hints periodically that peasant family farming was indeed differentiated. Thus, for example, his view that Pan-Germanism and the Christian Social movement – both populist far right political organizations – 'are supported by the prosperous and comfortable

---

was condemned by Trotsky (1953: 250). By contrast, Bauer's support for peasant economy was commended by populist writers such as Mitrany (1951: 156–57), according to whom it 'was the most realistic and constructive approach to the peasant problem made by a Socialist in that period', and for whom the views of Bauer 'almost echoed [those of] the Peasant writers [= populists]'.

15   'The Social Democratic Agrarian Programme' of 1925 is reproduced in Blum and Smaldone (2017: 483–96).

16   Because '[s]ocialism fights against the theft of property by the ruling classes, not against property used by peasants', Bauer noted (Blum and Smaldone, 2017: 495), 'peasant property is not endangered, but secured'. For this reason, 'peasants will live within the framework of socialist society…as free owners of their own land'.

peasants', and further that 'the parliamentary rule of the peasantry is only a mask for the economic domination of finance capital'.[17] As will be seen elsewhere in this volume, this is a method of decoupling peasant economy and accumulation, thereby expelling capitalism from the realm of family farming, the inference being that all cultivators belong to the same category of victim. An ethnographic account of peasant economy in the Austrian Empire during the mid-nineteenth century – its idealized depiction of rural life notwithstanding – suggests that petty commodity producers were indeed differentiated, and that a stratum of rich peasants was already in existence.[18]

According to the same account, the principal forms of surplus extraction in the countryside were imperial/seigneurial taxes and tithes, which 'press heavily on peasants'. Despite this, peasant farming is described as being in a 'flourishing condition'.[19] Seven decades later, a different image emerges, one that paints a picture of the economic plight structuring petty commodity production in rural Austria. Questions put by a visiting United States Senate Commission just before the 1914–18 war about the conditions in and policy applied to the agrarian sector in Austria, elicited replies stressing economic crisis in the countryside. This was attributed to two forms of capitalist competition affecting

---

17   Bauer (1925: 279). Again, it is necessary to question why peasant economy is linked by him only to finance capital, when better-off producers who hire labour-power and/or sublet tenancies in order to produce surpluses for the domestic market are themselves agrarian capitalists.

18   The account in question is by Kohl (1843: 102, original emphasis): 'The peasantry of Upper and Lower Austria have, with the exception of some of the peasants of Lombardy, certainly reached a higher degree of wealth and freedom than any other peasants in the Austrian Empire. Those of Galicia, Bohemia, and Hungary, are, on the whole, still serfs; the inhabitant of Illyria and the Tyrol is poor. There are *parts*, indeed, of all these provinces where the land is better cultivated, and the peasants more free and opulent. Hanna, in Moravia, is celebrated for this, so is Zips, in Hungary; Saxonland, in Transylvania; Egerthal, in Bohemia; and many rich Alpine valleys, are also remarkable exceptions. Neither ought we to pity or despise the peasants of other parts of the monarchy... To take them all in all, however, it is not less certain that the peasants of the Danube, in reference to mental cultivation, solidity of character, firmness of position, and a recognition of their rights as men, surpass the majority of their fellow-subjects, as far as they do in agricultural knowledge and opulence'.

19   See Kohl (1843: 105), who writes: 'The personal service which the peasants are held to render to their superior lord, is trifling in real amount. It is, for the most part, commuted for money. But the tithes, which are levied by the lords of the soil, the billeting of soldiers, the military conscription, to which the nobles are not subject, and the many imperial and seigneurial taxes, press heavily on the peasants. As the land, however, is, on the whole, fertile, the people sober and diligent, and the law, despite its oppressive enactments, is administered in a spirit favourable to the subject...agriculture, with all its disadvantages, is in the flourishing condition I have above described'.

producers, who faced on the one hand increased rivalry in cereal markets from American imports, and on the other scarcity of labour due to outmigration, both to towns and abroad.[20] Because of the latter, subdivision of peasant holdings in Austria was discouraged, since these properties had to be large enough to support a farm family and thus retain it on the land as a source of labour-power.[21] Just before the 1939–45 war, reports suggested that many of these same difficulties – among them labour shortages and outmigration – confronting the smallholding economy had not diminished.[22]

3 Half the Voters Plus One?

The idealized conceptualization by Bauer of peasant family farming, and the consequent decoupling of peasant economy from accumulation, led him and more generally Austro-Marxism to advocate reformist measures acceptable to rural petty commodity producers. Having discarded the revolutionary capture of the state apparatus as a political strategy, Bauer and other revisionists were as a result limited to a reform programme achieved only via the Parliamentary route. Electoral success, concluded Bernstein in 1899, therefore required that socialists henceforth obtain the support of the peasantry, an objective which

---

20 According to what was reported to the United States Senate Commission (1913: 201), therefore, 'the great agrarian crises, due especially to American competition in the cereal markets... As a general rule it can be said that rural property has been consolidated, especially in recent years, although the buying out of small peasant holdings by the great landowners has become a serious evil in many parts of Austria, leading to the depopulation of some sections and the detriment of agricultural development'.

21 Noting that '[a]gricultural workers in Austria may be classified as farm servants, who practically form members of the farmer's family, day labourers engaged by contract and employed occasionally, and permanent labourers who receive their wages partly in kind', the United States Senate Commission (1913: 201) was informed that '[a]s regards the agrarian policy, reference many be made first of all to the efforts to check rural migration to the towns, so as to insure the requisite amount of farm labour'. The complaint was that, from 1900 onwards, labour costs had increased by fifty percent. Answering a question from the visiting United States Senate Commission (1913: 202–3) as to whether in the agrarian sector of Austria 'the demand for labour is greater than the supply', the reply was 'yes'. Asked further 'what is the cause?', the response to that was '[t]he men prefer factory work, as the hours are shorter'.

22 Hence the account presented by Ludwig Löhr to the Fifth Annual Conference of Agricultural Economists (Elmhirst, 1939: 227–29) stressed that '[i]n recent years Austrian farming has suffered under a severe crisis in consequence of under-consumption and diminishing purchasing power of the rest of the population among whom unemployment was continually spreading. Limitation of agricultural production was the dominant note in economic policy'.

'will only happen if social democracy commits itself to measure which offer an improvement for small peasants in the immediate future'.[23] In keeping with this, and also the analogous policies advocated by Bauer, Sombart championed rural de-industrialization, the restoration of rural handicraft production, and the protection generally of subsistence agriculture undertaken by peasant enterprises and farm household economy.[24]

Such views were strongly opposed by other Marxists, then and subsequently. At the same conjuncture, therefore, Bernstein's data about the slowing down of class fragmentation were challenged by Parvus, who also criticized the former's argument that peasants bankrupted by capital would automatically join the socialist camp.[25] Kautsky pointed out that, because smallholders were a source of cheap labour-power, such units are never wholly displaced by large commercial enterprises.[26] It was this, and not economic efficiency, that determined the survival of 'peasant economy'.[27] The debate about whether or not European socialist parties should tailor their policies in order to attract the support of petty commodity producers resumed in 1920 during the Second Congress of the Communist International, when some delegates reported that middle peasants had 'become rich' as a result of the 1914–18 war, and were now to be found in the ranks of the counter-revolution.[28]

As important as the economic considerations was the political concern (raised by Trotsky) that an undifferentiated peasantry would continued to be invoked as bearers of national identity and culture by those opposed to revolutionary socialist transformation. This is because the far right not only possesses an international dimension to its own ideology, but the latter also allocates similar characteristics and a political role to the peasantry regardless of national context. An important consequence of the 1917 revolution, therefore, was to widen the political gap between on the one hand Bolsheviks who supported revolutionary agency as the only method to empower workers, and on the other reformist/revisionists who opposed revolution, insisting that 'from below' empowerment could be achieved only through electoral means of parliamentary democracy. The wide difference between these two

---

23   Bernstein (1961: 181).
24   Sombart (1937: 264–5).
25   See Tudor & Tudor (1988: 174ff.).
26   Kautsky (1984, 1988).
27   Employers continued to prefer the system of wages-in-kind linked to smallholding, even into the 1920s, since – as socialist trade unions pointed out – this enabled them to reproduce and reinforce unfree production relations (and with them low wages) in German agriculture (Wunderlich, 1961).
28   Second Congress of the Communist International (1977: 109ff.).

approaches, one based on seizing the state in order to establish the dictatorship of the proletariat, the other on the legal 'gradualness' of electoral politics, can be illustrated by reference to the debate that took place at the beginning of the 1920s between Trotsky and Kautsky.

Reversing the argument of Rosa Luxemburg, for whom barbarism was synonymous with unfettered capitalism, Kautsky applied the same term not to capitalism but to socialism. This was because in his opinion civil war generated by revolutionary agency was not just unacceptable but also avoidable.[29] Instead he supported a gradual/reformist transformation, a process whereby the working class only assumed power in keeping with the legality embodied in constitutional norms (= democracy): in short, with the consent of the bourgeoisie.[30] Observing that 'Kautsky has a clear and solitary path to salvation: *democracy*', Trotsky challenged this on the grounds that '[t]his fetishism of the parliamentary majority represents a brutal repudiation, not only of the dictatorship of the proletariat, but also of Marxism and of the revolution altogether'.[31] Against Kautsky, therefore, Trotsky advocated revolutionary agency aimed at capture of the state – a process and outcome described as 'to seize power, taking away from the bourgeoisie the material apparatus of government' – the object of which was to establish the dictatorship of the proletariat which would then carry out the tasks necessary for a transition to socialism.[32]

---

29 Hence the argument (Kautsky, 1920: 219–20) that 'the revolution is synonymous with civil war, with a war in which no pardon is given, in which one side attempts to crush the other without any lasting effect...[it] decimates the population, increases their brutality until it becomes the wildest barbarism... This masterly conception of the Socialist Revolution is certainly not that of a "learned expert", but of a professional revolutionary for whom insurrection is synonymous with revolution, and who really loses his health and life if such revolution assumes the form of democracy, and not that of civil war... As we have only the two alternatives – democracy or civil war – I myself draw the conclusion that wherever Socialism does not appear to be possible on a democratic basis...its time has not yet fully come'.

30 Perhaps this was the kind of view Gramsci had in mind when making the following observation (cited by Pozzolini, 1970: 58) in *La città futura* on 11th February 1917: 'To wait until one has grown to half the voters plus one is the programme of [those] who wait for socialism by a royal decree countersigned by two ministers'.

31 See Trotsky (1935: 22), who goes on to point out that '[i]f, in principle, we are to subordinate Socialist policy to the parliamentary mystery of majority and minority, it follows that, in countries where formal democracy prevails, there is no place at all for the revolutionary struggle'.

32 Trotsky (1935: 36). In his critique of the same revisionist trend within Marxism, Lenin (1961a: 353) commented: 'Denied was the theory of class struggle, on the grounds that it could not be applied to a strictly democratic society governed according to the will of the majority'.

Defending the 1917 revolution, but also making a case that applies to other contexts, Trotsky points out that in Russia 'the path divides into two: either the dictatorship of the imperialist clique, or the dictatorship of the proletariat', continuing that: 'On neither side does the path lead to "democracy"'.[33] He understands in a way that Kautsky does not that the true dynamic of the capitalist system is class struggle: rule ends up by being that of either the 'imperialist clique' or the working class, an instance of in the long run there being *tertium non datur*. Unlike Kautsky who maintained that it was only through democracy that 'the proletariat can come to complete emancipation', Trotsky argued that there was little chance of the working class anywhere and at any conjuncture being able to complete its emancipation (= achieving the implementation of its own class project) within the context of bourgeois democracy overseen by and serving the interests of capitalism. Neither the ruling class nor the workers, therefore, are in the view of Trotsky really interested in 'democracy' for the simple reason that each recognises it for what it is: a short-term truce in what is a broader historical process of class struggle.[34]

'Democracy' is categorized by Trotsky much rather as part of the political vocabulary of populism (although he doesn't use the latter term), in that it projects the meaning of a government that is 'popular' – that gets its support and legitimacy 'from below', in other words.[35] The term is acceptable to the rich and powerful, he continues, simply because 'the meaning of democracy rises above class distinctions'; as such it corresponds exactly to the political function and ideological trope of populist discourse, then as now. According to Trotsky, moreover, the efficacy of the concept 'democracy' derives from its particular appeal to 'the lower middle class' in urban and rural areas, where it has a powerful resonance among peasant farmers.[36] Having invoked 'democracy'

---

33   Trotsky (1935: 29).
34   This fact of democracy being nothing more than a historical truce in the wider class struggle is recognized even by the more perceptive conservatives. Thus, for example, T.E. Utley, a high Tory commentator, accepted this as long ago as 1957, when he noted (Moore and Heffer, 1989: 314–15): 'Look at England since 1945. The real problems which have beset this country have had nothing, or very little, to do with the problems that have been publicly ventilated; on the contrary, the real problem which has beset this country since 1945 is a problem which, by common consent...it has until yesterday been improper to mention in public. That problem is whether you can reconcile the aims of the Welfare State, which demands full employment, with an efficient economy, including the absence of inflation (without which, in the last resort, the Welfare State itself cannot be sustained)...This is not, at this moment, a particularly fashionable view among intellectuals'.
35   Trotsky (1935: 31).
36   Examples cited by Trotsky include the United States and Switzerland in the nineteenth century. The Russian peasantry in the immediate pre-revolutionary era were differenti-

against 'the powers of feudalism', the bourgeoisie then deploys the same concept against the working class ('the weapon of defence against the class antagonisms generated within bourgeois society').[37] That is, the view that workers are already sufficiently represented within and thus empowered by the existing (capitalist) state. Trotsky then goes on to say that that this so-called 'balance' which is the essence of democracy, or the ability to maintain the fiction of the bourgeois state as representing all its supporters equally, is increasingly perceived to be false as accumulation gathers pace, and generates both class differentiation within the peasantry and conflict based on this.

It is in the course of this defence of revolutionary agency that there emerge the political objections Trotsky had to the efficacy of 'democracy' and the role of the peasantry in propping this up. Seen as empowered both by formal democracy and by the state, therefore, peasants are depicted by Eduard Bernstein, Sombart, and others, as the 'mediators' between capital and labour. However, Trotsky – like Lenin – saw the peasantry as being fragmented as capitalism penetrated the agrarian sector, and consequently prey to reactionary politics and parties which undertook either to prevent this from happening, or to provide remedies in the form of land elsewhere (as did the Nazis in 1930s Germany).[38] As will be seen in later chapters, this is an argument that is ignored or downplayed currently in 'new' populist postmodern analyses which

---

ated economically and politically by Trotsky (1935: 103) along the following lines: '[T]he poor, living to a considerable extent by the sale of their labour-power, and forced to buy additional food for their requirements; the middle peasants, whose requirements were covered by the products of their farms, and who were able to a limited extent to sell their surplus; and the upper layer – i.e. the rich peasants, the vulture (kulak) class, which systematically bought labour-power and sold their agricultural produce on a large scale...the peasant poor represented the natural and undeniable allies of the town proletariat, whilst the vulture class represented its just as undeniable and irreconcilable enemies'.

37 See Trotsky (1935: 31).
38 'The more the middle classes lost their importance', argued Trotsky (1935: 32), 'the less they proved capable of playing the part of an authoritative arbitral judge in the historical conflict between capital and labour. Yet the very considerable numerical proportion of the town middle classes, and still more the peasantry, continues to find direct expression in the electoral statistics of parliamentarism. The formal equality of all citizens as electors thereby only gives more open indication of the incapacity of democratic parliamentarism to settle the root questions of historical evolution. An "equal" vote for the proletariat, the peasant, and the manager of a trust formally placed the peasant in a position of mediator between the two antagonists; but in reality, the peasantry [which is] politically helpless, has in all countries always provided support for the most reactionary, filibustering, and mercenary parties which, in the long run, always supported capital against labour'. During the early 1930s Trotsky (1979: 100) was adamant that, as fascism in Spain and Italy derived its support mainly from rural smallholders, similarly reactionary politics would not be capable of establishing itself in Britain because there was no equivalent peasant base there.

proclaim the need to uphold subaltern 'citizenship' of the 'multitude' in a democracy that remains capitalist.

4   Confused Chatter and Legislative Obstruction

In making his case, Trotsky recognized that peasants who have been depeasantized economically ('lost [a place] in production') as a result of the accumulation process would nevertheless attempt to effect *re*peasantisation – that is, to reverse this development and regain holdings that agribusiness and large commercial enterprises had acquired – by their access to the parliamentary system: that is, through the political representatives who required their support.[39] Despite being reviled for his supposed intransigence on issues to do with revolutionary action designed to realize a socialist programme, and specifically what the resulting dictatorship of the proletariat implied for social forces other than the working class, Trotsky made it clear that there would be concessions to and agreements with elements of the urban and rural petty bourgeoisie (= 'lower middle class'), a category formed mainly of peasants.[40] Equally clear, however, was his insistence that such concessions/agreements would not take place until after a workers' government had been established, since only then would it be possible to decide 'on which points to yield and on which to stand firm'. In order to illustrate why he was opposed to the reformist position which insisted on the necessity of keeping any 'from below' mobilisation within bounds defined by 'democracy', the words Trotsky puts into the mouth of the capitalist outline as precisely as need be the difficulty facing advocates of a parliamentary route to socialism, and ring as true today as they did when first made nearly a century ago.[41]

---

39   'Occupying in parliamentary politics a place which it has lost in production', he noted (Trotsky, 1935: 33), 'the middle class has finally compromised parliamentarism, and has transformed it into an institution of confused chatter and legislative obstruction'.

40   'The dictatorship of the proletariat is necessary', wrote Trotsky (1935: 21), 'because it is a case, not of partial changes, but of the very existence of the bourgeoisie'. This, however, 'does not exclude...either separate agreements, or considerable concessions, especially in connection with the lower middle class and the peasantry. But the proletariat can only conclude these agreements after having gained possession of the apparatus of power, and having guaranteed to itself the possibility of independently deciding on which points to yield and on which to stand firm, in the interests of the general Socialist task'.

41   So relevant is this discourse that it merits citing in full (Trotsky, 1935: 35): 'The capitalist bourgeois calculates: "While I have in my hands lands, factories, workshops, banks; while I possess newspapers, universities, schools; while – and this is the most important of all – I retain control of the army: the apparatus of democracy, however you reconstruct

Central to this debate, therefore, was disagreement over the way labour featured in the revolutionary programme: namely, the object of and form taken by planning, the role of the state in allocating workers to specific tasks, and the presence/absence in a socialist economy of a labour market. Hence the complaint by Kautsky both about the lack of 'high wages or extraordinarily short working hours' in order to make tasks attractive to those undertaking them, and that 'the bourgeoisie are compelled to work, but they have not the right to choose the work'.[42] This objection, which he levelled against the compulsory labour regime of the Bolsheviks, was itself linked to his advocacy of concepts not of class and class struggle but rather 'choice', 'humanity', 'liberty', and 'democracy': in short, terms associated not with socialism but with bourgeois notions of a capitalism that was benign.[43]

Countering this argument – not just that of Kautsky but also of the Mensheviks – Trotsky emphasized that one of the main objectives of working class revolutionary agency was precisely the elimination of market competition imposed on labour by capital: for this reason, the state that had been seized from the bourgeoisie was required to put into practice an economic plan no longer premised on *laissez faire* principles, amongst which was the kind of market

---

it, will remain obedient to my will. I subordinate to my interests spiritually the stupid, conservative, characterless lower middle class, just as it is subjected to me materially. I oppress, and will oppress, its imagination by the gigantic scale of my buildings, my transactions, my plans, and my crimes. For moments when it is dissatisfied and murmurs, I have created scores of safety-valves and lightning-conductors. At the right moment I will bring into existence opposition parties, which will disappear tomorrow, but which today accomplish their mission by affording the possibility of the lower middle class expressing their indignation without hurt therefrom for capitalism. I shall hold the masses of the people, under the cover of compulsory general education, on the verge of complete ignorance, giving them no opportunity of rising above the level which my experts in spiritual slavery consider safe. I will corrupt, deceive, and terrorise the more privileged or the more backward of the proletariat itself. By means of these measures, I shall not allow the vanguard of the working class to gain the ear of the majority of the working class, while the necessary weapons of mastery and terrorism remain in my hands'". Then as now surpluses are siphoned off by capitalist enterprises and/or those belonging to the ruling class. The obvious difference is that currently it is far easier to transfer and keep such wealth offshore in tax havens, beyond the legal capacity of individual states to recoup in the form of taxation. In this way, the state is deprived of revenue necessary for maintaining – let alone improving – existing levels of public expenditure.

42 See Kautsky (1920: 169, 171).
43 'Bolshevism triumphed', protested Kautsky (1920: 180), 'by degrading the social movement, by turning the cause of humanity into a mere cause of the working-man, and by announcing that to the wage earners alone belonged power...by transforming what should have been the social struggle for liberty, and for the raising of the whole of humanity onto a higher plane, into an outbreak of bitterness and revenge...'.

competition (= 'choice'/'freedom') that capital inflicted on its workforce.⁴⁴ In place of the capitalist anarchy of the market, therefore, socialist planning sought to prevent workers having to compete with one another at the behest of employers, the result being lower wages and declining conditions.⁴⁵

To these kinds of objection – that no difference separated the production relations imposed on the workforce employed by the Pharaohs when building the Egyptian pyramids from the labour regime of the Bolsheviks during the period of war communism – Trotsky invoked a crucial political distinction: the dissimilarity of control exercised over the state, and consequently on whose behalf, to what purpose, and in which class interests, such tasks were effected.⁴⁶ The same criteria distinguish labour regimes the object of which is private accumulation/appropriation by individual capitalists from those designed to benefit the mass of society in general and the working class in particular. Hence capitalists employ unfree labour because its cheapness and control enables larger quantities of surplus extraction, and thus generates higher profits for its individual or corporate owners.

By contrast, socialist planning requires the allocation of specific forms of labour to particular tasks, any benefits of which accrue not to private individuals but rather to the whole of society. Over time, workers and their offspring gain from a labour market controlled by the state no longer acting in the interests of private corporations, since – unlike capitalist enterprises subject to ever increasing competition from rival businesses – there is no requirement continuously to depress wages/conditions in order to survive economically. Instead of going into overseas bank accounts of individual capitalists, therefore, the fruits generated by labour-power mobilized in a planned economy operated along socialist principles are returned to its collective subject.

---

44   'For the Liberal', indicated Trotsky (1935: 130), 'freedom in the long run means the market. Can or cannot the capitalist buy labour-power at a moderate price – that is for him the sole measure of the freedom of labour. That measure is false, not only in relation to the future but also in connection with the past'.

45   'The transition to Socialism', explained Trotsky (1935: 131), 'means the transition from anarchical distribution of labour-power – by means of the game of buying and selling, the movement of market prices and wages – to systematic distribution of workers by the economic organizations of the county, the province, and the whole country. Such a form of planned distribution presupposes the subordination of those distributed to the economic plan of the state'.

46   Cited in Howe (1964: 20), the exchange involved 'the Menshevik leader Rafael Abramovich [who] opposed such forced labour battalions with the query: "Wherein does your socialism differ from Egyptian slavery? It was just by similar methods that the Pharaohs built the pyramids, forcing the masses to labour". Trotsky replied: "Abramovich sees no difference between the Egyptian regime and our own. He has forgotten the class nature of government... it was not the Egyptian peasants who decided through their soviets to build the pyramids...our compulsion is applied by a workers' and peasants' government"'.

The continuing relevance of the 1920s debate between Kautsky and Trotsky over the necessity of revolutionary agency to the implementation of progress involving political and economic development based on planning by the state, and whether the latter could also be achieved by adhering to a reformist path, realizing these objectives within parliamentary democracy, was underlined by the attempt of 1960s bourgeois modernization theory to do just this.

During the 1960s, movements in metropolitan capitalist nations were merely for 'bourgeois rights', including those components hitherto excluded from formal citizenship, while those in less developed countries were reformist and/ or nationalist, designed to do no more than promote or intensify economic growth. Neither objective fundamentally challenged the continued process of accumulation, elements in these kinds of mobilization frequently seeking nothing more than to improve their lot under the existing capitalist system. To the extent that the latter was at that conjuncture able to meet such aspirations without jeopardising its economic project, a desire for empowerment in metropolitan capitalist nations was not deemed to be revolutionary in intent, a threat to overturn property relations on the road to socialism. However, to the extent that what began as nationalist governments in Third World countries sought to go beyond that, and introduce what appeared to metropolitan capitalism as an actual/potential transition to socialism, they were perceived as a political threat. This conjuncture was characterized by attempts on the part of imperialism to oust reformist governments in Guatemala during 1952, in Indonesia during 1965, and Chile during 1973, where military coups were successful, and foreign interventions in Egypt during 1956, and Cuba during 1960, where similar attempts at destabilization were unsuccessful.

5 Modernity and/as Bourgeois Democracy

In political terms, therefore, modernization theory which rose to academic prominence in the 1960s was a bourgeois response to the perceived threat 'from below' of not promoting economic development in rural areas of the so-called Third World.[47] After the end of the 1939–45 war, rural populations were in the forefront of nationalist movements advocating decolonization and

---

47 A 1967 review in the *American Anthropologist* (Volume 69, page 417) underlined the influence of this approach, arguing that 'Modernization is probably the most potent force at work in the world today'. Although not usually regarded as part of 1960s modernization theory, it is perhaps significant that the two-volume examination of the Enlightenment by an historian of ideas (Gay, 1966, 1969) appeared at the same conjuncture. Among other things, it argued that the Enlightenment project was the authentic precursor of modernity, noting (Gay, 1966: 426) 'it is my conviction that it was the age of Enlightenment, not the age of Reformation and Renaissance, that may be called the first truly modern century'.

independence, and as such peasant mobilizations were regarded by many as actually/potentially socialist in political orientation. Advocates of development, whether supportive of bourgeois modernization theory or Marxism, challenged the prevailing images of peasant smallholders as unchanging and unchangeable, static depictions long associated with populism in pre-1939 Europe and anthropological monographs about underdeveloped nations in Asia, Africa and Latin America.[48] Such peasant-as-cultural-'other' approaches tended to portray rural society as an innate/eternal 'subculture of peasantry', deemed by modernization theory to pose obstacles to any development project. Among its components were 'fatalism', 'low aspirational levels', 'a lack of deferred gratification', 'familism', 'localiteness', and 'a lack of empathy'.[49]

Hence the research priorities outlined in the course of the 1967 International Conference of Africanists criticized the assumptions of what were termed 'rural romantics', whose emphasis 'tends to be on the noble peasant and on the qualities of the peasant that are "good": self-reliance, independence, and stoicism. The pristine existence, the beauties of traditionalism are all romanticized. Emphasis by the rural romantic is also on…the qualities of being self-contained and self-reliant under natural conditions'.[50] The implications for rural development of this approach were equally clear: 'The rural romantic fails to see the deprivations, the sickness and the hunger in perspective [and consequently] misunderstands the negative, choking effects of traditionalism'.

For this reason, modernization theory argued that in the case of Africa '[a] second major departure is the growing attention to…peasant peoples', based on the need to implement economic development ('[b]arriers to desired social changes are being inspected…questions of…success in a particular

---

48   Advocates of bourgeois modernization theory included Rostow (1960), Weiner (1966), and Rogers (1976). Summing up this approach, Halpern (1967: 97) noted that 'one of the most striking attitudes to emerge from the studies cited for India and China is that despite very real problems village people have at least some sense of progress and improvement in their lives. The total incorporation of the peasant into the national state is well under way…'

49   For such characteristics, see Rogers (1970). These were said by modernization theory to inform ethnographic studies by influential anthropologists such as Robert Redfield, George M. Foster, Eric R. Wolf, Edward C. Banfield, and Oscar Lewis. In keeping with the latter approach, Berger – on which see Chapter 10 – observes (Add. Ms. 8864/1/30): 'The idea of universal classification, taxonomy, makes no sense to the peasant. For example, he recognizes the plants or birds which are either useful or destructive to his work. He recognizes these as familiar presences: their names are commensurate with the names of the families in the area. Those, which may be common but have remained unnamed, are strangers because they do not significantly enter his life. Name follows function: not the contrary as with the classifiers'.

50   Miller (1969: 19).

modernization effort are being posed').[51] In terms of research, therefore, 'the newer departures are on problems of modernization and social change. These studies often touch on some aspect of gaining peasant participation [in] economic or political projects'. At that conjuncture, moreover, contributions by Marxism to the study of development were not demonized in the way that they later became. Noting that hitherto there had been 'a tendency to ignore... village micropolitics' which required 'study to further our understanding of... peasant society', even non-Marxist adherents of modernization theory were prepared to accept that Marxism had a contribution to make to this process, conceding that 'the interpretation of social change via social class, along the lines of Marx and others, is increasingly relevant to scholarship on Africa, by both western and African scholars'.[52]

Much the same approach challenging the efficacy of building a future on the basis of 'traditional' society informed ethnographic studies conducted in New Guinea. Noting that '[i]n each age there is a series of pressing questions which must be asked and answered', Margaret Mead dismissed as backwards-looking the tendency to reassert the efficacy of traditional society in the following manner: 'Yet the blandly certain questions provide...little solace: How soon will it take for men to come to their senses, realize that the old ways were best, return to nature and to God...and learn to live a proper life by always deferring consuming until tomorrow anything we can possibly save today? One has only to listen to this diluted utopia, which is all that it is possible to build out of the ghost of former ways of life, to know that it is a ghost as fleshless and inadequate as the way of life was once full-bodied'.[53]

Notwithstanding a shared perception of the necessity, desirability, and feasibility of the term 'progress', Marxism and bourgeois modernization theory nevertheless had very different views about its systemic direction and outcome. Informed conceptually by a broad notion of socio-economic development, by which was meant not merely that rural society could be changed for the better but further that such change ought to take place, modernization theory sought to improve the economic and political lot of smallholders, by

---

51   Miller (1969: 21).
52   Miller (1969: 22, 75, 87).
53   Mead (1956: 3–4). At the same conjuncture even an analysis by a conservative observer (Eliade, 1963: 3) of myth – including its Golden Age variant – announced that: 'In all probability phenomena of this kind will become more and more uncommon. We may suppose that "mythological behaviour" will disappear as a result of former colonies' acquiring independence'. Not only did chiliastic movements not disappear, but myth itself was in many instances reified in analyses of rural mobilization by adherents of the 'new' populist postmodernism.

promoting agrarian reform programmes. The latter, it was argued, would generate additional consumption in rural areas, thereby providing incentives for domestic capital investment and (consequently) fuelling economic growth.[54]

As interpreted by bourgeois modernization theory, however, development was confined to the political and economic incorporation of the peasantry, thereby leaving intact a rural culture that was subsequently mobilized against the State by the 'new' populist postmodernism. Excluding culture and religion from the structures that required modernization was the result of a failure to understand how non-economic identity might be deployed in the course of class struggle. Dismissing the view that cultural/religious values hindered change, on the grounds that tradition did not prevent rapid development and transformation in rural society ('basic religious and cultural ways are by no means incompatible with or obstacles to modernization'), anthropologists failed to spot the presence of a basic contradiction, and consequently missed the political significance of this antinomy.[55]

Whilst there was agreement that in the case of India economic change was indeed taking place, therefore, it was noted in passing that 'as far as the bulk of the original groups [studied] are concerned...they will also like to have their status validated *in traditional caste terms*'.[56] In other words, what was missed at that conjuncture was that in instances where class struggle generated by capitalist accumulation is acute, economic and political modernization can lead to the reaffirmation and/or intensification of traditional ideology. By the mid-1970s, therefore, some advocates of modernization were rolling back its original claim, arguing that instead of seeking to displace 'traditional institutions' with 'modern counterparts', development would henceforth entail 'a syncretization of old and new ideas'.[57]

Both the shortcomings of modernization theory, and the implications of its having left unaddressed (and thus intact) the ideological space occupied by

---

54 According to modernisation theory (Weiner, 1966: 282), therefore, '[t]he largest potential market for industrial products lies in agriculture, since the majority of people in the early stages of development are agriculturalists'.

55 The contribution by anthropologists (such as Milton Singer, M.N. Srinivas, and Bernard Cohn) to discussions about modernization is of particular interest, not least because fieldwork methods tended to privilege their perception of what was happening and – perhaps more importantly – what it was possible to do at the rural grassroots.

56 Weiner (1966: 66–67, original emphasis).

57 See Rogers (1976), who now promoted the idea of '[i]ntegration of traditional with modern systems, so that modernization is a syncretization of old and new ideas'. This, he continued, was because 'until the 1970s, development thinking implied that traditional institutions would have to be entirely replaced by their modern counterparts. Belatedly, it was recognized that these traditional forms could contribute directly to development'.

traditional culture, are revealed glaringly in the assumptions made by one of its hugely influential adherents. Perhaps the most optimistic of all modernization theorists, therefore, Rostow dismissed nationalism as 'a hangover from the world of traditional societies', arguing that as capitalism no longer required an industrial reserve army of labour, 'the patient acceptance of the framework of private capitalism by the working class' was to be explained by rising real wage levels.[58] This Panglossian *weltanschauung* continued that Lenin was wrong, therefore, because declining profits generated neither monopoly nor crisis, and consequently there was no tendency towards ever-greater competition for and military conflict over markets. Marxism, concluded Rostow, had underestimated the ability of bourgeois democracy to deliver 'progress [that] was shared between capital and labour [as a result of which] the struggle between classes was softened'.[59]

Although each of these interrelated claims made by Rostow can now be seen to be mistaken, given its assumptions the logic of his approach was consistent. For him, therefore, the absence at that conjuncture both of declining wages and of an industrial reserve army of labour challenged directly all the views of Marxism concerning the systemic instability of the accumulation process.[60] The latter – Rostow insisted – would not be affected by the private ownership of property, and thus in his view competition did not lead to monopoly, and even imperfect competition would not prevent wages from rising. Accordingly, trade unions would accept the market mechanism, a position effected through

---

58   Rostow (1960: 151ff.).This misplaced optimism was shared by Aron (1967: 92).
59   It should be emphasized that bourgeois theoreticians were not the only ones guilty of naïvete when it came to categorizing as benign the trajectory which the 1960s capitalist system would follow. Similarly overoptimistic prognoses were made at that conjuncture by a number of those deemed to be on the left, such as Stuart Hall (on which see Brass, 2017a: 16–19) and David Caute (1971: 60), for whom 'all the evidence points inescapably to this – the industrial proletariat has shed its revolutionary potential, its vulnerability to absolute pauperisation, its brief claim to occupy the last avenue of history'. Among the very few Marxists who accurately foresaw a darker systemic future, culminating in neoliberalism, was Maurice Dobb.
60   'There is every reason to believe', asserted Rostow (1960: 155, 158), 'looking at the sensitivity of the political process to even small pockets of unemployment in modern democratic societies, that the sluggish and timid policies of the 1920s and 1930s with respect to the level of employment will no longer be tolerated in Western societies. And now the technical tricks of that trade – due to the Keynesian revolution – are widely understood. It should not be forgotten that Keynes set himself the task of defeating Marx's prognosis about the course of unemployment under capitalism; and he largely succeeded... One failure of Marx's system...took the form of the rise in industrial real wages in Western Europe [which indicated that] the worker was content...that, by and large, he was getting a fair share from the lay-out of society as a whole'.

the democratic political structure, and any progress would be shared between capital and labour. Class struggle ceased to be a factor disrupting the smooth functioning and hence the tension-free reproduction of the capitalist system. In the next chapter, dealing with the subsequent rise and consolidation of far right political mobilization, the consequences of this erroneous model will become clear.

6   Conclusion

Central to the conceptualization by Marxism of the necessity for revolutionary action has been the formation/struggle/consciousness of class, a combination of selfhood and agency that emerges historically as a result of a twofold process: at one end of the agrarian hierarchy the separation of the direct producer from his/her means of labour, and the extension of ownership/control of private property in all its forms by better-off elements at the other. Differentiating the peasantry into its rich, middle, and poor components, therefore, Marxism argued that capitalist penetration of agriculture converted the former into a rural bourgeoisie and the latter into workers, while middle peasants (or petty commodity producers) were 'depeasantized'. This was the dynamic providing capitalism with its opposed class elements, the struggles between which gave the impetus both to revolutionary agency and to the necessity for a socialist transition. The gulf between the feasibility of achieving the latter objective through bourgeois democracy or by means of permanent revolution was highlighted in the 1920s exchange between Kautsky and Trotsky.

Insofar as undifferentiated rural smallholders could be seen as bearers of national identity and culture by those opposed to revolutionary socialist transformation, this category was viewed with mistrust by Marxists. The contrasting theory of populism, however, insisted that the family farm constitutes an undifferentiated pan-historical socio-economic category, largely impervious to outside economic forces. Unlike the exogenous one of Marxism, the dynamic as interpreted by populism is endogenous, governed simply by a producer/consumer balance. Despite this populist concept of an homogeneous peasantry being the 'other' of Marxist theory, it is shared by a variety of revisionist approaches, not least a number of those claiming a political affinity with Marxism itself. Chief amongst these was Social Democracy, the Austro-Marxist theorists of which not only advocated parliamentary reformism instead of revolutionary action but also sought the electoral support for this project of 'gradualness' from the peasantry. However, the focus of revisionism throughout that conjuncture was on how a landowning class, by holding on to its property, blocked thereby the possibility of economic development. This is the same point that advocates of bourgeois modernization and the semi-feudal thesis made in relation to Third World nations over the second half of the twentieth century.

The distinction between the way Marxist and modernization theory interpreted the peasantry, in terms of characterization and transformation, is easily discerned. Following in the footsteps of earlier leftist revisionists, bourgeois modernization theory downgraded class struggle because in its view capitalism was no longer crisis-ridden, and its workforce now enjoyed rising wages and secure employment. For modernization theorists, therefore, economic development occurred without generating class struggle, without reverses and defeats as well as victories. In short, without any longer necessitating 'from below' revolutionary action culminating in socialism. What they overlooked, however, was the link between the economy and ideology, and how accumulation fuelled 'from below' kinds of struggle that would take reactionary forms, or the very discourse that had been dismissed as an insignificant 'hangover from the world of traditional societies'. This resurgence of populism stemmed directly from a political and theoretical failure to understand the connection between the global spread of capitalism, the intensification of competition, an expansion of the industrial reserve army enabling producers to restructure the labour process, economic crisis, and the rise of the populist far right. Among those who similarly misinterpreted this process were adherents of the postmodern 'cultural turn', for whom populism was seen merely as empowering for rural populations.

An inability/unwillingness on the part of modernization theorists to address the actual/potential role of ideology existing at the rural grassroots in 'from above' class struggle waged by capital, and specifically the way this licensed the political formulation/reproduction/consolidation of populist discourse, contributed in no small manner to the 'cultural turn' which emerged some twenty years after the development decade of the 1960s. Privileging economic progress, modernization theory deemed this to be sufficient in terms of a development goal. It is perhaps difficult to appreciate the degree to which modernization theory was the orthodoxy in 1960s development studies, given the extent to which its epistemology has now been challenged and reversed by the 'new' populist postmodernism, the dominant paradigm that supplanted it from the 1980s onwards. How and why this happened, as well as the effects of this epistemological overturning, are issues examined in Part 2.

Moreover, the political impact of revisionism is not confined to revolutionary agency. It extends also to the way relations of production are misinterpreted, particularly as regards the presence, role, and object of unfree labour in both capitalism and socialism. Where accumulation is concerned, therefore, the unfree labour is recast epistemologically so as to make it acceptable to bourgeois ideology in a number of distinct ways: either to purge it of its coercive element and thus relabel it as nothing more than free wage labour; to claim that unfree production relations can be eliminated within capitalism, and are unconnected with a transition to socialism; or that such work arrangements are merely part of the way specific cultures operate, and thus possess no significance economically. Where socialism is concerned, however, the allocation by the state of workers as a result of economic planning is used to condemn any/all forms of Marxist theory and practice.

As will also be seen in Part 2, many analyses of the connection between capitalism and unfree labour still adhere to a familiar trope that informs much development theory. Thus unfreedom is seen as a pre-capitalist phenomenon, linked mainly/mostly to non-capitalist backwardness associated with colonialism/neo-colonialism/underdevelopment: it flourished because, in the absence of economic growth, workers from Third World contexts take whatever jobs they can, at whatever onerous conditions on offer, many as migrants who go to find employment in other nations. The problem with this view is that it either leaves out or downplays why employers in 'other nations' like – and in some instances prefer – such labour and working arrangements. The driving force in metropolitan capitalist contexts is threefold: a dislike of unionized/organized labour, which – because it is not unfree – is confident politically and well-paid; intense market competition amongst producers trying to sell their commodities on the global market; and intense competition amongst workers for jobs, trying also to sell their labour-power – their sole commodity – on the global market. When the latter processes combine, as they have done as a result of *laissez faire* policies implemented by neoliberalism, the consequence is the rise and rise of unfree production relations.

CHAPTER 3

Refusing Revolution, Empowering Counter-revolution

> 'The author will not even permit himself to say with certainty that such an organization will lead to a successful revolution. He can only say, with some confidence, that without it a peaceful (or other) revolution is highly improbable. Further, it seems proved that if no action like this is taken, action of another kind will be taken for us. The working class and the middle class are not today likely to suffer and struggle for a spineless Socialist or Labour Party, to put up uncomplainingly with another [Ramsay] MacDonald government. The continuance of uncertainty and feebleness will mean that existing organizations will crumble and the disillusioned will drift steadily across to a Fascist organization'.
>
> A concluding observation in a 1930s book by RAYMOND POSTGATE about revolution that has relevance for the present.[1]

∴

1 Introduction: To the Barricades?

Where and when the accumulation process experiences sustained economic crisis, licensing increased levels both of labour market competition and consequently of exploitation, the issue is no longer whether this will lead to radical direct action on the part of workers affected, but instead what political form this will take. In the absence of a leftist mobilization that effectively challenges capitalism, therefore, it becomes a question not of a missing 'from below' political movement but rather the agency which does emerge being harnessed by the populist far right. It is a problem examined in this chapter, with regard to the rejection by Austro-Marxists of revolutionary action designed to secure a socialist transition in favour of parliamentary reformism.

As has been outlined in the previous chapter, such complacency was matched subsequently by bourgeois modernization theory, which banished class struggle and economic crisis from capitalist reproduction. Among the

---

[1] Postgate (1934: 198–99).

concerns insufficiently addressed politically by the left in each case was an expanding industrial reserve army, a development accompanied by increased competition in the labour market. The result in both conjunctures has been the political rise of a populist far right movement presenting struggle not in terms of class but rather ethnic/national identity, and challenging not capitalism *per se* but only the 'abuses' perpetrated by specific variants (finance, foreign). In short, laying the ground for counter-revolution.

This chapter is divided into four parts, of which the first considers the impact on working class solidarity in late nineteenth and early twentieth century Austria of a burgeoning industrial reserve army differentiated along ethnic/national lines. Outlined in the second part is the way Austro-Marxism responded to this situation, while the third looks at how its parliamentary reformism contrasted with and was outflanked by the more direct counter-revolutionary agency of the populist far right. The fourth examines why the same kind of populist ideology has resurfaced now in Europe, a discourse that reproduces many of the claims made by its far right precursor.

It is a cliché that radical action the object of which is to empower peasants and workers is a 'from below' practice not confined to the left, but in fact a form of agency that can be shared just as effectively – if not more so – by those on the political right, in the shape of counter-revolution. To the oft-heard argument that currently revolutionary agency lacks a subject, therefore, it is possible to reply that the prevalence of working class representation now is to be found not in movements that are internationalist in outlook and designed to bring about socialism, but rather in the rise of the far right throughout Europe and North America. Clearly, much 'from below' mobilization which occurs currently takes the form of populist, 'nativist', and/or nationalist movements in metropolitan capitalist contexts. Historical antecedents indicate not just why and how this emerges, but also the political trajectory that such movements can follow. The resulting lessons are too obvious and important to be ignored, not least by Marxists with an interest both in a socialist transition, and thus also in potential/actual obstacles to this kind of transformation.

2 What History Taught Us

There are numerous historical instances underlying the centrality to political concerns expressed by workers' organizations of the actual/potential economic impact the industrial reserve army might have on their struggle to defend/improve pay and conditions, especially in cases where employers restructure the labour process. Of these instances, perhaps the most relevant to the issue examined here is how and why the role of immigration surfaced as a problem in Austria during the 1890s when employers there turned to Czech migrants so as to displace unionized German labour, undermining working class solidarity and fuelling the rise of nationalism.[2] Channelling the language of 'otherness' away from class distinctions and towards the differences of ethnic/national identity inevitably turned the struggle from one seeking the transcendence of capitalism – that is, the pursuit of a revolutionary transition to socialism – to the defence of what systemically was deemed to be the *status quo ante*.

This was clearly a *volte face* that entailed not the going beyond an oppressive/ exploitative labour regime and its economic system (= capitalism), therefore, but rather the restoration of specific and long-standing employment patterns/ practices within the same economic system that had nevertheless been transformed in a detrimental fashion. In short, it amounted to 'from below' agency that corresponds not to a revolutionary overturning of the accumulation process but to its counter-revolutionary defence. The latter was the approach of populist movements led by Georg Ritter von Schönerer and Karl Lueger in Austria towards the end of the nineteenth century, each of whom influenced the discourse and agency deployed subsequently in Germany by Adolf Hitler.[3]

Towards the end of the nineteenth century, a significant migration pattern emerging in Austria was composed of Czechs who came from farming backgrounds. Of this the largest immigration was into the districts of German Bohemia where coalfields and industry were located, and where the existing workforce – employed in all the relatively better-paid jobs there – consisted of those belonging to an indigenous German population.[4] Workers from the latter

---

2   See Whiteside (1962, 1975).
3   For the acknowledgement of this influence, see Hitler (1939: 58, 70, 93–95, 102). The importance of the contribution by Schönerer to the development in Europe of conservative ideology is outlined by Borkenau (1938: 128ff.), Rogger and Weber (1965: 308ff.), Carsten (1977: 9–29), Weiss (1977: 117ff.), and Schorske (1980: 120ff.).
4   On this point see Whiteside (1962: 38–39, 49), who notes: 'The new industrial labour force thus provided, made up as it was largely of unskilled farm hands, was necessarily at the bottom of the economic scale. The Czechs, moreover, were used to lower standards of living than the Germans and were therefore willing to accept lower wages. This gave them a competitive advantage in the labour market which led German workers to consider them as a great threat to wage standards as the employers' greed for profits. The enmity aroused on both sides created a popular psychology receptive to nationalist propaganda... It was the Czechs [who] appeared in a community as strangers, seeking work at any price. [...] The massive Czech immigration into the newly industrialised regions of Austria, especially Bohemia, threatened German Austrian workers in a long list of occupations with the loss of their jobs, status, and homes. The miners in the lignite fields, the factory workers in the growing industrial cities, the handicraftsmen in the villages, all felt the pinch of Czech competition in the crowded labour market. In the coalfields, where the influx of Czechs was extremely large, the pressure on the wage levels of the German Austrian miners was intensified after 1900 by the uncertain economic position of the industry, which was increasingly depressed by the importation of

ethnic category, for the most part unskilled labour, joined nationalist associations, where the focus of 'from below' agency shifted from collective bargaining with employers over wages and conditions to protecting themselves from being undercut by competition in the labour market from Czech and Polish migrants.[5] Among the results of this political shift was that workers henceforth sought to make common cause with employers of the same ethnic category, the replacement of class antagonism with ethnic conflict, and a decline in support for a leftist programme which promoted solidarity across ethnic boundaries.[6] Accordingly, over the late nineteenth and early twentieth century Austria witnessed the emergence of working class organizations based on nationalist identity, a process whereby 'German workers' protective associations formed to combat the menace of Czech competition.'[7] This was the situation confronting the left, in the shape of Austro-Marxism, which immediately raises the issue of

---

a higher-grade product from German, French, and English mines.' The result of this labour market rivalry based on ethnic difference, a situation taken advantage of by employers, is not difficult to discern (Whiteside, 1975: 81): 'In places like Vienna, northern Bohemia, and parts of Styria, where low-paid Slav workers competed for work with the traditionally higher – if miserably – paid Germans, ethnic antagonism flared up...'

5   The centrality of this issue to the subsequent rise of the far right in Germany is evident from the blame attached by Hitler (1939: 26, 27) to the Austrian ruling class for ignoring the effect of this market competition on its workers, and the vehemence of the language he used in doing this: 'What history taught us about the policy followed by the House of Habsburg was corroborated by our own everyday experiences. In the north and in the south the poison of foreign races was eating into the body of our people, and even Vienna was steadily becoming more and more a non-German city. The "Imperial House" favoured the Czechs on every possible occasion... As if struck blind, they [the Habsburgs] stood beside the corpse [= Austro-Hungary] and in the very symptoms believed that they recognized the signs of renewed vitality'.

6   Among the arguments deployed by German workers threatened with displacement in the labour market, therefore, was (Whiteside, 1962: 52) 'the tendency of master-craftsmen to use apprentices – untrained Czechs or what was virtually child labour – in place of journeymen. Some declared that the new Social Democratic idea of proletarian solidarity actually played into the hands of "Czech scabs"... [a textile worker] denounced employers who hired cheap Czech newcomers in preference to skilled German old inhabitants [describing] Czech workers as...putting up docilely with living conditions that no German would tolerate. Czech apprentices, he said, were willing to remain indefinitely in that inferior status and to forgo the better pay of journeymen, thus undercutting the legitimate demands of German craftsmen. German journeymen were in consequence forced to work on a precarious day-to-day basis without the traditional security and prospects of advancement'.

7   See Rogger and Weber (1965: 317), and also Carsten (1977: 35), who writes: 'The first German National Socialist Party which...came into being was, in its origins and composition, considerably more working class than its later Austrian or German namesakes... What it had in common with the later National Socialist parties was a mixture of radical national with socialist demands...' For the centrality to the concerns of Pan-German League of the link between on the one hand the presence of non-German migrant workers and on the other the impact of cultural erosion on German national identity, see Wertheimer (1924: 163ff.).

how adequate was its political response both to this burgeoning nationalism and also to the consequent divisions within the working class.[8]

It was this competition between German and Czech components of the working class in Austria that played an important part in the privileging by Otto Bauer, a prominent Austro-Marxist theoretician, of the national question.[9] Most significantly, therefore, leftist discourse itself began to adopt the language of 'otherness', framing struggle in terms not of class positions but rather of ethnic/national grievances.[10] These views fuelled a theoretical framework that emerged from Austro-Marxism – structured by qualifying terms such as 'interval in history', 'equilibrium', 'organic democracy', and 'co-determination' – validating a reformist politics conducted largely within the parliamentary system, an approach that promoted not struggle against but much rather collaboration with capitalism. In doing so, Austro-Marxism laid the ground for the circumventing of parliament in the form of a counter-revolutionary mobilization by the far right offering to provide both capital and labour a more radical and immediate form of political action.

In one sense, it is unsurprising that Austro-Marxism discarded revolutionary agency in favour of parliamentary reformism, given that many of its theorists were *katheder*-socialists, and as such comfortably ensconced in academic

---

8   According to Otto Bauer (Blum and Smaldone, 2017: 44), the year 1897 saw two significant developments in Austrian politics: Social Democracy not only entered parliament for the first time, but also began to fragment along national/ethnic lines ('national individualities became increasingly pronounced within the party as a whole'). About the latter Whiteside (1975: 177) notes: 'The explosion of nationalism in 1897 caused real trouble for the Social Democrats… The workers thought of themselves as German socialists or Czech socialists'.

9   In 1910 Bauer wrote (Blum and Smaldone, 2017: 56): 'This antagonism is rooted in the very real differences between the needs of the German and Czech proletariat… It will be eliminated only if the objective conditions of struggle allow us to commit our full power to the conclusion of a peace that results in a just solution to the national question. At such a moment we will surely be united.'

10 This leftist shift from a mobilizing discourse about class to one about ethnic 'otherness' is described (Borkenau, 1938: 167, emphasis added) thus: 'Not among a single non-German people [in Austria] did the socialists succeed in organizing labour so fully as did the German-speaking socialists, and *in order to have any success whatsoever they had gradually to adapt themselves to the nationalist impulses of the milieu in which they worked.*' Whiteside (1962: 54–56) points out that 'Czech workers felt that they were being not only exploited by their employers but persecuted by German fellow-workers; Germans complained that the Czechs' acceptance of lower wages and inferior working conditions depressed the German standard of living and handicapped strikes. Some Czech unions had actually offered to employers an agreement to work longer hours for less pay than the Germans in rival unions'.

posts.[11] In part, this accounts for the emphasis it placed on legalism, an approach to which revolutionary agency is antagonistic, since rather obviously laws framed by those in government invariably forbid and penalize non-parliamentary attempts to capture and rule through the state. Thus, for example, the approach of Karl Renner to legal and constitutional issues did not depart substantially from the historical meanings applied to them, and in particular as found in the legislative ordinances of capitalism. Among the political issues he deems absolute rights that transcend systemic differences, to be defended as such, is that of individual freedom at the root of not just liberal philosophy but also – and more significantly – the accumulation process.[12] Despite the fact that individualism licenses most – if not all – the self-validating ideology of the capitalist system generally (and neoliberalism in particular), it is categorized by him as an inalienable and trans-historical right, one that should be protected by any/all law.[13] This virtuous position is contrasted by Renner with that of the Bolsheviks, condemned by him for subordinating individual rights to that of the state.[14]

---

11 Why this academic background is significant is outlined below in Chapter 8, which considers both the fact of and the political response to the way a radical Marxist approach, which was developed on the margins by Bolshevism, was transferred to the academic mainstream, where it was depoliticized by the *katheder*-socialists of Austro-Marxism.

12 On this and the following points, see Renner (1949: 296): 'Our observations, however, have led us to recognize that every legal order must grant to everybody a private sphere into which the common will does not intrude. After the victory of a liberalist philosophy with its concepts of natural rights, to which the victory of the bourgeoisie over the feudal system corresponded in practice, a theory of constitutional law was evolved which set limits to the powers of the state, affecting even the public law. Public law may not transgress these limits; within them the individual is free and not subject to the control of the state... We hold this freedom of the individual in high esteem.' This is followed by a note on the same page, which elaborates: 'This has not prevented Bolshevism from again establishing the omnipotence of the state, from stringently curtailing human freedom in the spiritual sphere. I think this is a disastrous regression. It is not justifiable to surrender achievements of civilization even if they are branded as introductions of the enemy, the hated bourgeoisie.'

13 It comes as no surprise that Renner welcomed the Munich Agreement of 1938 as evidence of German 'strength' (Bukey, 2000: 79): 'Karl Renner, the semi-official spokesman of Social Democracy, even published a pamphlet exalting the "unparalleled strength and determination of leadership of the German Reich"'.

14 Clearly, where socialist planning depends on the capacity of the state not just to expropriate property but also to restrict competition by controlling food prices, a burgeoning black market, or access to the labour market, any or all of these may of necessity entail the curtailment of the individual freedom to continue owning property, trading produce, or purchasing/selling labour-power.

Bauer, another influential Austro-Marxist theorist, made it clear that, as the political focus of the working class movement in Austria was to be on the realization not of socialism but of democracy, this was to be achieved not by revolutionary agency but by electoral success consequent on the extension of universal suffrage.[15] To this end, he placed his hopes in 'a new Parliament', where the bourgeois democratic process of which he approved would be based on an 'equilibrium' in which the power of capital would be restrained by workers.[16] It was this much-desired and admired 'balance' between the classes, argued Bauer, that fascism ultimately destroyed. Another way of explaining this outcome, however, is that it was because of the political and economic compromises made by Austro-Marxists with capitalism, and the resulting constraints imposed by their adherence to parliamentary methods, that in a context of economic crisis elements from among the peasantry and the working class turned to those pursuing an alternative, non-parliamentary form of struggle that might conceivably address their plight. In short, it was the political timidity of an Austro-Marxism that sought conciliation with capitalism which paved the way for the success of what was a more radical form of agency on offer from the far right.

The political timidity of Austro-Marxism, and its consequent espousal of parliamentary reformism, stemmed additionally from two problematic assumptions: an overly cautious view amounting to a wish not to antagonize the opponents of socialism combined with an overoptimistic assessment of working class gains under capitalism. Noting the hostility of peasants towards the proletariat, therefore, Bauer insisted that as a social force they were too powerful for this antagonism to be ignored, and that consequently any attempt to establish a dictatorship of the proletariat would be doomed to failure. He also warned that French, British and Russian imperialism would similarly prevent any proletarian dictatorship installed in Austria from functioning.[17] For his

---

15 See the essay 'Intervals in History' (Blum and Smaldone, 2016: 315ff.), written by Bauer in 1910.
16 Bottomore and Goode (1978: 179).
17 Noting that it was 'impossible to govern the industrial district in opposition to the workers, but it was equally impossible to govern the great agrarian district in opposition to the peasants', Bauer (Bottomore and Goode, 1978: 162–63) continued: 'The economic structure of the country therefore created a balance of power between the classes which could only have been abolished by force in a bloody civil war. Large sections of the proletariat were eager for such a civil war... It was oblivious of the unshakeable power of the peasantry in the agrarian region, and equally blind to the menacing power of *Entente* imperialism externally. Consequently, it regarded the establishment of the dictatorship of the proletariat as a possibility. But the establishment of such a dictatorship would have meant nothing less than suicide for the revolution... The dictatorship of the proletariat would

part, Max Adler implied that anyway the accumulation process had benefited sections of the working class, which had as a result become upwardly mobile: no wonder, he concluded, 'that the Marxist theory of revolution came to be regarded by them as "impractical", "outdated", and in any case disruptive'.[18]

Accordingly, the perception that class fragmentation was not occurring, a claim that was central to revisionism (see previous chapter), and that consequently a terminal capitalist crisis would not emerge, led in turn to an abandonment of revolutionary politics in favour of electoral success. In the case of Bauer, a failure to differentiate the peasantry led him to an overestimation of rural elements opposed to a dictatorship of the proletariat; and, as the 1917 Russian revolution demonstrated, imperialist forces – although powerful – could be held in check once revolutionaries were armed.[19] However, no real difference was perceived by him to exist between revolutionary and counter-revolutionary agency, regarding the former as leading inevitably to the latter; since one was as bad as the other, both should be avoided.[20] Equally, the claim made by Max Adler that Austrian workers had benefited from the accumulation process applied only to the labour aristocracy, not the mass of the proletariat, which – he accepted – were still opposed to capitalism (albeit qualified along the lines of 'this revolutionary energy often remains dormant').[21]

3   The Nation's Great Concerns

The revisionist views held by Bauer about the peasantry and socialism are consistent with the general political approach of Austro-Marxism. The latter, as outlined in the previous chapter, eschewed both Marx's concept of the state as an instrument of class rule, and Lenin's model of revolutionary class struggle undertaken by the proletariat with the aim of capturing and governing through the state. Instead, Austro-Marxists argued that working class interests could be realized adequately by means of parliamentary reform, an objective involving an historical 'interval' or 'equilibrium' amounting to a balance not just between classes but also within a working class differentiated along ethnic

---

have ended with the dictatorship of foreign rulers. Large sections of the proletariat did not realize these dangers, but it was the duty of Social Democracy to see them.'
18   On this point, see Bottomore and Goode (1978: 228–29, 230).
19   For different reasons, Loew (1979) also thinks Bauer was mistaken in his belief that Austria would have been invaded by imperialist forces.
20   Bauer (1925: 225).
21   Bottomore and Goode (1978: 234).

lines. Because of this, primacy was to be accorded politically to the national question, to be resolved within the structure of parliamentary democracy.

Observing that the growth of Pan-Slavism 'only further sharpens the nationality struggles within the [Austro-Hungarian] Empire', Bauer nevertheless argued that for Austria this meant what he termed 'an interval in history, above all the continuation of the national struggles'. This despite his acceptance that "nationalism nourishes itself beyond Parliament', and further that 'nationalism... delivers the most powerful weapon against the working class'.[22] Although critical of those Social Democratic Party and trades union branches within Austria which privileged Czech identity, Bauer nevertheless supported the view of Victor Adler advocating cultural and financial concessions made to them on the basis of this ethnic/national 'otherness'.[23] It was done in the belief that a conciliatory policy was the way to defuse separatist trends within the ranks of the working class movement ('In this way – on the basis of national self-determination – minorities should get justice without intensifying the nationalist struggle'): in effect, buying off internal dissent.[24]

However, much like the reformist parliamentary strategy pursued by Austro-Marxism, designed not to antagonize either their own domestic capitalist class or imperialism (= avoiding external dissent), such concessions merely fuelled separatism based on cultural 'otherness', thereby undermining proletarian solidarity while simultaneously empowering owners of the means of production.[25] By the mid-1920s Bauer's 'interval' had metamorphosed conceptually into an 'equilibrium', explicitly between the classes, a balance of class strengths whereby it is possible for classes to share state power, but also implicitly

---

22   Bauer made the same point again in 1910 (Blum and Smaldone, 2017: 45): 'In Austria, where eight nations have conducted a bitter struggle for power since 1848, the most dangerous weapon of the bourgeoisie was the accusation that Social Democracy was disengaged from and ignorant of the nation's great concerns... To repel such attacks our comrades have to try to prove that they are the protectors of the true interests of the nation'.
23   Aspects of the separatist issue were addressed by Bauer in a 1910 article 'Internal Conflicts in Austrian Social Democracy' (Blum and Smaldone, 2017: 42–57), which among other things considered proposals such as financial support and the decentralization of trade union structures and party authority.
24   Linguistic and educational concessions – 'the Czech child belongs in a Czech school' – were among the special considerations extended to non-German components of the working class movement (Blum and Smaldone, 2017: 51–52, 53).
25   'The result of the Austrian Revolution was also a condition of things in which "the struggling classes held each other in check"', argues Bauer (1925: 244), adding: 'From the beginning it [state of 'equilibrium'] was based upon the contradiction between the powerful position of the proletariat in the country and the complete impotence of the country towards the capitalist powers outside our frontiers'.

between the ethnically different components of the working class.[26] That he perceived an 'equilibrium' as a lull in the class struggle is evident from his view that, in the pre-capitalist era when bourgeois and aristocracy were contending for state power, it 'was a condition of equilibrium in which the bourgeoisie were not yet strong enough or did not yet venture to take the instruments of governance themselves'.[27] The object became one in which the object of struggle by the proletariat in Austria was for 'a right of co-determination' in furtherance of 'organic democracy'.[28]

Because he was an advocate of reformism, pursued by parliamentary means, therefore, Bauer justified this theoretically by contending that the state was not an instrument of class rule – as Marxism had long insisted – but rather that it constituted an 'equilibrium', a balance of power between the bourgeoisie and the proletariat whereby neither exercised control over the other.[29] This enabled him not just to pursue reformist ends within a parliamentary structure, by claiming that since the bourgeoisie was unable to block or frustrate such progress, this was a politically efficacious form of agency, but also that

---

26 See 'The Equilibrium of Class Strengths', a 1924 essay by Otto Bauer where he states that (Blum and Smaldone, 2016: 323ff., 333) '[i]n many countries a condition has emerged in which neither the workers' party nor the bourgeois parties can govern the state by themselves in a parliamentary form'.

27 Blum and Smaldone (2016: 326–27). Taking issue with Lenin, whom he describes as a 'vulgar Marxist' because of the way he depicted the state as an instrument of class dominance and rule, Bauer (Blum and Smaldone, 2016: 332–33) downgrades the importance of class struggle, because in his opinion a better understanding of the relations between those who own means of production and those separated from this can be gained from deploying concepts like 'equilibrium' to explain the non-class specific role of the state. His reason for this is that '[a]n approximation of the facts which in the time of the first beginnings of the class struggle of the proletariat was sufficient, are not sufficient for our practical interests today'. The same kind of dismissing-by-chronologizing argument is echoed by Renner (1949: 208, note 2): 'Karl Marx's life work, especially *Capital*, his principal work, belongs to a definite period of history, the middle of last [i.e., the nineteenth] century, and must therefore be read with the eye of the historian.'

28 See Bauer (Blum and Smaldone, 2016: 327, 329), who underlines the fact that '[a]scendancy of the proletariat, the equilibrium of class strengths, the restoration of the bourgeoisie – these were the chapter headings of my history of the Austrian revolution'.

29 According to Bauer (Blum and Smaldone, 2016: 334, original emphasis), therefore, 'the class-based state of the bourgeoisie has not been followed by a dictatorship of the proletariat, but rather by a condition of the equilibrium of class strengths, which politically has been expressed in many different forms of state. This experience makes it possible that between the period in which the state was a class organization of the bourgeoisie and the period in which it will be class organization of the proletariat, there will be a transitional period in which the strengths of the classes in relation to each other are in equilibrium... And this is a condition of state in which no class can control the other, the power having to be shared, a passing *phase* in the development of the state.'

consequently there was no need to engage in revolutionary action outside this institution so as to seize and rule through the state.

4 The Balance of Class Power?

Not the least of the many problems with the concept 'equilibrium' are the following. When Bauer outlines what in his view corresponds to a 'balance of power' between the classes, it is clear that this is a misnomer: what he describes are developments which constitute an augmentation of the command exercised by capital over its workforce and the means of production.[30] In short, how is it possible to describe as a 'balance' of class power a situation when very clearly capitalism was reasserting its dominance: that is, a context in which state control over resources were abolished, private enterprise flourished, labour discipline was restored, and labour productivity increased.[31] Moreover, in support of his claim about the existence of an 'equilibrium', Bauer denies that Austria is 'fully capitalist', the inference being that employers are as yet insufficiently powerful to impose all the requirements of the accumulation project on their workers.[32] Not only does this justify the continuation *sine die* of what he terms a 'balance', but it anticipates the same argument made subsequently by exponents of the semi-feudal thesis.[33]

---

30 'Just as the year 1919 taught the proletariat [in Austria] that it could not establish its dictatorship but could only struggle for power within the limits of the democratic Republic', maintained Bauer (1925: 242), 'so the year 1921 taught the bourgeoisie that it could neither disrupt nor overturn the Republic...'. This begs the question as to why would it want to do so? The Republic was not opposed to accumulation, much rather the contrary. This is a specious argument, based on a false dichotomy.
31 For this description of what he presents as a 'balance'/'equilibrium' between the proletariat and the bourgeoisie, see Bauer (1925: 249): 'Economically, this period [1919–1921] was characterized by the revival of industry and commerce, which, on the one hand, lessened the widespread privations which supervened at the close of the war, and, on the other hand, abolished the State control of resources and restored the ordinary conditions of private enterprise. Socially this period was characterized by...the restoration of labour discipline, and a gradual improvement in the productivity of labour.'
32 'But the Austrian Republic', insists Bauer (1925: 280), 'has not yet assumed a completely bourgeois character. For more than four years the proletariat and the bourgeoisie in Austria have waged a war of position, and it has not been possible to dislodge any class from its decisive positions. Thus the Austrian working class is still able to prevent the establishment of the absolute rule of the bourgeoisie.' It scarcely needs mentioning that his claim about 'balance', to the effect that 'it has not been possible to dislodge any class from its decisive positions', is contradicted by the procedures Bauer indicates were followed by capital (among them, the restoration of labour discipline).
33 On the semi-feudal thesis, see Chapters 6 and 9 below.

Furthermore, the concept ‚equilibrium' is restricted by Bauer to its presence to the parliamentary system, which ignores what occurs outside this context, and with it whether that, too, corresponds to – or indeed negates – any notion of classes being in 'balance'. As important is the way his categorization as 'balance' – a crucial aspect of which is stability – conveys the impression that particular powers and/or social forces simply cancel one another out. This is similar to a situation described in chess as resulting either in stalemate or in *zugzwang*; that is, what is in fact struggle, and thus necessarily a process of conflict (= striving), that is incompatible with the notion of 'equilibrium'/'balance'. As conceptualized by Bauer, moreover, since an obvious cause leading to the transcendence of an 'equilibrium' appears to be lacking, there is no reason why a society could not operate with a perpetual condition of 'balance' between the classes.

This difficulty notwithstanding, Bauer differentiates the state in terms of class power, between an 'equilibrium' and a control phase. He then maintains that such a distinction can be applied to society generally, arguing that just as capitalist elements can be found in what are palpably non- or pre-capitalist modes, so it is equally possible to encounter non-capitalist elements (= 'remnants') within capitalism itself.[34] Although ostensibly true, this argument fails to address the specific nature of the concepts involved. Hence on the question of production relations, and their defining role with regard to the labour regime, it is all too easy to assume that unfree labour-power is simply a feudal or semi-feudal 'anomaly', systemically and/or historically out of place in the economic process which reproduces it. This avoids asking whether such production relations are indeed 'remnants', forms/arrangements 'left over' from – and thus systemically a characteristic only of (= belonging to) – a non- or pre-capitalist mode, or whether they are actually generated and reproduced by capitalism itself, and consequently intrinsic to the accumulation process.[35]

For Bauer, therefore, the task of Social Democracy was to represent (= 'make politically effective') the discontent of what amounted to a multi-class alliance, ranging from workers to bureaucrats, intellectuals, and small traders.[36] Not all

---

34   'In the society of the thirteenth century', declared Bauer (Blum and Smaldone, 2016: 335), 'there were already many capitalist elements; in spite of that we have no reservations in considering society of that time, in its predominant character, a feudal society. In the society of the nineteenth century, there were many significant remnants of feudal society; in spite of that we call this society, in accord with its predominant characteristics, capitalist.'

35   This is an issue that surfaces below in Chapters 4, 5 and 6.

36   See Bauer (1925: 281–2) who notes: 'The immediate task of Social Democracy is to make politically effective the growing discontent of the multitude of employers and small tradesmen who are hit by the economic crisis; the officials who are threatened with dismissal; the intellectuals who are resentful of alien domination; and the working class on whom the full brunt of the blow has fallen… We must avoid two equally disastrous errors: that of the Communists who would impose upon the working class during this period

of these are interested in socialism, however, and some – for example, traders, bureaucrats, and a number drawn from the ranks of the intelligentsia – will be strongly opposed to any prospect of a socialist transition. From among these elements were those who a decade later supported the populist far right in Austria. Equally contentious, yet politically symptomatic, is the first of the two 'disastrous errors' which Bauer insists Social Democracy must avoid. This is the desire on the part of the Communists to 'impose' on workers a push for revolutionary objectives (= 'tasks which are only appropriate to a new revolutionary epoch') from inside this 'equilibrium' (= 'period of transition').

In short, a confirmation of his reformist approach, and his opposition to the kind of revolutionary agency pursued by Bolshevism. Endorsements of gradualness (= 'step by step') coupled with a corresponding disdain for revolutionary agency (= 'the foolish malice of rabble-rousers') are difficult to miss.[37] What appealed to Bauer, it seems, was being in 'partnership' with capitalism, all the while insisting that the resulting 'balance' was only a transitory phase, which in effect stretched compromises with capitalism into the future.[38] In this discourse, therefore, not only was revolutionary agency postponed *sine die*, but – more significantly – Austro-Marxism was complicit with laying the ground for the emergence and consolidation (and thus empowering) the far right.

---

of transition [= 'equilibrium'] tasks which are only appropriate to a new revolutionary epoch, and that of the middle class democracy, which regards the period of transition as the close of an epoch, beyond which no new revolutionary period is looming.'

37   The following assertion by Bauer (2000: 326) captures both aspects: 'Certainly, it is hardly probable that national autonomy will be the result of a great resolution, of a single bold action. In a slow process of development, in long struggles that repeatedly paralyze legislation and maintain the rigidity of the administrative apparatus while also undermining its ability to survive, Austria will develop step by step in the direction of national autonomy. Rather than a great legislative act, it will be innumerable individual laws for the individual provinces and parishes that produce the new constitution...those for whom the national struggle is not the foolish malice of rabble-rousers but the necessary effect of altered national relations...'

38   There would be no end in sight to this supposed 'balance', which turns it in effect to a permanent form of stasis, whereby from the point of view of the proletariat its interests are not resolved – if, indeed, they are addressed at all. Bauer (1925: 245, 246, emphasis added) more or less admits as much when he writes that 'the classes could not carry their struggle to the point of forcible decision. They were obliged day by day to effect fresh compromises with each other... Thus the [Austrian] Republic was neither a bourgeois nor a proletarian republic. In this phase, the Republic was not a class State, that is, not an instrument for the domination of one class over other classes, but the outcome of a compromise between the classes, a result of the balance of class power.' Most cynically, it could be argued that the only ones to benefit from such a situation were those Austro-Marxist parliamentarians who continued to advocate reformist policies and further compromises with capitalism.

Although rightly noting that '[a]gainst this monstrous power of capital the masses finally rebel', Bauer and Austro-Marxism were mistaken as to the political form this would take: what they underestimated was that the far right was as capable as the left of attracting the support of the working class.[39] Insofar as Austro-Marxists had failed radically to oppose the development and consolidation of this 'monstrous power', therefore, they were not or no longer seen by many in the working class as offering a challenge – let alone an alternative – to capitalism.[40] The latter role – being prepared to take radical action because 'capitalism is not capable of insuring economic stability' – is one that, in the absence of a revolutionary project aimed at a socialist transition, gives rise to counter-revolution by the populist far right. And, indeed, this is what happened in Austria during the 1930s.[41] In Germany, too, among the recruits to the Brownshirts (SA or *Sturmabteilung*) were those who had formerly been socialists and communists.[42]

5 To the Barricades

Amidst radical nationalist organizations endorsing the innateness of ethnic/national 'other' identity in order to mobilize the support of peasants and artisans were conservative religious parties, such as the *Katholische Volkspartei*. In Austria, Catholicism was the mobilizing discourse used initially to obtain the support of peasants and artisans, by attacking liberals and Jews, the latter deemed responsible for the former, and consequently depicted as the embodiment of twin hates: capitalism and modernity.[43] This process was undertaken and

---

39 See the 1927–8 essay by Bauer, 'The Transition from the Capitalist to the Socialist Society' in Blum and Smaldone (2016: 341).
40 This shift is outlined by Whiteside (1975: 178) in the following way: 'The idea of a national socialism attracted both Czech and German workers... To some [German trade union leaders], allying themselves with the German middle class seemed a surer way to improve the workers' condition than sticking to proletarian solidarity... Proletarian nationalism, by weakening the socialist party and intimidating the Vienna leaders...not only forced the socialist deputies into the German nationalist camp...it also raised the question of where the workers' deepest loyalties really lay and whether Pan-Germanism might not in time express the hopes and fears of German workers more accurately than Social Democracy'.
41 In the case of Austria (Jeffery, 1995: 195), therefore, '[t]he mass, long-term unemployment of the depression years [from 1929 onwards] debilitated the [Social Democratic] movement, causing dramatic falls in membership... After 1932, when the Hitler bandwagon began to gather pace in Germany, the Nazi Party became a further beneficiary of such defections.'
42 On this point, see Fischer (1983).
43 For this and what follows, see Whiteside (1975: 82, 83–84). Borkenau (1938: 125) reports that '[i]t was impossible, apparently, to uproot Catholicism in Austria as a religious creed

organized under the aegis of the Christian Social Movement by aristocratic Catholic Democrats who promoted a radical nationalist programme, advocating increased economic and political equality. Liberalism was indicted by them on the grounds that its concepts of equality and freedom were false, since these undermined traditional institutions – such as family, guilds, and estates – which historically had been the source of 'socially valuable rules' governing work. Among the reasons for aristocratic opposition to liberalism was that an effect of *laissez-faire* economic policies was the replacement of duty to the community with struggle for individual gain, thereby releasing any social constraint on capitalist greed, which operated to the disadvantage of people in general.

The result was the destruction of Christian community which had regulated past society. In this discourse, therefore, liberalism and Judaism were triply at fault: for destabilizing a long-standing and successful form of social organization, then delivering workers into the accumulation project of capital as slaves, unleashing thereby a transformation that would eventually lead to revolution. By questioning and then undermining tradition/religion/hierarchy, therefore, liberalism generated class war that would be waged by those erstwhile peasants and artisans who now composed the 'mob-in-the-streets'. Claimed by aristocratic Catholic discourse was the view that opposition to Jews derived not from ethnic 'otherness' but much rather because they were harbingers of a liberalism and modernity (= capitalism) that weakened the traditional social order.[44] Blaming the disruption of existing hierarchy on 'Jewish greed', which then paves the way for revolution, is of course the familiar anti-capitalist ideology of the political right, and historically a central narrative trope of populism.

In keeping with this populist discourse, aristocratic Catholic democrats argued for a return to the solidarity as they saw it represented by the social order as it existed in the Middle Ages. Against the realization of the latter were arraigned liberals and Jews, who for reasons of personal gain encouraged the development of the free market. Instead, aristocratic Catholic discourse promoted an alternative concept of freedom, one which entailed adherence to the moral law (= choosing to be good within the rules laid down by those at the

---

and an everyday ritual... Karl Lueger, the most outstanding man in Austrian political Catholicism, stated himself that Catholicism, especially in Vienna, could only be made into a political movement through an intermediary stage of mass anti-semitism. In fact, anti-semitism has been the starting-point of modern political Catholicism in Austria.'

44 Rejecting anti-semitism as a form of irrationality (Whiteside, 1975: 85), aristocratic Catholic discourse maintained that it emerged 'because [together with peasants and artisans, it] regarded capitalism as a Jewish system and as destructive of the welfare of the sovereign people'.

apex of the existing social order). It was this populist vision – hatred of liberalism and the Jews on the one hand, advocacy of a return to the social order of the Middle Ages on the other – endorsed and sponsored by aristocratic Catholic Democrats, that offered workers a nationalist alternative to Marxist theory about the desirability of a revolutionary transition to socialism.[45]

It was this same discourse – targeted at ethnic 'others' (Jews, Slavs) while upholding traditional rural values and institutions as the embodiment of an 'authentic' cultural identity – that was deployed subsequently in Vienna to generate support for the reactionary political agency of Austrian populism: in the 1880s by the Pan-German movement of Schönerer, and in the 1890s by the Christian Social Movement of Lueger.[46] The deleterious impact of capitalist development, in the double form of on the one hand undermining peasant economy by separating petty commodity producers and village artisans from their landholdings, and on the other increasing the competition for jobs faced by workers entering the labour market, gave added force to the arguments made at that conjuncture by Schönerer and Lueger.[47]

---

45   In the somewhat different emphasis of Whiteside (1975: 84), therefore, '[t]he German radicals were also understandably interested, for ideological and practical reasons, in the German-speaking working classes...The radical politicians undoubtedly wanted to help the artisans, shop keepers, peasants, and workers whose livelihood was at the mercy of the capitalist economic cycle. At the same time, they saw that they could use the economic grievances of these groups to spread the somewhat abstract gospel of nationalism and build up the mass movement they needed to give political weight to their national cause. The class of urban and semi-rural artisans, small businessmen, and peasants constituted a potentially immense following, far more numerous at that time than the factory workers. In an age of increasing political and class consciousness and expanding suffrage, whoever could become their spokesman would be a power to be reckoned with.'

46   See Whiteside (1975: 152), who notes that: 'The [Christian Social] party's most powerful popular support before 1900 was furnished by the artisan class and peasantry of Lower Austria, who suffered from the competition of manufacturing industry and from capitalist landlords and dreamed of reintroducing a medieval economy, yet recognized that their only chance of achieving their reactionary objectives lay in universal suffrage.'

47   Of the two discursive components informing counter-revolutionary ideology – a discourse-for designating what is approved, and a discourse-against that indicates to what it is opposed – it is the negative one that in political terms is generally the most effective. Hence the view (Whiteside 1975: 139): 'Pan-Germanism was largely negative; it was more against capitalism, liberalism, Marxism, Slavs, Jews, and Habsburgs than it was for democracy, liberty, social justice and national unity. It was concerned as much with restoring the old as with introducing the new. For some, "old" meant German rule; for others, restricted capitalism. Restoration and revolution, order and oppression, were so intertwined in the thinking of the Pan-Germans that the movement could not produce or rest upon any constant theory of society. The promised land of Pan-Germanism remained a vague picture'.

Each of them called for a return to a medieval subsistence economy in rural areas, and also for urban recruitment practices and industrial employment decisions to reflect ethnic German solidarity. Similarly, both of them stressed that accumulation and modernity were themselves 'foreign', the alien (= non-German) product introduced by those within the nation bearing an ethnically 'other' identity (= Jews), who in turn were responsible for importing a migrant workforce that itself was also composed of ethnically 'other' labour.[48] These tropes of far-right political ideology received the backing not just of rural artisans and peasant smallholders, but also of German youth from the Austrian countryside searching for work in the cities.[49] It was on this discourse, moreover, that Hitler was to model his own mobilizing ideology deployed in Germany from the 1920s onwards.

Of significance, however, were the two modifications that were made subsequently by Hitler and the National Socialist Movement (*Nationalsozialistische Deutsche Arbeiterpartei*, NSDAP or National Socialist German Workers Party). First, it was only the discourse of Schönerer, not his target audience or form of political agency, that was adopted.[50] Whereas the Pan-Germanism of Schönerer was aimed largely at obtaining electoral support within the parliamentary system from among bourgeois and petty bourgeois elements, that sought by National Socialism was to be found outside the parliamentary system, amidst the working class and unemployed, amongst whom were those affected by labour market competition from ethnically 'other' migrants.[51]

---

48 The way in which Schönerer and Lueger both deployed anti-semitism as a mobilizing discourse is outlined by Schorske (1980) and Oxaal, Pollak and Botz (1987).
49 See Weiss (1977: 125).
50 The loss of revolutionary dynamic after 1901 on the part of Pan-Germanism as a result of the emphasis by Schönerer on electoral and parliamentary methods is outlined in Rogger and Weber (1965: 320), where it is noted that the 'movement degenerated into little more than a middle-class club for academic discussion, mutedly radical'. The parallel with the difficulties currently faced not by the right but by the academic left are too obvious to merit further elaboration.
51 This distinction, and the shortcomings of agency pursued by Pan-German Movement, was made clear by Hitler (1939: 96, emphasis added) when noting that 'the leaders did not have a clear concept of the importance of the social problem, particularly for a new movement which had an essentially revolutionary character. Schönerer and his followers directed their attention principally to the bourgeois classes. For that reason their movement was bound to turn out mediocre and tame. The German bourgeoisie, especially in its upper circles, is pacifist even to the point of self-abnegation – though the individual may not be aware of this – wherever the internal affairs of the nation or the State are concerned. In good times, which in this case means times of good government, such a psychological attitude makes this social layer extraordinarily valuable to the State. But when there is bad government, such a quality has a destructive effect. *In order to assure*

And second, this political difference itself licensed – and was to be reflected in – a more robust form of direct action: in short, a militancy that was manifested in conflict on the street. Although expressed in the language of cultural 'difference', therefore, at the root of this German/non-German distinction was an economic process which operated to the disadvantage of German identity and to the advantage of its non-German counterpart.[52] It was this populist combination – that is, capitalism = importation of 'foreign' modernity = potential/actual economic subordination of existing inhabitants = cultural erosion = loss of national/ethnic selfhood – which in the capitalist crisis in Germany over the late 1920s and early 1930s the National Socialist movement deployed to great political effect. Much the same kind of populist combination has resurfaced at the beginning of the twenty-first century, and for similar reasons as its earlier counterpart.

It is a truism that the global spread of capitalism has failed to follow the benign model envisaged by 1960s bourgeois modernisation theory (about which see Chapter 2). Contrary to its prognoses, therefore, in economic terms progress has not been shared between capital and labour, and consequently the class struggle has not 'softened' but much rather intensified. Politically, bourgeois democracy has not 'delivered', with the result that nationalism – dismissed as 'a hangover from the world of traditional societies' – has made a return in advanced capitalist nations, where far right populist discourse is on the rise. The latter is itself an effect of two further developments that modernisation theory failed to anticipate: the increase in migration flows, and the

---

the possibility of carrying through a really strenuous struggle, the Pan-German Movement should have devoted its efforts to winning over the masses. The failure to do this left the movement from the very beginning without the elementary impulse which such a wave needs if it is not to ebb within a short while. In failing to see the truth of this principle clearly at the very outset of the movement and in neglecting to put it into practice the new Party made an initial mistake which could not possibly be rectified afterwards. For the numerous moderate-bourgeois elements admitted into the movement increasingly determined its internal orientation and thus forestalled all further prospects of gaining any appreciable support among the masses of the people. Under such conditions such a movement could not get beyond mere discussion and criticism… Such was the fate of the Pan-German Movement, because at the start the leaders did not realize that *the most important condition of success was that they should recruit their following from the broad masses of the people.* The Movement thus became bourgeois and respectable and radical only in moderation.'

52 That behind the invocation of cultural 'otherness' lurked economic issues is evident from the 1897 language decrees giving Czech parity with German, thus making the Czech language a requirement for entry into and/or retention of state employment (Rogger & Weber, 1965: 316). As a result, bureaucrats who spoke only German feared the loss of their jobs.

way employment patterns and capitalist production relations themselves have changed.

6 The World We/(They) Have Lost

The two decades following the end of 1939–45 war were regarded in metropolitan capitalist nations as a period of economic affluence; hours worked fell while industrial conflict increased, both an effect of 'labour's stronger position'.[53] Struggles conducted by the working class had led not just to the consolidation of the welfare state, but also to full employment, prosperity and the consumer boom of the immediate post-war era.[54] It was these kinds of developments accompanying the accumulation process in advanced economies that caused exponents of bourgeois modernisation theory to conclude mistakenly that the welfare state, full employment, and better wages/conditions were here to stay,

---

53   See Glyn (2006a: 4–5, 24–5), who notes that 'with unemployment low over a prolonged period, union organization was strengthened... Employment protection legislation, against arbitrary dismissal and generally limiting employer prerogatives over hiring and firing, was also extended in this period... Radical demands for workers' control were channelled by the trade union leadership into negotiations which settled for a 10% wage increase, an increase in the minimum wage, and some extensions of trade union rights'. Among the arguments made by supporters of unregulated immigration is that the strongest opposition within the UK to immigration occurs in places where no migrants settle, the inference being that such antagonism is straightforwardly racist and nothing else. What is overlooked, however, is that although not affected economically by the presence of migrant workers in the immediate vicinity, such opposition is nevertheless still based on concerns about labour market competition. The latter process occurs not locally but in large urban centres far away – most notably London – to where those who oppose immigration would themselves (or their children) once have gone in search of work. This is especially true of regions where, due to industrial decline, there are no jobs for the young, who consequently have to travel to the metropolis in order to find employment. Because of increases in the industrial reserve army, and the consequent enhanced labour market competition in these distant urban centres, this option which used to be feasible is currently more difficult, not to say impossible. In short, antagonism in places where there is little or no migrant presence can still be based on economic considerations linked to the deployment by capital elsewhere in the same nation of a workforce composed largely or only of migrants who are cheaper to employ.

54   According to Glyn (2006a: 2), therefore, 'the very success of the "Golden Age" seemed to have undermined its basis. It brought extended full employment and thus the strengthening of labour...although the USSR and other planned economies had deep economic problems of their own, their continued existence still held out the possibility of an alternative path for development to that offered by free market capitalism.'

and thus signalled the end of economic conflict between capital and labour.[55] However, the gains made as a result of class struggle waged 'from below' during the 1960s triggered as a response class struggle 'from above', giving rise to what has been termed a 'counter-revolution in macroeconomic policy', consisting of monetarism, the decline of state intervention/expenditure, privatization/deregulation, and rising unemployment.[56]

The rising incidence of struggle waged by the working class in metropolitan capitalist nations from the late 1960s onwards and into the 1970s led in turn to a two-fold struggle – ideological and economic – waged by the bourgeoisie generally, and capitalists in particular.[57] On the ideological front, therefore, a scarcely concealed bourgeois anxiety pervaded the 1975 Reith Lectures, in which Dahrendorf argued for a change in the meaning of development, replacing 'quantitative expansion' (= economic growth, material consumption) with 'qualitative improvement' (= 'new liberty' enabling 'life-chances').[58] In a variation on the argument made by nineteenth century French liberal theory – that it was *laissez faire* economic growth which eventually would lead to the cessation of class struggle (see below, Chapter 4) – Dahrendorf opposed the same radical political

---

55 Lamenting the loss of authority by the ruling classes, an establishment academic (Annan, 1966: 7–8) writing during that period observed: 'In the second half of the twentieth century a further change has taken place. The mass of the population, who [earlier] were on the fringe of society, have now been incorporated in it. Though there are still black areas and pitiable impoverished groups such as coloured people, old-age pensioners, or mortgaged peasant communities, abject poverty in the West has gradually been eroded. As a result the great majority of citizens have acquired not only political status but equality of treatment by the government… As soon as nearly everyone was incorporated into society the sense of distance between ruler and ruled diminished. There was no longer a gulf fixed between the upper classes and the [rest]… As the distance between rulers and the ruled has diminished, so has authority. Authority no longer has such power to compel.' That such an idealized view about the trajectory followed by post-war capitalist development was not confined to establishment academics or bourgeois modernisation theorists is evident from the fact that much the same kind of argument can be found in Hobsbawm (2011: 261).

56 See Glyn (2006a: 28), who notes that in the UK unemployment increased from 5% in 1979 to 11% in 1983.

57 For case-studies of increasing class struggles waged by organized labour in Western European nations at this conjuncture, see Crouch and Pizzorno (1978a, 1978b).

58 'In the advanced societies of the world', explained Dahrendorf (1975: 14), 'with their market economies, open societies and democratic politics, a dominant theme appears to be spent, the theme of progress in a certain one-dimensional sense, of linear development, of the implicit and often explicit belief in the unlimited possibilities of quantitative exapnsion'. He continues: 'The motive force of the political economy of liberty in the 1970s is no longer expansion but what I shall call improvement, qualitative rather than quantitative development'.

trinity (Marxism, revolution, socialism) on different grounds: that cultural empowerment, not economic development, would achieve the same result.[59] To this end, he rejected not just Marxism but also modernisation theory (= progress in its economic sense), and advocated replacing them both with a non-economic concept of empowerment (= progress in a non-material sense).[60]

The latter amounted to an emphasis on 'difference', a right to be enshrined in the 'new liberty'. What was being advanced by Dahrendorf, therefore, was the view that, although everyone is equal as a citizen, this does not preclude distinctions in terms of 'abilities' and 'aspirations'.[61] He omitted to ask how the latter are formed in the first place, and how aspects of this difference (for example, being educated at a fee-paying public school) creates and/or cultivates these 'abilities'/'aspirations'. Dahrendorf then argues that denying 'such difference' is 'to deny life-chances', again without problematizing the way 'difference' comes about, and how it in turn privileges certain kinds of 'life-chances'. He reveals his agenda, and in effect its conservative underpinnings, by arguing that for him equality meant 'difference', not the elimination or abolition of 'difference' through a process of levelling.[62] Accordingly, during the 1970s ideological struggle waged 'from above' not only recognized that in a context where capitalism was facing crisis in the form of a sustained 'from below' challenge, the emphasis should switch, away from economic development and towards cultural forms of empowerment, a 'new' populist postmodern approach *avant la lettre*.

This change of ideological emphasis was accompanied by a similar transformation in economic struggle waged 'from above'. To a large degree, the efficacy of the counter-revolution in metropolitan capitalist nations at this conjuncture

---

59 'It is all the more necessary', maintained Dahrendorf (1975: 25), 'to take [Marxist theory] down and replace it by one which bears more semblance to what is actually happening. For class conflicts reflect the development of social structures: they too become irrelevant when a new potential of human life-chances has emerged.'

60 Observing that 'some people would prefer a revolution to gradual change [but] I am not one of them', Dahrendorf (1975: 23, 24) criticizes Marx both for being 'obsessed' with economics and production, and for having 'underestimated the capacity of societies to change without drama'. Instead, Dahrendorf wishes to focus on 'an existing potential of human life-chances...a liberal option'.

61 Echoing the defence of individualism by revisionist and Austro-Marxist theory, Dahrendorf (1975: 30) argued that there existed 'the potential of support for the assertion of individual rights against anonymous powers, private or public'.

62 'All men are equal in rank and right as human beings and as citizens', insisted Dahrendorf (1975: 44), 'but they differ in their abilities and aspirations. To deny such difference is to deny life-chances, thus liberty... The new liberty means that equality is there for people to be different, and not for the differences of people to be levelled and abolished.'

depended on developments taking place elsewhere, in the so-called Third World. The latter took the form of the new international division of labour, comprising the shift of manufacturing, away from metropolitan capitalism and towards Asia (Japan, Korea, India and China). It was a shift made possible in turn by on the one hand the Green Revolution (which drove peasants off the land, and made them available to capital as workers), and on the other technological/transport improvements such as containerization (which erased distance as an obstacle to marketing). This process has had profound implications both for metropolitan capitalist nations, newly industrializing nations, and for an understanding of the way accumulation would itself develop.

The most profound impact of this shift was on what was now a global labour regime, as outsourcing/downsizing the capitalist labour process became possible due to an expansion in the industrial reserve army of labour.[63] A corollary of the deskilling that accompanied this transformation was that much of the labour force in metropolitan capitalist nations is no longer composed of permanent workers who are free labourers employed in well-paid jobs, but rather casual labourers – many of whom are unfree – in poorly-paid temporary jobs.[64] The economic impact of the new international division of labour, in the form of work going to nations where labour-power is available and cheap, has itself been reinforced by workers coming the other way, from Eastern European countries previously part of the USSR and now members of the EU.[65]

---

63   When compared with the change made by current migration flows to the size of the industrial reserve army, the relative unimportance of earlier amounts of surplus labour available to capital is outlined thus (Glyn, 2006a: 3): 'Although net inward migration was significant, by the end of the 1960s and early 1970s, when labour markets had become very tight, it was only contributing 0.1% per year to the population of the highly industrialized economies or a tenth of the total increase in the population of working age.'

64   The significance of using labour-power that is unfree, both when outsourcing/relocating work and when employing migrants, is considered in Part 2. Not the least important economic effect is that it takes purchasing power from the workforce as a whole, since those who are employed as unfree and thus cheap labour-power, in temporary/seasonal/insecure jobs, lack the purchasing power of well-paid free workers in permanent jobs. The resulting shortfall in consuming power where the domestic market is concerned gives rise to borrowing, which in turn generates further lending that becomes ever more risky.

65   '[F]ollowing Kalecki', Glyn (2006a: 31) points out rightly that such a development 'is really Marx's "reserve army of labour" in disguise – the unemployment whose function in capitalism is to keep wages in check. Unemployment could then be seen as a response to industrial conflict, and its various destabilizing manifestations like inflation and profit squeeze, as business investment would decline with the fall in confidence and governments would turn to restrictive policies to restore discipline. Such an interpretation is quite consistent with the pattern of unemployment... Despite all intervening events...and

Analysing immigration in terms of culture rather than political economy has resulted in mistaken interpretations as to its effect. To begin with, an expanding industrial reserve army does not actually have to take jobs, its members merely have to be, and thus available to undertake this function. The threat its components pose derives not so much from entering the labour market, therefore, as from the capacity to do so were this necessity to arise. What is of importance is – having ignored/underestimated the political impact of culture/ideology, which as a result stayed unchallenged by modernization theory – that it was precisely this 'hangover from the world of traditional societies' which in the context of economic growth unaccompanied by permanent and well-paying jobs became the oppositional discourse that was deployed politically in metropolitan capitalist nations.

7 A (Marxist) Warning from History

On working class agency, the impact has been just as profound, the combined effect of the new international division of labour, an expanding industrial reserve army and expanding immigration being an intensification of competition for jobs, union busting, a dampening down of class struggle, and rising incidence of political and electoral support for populist far right parties. Hence the negative influence on class struggle and political consciousness, as recourse to national/ethnic identity on the part of both migrant and local labour displaces class in each component of the work force – a response not dissimilar to that in Austria towards the end of the nineteenth century. As in the latter case, therefore, what emerges politically is not socialism but false consciousness, together with the rise of populism and far right. Instead of revolutionary action, the only agency countenanced by workers and poor peasants is counter-revolutionary.

However, bourgeois modernization is not the only theoretical approach that has underestimated the relevance of the Marxist argument regarding the continuing dependence of the accumulation process on the industrial reserve army, the deleterious impact of the latter on working classes in metropolitan capitalist nations, and the resulting political direction of grassroots mobilization in such contexts. Because they perceive migrant identity in non-economic terms, simply as an issue of cultural 'otherness' and not political economy, therefore, sections of the contemporary left persist in ignoring or downplaying

all other differences between countries [therefore] a country's unemployment is significantly related to the degree of industrial conflict a quarter of a century earlier'.

the role of a burgeoning industrial reserve army.⁶⁶ Nowhere is this difficulty more on display than in leftist discussion in the UK, about opposition to immigration as the main reason for the leave vote in the Brexit referendum of June 2016, about how to characterize and respond to this situation, and about the role in all this of the populist United Kingdom Independence Party (UKIP).⁶⁷

Hence the indictment as racist by a recent leftist analysis of those who question immigration on the grounds of political economy; the Labour Party is then attacked as 'spineless' for not giving its full backing to what in effect is the current deregulated/decontrolled labour market; finally, the same analysis dismisses as exaggeration the view that UKIP draws much of its support from the working class which usually votes Labour. Failing even to mention the industrial reserve army, let alone its role in propping up capitalism, the same analysis then maintains that elements within the British capitalist class have no desire to remain within the EU, and inferentially are opposed to increases in the industrial reserve.⁶⁸

---

66   In a sense, this makes such leftist elements more culpable than 1960s bourgeois modernisation theorists. The latter at least had the excuse that their prognoses were made during a period when in the immediate post-war decades working class living standards and wages appeared to be improving, whereas it is – or should be – clear to all that nowadays the opposite is the case.

67   The UK vote to leave the EU can be seen as confirmation of the following prescient observation made over a decade ago by Glyn (2006a: 153–4, emphasis added): '…there is the impact of surplus labour in China and elsewhere, significant segments of which will be highly educated but with much lower wages than in the North. Access to this cheap labour could encourage a much higher level of direct investment from the North, in effect an investment drain away from the rich countries. In effect the capital-labour ratio would decline on a world scale, by one-third or more…as the vast reserves of labour in those countries become inserted into the world economy. The result could be a major fall in the share of wages in the rich countries as workers find their bargaining position weakened. The political consequences of such developments are hard to forsee. *Growing demands for forms of protection for Northern workers from Southern competition seems very probable.*'

68   For these views, see Jones (2014: 38, 44–45, 48, 50), who accepts that business does well out of immigration, but then claims that migration contributes economically to the nation (significantly, not the working class) 'through taxation'. Not only is this what employers themselves claim, but it also misses the point. The latter concerns a number of connected economic issues. To begin with, the *level* of taxation will be lower where migrant workers are paid less than local counterparts, since migrants – unlike locals – are more likely to accept existing wages/conditions, as these compare favourably with equivalents in the sending nation. Furthermore, those migrants in unskilled employment will require subsidies from the state to offset their low wages, which brings into question the argument about migrant contributions. Such workers certainly do contribute, but to the profitability of capital, not taxation by the state: that is, to *private* coffers, not public ones. Local workers who might otherwise have got these jobs, and pushed for improved wages/

Much rather the contrary is the case, however, in that many components of the capitalist class do indeed want to retain immigration at present levels, since this permits employers to damp down wages/conditions of those in work: that is, to maintain, if not to enhance, the size and function of the industrial reserve army.[69] Similarly, on the question of whom UKIP represents, it has unfortunately given voice to the concerns of workers faced with yet more competition for jobs they already have, hope to have, or hope their children will have, for the very same reasons that a century ago elements of the German working class in Austria transferred their support from Social Democracy to the far right.

8 Conclusion

Underlined here is the extent to which a 'from below' struggle that is simply for better wages/conditions – a struggle the narrow objectives of which Lenin criticized for a failure to address the systemic causes of impoverishment and oppression – can in specific circumstances veer off into ethnic conflict, in the process empowering the politics and agency of the counter-revolution. This is particularly the case where the left has failed to argue for the systemic transcendence of capitalism, and opted instead to confine opposition to the limits imposed on its project by bourgeois democracy exercised from within a parliamentary system. Hence the espousal by Austro-Marxism of a reformist political strategy conducted within the confines of the parliamentary system was premised on the desire not to antagonize – and provoke a 'from above' reaction from – capitalists and imperialism.

---

conditions, have now to be supported by the state in terms of welfare provision, and this constitutes an *indirect* cost on the state of migration, a cost that is not usually mentioned. It is a difficulty that also fuels conservative calls for yet more austerity, along the lines of 'we can't afford this', which weakens yet further both welfare provision for workers and their political confidence.

69 Evidence for this is presented in Brass (2017b: Chapter 19). In ways that anticipate current argument about withdrawal from EU membership so as to stem competition from the industrial reserve army, a century and a half ago Marx (Marx and Engels, 1934: 289–90) advocated severing the link with Ireland precisely in order to prevent migrants from competing with and undercutting English workers. He insisted that working class emancipation in England depended ultimately on Ireland following its own path of capitalist development, and to this end international solidarity would take the form of support from English workers for Irish equivalents in their struggle for economic and political independence, as distinct from migrating to where this had already occurred.

This peaceful form of gradualism, inferred in the arguments of its principal theorists such as Otto Bauer, Victor Adler and Karl Renner, would (they argued) in the end achieve the same working class objectives as the Bolsheviks in Russia but without the necessity of the kind of direct action practiced by revolutionaries like Vera Figner and Lenin. This strategy of conciliation was extended similarly to those within the ranks of Austrian Social Democracy and the trade unions advocating separatism on the basis of an ethnic/national 'other' identity. The result was that not only were proletarian organizations and politics fragmented along ethnic/nationalist lines, but labour market competition between Czech migrants and German workers, together with the intense economic rivalry to which it gave rise, remained to a large degree unaddressed and thus unresolved by leftist strategy.

A somewhat predictable outcome of this twofold passivity, designed to alienate neither 'those above' nor 'those below', was that social forces in each of these opposed camps sought political solutions to increased competition linked to capitalist crisis – affecting in different ways producers and workers alike – by shifting their political allegiance from conservatism or social democracy to far right national socialism. Even where a workforce is unionized, therefore, a defensive response to the introduction by capital of cheap migrant labour can take a politically reactionary turn. This was how the seeds of fascism were sown at the end of the nineteenth century, when German workers attempted to protect themselves from economic competition in the labour market by Czech migrants. In Austria this was a fate that conservative populists (Schönerer, Lueger) shared with Social Democracy (Austro-Marxists), since in the end the inability/unwillingness of a reformist left and right to adopt a more radical form of mobilization were outflanked at both ends of the political spectrum by those who did: the revolutionary agency of the Bolsheviks in Russia, and the counter-revolutionary action of National Socialists in both Austria and Germany.

In short, parliamentary reformism proved to be a catalyst with respect to the very process Austro-Marxism feared most. Rather than pursuing a gradualist strategy within the parliamentary system (= in effect 'doing nothing' very much) and successfully avoiding thereby offending capitalists, imperialists, and working class separatists, therefore, it had the opposite effect. Timidity on the part of Austrian Social Democracy instead paved the way for the emergence and consolidation of counter-revolutionary political mobilization committed to a more radical form of direct action (= 'doing something'). Both the language and theory of political compromise ('equilibrium', 'balance of class power', 'co-determination'), together with the kind of agency to which this reformist discourse gave rise, were rejected by components located at either end of the social hierarchy. Namely, elements of the working class whose struggles Austro-Marxism wanted to prevent from leading to a parliamentary confrontation with representatives of the bourgeoisie, and capitalists who had hitherto eschewed non-parliamentary forms of action in defence of their property and wealth.

Contrary to received wisdom, therefore, what leads to fascism is not the curbing of immigration – an economic policy dismissed by many on the left for non-economic reasons (the need to empower cultural 'otherness') – but much rather a failure to do so. In contexts where accumulation is accompanied by increasing competition between producers a deregulated labour market necessarily leads to intense competition between workers, enabling capitalist producers to exercise downward pressure on wages/conditions in order better to contend with rival corporations. When this dynamic involves an expanding industrial reserve army that sets against one another locals and migrants belonging to different ethnicities/nationalities – as is occurring in Europe and North America currently, and as happened in Austria during the 1880s and 1890s – workers unsurprisingly invoke in their defence the only identity that still privileges access to contextually-specific jobs: a non-economic or cultural one ('British jobs for British workers', 'Bring jobs back to America'). Perceiving that their existing parliamentary representatives are unable/unwilling to do anything about their worsening economic prospects, workers turn away from Social Democratic or Labour parties and give their political support to any rightwing populist who undertakes to exclude migrants simply on the grounds of a different culture, ethnicity or nationality.

PART 2

Other Marxisms, Other Priorities/Identities

© ANNA LUISA BRASS

CHAPTER 4

The (Revolutionary) Path Not Taken

'This tragic result was inevitable because of a profound though, perhaps, historically necessary contradiction in the conception of the goal towards which the anti-feudal – the liberal – liberators were working...the beast of the jungle is the ultimate ideal of freedom for the liberal who has taken liberalism to its ultimate conclusion... These are the social relations of capitalism, the social relations of the market. Every man is now free, none has legal, compulsive powers over any other. Society is composed of free atoms'.

A description by CHRISTOPHER CAUDWELL (1938: xii–xiii) of the kind of transformation which *laissez faire* capitalism eventually brings into being.

∴

1 Introduction: Promoting Capitalism, Not Socialism

Accounting for the way revolution and socialism have vanished from the agenda of the left requires that their epistemological disappearance be traced to the kind of arguments within political economy that emerged following the 1789 French Revolution. That conjuncture marked the consolidation of opposition to the landlord class so as to facilitate a transition not to socialism but only to capitalism. Of particular significance is that advocacy of *laissez faire* theory in this manner, which combined a simultaneous defence of peasant economy with promoting economic development, subsequently informed a variant of Marxism. This was the semi-feudal thesis which, like the *laissez faire* ideology of French liberalism, opposed landlordism so as to bring about economic growth. Because accumulation and bonded labour were perceived as incompatible, 'pure' capitalism was deemed to be absent until all unfree production relations had been replaced with free equivalents. Revolution and socialism was on the agenda of neither of these two approaches: unsurprisingly in the case of French liberalism, but surprisingly in the case of the semi-feudal thesis.

For understandable reasons, the main focus of those analysing opposition to the 1789 French Revolution has been on the ideology and agency of the dispossessed nobility and clergy.[1] One consequence of this focus has been that the political object of such opposition has been depicted merely as negative: that is, the attempt to reinstate a backwards-looking and discredited feudalism. In keeping with this, the main alternative to this reactionary ideology/agency, one that advocates a progressive forwards-looking politics, has been seen as radical 'from below' movements designed to achieve some form of alternative (= non-feudal) production relations and property ownership.[2] What is usually overlooked by this kind of approach is the emergence at that conjuncture of another forwards-looking (and in this sense positive) alternative, but one that was itself a vehemently anti-socialist political economy, the discourse of which advocated class struggle waged against a backwards-looking feudalism in the name ultimately not of socialism but simply of capitalist development.[3]

Over a period extending from the mid-eighteenth to the mid-nineteenth century, therefore, market expansion and consolidation was formulated and advocated by the liberal political economy of Anne-Robert-Jacques Turgot (1727–1781), Henri Saint-Simon (1760–1825) and Charles Dunoyer (1786–1862).[4] In what might be termed the 'other' of Marxist theory and socialist politics, this liberal political economy corresponded to – and indeed put in place – a *laissez-faire* project in defence of 'pure' capitalism, leading to neo-classical economic theory and culminating in present-day neo-liberalism. Its importance is twofold: the attack by liberal political economy on feudalism in the name of 'pure'

---

1 On the opposition to the 1789 French revolution, see Tilly (1964), Godechot (1972) and Johnson (1976). No attempt is made here to foreground the debate about this episode, since the reference to this is no more than a peg on which to hang the emergence of the left/right political divide that became important during the following two centuries. Hence the revisionism of Cobban (1964) and Furet (1981, 1998) does not alter the point being made here: namely, that for advocates of capitalist development in general and *laissez-faire* policies in particular, the argument at that conjuncture was centrally about the validity of a landowning aristocracy continuing to hold on to its privileges, thereby blocking the possibility of economic development. This is the same point that advocates of the semi-feudal thesis made in relation to Third World nations over the second half of the twentieth century.
2 For these grassroots movements, see Rudé (1959), Williams (1968a) and Guérin (1977).
3 Ironically, this interpretation – that among the things the 1789 French revolution unleashed was a discourse promoting capitalist development – is one that is attacked by Cobban (1964: 172), who mistakenly attributes it simply to Marxist theory, and thus a view to be opposed ('In so far as capitalist economic developments were at issue, it was a revolution not for, but against capitalism. This would, I believe, have been recognized long ago if it had not been for the influence of an unhistorical sociological theory').
4 An advocate of *laissez-faire* economic theory during the immediate pre-revolutionary era, Turgot was briefly the Finance Minister of Louis XVI (1774–6).His views are contained in Meek (1973) and Stephens (1895), those of Saint-Simon in Markham (1952) and Manuel (1956), and those of Dunoyer in Ferrara (1859), Lochore (1935), and Hart (1997).

capitalism is not only shared by a particular variant of Marxism, but is also based on the mistaken view that unfree production relations are pre-capitalist relics, destined to be swept away as accumulation spreads.

In the name of *laissez-faire* capitalism, Turgot, Saint-Simon and Dunoyer all opposed feudal dues exacted by landowners, which in their view constituted appropriations from peasant proprietors who would otherwise be or become commercial producers. Together with craft guilds, unfree relations such as *taille* and *corvée* were categorized as obstacles to economic growth. Once these institutional forms were abolished, and the consequent hindrances to national/international free trade and market expansion removed, their critique tended to halt, and with it any notion and advocacy of class struggle. This was because, politically and ideologically, each of them regarded capitalist development as a desirable end in itself; the realization of a 'natural' systemic form that represented the economic growth based on free wage labour each of them advocated, beyond which there was consequently no need to go.

Epistemologically, much of this *laissez-faire* theoretical approach is shared by the semi-feudal thesis. Like eighteenth and nineteenth century advocates of *laissez-faire*, twentieth century exponents of the semi-feudal thesis regard capitalism and unfree labour as fundamentally incompatible, and for the very same reason: contemporary Third World equivalents of *taille* and *corvée* are said to deprive potential agrarian capitalists of the investment needed for further accumulation, thereby preventing economic development from continuing as it should. Again like free market theorists, the main focus of the semi-feudal thesis is on class struggle against (feudal) landownership and for a 'pure' or 'fully functioning' capitalism.[5] Although Marx also regarded capitalism as systemically more advanced than feudalism, unlike *laissez-faire* theorists he did not stop there. His analysis of class struggle leading to political and economic change continued, the point being that, just as feudalism gave way to capitalism, so the latter in turn would be replaced by socialism.

In the end, the politics of both the *laissez-faire* and the semi-feudal approaches are simply another way of negating, postponing, or abandoning a transition to socialism. This they do by maintaining – incorrectly – either that 'pure' capitalism entails harmony not class struggle, or that as long as unfree production relations are found anywhere in the countryside, what is on the agenda is a transition to capitalism (not socialism) and alliances with

---

5   Not the least problematic outcome of such an approach is that – as has been argued elsewhere (Brass, 2014a) – it enables bourgeois development studies to claim erroneously that, because Marxism failed to spot the acceptability to capital of unfree labour-power, this casts doubt on the entire theoretical viability of leftist political economy.

(not struggle against) a 'progressive' national bourgeoisie in order to establish a benign capitalist democracy. However, because Marxism sees class struggle as not merely continuing under capitalism but as an integral aspect of the accumulation process, signalling a *further* systemic transition, this time from capitalism to socialism, unfree production relations do not – and cannot – cease with the onset of capitalism. Much rather such relations continue, one weapon in the employers' armoury used to roll back any gains free labour may have made in its conflicts with those owning/controlling means of production, distribution, and exchange.

The presentation which follows is divided into four sections, the first two of which examine what kind of economic process and political agency has been opposed (discourse-against) and advocated (discourse-for) historically by *laissez-faire* theorists. Both the third and fourth sections consider the same epistemology as this informs current yet radically different variants of Marxism, together with the implications for arguments about a socialist transition made by these divergent interpretations.

In an attempt initially to forestall the approach of the 1789 French revolution, and subsequently to avoid further such 'from below' agency, the *laissez-faire* ideology of Turgot, Saint-Simon and Dunoyer expressed a consistent set of theoretical positions. What free market theory opposed, or its discourse-against, is evident from the negative views they held about the feudal aristocracy, unfree production relations, and the state.

Despite claims that it is informed solely by hard economic calculus, the championing by Turgot of *laissez-faire* theory was premised on moral arguments.[6] As well as upholding religious freedom, he insisted that famine and starvation in France could be avoided by free trade in corn, transferring this commodity from surplus producing areas to ones of scarcity. Turgot defended the right of corn merchants not merely to engage in commerce of grain but also to profit from this, arguing that were they not permitted to do so, famine and starvation would continue to be the norm.[7] Preventing both free trade in corn and merchants benefiting from this, therefore, meant that famine victims would continue to suffer. Daring opponents to ignore the plight of famine victims, Turgot further justified *laissez-faire* theory on the grounds that impeding this would mean additionally that the proprietors who grew corn would also lose wealth and income. The latter in turn would lead to a decline in the value of harvests, as a result of which 'all agriculture would be discouraged'.

---

6   As will be seen in the next chapter, the opposite is true of Breman, who similarly deploys moral arguments, but in order to criticize neoliberalism.
7   On this point see the volume edited by Stephens (1895: 46ff.), where the views expressed by Turgot on all the political and economic problems facing France are set out.

This discourse-against, whereby famine imbued the market with virtue, underwrote the physiocratic model of agricultural production. When Intendant of Limoges, Turgot attributed the impoverishment of peasants to taxation, 'which left the cultivator no saving to form capital, and bereft him of all hope of improvement'.[8] The main cause of this was feudal exaction by the nobility from smallholders, in particular *taille* (head tax) and *corvée* (unpaid work), the latter described by him as 'more odious still, [compulsory labour that] crushed man and beast, and left the fields uncultivated [the result of which was] no activity, no industry, everywhere desolation'. Because of the *corvée*, Turgot argued, rural inhabitants 'had lost much of their former prosperity... [they] drew formerly, from the soil and their industry, considerable profits...the excessive burden laid upon them in their prosperity has been more than anything else, the cause of their present misery'.[9]

The link between on the one hand the abolition of *taille* and *corvée*, and on the other *laissez-faire* theory as the path to national well-being, emerges clearly in the defence by Turgot of peasant economy.[10] Although better-off peasant farmers who are 'the most profitably industrious' pay the highest levels of labour-rent, he denied that they possessed sufficient resources to meet this. Were it not for these rental demands, he maintained, cultivators would be free to invest in the kind of farm improvements (irrigation, drainage, fencing) leading to increased productivity and agricultural development. By pursuing their own prosperity, therefore, these better-off peasants would be able to contribute to the economic growth of the nation, from which at present they were prevented from doing by the existence of labour-rent. By categorizing feudal dues as a form of taxation, therefore, Turgot laid the foundation for the subsequent conceptualization by *laissez-faire* theory of tax in general as an illicit exaction from producers on whom national economic growth depended.

Like Turgot, Saint-Simon advocated ending feudal privilege, the object being to shift the role of economic activity from war (conducted by the nobility) to commerce and production (undertaken by the bourgeoisie).[11] Again like Turgot, he championed *laissez-faire* on the grounds that only the eradication of *rentier* landlords would enable an increase in agricultural output. Among those gaining from this process, Saint-Simon argued, were peasant cultivators who would benefit both from the abolition of feudal land tenure and from policies designed to promote competition based on economic efficiency. During the Restoration era (1814–24), he urged that the propertied form a united front,

---

8   Stephens (1895: 22).
9   Stephens (1895: 39–40).
10 Stephens (1895: 96).
11 Markham (1952: 57–58, 78, 80); Manuel (1956: 241, 285).

joining with the propertyless and intellectuals against a resurgent landowning class and clergy, deemed by him as 'idlers'. The latter, contrasted with productive 'industrials' identified as embodiments of the nation, were further categorized by Saint-Simon as anti-national, ranged against the economic and political interests of the whole country.[12]

Much the same is true of Dunoyer who, in his 1817 foreword to *Le Censeur européen*, asked '[c]an we say that the current state of Europe represents anything other than widespread feudal anarchy?', and proceeds – like Turgot and Saint-Simon – to argue that feudalism was an anti-industrial system founded on privileges and monopoly enforced by the state but incompatible with economic development.[13] That exercised by aristocratic landowners whose refusal to engage in commerce and manufacturing was reinforced by their monopoly over state power. Guilds similarly reinforced their occupational monopoly, excluding outsiders from such jobs. Blocked thereby was the development of 'industrialism' based on free market competition. It was this dual role – supporting feudal privileges/monopoly and opposing the capitalist market expansion – which for liberal political economy delegitimized the state as a regulating institution.

A corollary of the antipathy expressed by *laissez-faire* economic theory towards the landowning class, its state and its coerced workforce was the familiar argument deployed against slavery that, compared with free workers, unfree labour was inefficient.[14] Thus Dunoyer subscribed to the idea of historical progress, in which the pinnacle of human development coincided with the absence of slavery, because the latter was incompatible with the realization of individual liberty. Perceived as a characteristic of pre-industrial society, the

---

12   In terms of discourse, and when combined with other categories deployed by Saint-Simon, the 'industrial'/'idler' dichotomy generates the following oppositions:

Industrials	'Idlers'
businessmen, bankers	nobility, clergy
productive	unproductive
new class	defunct class
future	past
bourgeois	émigrés
national	anti-national
good	bad

13   See Leroux and Hart (2012: 51) and Hart (1997: 147–148).
14   A staple of non-Marxist political economy, the argument categorizing unfree labour as inefficient or too costly extends from Adam Smith in the 1770s to cliometric historiography in the 1970s (on which see Brass, 1999: Ch. 5 and 2011: Ch. 1).

existence of unfree labour – not just slavery, but serfdom and debt peonage – was attributed by him to the actions of the state, an institution which legislated on behalf of a feudal aristocracy.[15]

Saint-Simon, too, regarded the State as a malign institution, since it was the source of power exercised nationally by feudal landowners in order to block change so as to maintain their privileges and economic position.[16] He attributed social upheaval and its attendant economic disruption not to the actions of a new industrial class but rather to the attempt by the old landowning class illegitimately to hold on to their privileges/monopoly. Described as 'extreme anti-statism' corresponding to free market anarcho-capitalism, the views of Dunoyer were similar to those not just of Saint-Simon but also of Herbert Spencer.[17] Together with the aristocracy, the state was regarded by Dunoyer as non-productive, and thus parasitical on economic growth.

By contrast, a positive view (= the discourse-for) held by these same advocates of the free market is evident from their conceptualization of class, class struggle, and an all-embracing 'pure' capitalist system (= industrialism).

2   *Laissez-faire* Discourse-for

For Turgot, therefore, economic development generated three classes, or 'orders', consisting of landowners, wage-earners and capitalists.[18] In keeping with the two sides of the *laissez-faire* coin, he proposed that suppressing unfree relations like *taille* and *corvée* would permit the free movement of labour to flourish.[19] On the grounds that inhabitants of other nations brought with them economic benefits, Turgot advocated removing disadvantages operating against foreigners resident in the country. To this end, he sought to 'abolish the *droit d'aubaine*, which debarred the settling in France of a great number of clever men and industrious artists, of capitalists and useful merchants, who would have desired nothing more than to make France the centre of their affairs'.

For the same reason, Turgot also opposed craft guilds (*jurandes*), regarded by him as one more variant of privilege which prevented market expansion. This particular abolition was done in the name of the 'rights of industry', and on the basis of his *laissez-faire* belief that it was 'the right of every man to work

---

15   Hart (1997: 59–60, 94).
16   Manuel (1956: 242).
17   See Spencer (1881), and for Dunoyer, see Hart (1997: 66, 165).
18   Meek (1973: 119ff.).
19   Stephens (1895: 94ff.).

without restriction'.[20] Only in this way would peasants and artisans be 'free to make the best of their labour' – that is, to sell their labour-power to the highest bidder.[21] In short, Turgot was opposed to all work associations/combinations, whether by employers or those they employed. To this end, Clause XIV of his 1776 edict stated that 'it is forbidden to all masters and all journeymen, workmen, and apprentices to form among themselves any association or assembly'.[22]

As with other kinds of feudal dues, therefore, ending *jurandes* was defended by Turgot in moral terms, in effect obeying what was 'natural' as ordained by divine law. His argument was that abolition was done in the name of God (= Nature), who – by providing humanity with wants – provided also the means of satisfying those wants: the capacity to work.[23] Hence the unleashing of this capacity – 'the property of every man' (shades of Hegel and Marx) – was and should be the object of any/all *laissez-faire* policy. Introducing a moral dimension into the argument was thus in effect a Trojan horse, enabling Turgot to apply the same *laissez-faire* principle to economics. If policies such as free trade in corn, the abolition of feudal dues, and the free movement of labour were justified at the national level, why not extend the same dynamic to relations between countries, thereby paving the way for capitalism as a global system.[24]

Class and class struggle were also for Saint-Simon the main categories/processes informing systemic development, and – as with Turgot and Dunoyer – it was a dynamic pitting a rising bourgeoisie against declining feudal landowners.[25] The latter, together with the clergy, were regarded as peripheral to the three main components of the social structure: the property owners, consisting of manufacturers and businessmen; the propertyless, corresponding to the rural and urban working class; and the 'savants', or intellectuals. According to

---

20   Stephens (1895: 129).
21   Stephens (1895: 124).
22   Stephens (1895: 130).
23   Thus the first clause of Turgot's 1776 edict declared that: 'It shall be free to all persons, of whatever quality or condition they may be, even to all foreigners, to undertake and to exercise in all our kingdom, and particularly in our good city of Paris, whatever kind of trade and whatever profession of art or industry may seem good to them, for which purpose we now extinguish and suppress all corporations and communities of merchants and artisans, such as the *maîtres* and the *jurandes*. We abrogate all privileges, statutes, and regulations of the said corporations, so that none of our subjects shall be troubled in the exercise of his trade or profession by any cause or under any pretext whatever'.
24   Exactly the same kinds of argument surface in current neoliberal discourse, large capitalist corporations in the UK insisting that by attracting external talent the free movement of labour will assist national economic growth, a view which omits to mention both the impact on the existing workforce of these additions to the labour market, and the fact that migrants employed in agriculture are frequently not free labour.
25   Manuel (1956: 244ff., 248ff.).

Saint-Simon, the struggle for 'industrialism' would generate conflict between property owners and the propertyless (= 'the mob'), for which reason it was necessary for those with power/wealth to bring intellectuals onto their side, so as to counter the persuasiveness of 'egalitarian preachments'.

As formulated by Saint-Simon, the concept 'industrialism' provided the bourgeoisie in post-revolutionary France with its own ideology. The centrality of his role is evident from the following: 'A class of merchant-manufacturers who usually did their own financing were pushing to the fore of French Restoration society and a new terminology [= industrialism] was being created to define their achievements and to articulate their class desires. In this process Saint-Simon was a historic mid-wife'.[26] Describing it as 'the new organic epoch', he viewed future society not as classless but an 'ideal society based on natural classes'. These would be based an innate 'capacity', which he thought would find its 'proper and essential place' in an 'industrial' hierarchy.[27] Like Turgot, Saint-Simon hoped both that the king would ally with the industrial bourgeoisie against the nobility, and that consequently the transition to capitalism would make further revolution 'from below' unnecessary.[28] As Manuel observes, this was 'an ideal bourgeois credo for a culture that required something more positive than an affirmation of the Rights of Man'.[29]

Many of these arguments also informed the term 'industrialism' as conceptualized by Dunoyer. Outlined by him in *Le Censeur européen* and other published works, his view of 'industrialism' or 'pure industrial capitalism' envisaged the last stage of modern society as one in which the market finally reigned supreme, unfree labour had been abolished and replaced by free equivalents, and the state as a centralizing/planning/regulating institution had ceased to exist.[30] Preceded by different historical stages – savagery, nomadism, slavery, feudalism and mercantilism – each of which possessed a specific pattern of intellectual, cultural and religious forms, 'industrialism' constituted for Dunoyer 'the fundamental object of society'.[31] Unlike Marx, for whom the service sector and entrepreneurs were unproductive categories, Dunoyer classified them as productive components of the accumulation process, whose

---

26   Manuel (1956: 189–90).
27   Markham (1952: 76ff.).
28   Markham (1952: 62).
29   Manuel (1956: 253).
30   See Dunoyer (1859), Liggio (1977), Hart (1997), and Raico (2012). According to Lochore (1935: 31), therefore, 'Dunoyer gives to material progress the functional primacy, as precondition for moral progress. In all other respects he shelved the question of values by supposing that everything that he, the bourgeois of July [Monarchy] approved, should have "liberty" to continue to be what it was, and so he ended in perfect conservatism'.
31   Hart (1997: 67).

activity contributed to economic growth. Capitalist rewards, in the form of surplus and profits, were in his view justified. With the onset of 'pure' industrial capitalism, moreover, workers too would become productive, because – unlike slaves – they were now free, and consequently toiled hard in response to self-interested pecuniary incentives.

In keeping with nineteenth century economic liberalism, Dunoyer perceived class struggle as a process waged only by a nascent bourgeoisie against feudal landowners blocking capitalist development by means of political monopoly over the state. His view was that a transition from feudalism would take an evolutionary form, non-revolutionary means to realize market domination making the seizure of state power unnecessary.[32] Once a 'pure' industrial capitalist stage had been established, class struggle would in his opinion cease. This absence of conflict between classes under a system of *laissez-faire* accumulation Dunoyer attributed in turn both to a minimal state, for him the locus and cause of struggle, and to a consequent harmony of interests between the classes.[33] Despite inequalities, therefore, because 'in a society where each individual lived off the fruits of their own labour in a completely *laissez-faire* economy', there would be no reason for conflict.

Neoliberal supporters of *laissez-faire* policies delight in claiming that, in many respects, the ideas of Turgot, Saint-Simon and Dunoyer anticipated those of Marx. Hence the claim by Manuel that the 'tactical formulations proposed [by Saint-Simon] to the French industrials were later made applicable to the proletariat, with minor alterations, by Marx and Engels', while Hart argues similarly that Dunoyer conceptualized the mode of production long before Marx.[34] This applies especially to non-Marxist interpretations of class struggle, which libertarians such as von Mises, Rothbard, Hoppe, and Raico, all insist predated this historical dynamic associated exclusively with Marxist political economy.[35] Not only did Marx acknowledge that earlier bourgeois theorists conceptualized the term class struggle, but – as will be seen below – he also conceptualized it in a very different way, one that departs substantially from that found in the *laissez-faire* framework.[36] The latter approach, however, does

---

32   Hart (1997: 121, 158ff.).
33   Raico (2012: 198). For a similar view made subsequently, see von Mises (1966: Ch. XXIV).
34   See Manuel (1956: 282) and Hart (1997: 1, 113, 126–127, 135ff.).
35   See von Mises (1966: 674–5), Rothbard (1995: Ch. 3), Hoppe (2012), and Raico (2012).
36   In a letter to Weydmeyer, dated 5 March 1852, Marx accepted that (Marx and Engels, 1934: 57) 'no credit is due to me for discovering the existence of classes in modern society nor yet the struggle between them. Long before me bourgeois historians had described the historical development of this class struggle and bourgeois economists the economic anatomy of the classes'.

possess rather surprisingly a follower amongst Marxist variants: the semi-feudal thesis.

3 In the Footsteps of *Laissez-faire*

Although it predated this, the semi-feudal thesis re-emerged during the 1970s mode of production debate, when the existence of capitalism in the Third World countryside – particularly rural India and Latin America – was linked to the presence or absence there of unfree labour relations.[37] Because moneylending and debt bondage were regarded by exponents of the semi-feudal thesis as archaic forms amounting to an obstacle to 'pure' capitalist development, unfree labour was categorized as a pre-capitalist remnant to be eliminated by commercial producers at the first opportunity.[38] In keeping with earlier libertarian views, therefore, not only is coercion equated with economic inefficiency, and thus a backward agriculture, but any labour relations connected with accumulation are by contrast perceived as non-coercive, and thus freely entered into by the workers concerned.[39]

Significantly, the semi-feudal thesis is opposed to landlordism for the very same reason as *laissez-faire* French liberalism of the nineteenth century. Each maintains that by its control of the state, the landowning class perpetuates economically backward institutional forms that prevent the emergence and/or operation of market forces, and thus constitute an obstacle to the development of 'pure' capitalism. Like free market economists, therefore, opposition by Patnaik to the role of the Indian State stems from her perception of it as an institution reflecting the political interests of a still dominant unproductive 'feudal' landowning class, which on its own large rural properties blocks further capitalist development, pauperizing potentially productive smallholding cultivators by extracting rents from them, not only reproducing their subordinate

---

37 Rudra *et al.* (1978); Thorner (1982). Other aspects of the semi-feudal thesis are considered in Chapter 6 below.
38 Exponents of the semi-feudal thesis as applied to the so-called Third World include Patnaik and Dingwaney (1985), Patnaik (1990), and Byres (1996).
39 In the case of the debate about chattel slavery in the American South, it was because antebellum cotton plantations were economically efficient that neoclassical analysis by Fogel and Engerman (1974: 67–78) categorized such units as capitalist, as a result of which it was necessary to claim that slaves chose to remain on them in what could only be non-coercive working arrangements and conditions.

position as unfree labour but also stopping petty commodity producers from investing in better technique, thereby undermining 'food security'.[40]

Seeing class through nationalist lens, Patnaik claims that workers in the capitalist heartland remained free at the expense of their counterparts on the periphery, where unfree production relations were imposed. This not only overlooks the presence of the latter in core areas (which continues), but also implies free workers were somehow complicit participants in the exploitation of unfree labour in the colonies. It also reproduces the semi-feudal dichotomy between developed core = capitalism = free labour-power, and underdeveloped periphery = non-capitalist = unfreedom. When considering class conflict, therefore, her focus is on resistance by (unfree) peasant smallholders to (feudal) rental extraction, and not on the struggle by (unfree) workers to become, remain and act as a proletariat in the full sense of the term.

Accordingly, the semi-feudal thesis is structured by the same epistemology as *laissez-faire* theory: unfree labour is conceptualized simply as a pre-capitalist relation, and thus as an obstacle to economic growth, to be replaced by free wage labour as capitalism develops. And just as the target of *laissez-faire* theory was the French landlord class responsible for and benefiting from *taille* and *corvée*, against which any progressive struggle must be waged, so the object of class struggle as interpreted by exponents of the semi-feudal thesis is also the landlord class in Third World nations, similarly blamed for the continued existence there of debt peonage and bonded labour relations. In each case the systemic transition is to be toward capitalism, whose employers are viewed as progressive, interested in recruiting free wage labour, and consequently striving to replace production relations that are unfree. Hence the American path of the agrarian question as interpreted by Byres, an exponent of the semi-feudal thesis, involves the defence of efficient commercial farming undertaken by peasant proprietors against backward 'feudal'/pre-capitalist landowners, in which capitalism gives rise to political democracy.[41] For this reason, *laissez-faire* theory and the semi-feudal thesis also perceive nationalism as progressive, since it forms the democratic political context in which accumulation will take place.

In the case of late eighteenth-century France, the defence both of privilege and of the landowning class took two forms. The first consisted of highlighting their importance in protecting the nation, the inference was that were such privileges to cease, and with them the position of the landowning class, then the nation would be vulnerable to foreign conquest. opposition by landowners

---

40   Patnaik (1999, 2007: 208ff.).
41   Byres (1996: Part III).

and clergy – 'the two great classes who had long held in their hands the control of all public affairs' – to free trade from which actual/potential better-off peasants would benefit was described by Turgot as a defence of privilege.[42] The second took the form of a warning: the landowning class maintained that the abolition of *corvée* would promote equality by erasing distinction between themselves and 'the lowest class of the nation', thereby leading to the overthrow of the existing social order. In this they were right, since it was only with the 1789 revolution that privileges were abolished.[43]

A corollary is that – like Turgot, Saint-Simon and Dunoyer – exponents of the semi-feudal thesis continue to regard capitalism as a 'progressive' force, to be promoted economically and supported politically. Restricting his analysis of capitalist development and the agrarian question to a national context, Byres maintains that unless labour-power employed there is free, capitalism is deemed to be absent or insufficiently developed, a view which discounts accumulation by international corporations using unfree workers to restructure the labour process. Since bonded labour is misinterpreted by the semi-feudal thesis as a 'pre-capitalist' relation, its presence signals wrongly that a transition is to be to yet more efficient capitalism, not socialism. Confining the agrarian question to national contexts, therefore, allows capitalism off the hook, banishes revolution and socialism from the political agenda, and permits the myth of a 'progressive' national bourgeoisie to flourish.

The semi-feudal thesis also echoes libertarian hostility to the state, and for the same reason: seen as an institution under the control of an unproductive landlord class, the state is deemed responsible both for political blockages to a 'progressive' bourgeoisie, and thus also to holding back a capitalist transition, and consequently for the resulting economic backwardness of the nation as a whole. Again like the 'industrialism' of Turgot, Saint-Simon and Dunoyer, a 'pure' form of capitalism is for the semi-feudal thesis the next necessary transition, based as it is on the view that capitalists would be 'progressive' under such a bourgeois democratic stage, and that as a consequence unfree labour would then be eliminated. Rather than occupying a heretical position during the era following the 1960s development decade, therefore, the semi-feudal thesis was

---

42   Stephens (1895: 103). According to the latter (Stephens, 1895: 119), '[t]he French Court hated Turgot for daring to think that the weight of taxation bore too heavily upon the poorer, and too lightly upon the richer classes. They hated him because he had abolished sinecures, the very object of a courtier's most sacred respect. They hated him because he was preaching economy – was pressing the King, in the interests of the State, to reduce the extravagant expenses connected with the Court and to revise the lavish list of pensions, which had grown to an extraordinary number and amount'.
43   Stephens (1895: 132–33, 148).

part of the economic orthodoxy of that period: together with bourgeois political economy, it argued that economic growth and capitalist development in the so-called Third World required the elimination of unfree production relations.

Because landowners are categorized by free market theory in nineteenth century and the semi-feudal thesis in the twentieth as unchanging bastions of pre-capitalist economic values, politics and production relations, therefore, they have been – and are – perceived consequently as the main (or sole) targets of forward-looking (= progressive) class struggle. Insofar as the economic power of a landlord class merges with and becomes part of that of capital generally, this underlines the fallacy of treating the former as separate from – and indeed opposed to – the latter, to the degree of attempting to mobilize 'progressive' capitalists against reactionary landlords. The argument about separate entities (landlord, capitalist) holds good only as long as capitalism has not developed. Once it has, aristocratic and/or royal landlords can – and do – invest in commercial activities, while capitalists for their part purchase rural estates.[44] For this reason, it is no longer possible to insist categorically on their economic distinctiveness, and consequently to locate them on different sides in the class struggle. Nor is it the case that, once engaged in accumulation, capitalist landowners replace unfree labour with a workforce that is free.

Supporters of free markets in the nineteenth century, marginalist economic theory in the twentieth, and neoliberalism in the twenty-first, all maintain that the realization of individual liberty under capitalism necessarily signalled the end of slavery and other forms of unfree labour. Structured by a concept of historical stages, this claim insists that such production relations are incompatible with a 'pure' or 'fully mature' accumulation process. Shared also by the semi-feudal stages framework, this view is held only by those who see the attainment of capitalism as an end in itself. According to *laissez-faire* theory, class struggle waged hitherto by the (productive) bourgeoisie against

---

44 Brass (2014b: Chapter 5). Whilst it is true there may indeed be a turnover as regards social composition – erstwhile merchants and/or financiers become landowners – the class position and interest, which stems from property rights, stays the same. It is not the case that consolidation of land ownership indicates an onward march of anything to do with 'feudalism' or 'semi-feudalism'. Following the subprime economic crisis, many profit-hungry capitalist corporations have shifted their investment strategies, and now make large scale purchases of agricultural land, anticipating food price rises consequent on their ability to monopolize an inelastic global demand that is on the increase. See, for example, 'English farmland offers better returns than gold', *The Guardian* (London), 23 September 2015. The economic logic in such circumstances is no different from the one that drives capital investment in its search for non-agricultural resources.

the (unproductive) landlord class to establish the market, ceases once this objective has been realized and a capitalist transition effected.

4   Capitalism – or Socialism?

The antithesis of the stages approach is the process of combined and uneven development which, as Trotsky made clear, meant that backwardness resulted in things from the past being used alongside those of the present.[45] As has already been noted above in Chapters 2 and 3, not the least advantageous consequence for commercial enterprises of this juxtaposition takes the shape of the industrial reserve army of labour, available in one of two forms: either boosting the supply of workers in underdeveloped contexts themselves, to which capital is then able to outsource production; or, alternatively, fuelling migration flows into metropolitan capitalism, where such workers join the existing labour market.

To illustrate the point about the impact of combined and uneven development, Trotsky noted that in Russia 'the introduction of certain elements of Western training and technique...led to the strengthening of serfdom as the fundamental form of labour organization'. This in turn puts permanent revolution on the agenda – or to use his phrase, the 'skipping of stages' – since the conditions for a transition to socialism are now already in place. It is precisely this view, advanced by Trotsky against the promotion by Stalin of the stages theory, which informs the semi-feudal thesis, adherents of which see unfree labour as a pre-capitalist relic.[46]

Whereas Trotsky maintained that such relations were perfectly compatible with accumulation, and thus also with a situation where a socialist economic

---

45   About the significance of the law of combined and uneven development, Trotsky (1972b: 117) noted: 'We do not need to deny the existence of the law but we must explain it...by the formula of "combined development". Uneven development consists in the main in the fact that the different countries pass through different epochs. Advanced and backward countries – that is the most elementary expression of the law. Evolution, however, has also shown that the backward countries supplement their backwardness with the latest advances. From this emerges the combined development which I have proved for Russia as an example in the *History*'. On the theory of 'permanent revolution', see Trotsky (1934: 26–27), and also above in the Introduction.

46   Unlike Trotskyism, such a policy (Stalin, 1928: 124ff., 276ff.) was based on the notion of an intervening bourgeois democratic stage, the existence of which would be characterized by 'progressive' capitalists using free wage-labour regarded as the sine qua non of 'pure' capitalism. As Trotsky (1936, 1973b) pointed out at the time, this led directly to the massacre of workers in China and Spain during the 1930s, when capital demonstrated to all concerned just how 'progressive' it was prepared to be.

development transition was *already* on the political agenda, exponents of the semi-feudal thesis argue the opposite. They maintain – wrongly – that unfree production relations are an obstacle to, and consequently not only have to be eliminated before capitalist development proper (that is, a 'pure'/'fully-functioning' process of accumulation, what we now recognize as being the global spread of the market, or neoliberalism) can occur but also make the political agenda one of transition not to socialism but to capitalism.

The political difference between Trotsky's interpretation and that of the semi-feudal thesis is clear. Having pushed for Third World accumulation – much like bourgeois political economy – exponents of the semi-feudal thesis insisted that the agrarian sector of these countries was 'not yet capitalist' or 'not capitalist enough'. Its proponents still argue, even now, for the necessity of boosting agricultural performance in India, so that the ever elusive agrarian capitalist – the absent 'other' of the semi-feudal framework – may finally emerge onto the historical stage and begin to provide a surplus for what in their view is an as-yet insufficiently realized drive to industrialization. This, it seems, will continue to be their view as long as the production relations regarded by exponents of the semi-feudal thesis as capitalist – 'pure' wage labour that is free, in other words – are not encountered in agriculture. Since in many parts of the so-called Third World unfree labour is the relation of choice where agrarian capital is concerned, this means in effect postponing opposition to capitalist development there until the Greek Calends. Such a position, it is argued here, is little different from that of Dunoyer.

Since for Dunoyer 'industrialism' reached its apogee under *laissez-faire* capitalism, this was where systemically the development process ended, both economically and politically. Given the corresponding absence of contradiction and struggle arising from this, there was accordingly no need in his model for systemic transcendence. Unlike Marxists, for whom class struggle reaches its apogee in a *laissez faire* economy, leading to a socialist transition, therefore, liberals such as Dunoyer failed to address a crucial issue. Insisting an 'harmony of interests' meant that conflict was absent from a 'pure' industrial system, he overlooked (or downplayed) the effects of different forms of property owned. Inequality based on property – not to be redistributed or owned collectively – went unchallenged.

Given that Dunoyer regarded capitalists as productive, no less than workers, his view was in a sense consistent: under 'pure' industrial capitalism, employers – like workers – do nothing more than enjoy the fruits of their own labour. This despite the fact that means of production (land, machinery, factories) will still be owned by some, who sell the product of labour, while others will have only their personal labour-power to sell, the latter consequently working for (and yielding a surplus to) the former. Each is a form of property ownership, to be sure, but of very different economic resources, a situation which – as Marxism points out – has profound political implications. Furthermore, an equivalence between capital and labour, implied in the view that both live off the fruits of their own labour, misrepresents what proprietors of means of production actually do. Hence the impossibility of an 'harmony of interests' and an absence of conflict in such a system: 'pure' *laissez-faire* capitalism.

5   The Path Not Taken

The assumption of both *laissez-faire* theory and the semi-feudal thesis was, and remains still, that in a 'pure' capitalist system working arrangements would be free in the double sense understood by classical political economy: a worker would be free both of the means of labour and of the control exercised by a particular employer. As such, dispossessed peasants were transformed into – and remained thereafter – a proletariat, in that they were henceforth able personally to sell their only commodity, labour-power. Again as is well known, this transformation corresponded to a process of class formation, whereby buyers and sellers of a particular commodity – labour-power – faced one another in the market place.

At that particular moment, however, and following the initial process of class *formation*, the transaction between capital and labour gave rise to an additional process: class *struggle*. The capacity of workers – once free – not just to combine and organize in furtherance of their class interests but also to withdraw their labour-power, either absolutely by going on strike, or relatively by selling their commodity to the highest bidder, posed a fundamental challenge to capitalist discipline and profitability. It is hardly surprising, therefore, to find limiting or curbing the ability of workers to commodify/recommodify labour-power among the weapons deployed by capital in its struggle with a proletariat seeking to improve pay and conditions. It is precisely the latter situation that is explained by the class struggle argument, based on deproletarianization of labour-power.

Class struggle involving deproletarianization, it is argued here, constitutes the Marxist path not taken. It entails the reproduction, the introduction, or the reintroduction by capital of unfree labour, and corresponds to a form of workforce decomposition/recomposition frequently resorted to by employers in their struggle with labour.[47] Conceptually, deproletarianization is based on Marxist theory about labour-power as the personal property of the worker, indeed his/her only one.[48] In keeping with Marxist theory about the capitalism/unfreedom link, therefore, deproletarianization defines a relation of production in terms of whether or not a worker is able personally to commodify his/her own labour-power. Accordingly, it was this need to maintain or enhance profitability in the face of 'from below' class struggle that, dialectically, triggered an antithetical 'from above' response by employers interested in disciplining and cheapening the cost of their labour-power: either converting free workers into unfree equivalents, or replacing the former with the latter. Hence the acceptability of unfree labour to capital: it is the process of class struggle subsequent to class formation which results in proletarianization giving rise to its opposite, deproletarianization.

What exponents of the semi-feudal thesis do not confront is the impact of outsourcing/restructuring on the production relations available to capital. They still think a group of permanent workers enjoying trade union rights and employed for a good wage under one roof in a big factory is the next step, whereas the reality nowadays is very different. Subcontracting of production by large off-shore corporations to many smallscale sweatshops (frequently located in the countryside, out of sight of government regulation, the workforce consisting mostly or entirely of women) where coercion and bonded labour relations are rife. Coming across the latter, advocates of this approach declare them to be evidence for semi-feudalism, and thus the absence of a 'fully functioning' (or 'pure') capitalism, rather than what such units actually are: evidence precisely for the existence/operation of a 'fully functioning' capitalist system.

This capacity on the part of capital currently to employ workers that are unfree is in turn facilitated by two conditions that are both currently a feature of neoliberal capitalism. The first is that in many contexts of the Third World, agricultural production is for export. This means that one of the usual objections to employing unfree labour – that driving down the wages of a domestic workforce simultaneously deprives agrarian capitalists of consumers, thereby

---

47 See Brass (1999, 2011), and also elsewhere in this book.
48 As has been argued in Brass (2010), not just Marx and Engels but also Lenin, Trotsky and others all subscribed to the view that, in the course of class struggle between capital and labour, unfree relations were central to the way owners of the means of production organized and protected their accumulation process, and thus not part of any pre-capitalist system that commercial producers sought to discard. As such, these work arrangements become a problem of capitalism *per se*, not an indicator that a benign form of the latter is still on the political agenda.

negating the economic advantages of using bonded labour – no longer holds. And second, a consequence of seemingly limitless global migration patterns is that rural producers in many contexts – metropolitan capitalist nations no less that developing countries – now possess an ability to drawn upon a large industrial reserve army of labour.

Since each of these conditions was either unmet or unrecognized at an earlier conjuncture, however, some Marxists questioned whether it was possible for capital to continue employing a workforce that was unfree. For this reason, they persisted in regarding unfree labour simply as 'other', a relational anomaly somehow located within – but not actually part of, let alone actively reproduced by employers in – the wider capitalist system. What they missed thereby was the way in which unfree labour currently fits into an employment matrix forming an optimal combination where agribusiness enterprises are concerned.

The global spread and integrated nature of capitalism does indeed undermine the semi-feudal thesis, no less than the *laissez-faire* approach. In methodological terms, semi-feudalism thrived during the 1960s, when social scientists were engaged in trying to explain why economic development had seemingly bypassed rural areas in the Third World. This generated the notion of non-capitalism (at village level) in the midst of capitalism (the city), a form of dualism common then (particularly for those discussing the mode of production) but untenable now. Even when this kind of view initially emerged, around the start of the twentieth century, Rosa Luxemburg questioned its applicability, as did Trotsky. One hundred years later, it simply cannot be sustained, although those (such as Harvey and Negri) who maintain what we are seeing now is a form of primitive accumulation are merely reinstating the old dualism, albeit in a different form.

6 Conclusion

By advocating the principle of a free labour market, and defending this in terms of a moral discourse, *laissez-faire* theory from the mid-eighteenth to the mid-nineteenth century cleared the ground and laid the economic conditions for capitalist accumulation. Moreover, this element of freedom was not confined to workers of a particular nationality, since the right of free sale of labour-power extended also to foreigners coming to or residing in the nation concerned. Established thereby was the principle underwriting the formation and operation – on a global scale, eventually – of the industrial reserve army of labour. Any restrictions deemed to hinder this process – not just feudal dues but also worker associations or trade unions – were declared a social privilege, incompatible with national well-being and economic development, and thus illegal.

Turgot, Saint-Simon and Dunoyer all invoked *laissez-faire* theory against a landowning class that controlled both trade and labour by means of feudal legislation and monopoly over State power. It was to oppose this that the freedom of the population to sell their commodities – goods and labour-power alike – was endorsed. This view has underwritten *laissez-faire* economic theory ever since, and it is based on the notion that capitalism is a positive good, an end in and of itself. Marx departed from this, and argued that freedom was desirable because it prefigured the next step for workers *as a class*: namely, a transition to socialism. Insofar as workers who are unfree have difficulty organizing against capital, becoming and remaining free – being and acting as a proletariat, in other words – is desirable, therefore, not as an end in itself but rather as a means to another end: a socialist transition.

Notwithstanding continued inequality based on class, reflected in the distinction between ownership of and separation from means of production, liberal political economy formulated between the mid-eighteenth and the mid-nineteenth century nevertheless maintained that in a 'pure' industrial capitalism an harmony of interests would prevail between capital and labour. Its discourse-for includes the advocacy of 'pure' industrial capitalism, to be realized by a peaceful transition to a *laissez-faire* economic system, in which producer and free labour compete in perfect market conditions. By contrast, the target of its discourse-against is the feudal landowner, whose control of the state enables this unproductive class to exploit a workforce composed of unfree labour, preventing market formation/expansion, thereby fuelling 'from below' calls for socialism and revolutionary agency.

The *laissez-faire* view about class struggle – all against the State and its rulers, who are 'feudal' landowners blocking capitalist development which will benefit everyone, producer and free worker alike – is not so different from the semi-feudal thesis, which similarly perceives labour emancipation being achieved under capitalism by efficient agribusiness enterprises waging class struggle against inefficient landlords. This is where advocates of the semi-feudal thesis and free market economics both stop. By contrast, Marxist theory about deproletarianization goes beyond this, and argues that capital actually does the opposite: it reproduces, introduces or reintroduces unfree labour into the capitalist labour process in the course of the class struggle. The corollary is that class struggle continues, but now waged against capitalism itself, rather than against feudalism, as Dunoyer and the semi-feudal thesis maintain.

Contrary to what both *laissez-faire* theory and the semi-feudal thesis argue, therefore, as accumulation spreads across the globe class struggle and its attendant unfreedom not only continues to be reproduced but becomes more intense. As the class struggle argument, a central element of Marxist theory about the dynamics of the accumulation process, this constitutes the path not taken.

CHAPTER 5

Avoiding Revolution: A Return to Patronage

'The truth is that Dickens's criticism of society is almost exclusively moral. Hence the utter lack of any constructive suggestion anywhere in his work. He attacks the law, parliamentary government, the educational system and so forth, without ever suggesting what he would put in their places... There is no clear sign that he wants the existing order to be overthrown, or that he believes it would make very much difference if it *were* overthrown. For in reality his target is not so much society as "human nature". It would be difficult to point anywhere in his books to a passage suggesting that the economic system is wrong *as a system*. Nowhere, for instance, does he make any attack on private enterprise or private property... There is not a line in the book [*Hard Times*] that can properly be called Socialistic; indeed, its tendency if anything is pro-capitalist, because its whole moral is that capitalists ought to be kind, not that workers ought to be rebellious... If men would behave decently the world would be decent... Hence that recurrent Dickens figure, the good rich man'.

> An observation made by GEORGE ORWELL in a 1939 essay concerning the ineffectiveness of a moral critique that applies equally to the invocation of patronage, sought either from the landlord class or from an 'uncaring' capitalist state.[1]

∴

1 Introduction: From Periphery to the (Academic) Core

The jettisoning of revolution and socialism as desirable outcomes of the development process by those in academia has given rise to an enduring paradox: the confluence of what were initially parallel but antithetical narratives, as an earlier interpretation is unaccountably replaced by a later and very different one. However, this transfer of a more radical Marxist argument from the margins to the mainstream raises further problems, in that once in the latter context it is reproduced with a different political framework and objective.[2] In the

---

[1] Orwell (1965: 83–4, original emphasis).
[2] In the course of this transfer, therefore, a politically radical but institutionally peripheral argument is converted into its opposite: now institutionally central, it has become deradicalized

case of the views examined in this chapter, therefore, a number of radical Marxist arguments circulating at the margins have metamorphosed politically when adapted by the mainstream.

Of these the most important concerns the way the meaning of production relations constitutive of the capitalist labour regime has itself been transformed. Hence an initial interpretation of bonded labour as a benign form of 'subsistence guarantee' and employer 'patronage', whereby workers struggled to retain such unfree production relations, has been replaced with a more radical Marxist interpretation – the class struggle argument – formulated on the margins. Rather than leading to socialism via revolution, however, what was the class struggle argument becomes instead one about patronage, sought from and exercised by a 'nicer' form of capitalism.

Most of those who have written, and still write and publish, about Third World development cannot but be aware of a twofold closure taking place. Many who belong to the generation which participated in the development debate about the Third World from the 1960s onwards, approaching issues from a broadly progressive viewpoint, are now doing one of two things, and often both. First, lamenting the end of the development project itself, they have abandoned both the possibility of transcending capitalism and a socialist politics. And second, collecting academic honours they perhaps feel are due them for their valuable contributions to these discussions.[3] Since acknowledging setbacks is always uncomfortable, a recognizable pattern is currently unfolding inside a number of university social science departments where, in true postmodern fashion, the political failure of the development project is being redefined as a form of success: not, however, of the project itself but rather of the prescient contributions to the debate.[4]

One senior academic who participated in the development debate is Jan Breman, a Dutch anthropologist whose contributions are, in the words of Saith, currently being recognized 'with a bagful of national and professional honours'.[5]

---

and thus conservative, and is consequently no more than peripheral in terms of debates in political economy. This culminates in the kind of mainstream argument considered here: namely, eradicating unfreedom by appeals to the 'patronage' of an 'uncaring' neoliberal state.

3 These academic honours take many forms, extending from university vice-chancellorships to *festschriften*, deferential interviews, and having journal prizes named for one.

4 An interpretation of this process far more cynical than mine would point out that, by contrast, the receipt of honours and plaudits are in a sense justified, insofar as the recipients were instrumental in steering the development debate away from a radical and/or a revolutionary socialist politics.

5 Saith (2016: 876).

He belongs, in short, unambiguously to the academic mainstream (or core). From the early 1960s onwards, Breman has undertaken many fieldwork trips to rural Gujarat in western India, the findings of which have resulted in numerous articles and monographs, the text examined here being only the latest. About his own research and its impact, Breman not only observes that 'I have endeavoured to raise the visibility of the lower classes in the countryside and to speak up on behalf of people whose voices have remained muted', but also compares himself to a whistle-blower who 'stands out as an exemplary figure in the landscape of social activism', adding that 'I feel at ease to share the same wavelength with such dissenters'.[6]

Throughout his most recent analysis, Breman upbraids others – principally development economists – for their failure, as he sees it, to spot changes in the agrarian structure that, inferentially, non-economists (such as him) identified early on. Among those he criticizes are colonial historiography and the World Bank, the former because it perceived the village as a closed community, the latter because it 'wanted us to believe that employer-worker relations in the informal economy were governed by a wide range of social customs and traditions which mitigated the insecurity of the labouring poor'.[7] Unlike economists studying development, who thought that unfree production relations would vanish, to be replaced with free equivalents as capitalism spread (such as adherents of the semi-feudal thesis), non-economists – like himself – accurately saw that this would not happen.[8] Migration studies and researchers on rural labour mobility are similarly taken to task for not understanding the crucial distinction between migrants recruited to supplement as distinct from supplant an existing workforce.[9] In each case, the impression conveyed is that Breman himself has never advanced such obviously erroneous views.

Rural and urban poverty, its causes, effects and political solutions are the focus of the analysis by Breman. Along the way he considers issues such as

---

6 Breman (2016: 52).
7 Breman (2016: 25–26, 35–36, 59–60). Chiding the World Bank for believing that employers would 'continue wage payments during the slack season…provide loans to workers who faced unexpected expenses, and…support aged workers', Breman continues: 'These statements…showed an outrageous degree of ignorance [and] also a deliberate neglect of all the countervailing evidence about the lives of the working poor'. What the World Bank is being criticized for, is mistakenly subscribing to the 'subsistence guarantee' argument.
8 Breman (2016: 47) observes: 'Not much thought happens to have been given…to the predicted transition in the social fabric. It was mainly non-economists who brought up the issue in their writings', adding '[t]hat glaring omission needs to be repaired to some extent. After all, shifts in the relations of production have to be contextualized in the wider canvas of social stratification'.
9 Breman (2016: 35–36, 148).

the appropriateness of anthropological research methods, the supply of and form taken by labour-power, the patterns of migration, and the role in all this of the capitalist state. Accordingly, the three sections which follow will look at each of the claims and arguments he now makes, in terms of their theoretical consistency and political efficacy.

2   Empiricism, Patronage and Subsistence

The sorts of difficulties confronting Breman surface almost immediately, when evaluating anthropological fieldwork, and his own participant/observation methods. Underlining the impossibility of remaining neutral in the course of his research, he gives as the reason that 'I have from the very beginning of my fieldwork half a century ago consistently located my investigations in the lower echelons of village economy and society'.[10] This grassroots vantage-point is also the reason why Breman privileges the approach of non-economists to the issues he studies, maintaining that anthropological fieldwork participant/ observation methods are capable of uncovering realities that development economists and other social scientists tend to miss. Although true in part, there are two inter-related problems with this claim.

To begin with, this stress on long-term methodological research, in the form of his many return fieldwork trips to Gujarat, inadvertently bolsters the impression of a very different sort of continuity: that there has also been an unbroken theoretical consistency, which as will be seen below is not the case. More significant epistemologically, however, are his observations elsewhere about his research training and groundwork: Breman confesses that he went to India to do fieldwork 'fairly unprepared', adding that 'I knew so little, I...did not know how to get a hold of that society'.[11] Contrasting his own fieldwork approach with another one that was 'far more theoretical, analytical', he comments that '[t]he works I wrote on my fieldwork experience hold. They are empirical'. The importance of this admission is that it identifies why Breman – an anthropologist who not only accepts that he knew next to nothing about the issues and context he was to study when embarking on his first fieldwork in the 1960s, but was also resistant to a theoretical approach – explained what he saw the rural grass-roots somewhat uncritically. That is, in terms of the two prevailing orthodoxies in development studies current at that time: the semi-feudal

---

10   Breman (2016: 49ff.).
11   These observations are contained in Patel (2008: 14–15, 28).

thesis (unfree production relations would be replaced by free equivalents as capitalism spread) and the 'patronage'/'subsistence guarantee' argument.

Among the most problematic claims Breman makes now, therefore, is that from the very first he regarded unfree labour as exploitative, '[t]he opposite assessment of bondage [which] articulated the benevolence of the master who was obliged to provide subsistence for the servants he had engaged'.[12] This distancing by him from those analyses which took a benign view of bonded labour is supported by references such as '*pretended* patronage' and 'a *semblance* of life-long benevolence', the inference being that unlike others for whom 'patronage' and 'subsistence guarantee' were in material terms real, and to the advantage of unfree workers who saw such arrangements to their advantage and desirable, he himself has always recognized these concepts were no more than special pleading on the part of landlord ideology.[13] That is, to use a word he has applied elsewhere, as terms which lack a material referent, and are thus 'bogus'.

Before the 1980s, unfree labour in the Third World was regarded by many as a benign relationship which traditionally provided its subject with a 'subsistence guarantee'. In keeping with this view, Breman at that conjuncture accepted that the *hali* system lacked freedom, but nevertheless downplayed its coercive element and instead emphasised strongly the benign and mutually-beneficial aspects of the relation.[14] 'It is therefore doubtful', he maintained, 'that the *hali* strove to end attachment', concluding unequivocally that 'servitude was sought rather than avoided by the Dublas'. Accordingly, Breman interpreted *hali* labour initially as a form of 'patronage' extended by a landlord to his bonded labourer, an exchange conceptualized by him as 'a pattern of relationships in which members of hierarchically arranged groups possess mutually recognized, not explicitly stipulated rights and obligations involving mutual aid and preferential treatment. The bond between patron and client is personal,

---

12   Breman (2016: 196).
13   Breman (2016: 4, 16, emphasis added).
14   Thus he insisted (Breman, 1974: 43–44, 45): 'it is difficult to maintain that the servitude of the Dubla agricultural labourers was forced upon them against their will. On the contrary...those who had managed to find someone to provide for them had every reason to consider themselves lucky. It follows that servitude was in fact preferred to free labor by landowners and agricultural laborers alike... Economically, the *hali* system was an attractive proposition for both parties... As farm servants, they [the Dublas] did not receive any remuneration, but were entitled to credit. Under the circumstances it was hardly relevant that their debt increased in this way. More important was the fact that their subsistence was assured in an economy of scarcity'.

and is contracted and continued by mutual agreement for an indeterminate time'.[15]

Since the *halipratha* relation was unfree and based on 'patronage', Breman unsurprisingly not only conflated both the latter characteristics but also equated them epistemologically with 'reciprocity' and 'subsistence' (patronage = unfreedom = reciprocity = subsistence). Although he has subsequently denied this, and indeed presented contradictory information about the meaning of 'reciprocity', it is clear that – initially at least – Breman did indeed interpret patronage/unfreedom in a positive manner: as a benign relationship to the benefit of each party, structured by 'reciprocity'.[16] The fact that for Breman the 'other' of patronage was economic rationality, and further that patronage was itself equated with the *hali* system and thus with feudalism (patronage = personal = non-economic = feudal/pre-capitalist relation), meant that the onset of this 'other' in the form of capitalist development gave rise in turn to a multiple and interlocking process of socio-economic erosion.[17] Accordingly, the decline of the *hali* system licensed not only a process of 'depatronization' but also and thereby the destruction of what he regarded as positive elements (personal/benign, patron/clientage) that previously characterized relationships between worker and landowner.[18] In short, a situation in which the 'right to work is no longer recognized,...social security no

---

15 See Breman (1974: 18, 20), who concludes that 'servitude in the past cannot be simply described as a system of unfree labor. The servant was not only a laborer but also a client, and as such he was entitled to affection, generosity, and intercession on the part of his master, who, as a patron, had to guard and promote the interests of his subordinate'. For more along the same lines, see Breman (1974: 143ff.; 1985: 129). Elsewhere he describes servitude as possessing a 'familial character' (1974: 185), which implies incorrectly that kinship is a benign institutional domain in which coercion associated with unfreedom has no meaning or role.

16 In an article entitled 'The Renaissance of Social Darwinism', originally published in 1988 and subsequently reprinted twice, first in 2003 and more recently in Patel (2008: 32–33), is found the following unequivocal description by Breman: 'Concepts such as debt, interest, loan, or advance were, in any case, only of nominal significance. Neither party wanted the relationship of dependency to be terminated by the repayment of the debt. Bondage was attractive to the landowners because they were assured of a permanent and cheap labour force. In turn, the Halpatis preferred this mode of attachment because it provided them with security, however minimal'. That is to say, an exchange involving the provision of labour-power by the client to the patron, who in turn extends to his client a 'subsistence guarantee'.

17 Breman (1974: 139,141,193).

18 On 'depatronization' see Breman (1974: 220ff.).

longer guaranteed', and the 'personal tie of affection between master and servant is tenuous'.[19]

3 Personal Tie of Affection?

Breman's idealized view that the decline in the incidence of attached labour corresponded to a process of 'depatronization' which adversely affected workers, and was therefore resisted by them, has been challenged by the findings contained in Vyas.[20] Ignoring the element of self-contradiction that structures many of the pronouncements about *halipratha*/'patronage'/unfreedom, what seems to have occurred epistemologically is a double paradigm shift: having initially identified an end not of unfreedom but of patronage, a result of conflating both concepts was that the decline of patronage subsequently became for Breman a metaphor for the decline of unfreedom. There are at least four difficulties with this clear endorsement by Breman of 'patronage' as a form of 'subsistence guarantee', of advantage to and sought by landowner and bonded labourer alike, a production relation in which debt was unimportant.

First, it is a staple of pro-slavery discourse, advanced historically by neoclassical economists, liberals generally, and Social Darwinists, all of whom similarly maintained that slaves actually preferred unfreedom, and sought out such working relations because – unlike workers who were free – they were provided thereby with a 'subsistence guarantee'.[21] Claims about the efficacy of the latter inform pro-slavery discourse in antebellum America, where – just as in the case of interpretations regarding bonded labour as a benign form of 'patronage' – it was argued that unfreedom benefited slave and master alike.[22] Hence the concept of 'positive good' maintained that, as slaves were 'protected against every contingency of life', they were in fact economically better-off than free labour.[23] In a similar vein, evidence of pro-slavery witnesses to the 1832

---

19   Breman (1974: 239).
20   Vyas (1964).
21   This is an argument that extends from Elliott (1860) and Fitzhugh (1960) in the midnineteenth century, via Page (1910) and social Darwinists such as William Graham Sumner (1959: 304–306) in the early twentieth, to Fogel and Engerman (1974) in the late twentieth.
22   Tise (1987: 97–123).
23   See Tise (1987: 1987: 110ff., Tables 5.2, 5.3 and 5.4) who observes that pro-slavery discourse exhibited 'a universal tendency to idealise the master-slave relationship as the most beneficial and benevolent condition for capital and labor', adding that it 'is striking how little time [pro-slavery] writers spent in demonstrating the cheapness and efficiency of slavery'.

British House of Lords Committee on *The Condition and Treatment of Colonial Slaves* insisted both that '[t]he treatment of the slaves was excellent; their food and clothing abundant; and their dwellings remarkably good in general', and that on estates 'old slaves [were] comfortably provided for'.[24] Over a century later the same kind of arguments were advanced in the revisionist cliometric historiography of Fogel and Engerman.

Second, there is abundant evidence supporting the opposing view, that claims about the efficacy in rural India of 'patronage'/'subsistence guarantee' were incorrect. Breaking with assertions that entering bonded labour relations was necessary because in a context of 'closed villages' alternative employment was lacking, evidence suggests that rural migration in search of urban employment opportunities was a constant feature of 1920s/1930s Gujarat.[25] Equally significant is the fact that there has been little need on the part of workers for a 'subsistence guarantee', and when there has, it was the creation of landowners, who then refused to supply it.[26] In the case of the antebellum South, the 'positive good' argument – the equivalent of the 'subsistence guarantee' – applied to slavery was similarly wrong. 'Contrary to the conventional wisdom of generations of historians', argues Tise, 'all parts of the positive good thesis are false and without foundation'.[27]

Third, it is clear that initially Breman regarded 'patronage'/'subsistence guarantee' in positive terms, maintaining that attached labourers preferred servitude, and considered themselves 'lucky' to be employed thus, that bondage was for them an economically attractive proposition in which the element of debt was unimportant. Such an interpretation throws into question his current view that he perceived unfree relations in negative terms (patronage was 'pretended', 'a semblance' of benevolence). It also casts a revealing light on the accusation levelled at the shortcomings of the World Bank – 'an outrageous degree of ignorance' for mistakenly advocating just such an argument – not least that at a subsequent point, and for some reason, he changed his mind. And fourth, it will be seen below that Breman has still not broken with the concept 'patronage', in that when considering the role of the capitalist state he returns to this earlier notion, albeit now with a different subject: instead of the landowner, therefore, it is the capitalist state which in his view ought to be the provider and source of 'patronage'.

---

24 For this testimony, see Anti-Slavery Reporter (1833: 477, 481). It underlines the veracity of the view (Tise, 1987: 97) that 'the notion that slavery could be a positive good for slaves and slave society appears in pro-slavery literature of all nations and in nearly all eras...'
25 For details, see Mukhtyar (1930) and Shukla (1937).
26 Brass (1999: 226ff.).
27 Tise (1987: 98).

Lest it be thought that the defence by Breman of patronage as a benign relational form – initially, as involving the landlord class, and currently as emanating from the neoliberal state – is in some sense a theoretical and political anomaly, a single case of untoward harking back to an earlier analytical framework, evidence suggests otherwise. Much the same kind of approach lamenting the loss of patronage, recast as a form of landlord benevolence, informs a recent account of present-day agrarian relations in Bolivia.[28] Clientage is presented as a 'from above' struggle over 'unfulfilled patronage duties', a depiction which – like that adhered to by Breman in his earlier analyses of bonded labour – entails the persistence of 'from below' claims to landlord patronage.[29] Much like Breman in Gujarat, therefore, who argued initially that landlords wanted to eliminate patronage but debt bonded labourers struggled to retain this, Winchell assumes that all former hacienda tenants in Bolivia hankered after – and lamented the loss of – earlier patronage relations.[30] However, this seems to have been true mainly of one particular individual described by her as a 'favourite servant' of the landowner in the pre-reform era.[31]

---

28   The account privileging what is depicted as a 'benign' form of patronage in present-day Bolivia is by Winchell (2018). The problematic nature of its claims in this regard are twofold. First, the kinds of sources invoked: these consist for the most part of an uncritical acceptance of arguments found in traditional anthropological texts (Sallnow, Murra). No reference is made to long-standing critiques of these same approaches, by Sanchez (1977, 1982) and Bradby (1982). And second, some of the fieldwork methods used generate similar misgivings: the latter derive from the fact that she was accompanied on fieldwork trips by landlord kin ('Raul belonged to a family infamous for its cruelty and violence').

29   See Winchell (2018: 14, 16), who maintains that in Bolivia 'today the hacienda serves not only as an historical referent but also as the relational hinge at the centre of an informal economy of exchange and aid. These exchange practices were loosely organized by an ethic of elite accountability to former servants, the kin of former hacienda landlords often providing ex-servant families with access to transportation, medicine and education as well as goods like clothes and food…rather than dismiss such practices as evidence of false consciousness, we might consider them distinct articulations of authority and duty'.

30   Hence the view (Winchell, 2018: 7, 13) regarding 'the elite's failure to act appropriately within the shared moral framework of redistributive exchange', and 'the demands of former servants for the aid of their prior employers'.

31   Much of the case about the benign nature of patronage was told her (Winchell, 2018: 13, 14, 15) by a 'favourite servant' of the landlord who was perceived by other peasants on the estate as sharing the interests of the landowner. Significantly, therefore, earlier the 'favourite servant' had 'been beaten unconscious by a…union leader when villagers stormed the hacienda', and his 'neighbours referred to him disparagingly as "he who remains a slave"'. In Peru such a 'favourite servant' on the estate was invariably regarded by other tenants as an informer (*soplón*).

4   Two Concepts, or One?

There has been a discernable shift in the way production relations in Gujarat have been interpreted by Breman. From the 1960s to the 1970s, his insistence on the efficacy of a 'subsistence guarantee' generated a number of interrelated claims: that as capitalism spread to the countryside, rural producers replaced their unfree workers with free equivalents, on the one hand accelerating the growth of proletarianization and on the other withdrawing 'patronage' on which attached labour depended. This development was presented by him as a process to the benefit of capital but to the disadvantage of unfree labour. Commercially-minded employers attempted to rid themselves of an economically unprofitable relational form (a 'subsistence guarantee' making permanently bonded labour expensive to maintain) with a less costly variant (a daily wage payment to casual or seasonal workers being much cheaper). By contrast, unfree workers were deprived of permanent jobs that delivered them and their families an economically valuable 'subsistence guarantee', as a result of which they became impoverished.

During the 1980s, however, the positive view of debt bondage equating it with a desirable form of 'patronage'/'subsistence guarantee' sought by workers, together with the claim that capitalist producers would automatically replace such unfree production relations with free equivalents, were challenged by Marxist theory.[32] The latter argued that, bonded labour was reproduced not 'from below' by workers, but much rather 'from above' by employers due to the acute nature of the class struggle. Labelled deproletarianization, this was a process of workforce decomposition/recomposition frequently resorted to by employers in their conflict with rural labour. The object was to discipline and cheapen labour-power, an undeniable economic advantage in a context where global capitalism meant that agricultural producers had to become increasingly cost-conscious in order to remain competitive. This alternative interpretation was dismissed by Breman, who was adamant both that unfreedom was on the decline, and consequently what was occurring was not deproletarianization but proletarianization.[33]

---

32   For this Marxist approach, see previous chapter.
33   Breman (1993, 1996). It 'is no longer the case' argued Breman (1985: 311) that permanent farm servants are bonded, 'even when...indebtedness is a persistent feature of the labour relationship', and although casual workers receive loans and maidservants live in the house of their employers, 'their situation does not constitute an unfree working relationship, either'. As to the question of a link between capitalism and unfreedom, his view was categorical and unambiguous: 'To my mind', he asserted, 'it is unsound to deduce from this [the existence of debt] that unfree labour continues in either the same form *or a*

Notwithstanding his opposition to this Marxist link between labour attachment and class struggle waged 'from above', the 1990s saw an unacknowledged *volte face* by Breman, who now discarded his original position (unfreedom declines as capitalism develops) and replaced it with a diametrically opposite one (capitalist producers prefer bonded labour). Since then he has maintained that what is termed 'neo-bondage' is, after all, not just compatible with the accumulation process but actually central to agrarian capitalist growth in Gujarat. Currently, the characteristics ascribed by him to 'neo-bondage' – among them 'the loss of control over their own labour power [is] a final step in the trajectory of dispossession among the landless workforce' – are epistemologically indistinguishable from those of deproletarianization, a concept he earlier rejected as inapplicable.[34]

Despite his initial objection to the concept, therefore, Breman has clearly been influenced by what has been written about deproletarianization, to the extent of adopting not just its arguments about unfreedom (definition, causes, incidence), but also taking issue with others who have failed to spot its relevance. Endorsing the application by Harvey of the concept 'dispossession' to state appropriation of land belonging to smallholders so as to make this resource available to capital, Breman adds: 'I...would also go a step further and claim that the labouring poor in India who have no means of production other than their labour-power still are victims of further dispossession [since they] are forced to bargain their freedom away by selling their labour power in advance and thus lose control over how to make the best price possible for the incidental use of their hands and feet'.[35] Exactly the same critique of Harvey, noting that he could have, but didn't, extend the concept 'dispossession' to the ownership by workers of their sole commodity labour-power, was made earlier in connection with deproletarianization.[36]

---

new one...[t]he binding which accompanies this cannot...be equated with unfree labour' (emphasis added). Similarly, 'I shall regard as unfree only that form of debt-labour which is rooted in non-economic coercion...*this relationship has nothing to do with the essence of present-day control over agricultural labour*' (emphasis added). What was happening, by contrast, was 'the transition from a traditional agrarian economy to *a free labour market* in the countryside [and] the acceleration of a capitalist mode of production in agriculture' (Breman, 1985: 443–4, emphasis added).

34 Breman (2016: 17, 35, 44, 60–61, 148, 199).
35 Breman (2016: 255–56).
36 See Brass (2011: 148): 'There is an irony here, in that Harvey fails to spot the space unfreedom might occupy in his theoretical framework. Why should unfree relations of production not be seen also as a case of "accumulation by dispossession" (to use the term preferred by Harvey), where owners of labour-power are concerned? That is, literally 'dispossessing' workers ultimately of a capacity personally to commodify or recommodify

Having attacked deproletarianization, saying unfreedom was no longer a factor in capitalist agriculture of Gujarat, therefore, Breman has adopted most of its arguments, presented by him under the label 'neo-bondage'. However, unlike the deproletarianization approach, which sees solutions to unfree labour only in a socialist transition, he persists in arguing for a solution within capitalism, in the process criticizing the capitalist state for not caring sufficiently about the poor and workers – an argument which in effect brings him back to his original framework of seeing patronage as the answer to poverty and unfreedom.

5 A Caring State...

Two interrelated themes structure the narrative of the analysis examined here. First, that pauperism is an effect of an increasingly large segment of the Indian population no longer having an economic role in production.[37] And second, both employers and the State are blamed for not caring about them.[38] These positions confirm the extent to which Breman misunderstands the economic role of the poor. Contrary to his view that 'they aren't needed anymore', they are: specifically, as components of the industrial reserve army.[39] In the latter capacity, they don't need actually to enter the productive process: much rather, their presence is there as a threat – that they could be called upon to replace existing workers. In this way, they help capital not only suppress the wages of those already in work, but also dissuade them from organizing in order to improve pay and conditions. That is, they *do* have an economic function, and from the point of view of capitalists engaged in accumulation a very important

---

their only commodity. This, surely, is a logical final step in the class struggle waged by capital, one that would ensure that workers are deprived of the sole remaining weapon in their conflict with owners of the means of production: making or not making available their labour-power, according to the conditions stipulated by the market'.

37 See Breman (2016: 3, 13, 14–16, 18–19, 23ff.), according to whom (Patel, 2008: 32) '[t]here are too many poor and they aren't needed anymore. There's no way for them to be included in the labour and production process. They have become useless; they have lost, in fact, a reason for existing at all'.

38 Breman (2016: 40ff., 44–45, 54ff., 60ff., 66, 72, 76, 133–34).

39 On the crucial role of the industrial reserve army, in terms of the way capitalist accumulation is reproduced, both historically and currently, see Chapter 3 below. It scarcely requires mention that for someone undertaking an analysis of economic development and its connection to impoverishment not to know about how the industrial reserve functions is problematic in the extreme.

one.[40] Ironically, right at the start of his analysis he describes casual workers as 'hanging around but ever ready to go wherever their presence for the moment is required', without realizing this is precisely the object of the industrial reserve.[41]

Seemingly unaware of this Marxist interpretation, Breman is critical of Himmelfarb for not appreciating that Tocqueville was a critic of capitalism who took the rich to task for not caring sufficiently about the poor.[42] This confirms that what Breman shares with Tocqueville is an emphasis on the *moral* dimension of the capital/labour relation, in that in their view the wealthy and powerful ought to show a little more concern than they do for the plight of the poor.[43] In short, both argue that solutions to poverty and exploitation can still be found within the capitalist system as it currently exists, which is the classic reformist position. The latter insists a better capitalism is possible, despite being a claim that is now widely discredited by Marxists who argue that a better capitalism is not possible. Its current operation is not, as reformists think, a systemic anomaly – an untypically 'nasty' capitalism – that is open to amelioration, thereby restoring a more benign version (a 'kind'/'caring' capitalism)

---

40   That Breman misunderstands economic concepts is evident, for example, from his (Breman, 2016: 48, 76) application of the term 'tight labour market' to situations where many workers are chasing few jobs, whereas it actually means the opposite: employers compete fiercely for workers, because there are more jobs available than labour to fill them.

41   Breman (2016: 1).

42   Breman (2016: 6, 239–40). Hence the view (Breman, 2016: 243, 248) that '[i]n order to bring about social peace, Tocqueville spoke out in favour of inter-class solidarity', and further, '[w]hat he diagnosed as a broken moral bond, an alliance of trust between elite and underdogs which he projected back to a rustic past, has not been repaired'. Significantly, Tocqueville is claimed by neoconservatives as one of their own (Stelzer, 2005: 35, 216, 310).

43   Hence the applicability of the critique of Dickens made by Orwell, as outlined in the epigraph at the start of this chapter. 'The one thing that everyone who has read A Tale of Two Cities remembers is the Reign of Terror', continues Orwell (1965: 89–90), adding that: 'If, [Dickens] says, you behave as the French aristocracy had behaved, vengeance will follow... In other words, the French aristocracy had dug their own graves. But there is no perception here of what is now called historic necessity. Dickens sees that the results are inevitable, given the causes, but he thinks the causes might have been avoided. The Revolution is something that happens because centuries of oppression have made the French peasantry sub-human. If the wicked nobleman could somehow have turned over a new leaf, like Scrooge, there would have been no Revolution, no jacquerie, no guillotine – and so much the better. This is the opposite of the "revolutionary" attitude. From the "revolutionary" point of view the class-struggle is the main source of progress...'. Accordingly, what Breman shares with Dickens is the avoidance of systemic causation; hence the idealized perception that something 'nasty' – that is, neoliberalism – can be avoided simply by getting employers and their political representatives in the state apparatus voluntarily to adopt a different and more benign moral approach.

of this mode of production as it existed seven decades ago (state regulation of capital, central planning, near-full or full employment, permanent well-paying jobs). Neoliberalism is the logical outcome of capitalist development on an international scale, and as such signals that, considered in terms both of economic theory and working class political interests, its time has passed.

Accordingly, Breman fails to understand that the problem of rural poverty cannot be solved by capitalism of any kind, not least because the accumulation process depends precisely on the presence of large numbers of the rural poor, who in their capacity as an industrial reserve army of labour undermine the bargaining power of employed workers, thereby keeping wages down and profits up.[44] This is because the reproduction of capitalism no longer depends on the consuming power of peasants in the so-called Third World. What an increasingly international capitalism *does* require, however, is their labour-power, either to produce agricultural commodities that can be exported and consumed elsewhere, or to exert downward pressure on the wages/conditions of those in work. This is an old argument, made by Kautsky a century ago, and still relevant today. It contrasts absolutely with the view held by Breman, which, ironically, has come full circle. His initial argument about patronage implied that the landowners ought to care more about their bonded labourers than they did, while the one he now makes is that the state ought to care more about the poor than it does, which is a *de facto* return to the earlier position, with the difference that instead of the landowner as 'uncaring' we now have the capitalist state as 'uncaring'.

---

44   Where the industrial reserve army is concerned, both the economic benefits and the social costs of migration have long been recognized in India. The two-sidedness of official attitudes towards labour migration, seen on the one hand as providing employers facing intense competition from other producers with cost advantages where market rivalry is intense, yet on the other generating antagonism from those already in the labour market, is clearly demonstrated in the following account by Toynbee during the late 1920s capitalist crisis. Hence the view (Toynbee, 1928: 12–13) that '[f]or Great Britain, oppressed since the [1914–18] War by the burden and menace of unemployment among her industrial population on an unprecedented scale, the incentive to find outlets for emigration was particularly strong... In the matter of Oriental migration...there was a conflict of interest between India on the one hand and the overseas Dominions of European origin on the other [since] in the case of Oriental migrations the economic issue was complicated by a marked difference in the standard of living and this difference itself was the outward symptom of racial and cultural differences which were capable of arousing the strongest of all social passions'. Given the spread to underdeveloped countries of nationalism and democracy, where such processes might lead is made equally clear (Toynbee, 1928: 36), in that these nations 'were being rudely awakened from a long political slumber by the Principles of the French Revolution – long since a platitude in the West, but still a trumpet-call in unaccustomed ears'.

6   ...or Permanent Revolution

The difficulties confronting Breman's analysis underline as neatly as possible the veracity of the arguments deployed by Trotsky generally against the exponents of *katheder*-socialism and Kautsky in particular during the 1920s.[45] Thus Breman continues to look in vain to the existing capitalist state for solutions to rural poverty, and when these are not forthcoming labels the bourgeois state as 'uncaring'; his expectation is that a neoliberal regime ought to put into practice its expressed concern about impoverished workers and peasants, and is mystified as to why this does not happen. In making this assumption, the appeal by Breman to the 'patronage' of the capitalist state is in effect no different from the reformist views of Bauer, Sombart and Austro-Marxists who advocated working class empowerment in all its forms not through revolutionary agency but simply by adherence to democratic procedures – that is, with the consent of the bourgeoisie.

The futility of such appeals to a moral order – that is, to what in reality are non-existent obligations of neoliberalism and its state – so as to implement change desired by the proletariat was central to the theory of permanent revolution. Arguing for the necessity of the latter, Trotsky showed that tasks solving economic stagnation, inequality, poverty, unemployment, exploitation, low wages and poor conditions, would – and could only ever be – carried out once socialism was on the political agenda, by a workers' government and its state. No capitalist regime – and most certainly no neoliberal one – was going to put in place the kind of reforms the implementation of which might in the end threaten the property relations underpinning its own holders of power and wealth. At a general theoretical level, therefore, two interpretations exist as to why revolution is a necessary step not just in the transition to socialism, but also in addressing the kinds of issues raised by Breman.

The first maintains that such tasks fall to the proletariat because the bourgeoisie has been too weak to push through the change that is required. Because the profit margins of the bourgeoisie in less developed countries are smaller and more precarious, their exploitation of workers is necessarily more oppressive. For this reason, they will not voluntarily discharge the tasks of a progressive/democratic bourgeoisie, which accordingly fall to the workers.[46] Against this, a second interpretation argues that, by contrast, a bourgeoisie was never going to undertake such change, because by doing so it would either bring into being or consolidate the power of a proletariat – that is, a workforce composed

---

45   For the 1920s debate, see Chapter 2 above.
46   On this point, see Trotsky (1936: 179).

of labour that is free – conscious of its political objective and at last possessing the agency to bring this to fruition, by pushing for socialism. In short, the bourgeoisie does not undertake change not because it is too weak to do so, but rather because if it does it in effect signs its own death warrant.[47] It was for this reason, amongst others, that Trotsky advocated permanent revolution, or the theory that, following landlord expropriation and the defeat of feudalism, the object of struggle is to proceed directly to the dictatorship of the proletariat, rather than to an intervening bourgeois democratic stage.[48] Against the latter – an approach which maintained the necessity of proceeding to democracy and a 'fully functioning' capitalism – he justified permanent revolution because of potential/actual hostility encountered by workers at that crucial point from rich and middle peasants opposed to attempts at converting all private holdings – not just those confiscated from a landowning class – into state property.

7 Conclusion

Traced here is the way a radical Marxist argument formulated on the margins undergoes a substantial political metamorphosis once it reappears in the academic mainstream. As conceptualized by radical Marxist theory, therefore, the object of deproletarianization – replacing free workers with unfree equivalents – undertaken by employers constitutes the way in which class struggle is conducted by 'those above' in order to pre-empt or curb the emergence or

---

[47] This much is clear from what Trotsky (1972a: 52–3, emphasis added) writes about the bourgeoisie during the 1848 revolution in France, where '[i]t did not want to, and could not, assume the responsibility for a revolutionary liquidation of the social order which barred the way to its own dominance. Its task – and this it fully realised – consisted in introducing into the old order certain essential guarantees, not of its own political dominance, but only of co-dominance with the forces of the past. It not only failed to lead the masses in storming the old order; it used the old order as a defence against the masses who were trying to push it forward. Its consciousness rebelled against the objective conditions of its dominance. *Democratic institutions were reflected in its mind, not as the aim and purpose of its struggle, but as a threat to its well-being. The revolution could not be made by the bourgeoisie, only against the bourgeoisie*'.

[48] For the theory of permanent revolution, see Trotsky (1962) and also above, Chapter 2. Trotsky (1972a: 322, original emphasis) defended it on the following grounds: 'The question of bourgeois democracy has been argued over many times, and anyone who does not yet know the answer to it is bound to be in the dark. We have supplied the answer. *A national bourgeois revolution in Russia is impossible because of the absence of a genuinely revolutionary bourgeois democracy*. The time for national revolutions is past… it is no longer a matter of a bourgeois nation opposing an old regime, but of the proletariat opposing the bourgeois nation'.

consolidation of a consciousness of class among the workforce. This in turn forms an obstacle to the transformation of a class-in-itself into a class-for-itself: that is, it serves to block a socialist transition and any chance of revolutionary agency designed to achieve this end. As long as deproletarianization succeeds in this objective, by dividing the workforce and undermining the efficacy of its political organization, the accumulation process is able to avoid at least one potential challenge to its reproduction.

However, the re-emergence within the academic mainstream of the same framework – albeit with a different label attached – positing a link between the presence of unfree labour and class struggle waged by capital, gives rise to a different outcome. Instead of being connected to a socialist transition, a similar case about capitalism/unfreedom now looks to the neoliberal state for a resolution, in the form of patronage. This, it is argued here, merely reproduces the same central tenet of the bourgeois argument concerning the desirability of patronage, but with a single difference: the patronage from which the impoverished worker is supposed to benefit shifts from the feudal (or semi-feudal) landlord class to the capitalist state.

As formulated on the margins, the more radical interpretation maintained that unfree labour was much rather imposed on workers, not sought by them, and was thus to be seen as part of the class struggle waged by employers against their workers. Whereas in the more radical Marxist version solutions to bonded labour could only be realized by a socialist transition, the mainstream version argued by contrast that unfreedom could – and should – be eradicated within capitalism (by a 'caring' state). Lacking the concepts revolution and socialism, however, the mainstream analysis examined critically above remains unable to provide any reason as to why the capitalist state would eradicate a production relation (and its attendant rural poverty) that confers economic advantages on employers, other than an appeal to the moral order: the neoliberal state really ought to 'care' about the workforce.

Despite being influenced by the deproletarianization argument, to the extent of reproducing its entire analysis, therefore, the mainstream analysis has nevertheless shorn this Marxist interpretation of its revolutionary politics. It rejects socialism as an outcome, adopting instead calls for a more 'benign' capitalism. This is what happens once a socialist transition as an objective has been abandoned by those who – like Breman – study and write about the agrarian sector in Third World nations. What remains, unfortunately, is nothing more than a fruitless (and politically naïve) appeal to the capitalist state to be 'nicer' and 'kinder' to impoverished rural workers, an approach that cannot be seen as anything but the nadir of development theory.

CHAPTER 6

Misunderstanding Revolution: (Re-)Defining Labour Coercion?

> 'All I wanted to say is that my circuits are now irrevocably committed to computing the answer to Life, the Universe and Everything, but the programme will take me seven and a half million years to run... And it occurs to me that running a programme like this is bound to cause sensational public interest and so any philosophers who are quick off the mark are going to clean up in the prediction business [by] violently disagree[ing] with each other about what answer I'm eventually going to produce'.
>
> The computer Deep Thought advising philosophers as to the best course of action, in the cult BBC Radio adaptation of *The Hitch-Hiker's Guide to the Galaxy*.[1]

∴

1 Introduction: A Necessary Journey?

The rest of this section continues to trace the effects of conceptually discarding revolutionary agency and with it a socialist transition, considered in terms of their impact on academic debate about the systemic form taken by and object of economic development. Of particular interest is the way the more radical ideas formulated on the margins are transformed once these reappear in the academic mainstream, a process that reproduces many of the issues and arguments raised by the Bolsheviks in their disputes with Austro-Marxists (see Part 1 of this volume). Like the Austro-Marxists at an earlier conjuncture, therefore, many of those in academia – particularly in the social sciences, and especially undertaking a study of development in so-called Third World countries – who continue to regard themselves as leftists are currently still trying to find solutions within capitalism to the very obvious kinds of plebeian disempowerment encountered.

This quest takes the form either of ameliorating the *laissez-faire* labour regime or – as will be seen in the next chapter – advocating the empowerment

---

1 Adams (1985: 77).

of non-class identities, neither of which is thought by those making this case to necessitate the transcendence of the accumulation process. In doing so, they make the same theoretical and political mistakes as their early twentieth century counterparts. Both the theoretical problems and the political stasis raised by this quest emerge in Section 3 below, when such arguments surface in the domain of popular culture, in the form of specific case-studies (Peru, France) that attempt an interpretation of peasant movements and peasant economy.

Among the questions that have to be asked of any book are: does it make a case not made before, or does it merely repeat what is already known; and is it sufficient to avoid rigorous theoretical interpretation and focus instead on empiricism? Both these questions must be asked of the two volumes examined here, since they not only cover what has now become well-trodden ground, but also raise issues concerning the direction taken by transformations in the global labour regime. Each volume presents case-studies of unfree labour over a period from the eighteenth century to the present day in almost every region of the globe, extending from Asia (China, Japan, the Philippines, India) and Africa, through the Americas and the Caribbean, to the Middle East. A notable absence is Europe, which features mainly as the colonial power responsible for the presence of coerced workers in many of these contexts; this absence is significant, in that it is now clear that metropolitan capitalist nations are no more immune to the imposition of unfree production relations than countries in the so-called Third World.

It is surprising yet unsurprising to encounter at the outset claims that 'less consideration' has been given to the types of unfree production relations – such as sharecropping, debt peonage, indenture, convict workers, attached and/or bonded labour – lying between free and slave labour, a lack which justifies and requires further investigation since 'they have received little scholarly attention [and] their historiography is only now beginning to emerge'.[2] Surprising in the sense that the claim is quite simply incorrect: if anything, discussions of unfree production relations located between these 'two extremes' can be found in many books and almost every social science journal over the last three decades, so much so that concerns have been expressed lest the focus of the development debate may now have shifted too far in the direction of the link between capitalism and these kinds of unfree labour.[3] Unsurprising in that claims about the lack of analysis and investigation serve to justify the appearance of yet another volume covering the same ground as many earlier ones. Hence the equally startling claim by van Melkebeke that, where colonial

---

[2] van der Linden and Rodríguez García (2016: 1–2).
[3] For these concerns, see Das (2014: 91).

labour regimes are concerned, an 'analysis of the concept of coerced labour... is still lacking'; again, much rather the opposite is the case, in that many continue to analyse unfree work arrangements *only* in relation to colonial labour regimes.[4]

Notwithstanding a shared desire on the part of the essays in each of the edited collections to go beyond the free/unfree dichotomy that has informed political economic theory about the way production relations change, Tappe and Lindner start from the premise that non-slave labour is free, while van der Linden and van Melkebeke by contrast maintain that most are unfree.[5] However, all of them concede that, in the end, the free/unfree dichotomy is not transcended.[6] The reasons for this are examined in the four sections which follow, the first of which sets out the parameters of the debate about unfree labour, while claims that this discussion has been transcended are considered in the second. Identified in the third section are the theoretical difficulties at the root of these claims, and the resulting focus on empiricism is outlined in the fourth.

2   The Debate

Unfree labor re-emerged as an issue in the debate about rural development during the years following the end of the 1939–45 war, when a political concern of Keynesian theory was not just economic reconstruction (mainly in Europe and Asia) but also planning (in the Third World). A crucial aspect of the ensuing discussion concerned the extent to which different relational forms constituted obstacles to capitalist development, and why. During the 1960s and 1970s unfree labour was regarded as incompatible with capitalist accumulation, and thus an obstacle to economic growth, an interpretation advanced by exponents of the then-dominant semi-feudal thesis.[7] According to the latter, unfree

---

4   van Melkebeke (2016: 189).
5   See Tappe and Lindner (2016), van der Linden and Rodríguez García (2016), van der Linden (2016), and van Melkebeke (2016).
6   In this, they merely follow the earlier trajectory of Jan Breman, who switched from the view that capitalism necessarily requires free workers to his current position, that accumulation is perfectly compatible with unfree labour. For evidence of the latter, see previous chapter.
7   Applying the semi-feudal thesis – a stages theory defined rigidly in terms of relational forms exclusive to and necessarily ubiquitous within a specific mode of production – to nations as different as India and the United States, its more recent exponents include Patnaik (1990), Byres (1996), and Laibman (2015).

labour was a pre-capitalist relation, destined to be replaced by a workforce that was free as capitalism spread throughout the agrarian sector of Third World nations. Like much non-Marxist theory, this variant of Marxism saw unfree labour as incompatible not just with capitalism but also with advanced productive forces, economic efficiency, skilled workers, and market expansion.

The corollary of the inefficiency argument is that capital is seen as opposed to using unfree labour, and in contexts where the latter relational form is found, invariably strives to replace it with free labour-power. Not the least difficulty facing those who advocated the semi-feudal approach is that it resulted in an indefinite postponement of a socialist transition, while everyone waited until free wage-labour was systemically ubiquitous.[8] An inevitable consequence of rigidly-defined unilinear stages, therefore, was – and is still – political stasis (= alliances with a 'progressive' national bourgeoisie) incurred by the long wait for the arrival (or return) of a 'nice' capitalism that everywhere uses only free wage-labour. Downgraded or ignored thereby is a central tenet of Marxism: namely, the dialectical interplay between free and unfree labour-power generated by capitalist class struggle, waged 'from above' by – among others – the 'progressive' national bourgeoisie.

From the 1980s onwards, however, another and very different view emerged, arguing that evidence from Latin America and India suggested agribusiness enterprises, commercial farmers and rich peasants reproduced, introduced or reintroduced unfree relations. Conceptualized as 'deproletarianization', this approach to the debate restored the sale/purchase of labour-power by its owner to definitions of work arrangements that were not free.[9] In contexts/

---

[8] As pointed out by Trotsky (1936: 208–9, original emphasis) long ago, when disagreeing with the tendency of Comintern to label production relations in less developed nations as 'feudal', in order to postpone both revolution and socialism, 'matters would be quite hopeless [= revolution postponed indefinitely] if feudal survivals really did *dominate*. But, fortunately, survivals in general cannot dominate.' This is precisely the central issue: 'survivals' cannot dominate – if they do, they are *not* 'survivals'.

[9] Further aspects of deproletarianization are considered in previous chapters. The concept takes its theoretical impetus from the Marxist dynamic of class struggle, arising from the need of employers to cheapen labour-power in increasingly competitive global markets. Class struggle waged 'from above' involves the employment of unfree labour, capitalist restructuring, and workforce decomposition/recomposition, all of which entail deproletarianization. Hence the shifting of unfreedom from permanent, unpaid and local workers to temporary, paid and migrant equivalents. Class struggle 'from below' entails strong worker opposition to restructuring, and equally forthright attempts by employers to proceed with this, in order to cut production costs. Numerous contextually and historically-specific instances exist of the central role played by unfree labour in the process of capitalist restructuring, a procedure whereby employers used it to replace free workers bargaining over pay and conditions or engaged in strike action.

periods where/when further accumulation is blocked by overproduction, therefore, economic crisis may force capital to restructure its labour process in one of two ways: either by replacing free workers with unfree equivalents, or by converting the former into the latter. Generated as a result of class struggle, both these kinds of transformation correspond to deproletarianization, or the economic and politico-ideological decommodification of labour-power.[10]

This dynamic is missing from those who interpret history as an unproblematic and irreversible progression from unfree to free production relations. What the 'deproletarianization' approach maintains is not that somehow free labour has ceased to exist, and consequently Marx was wrong to regard it as the defining characteristic of capitalism, but rather that, in the course of class struggle, employers on occasion attempt to claw back the advantages – economic, political, ideological – that being free confers on their workers.[11] It is precisely this element of ownership, exercised personally by workers over their labour-power, that an employer has to deprive them of so as to exert in turn full control over production. Deproletarianization captures this fact, by underlining the extent to which it is necessary for capital to close off even this limited economic autonomy. It recognizes conceptually that what has happened to

---

10 As has been noted previously, this divergence between deproletarianization and the semi-feudal thesis also structures the different meanings attached to the process of combined and uneven development. In the deproletarization analysis, therefore, capitalism in both advanced and less developed contexts utilizes unfree labour-power because of its cheapness and as a weapon in the class struggle with workers who are free. Seen thus, unfreedom is not a relational anomaly situated within capitalist development, one that is destined to be eliminated by commercial enterprises intent on replacing it with labour-power that is free. Epistemologically, the conclusion is that unfree labour-power cannot be other than a capitalist relation. By contrast, the semi-feudal thesis maintains that, because capitalists in more advanced countries unproblematically employ only free labour-power, their use of unfree variants in less developed nations is done reluctantly. That is, in the latter contexts such production relations are resorted to only because they are the only kinds available. In this interpretation, unfreedom is not a relation of choice for accumulation, but used only because nothing else – no free labour – is on offer. Epistemologically, the conclusion is that labour-power which is unfree is necessarily a pre- or non-capitalist relation.

11 The centrality of 'from above' class struggle to the reproduction of unfree relations is still not fully recognized. Attributing the origins of unfree labour to a situation where '[u]nfree labour emerges when 'normal' wage labour relations break down', Munck (2009: 9) conveys the misleading impression almost of an accidental, haphazard occurrence, thereby overlooking/downplaying the way in which producers engineer such an outcome. Namely, that in the course of the class struggle capitalists employ workers who are unfree in preference to 'normal' or free wage-labour relations, precisely because – unlike the latter – those in the former category are less costly, more easily controlled, and therefore cheaper and more profitable.

workers is that, finally, they have become what Marx said they would: men and women of no property. Capital has taken from them their sole remaining property, the ownership by workers of their own labour-power. It signals the completeness both of the subordination of the worker to the employer, and thus also of the *class* inequality between capital and labour.

Consequently, it could be argued that in this debate the epistemological break, shifting the paradigm from on the one hand unfree-relations-incompatible-with-capitalism together with unfreedom-as-obstacle-to-accumulation to on the other capitalism-compatible-with-unfree-relations and accumulation-thrives-on-unfreedom, occurred long ago, back in the 1980s. Most of what has been published since then merely confirms the extent and economic impact of this shift. Contributions to the debate about the meaning and causes of unfree labour have on occasion either questioned or attempted to exclude deproletarianization from the discussion, while others have changed their minds, and espoused its arguments. Despite initial objections to the concept deproletarianization, therefore, some have clearly been influenced by what has been written about this theoretical approach, to the extent of adopting not just its arguments about unfreedom (definition, causes, incidence), but also taking issue with others who have failed to spot its relevance.[12]

Although this paradigm shift is now broadly accepted by most of those who study development from the viewpoint of political economy, it has not gone unchallenged. A number of those who now accept the epistemological validity of capitalism/unfreedom link nevertheless insist wrongly that, because Marxist theory failed to understand the centrality of unfreedom to modern capitalism, a new explanation of this link was needed.[13] For their part, some advocates of the semi-feudal thesis still adhere to a form of stages theory, privileging the ubiquity of free labour and denying the presence of unfree relations.

---

12   See, for example, Breman (on which see Chapter 5 above). Although originally he, too, insisted that production relations in rural Gujarat entailed the replacement of unfree labour with a workforce composed of free equivalents, and attacked the deproletarianization approach, saying unfreedom was no longer a factor in capitalist agriculture, therefore, Breman has now adopted most of its arguments, presented by him under the label 'neo-bondage'.

13   See, for example, the exchange between Barrientos, Kothari and Phillips (2013) and Brass (2014a). As in so many instances, an unawareness of a long-standing debate about the unfreedom/capitalism link is combined with an entirely unjustified attribution of blame to Marxism for having failed to spot this connection. Hence the following view: 'Coercion may also be exercised in more indirect ways', notes Huws (2013: 95), adding – mistakenly – that it 'has however received only rather fitful attention from Marxian scholars, except as a kind of vestigial repository of pre-capitalist social relations from which waged labour later emerged.'

Neoclassical economists and postmodernists similarly revise the meaning of debt bondage, and continue to argue that, far from being a disempowering coercive/oppressive relation it was and remains much rather an empowering outcome of worker 'choice'.

3   The Debate Transcended?

One would never guess from the current near unanimity among those writing about the acceptability to capitalism of unfree production relations that it is a view which – as the above section underlines – has in the recent past had to be fought for, vigorously and against the grain. A symptom of this is a tendency by some analyses simply to make the same point as has been made before, without realizing (and thus acknowledging) its provenance. Thus, for example, in support of the claim that the free/unfree distinction does not hold, Rodríguez García maintains every kind of working arrangement involves some form of coercion, a situation faced as much by notionally-free highly-paid professionals employed by large urban corporations as by debt bonded agricultural labour.[14]

Without realizing it, Rodríguez García repeats the argument first made during the 1970s by a revisionist historian, who posited an equivalence between on the one hand wealthy executives 'tied' to a company by bonus payments and pension schemes, and on the other impoverished labourers compelled to work for long hours in poor conditions in order to repay a loan borrowed from a landowner or labour contractor.[15] Criticisms made of this revisionist claim at that conjuncture pointed out that, unlike bonded labour, corporate executives are not dependent on cash advances for subsistence, nor are they required to repay debts such as bank overdrafts in the form of low-wage hard manual labour on rural properties or construction sites owned by the bank at a low wage fixed by the latter. To regard the situations as the same, and therefore as evidence for the non-existence of a difference between free and unfree production relations, is quite simply incorrect, a point conceded subsequently by Rodríguez García. Quite why this comparison, made and dismissed long ago, reappears yet again is something of a mystery.

14   Rodríguez García (2016: 13–14, 18).
15   The revisionist in question was Arnold Bauer (1979: 41), who deployed this argument in order to cast doubt on the coerciveness of the Latin American *enganche* system. Ironically, the conclusion he drew from the same comparison was the opposite one from that arrived at by Rodríguez García. Unlike her, for whom all working arrangements are unfree, Bauer maintained by contrast that – as in the case of executives 'tied' to corporations – even debt bondage was free.

Unfamiliarity with what was said in this earlier debate also leads to frequent error, a result either of misinterpreting sources, or of being unaware that issues were raised and disputes resolved previously. In support of the view that the Pacific Island labour trade was 'contract slavery', therefore, Zeuske cites the work of Munro and Moore, seemingly unaware of the fact that both the latter deny it was based on coercion, and therefore composed of unfree migrants, being much rather in their opinion voluntary, and hence for the contract worker empowering. In short, the opposite of what Zeuske maintains is the case.[16] A particular source of confusion is the connection between family labour and wage labour, since this distinction does not always hold true: this is especially the case when kin are deployed to work for others in order to repay loans incurred by the household head.

Although he accepts that women and children in the peasant household are unfree – they work for the household head – van der Linden regards the household head himself as free ('the work of the patriarch is free, since it is autonomous').[17] This ignores cases – frequent in Latin America and Asia – where the household head not only has to work to pay off a debt owed his employer, but is also required to contribute the labour-power of family members who work alongside him under the direction of the employer. In short, the household head is no more 'autonomous' than his kinfolk. By contrast, Rodríguez García categorizes the enforcement of unfreedom by pressure exercised from within the kinship domain as 'non-material', which ignores the material dimension to this kind of compulsion, in the form of denying access to or disinheritance of economic resources (such as land).[18]

Much the same difficulty confronts Tappe and Lindner who advocate replacing terms like 'new slavery' and 'modern slavery' with 'new coolies' on the grounds that conceptually the latter – unlike both the former – include no 'idea of property'.[19] The inference is that slaves are owned, but coolies are not. What Tappe and Lindner miss thereby – oddly, since they follow the

---

16 See Zeuske (2016: 36–7). In the debate about Pacific Island labour, which ranged across a number of publications (*Slavery & Abolition, The Journal of Pacific Studies*) during the 1980s and 1990s, Munro and Moore were part of a revisionist historiography which, together with Schlomowitz – another contributor to the same debate – applied to the plantation labour regime much the same kind of neoclassical economic framework as that used earlier by cliometricians like Fogel and Engerman when reinterpreting the meaning of chattel slavery employed in the antebellum American south.
17 See van der Linden (2016: 296). That females and children in the peasant household are unfree workers has long been reported in the literature on rural development.
18 Rodríguez García (2016: 13–14).
19 Tappe and Lindner (2016: 25–6).

deproletarianization approach and subscribe to unfreedom as a 'class-based phenomenon' – is that there *is* a property element involved, one that dissolves the distinction they claim separates coolies from slaves. Like other workers, the coolie does indeed have property: as pointed out by Marx, this takes the form of labour-power, the only commodity which s/he is either able personally to sell, or prevented from so doing. Where a worker has been deprived of this ability, as is the case with coolies, s/he has lost the capacity personally to commodify (or not commodify) his/her own labour-power. As noted above, in a capitalist system this process of separating workers from ownership of their sole commodity is for employers both a necessary and in many instances a last step in gaining control over the accumulation project.

Another consequence of the non-reading or misreading of these prefiguring contributions to the debate is a tendency to repetition, attributing only to recent publications arguments that have long been known about. Thus, for example, both Zeuske and van der Linden are mistakenly credited by Tappe and Lindner with the 'discovery' that unfree labour did not actually end with slave abolition, but continued long after because it contributed to capitalist profitability.[20] Because Tappe and Lindner assume that, with the exception of slavery, labour is free, they are surprised by the fact that many post-slave relational forms are unfree, to the extent of presenting this too as a 'discovery'. Hence the many references throughout the volume edited by Damir-Geilsdorf *et al.* to the existence of 'blurred boundaries' between slave and non-slave labour.[21] Had they not made this assumption, and accepted the free/unfree dichotomy, Tappe and Lindner (and others) might have avoided this mistake.

A similar mistake is made elsewhere and more recently by LeBaron and Phillips, who maintain – wrongly – that no attention has been paid to the role of the state in the reproduction of unfree labour.[22] As before, Marxist theory is

---

20   Tappe and Lindner (2016: 17, 18). For the same misattribution, see also Tappe (2016: 206). Others who mistakenly believe that it is they who have just 'discovered' that unfree labour-power is, after all, perfectly compatible with capitalist production include Graeber (2011: 351), Barrientos, Kothari and Phillips (2013), and Žižek (2016: 50–51).
21   Damir-Geilsdorf *et al.* (2016: 12, 17, 25–6, 50–51).
22   See LeBaron and Phillips (2018), who assert that there is 'very little scholarship' about the state/unfreedom link. It should be noted that this is not the first time they have made claims about a missing approach which, on subsequent examination (see Brass, 2014a), turn out to be unsustainable. Disregarding the presence of what is now a vast literature outlining in the clearest possible terms as to why unfree labour-power is acceptable to modern capitalist producers (= the class struggle argument), LeBaron and Phillips declare that 'there is a need for much greater clarity regarding why and how neoliberal globalization has contributed to the dynamics of contemporary unfree labour'. Equally bizarre is their insistence on the one hand that because the term 'is contentious', no attempt will

blamed for what they perceive as being an absent state ('[e]specially in recent Marxist scholarship on unfree labour, this has led to a certain invisibility for the state').²³ This is quite simply nonsense, and an astonishing claim to make, for two reasons in particular. First, an historical constant in most global contexts (India, the United States, Southern Africa, and Latin America) is the plethora of legislative ordinances issued periodically by the state – local and national, colonial and post-colonial, non-capitalist and capitalist, apartheid and non-apartheid – declaring specific forms of unfree labour either legal or illegal (and consequently abolished).²⁴ And second, Marxist theory has from the very outset always linked the reproduction of unfree labour-power to the role of the State, for the obvious reason that the latter institution is regarded as central to – and, indeed, a guarantor of – the continuing process of capital accumulation.²⁵

Ironically, having argued that what the state does or does not do is the component part missing from the dynamic in all recent analyses of unfree labour, and in their view ought to be central to any discussion about this production

---

  be made at conceptualizing unfree labour, yet on the other that they intend to 'resist the notion that there is a neat separation between "free" and "unfree" labour'. How is it possible to focus on the state/unfreedom link, having first refused to address debates over the meaning of unfree labour-power, then privileging one particular (and contentious) interpretation of this relational form?

23 Marxism was also the target of a previous claim by them (Barrientos, Kothari, and Phillips, 2013), to the effect that it was a theoretical approach which had failed to spot the capitalism/unfreedom connection, a claim shown to be incorrect (see previous endnote).

24 It is difficult to think of a single Marxist analysis of the South African apartheid labour regime that does not make the link between state agency and the reproduction of labour-power that is unfree. Legislative ordinances enacted by the state in India and Peru, all addressing the issue of bonded labour, are listed in Brass (1999: 33 notes 17 and 19), while details about the state/unfreedom link in Europe and North America are outlined in Brass (2011: Chapters 6 and 7). None of the latter is mentioned by LeBaron and Phillips.

25 Thus, for example, in a section entitled 'Soldiers as competitors of free labour', Liebknecht (1973: 53) – a Marxist – outlined at the beginning of the twentieth century how the state in Germany allocated soldiers (by definition unable personally to commodify their own labour-power) to rural employers facing labour shortages: 'Militarism is well aware, as a functionary of capitalism, that its highest and most sacred duty is to protect the employers' profits. So it considers itself quite free, even bound, officially or unofficially, to place the soldiers like beasts of burden at the disposal of the exploiting classes and especially of Junkerdom. This is meant to solve the problem of the shortage of agricultural workers, a shortage brought about by the inhuman exploitation and brutality to which they are subject.' More recent analyses of the state/unfreedom link – including ones by Marxists – extend from Davies (1979), Lacey (1981), Lichtenstein (1996), Hochschild (1999), and Brass (1999) – one section of which is entitled unambiguously 'Unfreedom, the Law, and the State' – to Marchal (2008), Brass (2010, 2011), and Das (2014, 2017).

relation, LeBaron and Phillips nevertheless misunderstand both how and why the role of the state has itself changed over time, and also the connection between the absence of the state and its agency. In the case of India, therefore, from initially opposing the presence of unfree labour during and immediately following the colonial era, because it was thought to be an obstacle to economic development, the present-day neoliberal state turns a blind eye to such working arrangements since these are recognized as contributing to profitability and thus also to the process of capital accumulation. There is, in short, no mystery as to the fact and cause of this shift on the part of the state: acute market competition between capitalist producers in an increasingly *laissez-faire* global economy, a commonplace in recent Marxist analyses of unfree labour.

Moreover, because they posit what is a false dichotomy between state agency and state absence, LeBaron and Phillips miss the chronological link between these two moments. Hence their complaint, both that the 'prevailing assumption in several strands of scholarship is that unfree labour occurs [due to] the *absence* of labour market regulation', that 'it is frequently presumed that unfree labour flourishes in the absence of the state, where regulation and enforcement are low or non-existent', and, finally, that '[a]n absence of regulation or the presence of the state…may well be connected with the incidence of unfree labour'.[26] Pace LeBaron and Phillips, there is no mystery whatsoever about this causal link, which appears to them as an issue only because of their failure to problematize the chronology: the state is absent precisely *because* of its earlier agency in stripping back or curtailing labour rights protected by legislation, once again a commonplace observation found in most – if not all – the recent Marxist analyses of the capitalism/unfreedom link.

4   Problems with Theory

Both van Melkebeke and Rodríguez García endorse the view that all those who work for others are subject to coercion, a position attributed to van der Linden who in turn attempts unsuccessfully to invoke the authority of Marx himself for the same view: namely, that 'anyone who works as an agent for a principal is unfree'.[27] For van Melkebeke, Rodríguez García, and van der Linden, therefore, the distinction between free and unfree labour-power does not hold. This is problematic, for four reasons. First it ignores the many affirmative references throughout the work of Marx not just to the existence of the free/unfree

---

26   LeBaron and Phillips (2018: 10, 16, original emphases).
27   van Melkebeke (2016: 188) and Rodríguez García (2016: 11, 27).

distinction but also to its crucial role in the class struggle.[28] Second, elsewhere van der Linden strongly rejects Marxist theory, insisting that it no longer has any explanatory role in the social sciences.[29] Third, in criticizing Marxism for privileging free wage labour as the capitalist relation of choice, it fails to distinguish between the semi-feudal thesis (which does) and the deproletarianization approach (which doesn't). And fourth, a result of epistemologically dissolving the free/unfree distinction is that – by declaring everyone a 'subaltern worker', regardless of whether those included in this category are free or unfree labour, or own/control means of production – it clears the way politically for the construction of multi-class alliances and epistemologically for the 'new' populist postmodernism.

Like van der Linden, therefore, van Melkebeke advocates locating petty commodity producers within the ranks of the proletariat, thereby considering an undifferentiated peasantry as part of the working class. Because they ignore long-standing and still relevant debates between populists and Marxists about the socio-economic differentiation of rural community and its political effects, both of them unwittingly reproduce the views of populists. Whereas the latter maintained that undifferentiated peasant economy was an innate organizational form (= peasant essentialism), Marxists by contrast, argued that in the course of economic development the peasantry was differentiated along class lines, its top stratum (= rich peasants) consolidating means of production and becoming small capitalists, while its increasingly landless bottom stratum (= poor peasants) joined the ranks of the proletariat.

The Subaltern Studies approach replaces class difference with an opposition between on the one hand the 'elite' and its 'state', and the on the other the 'masses'/'popular masses'.[30] The politically and sociologically problematic nature of the 'subaltern' is evident from its all-embracing social composition: among its ranks, therefore, are to be found 'the lesser rural gentry, impoverished landlords, rich peasants and upper middle peasants'.[31] The fact that it includes those whose *class* position and interest correspond to those of an agrarian petty-bourgeoisie, opposed historically only to certain kinds of capital

---

28 For details, see Brass (2011: Ch. 2).
29 Roth and van der Linden (2014: 445–485).
30 There are still those – for example D'Eramo (2013) – who, even now, persist in categorizing populist movements by the 'popular masses' as progressive, and the way forward politically, simply because the target of such mobilizations is *laissez faire* capitalism. What is forgotten is that opposition to capitalism can, and does, encompass components of the bourgeoisie who nevertheless are just as opposed to socialism.
31 For the social composition of the subaltern category, see Guha (1982: 8). The debate about the politics of the Subaltern Studies project is outlined below, in Chapter 7.

(financial, foreign) and not – as in the case of the proletariat – to capital *per se*, rightly identifies the 'subaltern' as an agrarian populist category.

Significantly, the category 'subaltern worker' also contains employers who oppress/coerce/underpay labour which is unfree. Although family and kinfolk deployed by the household head as substitute workers on coffee plantations in the Congo are labelled as 'non-wage labour' by van Melkebeke, it turns out that these replacements were in fact compelled to meet labour-rent payments owed by peasant tenants.[32] As is clear from what happens in other coffee-growing areas, it is at this grassroots level where coercion/unfreedom occurs, generated and enforced not by the state – which is where he locates the relational impetus – but from within the peasant household or kin group itself. Despite van Melkebeke arguing that rural families willingly chose such arrangements, and their preference for subsistence agriculture was the reason for low plantation wages, it transpires that there existed a strong demand for labour-power from local plantations, mines and urban enterprises.[33]

Employer competition for workers in the Congo noted in passing by van Melkebeke suggests that, had the labour-power of peasant family/kin been free, wages would have been much higher. It is precisely in such circumstances that commercial producers – among them better-off peasants growing cash crops for export – resort to unfree labour relations, not to bring a labour market into being but much rather to prevent it from developing. This dynamic is missed by van Melkebeke, because – like populist theory – he thinks of the rural family as composed entirely of 'natural' peasants; in short, he fails to differentiate the peasantry, and consequently subscribes to what is an essentialist view of smallholding agriculture. The latter reproduces the familiar trope – shared with agrarian populist, imperialist and NGO discourse – that all indigenous rural inhabitants throughout Africa are basically peasants, an identity which determines their ideology, economic strategies and political agency. That some form of worker consciousness and identity – however tentative – may have been emerging at the start of the nineteenth century in the Congo, even then, is not considered.[34]

---

32 van Melkebeke (2016: 189, 193, 197).
33 van Melkebeke (2016: 201, 204–5).
34 That a labour market already existed in the Congo at this early conjuncture, in which labour-power was offered for sale by its owners, is clear from a 1904 letter written by the British Consul (The National Archives, Kew, FO 367/4, fo 354–363, File 18348) which goes as follows: 'The unsatisfactory treatment meted out to the natives of the West Coast Colonies employed here in the Congo Free State induces me to ask your Excellency to use all means possible to dissuade men from your Colony from seeking employment in the Congo. The wages offered today are only one-fourth of what a man could earn a few years

Also not considered is the distinction between different Marxist approaches to the capitalism/unfreedom link, the result being that Rodríguez García dismisses Marxism *tout court*, both for equating free labour with the accumulation process and concluding that only such workers are able to organize in order to transcend capitalism.[35] On the grounds that free labour is 'rare', the efficacy of current anti-slavery and/or human rights campaigns and legislation is also dismissed, for two reasons in particular: because definitions of coerced labour 'have no legal standing' and consequently do not comprehend that 'trafficking is not a form of exploitation [but] a process'; and by virtue of the fact that current abolitionist discourse interprets unfreedom as a specifically non-Western phenomenon, confined to less developed countries.[36] The difficulties confronting these views are easily discerned.

To begin with, by dismissing Marxism for not recognizing that unfree production relations are compatible with accumulation, Rodríguez García follows van der Linden and van Melkebeke in ignoring the opposite Marxist view associated

ago...Men come here thinking to obtain employment for the good wages of the days of yore, only to find, to their surprise, that things have greatly changed; and, as they are without means to pay their passage back to their own Colony, they find themselves forced to accept an engagement on a contract for two years on the reduced scale. The men, once their contracts are signed, are liable to be sent to the far interior, where they are subjected to treatment almost amounting to military discipline. I am constantly receiving numerous complaints from...British subjects who are employed on the Great Lakes Railway beyond Stanleyville, and, if only one-tenth of those complaints is true, all means possible should be used to prevent the people of your Colony from coming here.' As set out in this letter, what is being described constitutes a shift from free to unfree labour: migrants are attracted to the Congo in order personally to commodify their labour-power, but are misled as to the wages/conditions on offer. Once in the Congo the low pay means they are unable to afford the return fare, and consequently are forced to sign up for a two-year contract at a low wage. Trapped in this manner, such migrants are then sent into the interior 'where they are subjected to treatment almost amounting to military discipline'.

35   Rodríguez García (2016: 11, 21–22, 23–24).
36   Among the reasons Rodríguez García (2016: 24ff.) objects to equating human trafficking with exploitation is that it entails an indiscriminate trawl of 'perpetrators', ending up indicting those not directly responsible for the unfreedom of others. What is overlooked here, however, is that it is precisely for this reason that – historically and currently – employers resort to intermediaries (labour contractors) or outsource recruitment/production (smallscale sweatshops) under the direct control of third parties. In this way, if the question of legality concerning production relations is raised, and with it the possibility of prosecution, capitalists can disclaim knowledge of what is occurring on the ground, and consequently shift responsibility and culpability onto those directly in charge of the labour process. Instances of this extend from carpet manufacturing in 1930s India to present-day clothing manufacturers who sign up to ethical codes and – when unfree labour is uncovered in the sweatshops to which production has been outsourced – proclaim ignorance of this fact.

with deproletarianization. The claim that all opposition to unfree labour fits it into a colonial framework, thereby defining coercion as a non-Western phenomenon, overlooks the fact that many Marxists – starting with Marx himself – have long argued that unfree labour-power is as much a feature of metropolitan capitalist nations as in so-called Third World nations, for the simple reason that it arises precisely where economic competition and class struggle are at their most acute. Again, the objection levelled at human rights legislative ordinances – that it targets individuals rather than the economic system – is yet another critique made during the earlier debate about unfree labour.

Privileging empiricism over theory, Rodríguez García advocates even more research into grassroots conditions because 'a micro-level approach…can provide more reliable…experiences of the persons concerned'. This, she maintains, would 'lead to a new legal framework that is based on a proper theory of coercion in labour relations rather than on pseudo-universalist discourses' that exclude 'cultural realities'. Not the least problematic aspect of this view is the inference that Marxism and what is termed 'pseudo-universalist discourses' are not themselves based on 'a proper theory of coercion in labour relations' derived in part from (and thus supported by) fieldwork at the grassroots. However, championing empiricism in this manner avoids engaging with the central question – the extent to which issues like unfreedom and exploitation can be 'solved' in a capitalist system – and simultaneously reveals the target of such an approach. The latter is not just Marxism but 'pseudo-universalist discourses', by which is meant political economy that addresses the very systemic processes reproducing coerced labour. In short, the framework espoused by Rodríguez García is – like the subalternism of van der Linden and Melkebeke – a 'new' populist postmodern one.

Privileging culture in this manner, Rodríguez García merely replicates a similarly problematic approach untaken earlier by Taussig and Prakash.[37] Each of the latter applied a postmodern framework to the analysis of unfree labour, and consequently recast debt bondage/peonage relations in India and/or Latin America as a benign form of cultural 'otherness'.[38] Like Rodríguez García, therefore, Prakash dismisses what he terms 'foundational' Marxism for focussing on 'the economic'; he regards the Eurocentric/Enlightenment/Emancipatory

---

37   Their arguments are examined critically elsewhere (Brass, 1999: Chapter 8).
38   The privileging of non-class identities, in the form of the 'otherness' of culture as distinct from the sameness of class, is central to postmodern theory. This is conceded (Ashcroft, Griffiths and Tiffin 1995: 125) in the following manner: 'We can…characterize postmodern thought…as that thought which refuses to turn the Other into the Same…post-colonialism is regarded as the need, in nations or groups which have been victims of imperialism, to achieve an identity uncontaminated by universalist or Eurocentric concepts and images.'

notion of class as inapplicable to the Indian countryside, and rejects this in favour of a postmodern approach which emphasizes the 'cultural' formation of labour. Because for him unfreedom is the significant and invented other of colonial discourse, Prakash concludes both that free labour is a correspondingly unacceptable embodiment of Eurocentric notions of human destiny, and that unfree labour was part of a 'real' India undisturbed by the coming/going of colonialism.

A similarly revisionist view of Latin American debt peonage is advanced by Roseberry in a collection endorsing the Subaltern Studies project.[39] That the latter has little of value to add to earlier analyses of unfree labour – see, for example, Bose – is evident from the fact that, even where the presence of coercion is acknowledged, the focus remains on the process of deculturation.[40] In another volume of the series, a contribution examining the dynamics structuring the recruitment of migrant indentured labour from northeastern India laments that '[a]ll the specificities of language, of religion, of proud histories of autonomy from sedentary states [were] wiped out rapidly and...replaced by a monolithic identity beaten out from the labour contracts [, this being] the logic of the civilizing mission of colonial capitalism'.[41] Such a view overlooks the degree to which, historically, colonial planters and other rural capitalist producers have followed a very different path, and encouraged ethnic/regional/tribal identity (in order to divide and rule the workforce) while simultaneously discouraging class solidarity (the political and economic effects of which employers feared).

In keeping with this kind of postmodern approach, Tappe and Lindner endorse the conceptualization by Müller and Abel of 'coolitude' – a positive interpretation of unfree labour – recommending the epistemology of 'cultural studies' and 'postcolonial theory' for providing 'cultural representations' of the coolie as a way of arriving at 'a new dimension in understanding' unfree labour.[42] This amounts to shifting the debate from unfreedom-as-a-disempowering-economic-relation to unfreedom-as-an-empowering-cultural-relation, or the displacement/downgrading of class analysis in favour of a postmodern one that focuses on 'from below' culture. Because unfree workers have a culture, they are deemed to be empowered, a familiar revisionist trope. From this it is but a short step to the claim made by cliometric historiography: namely, that because slaves and/or indentured workers had a culture, life on the

---

39   Roseberry (1993: 349–50).
40   Bose (1954).
41   Ghosh (1999: 18).
42   Tappe and Lindner (2016: 16); Müller and Abel (2016: 221).

plantation could not have been that bad, and consequently what existed there was a form of free labour, chosen by the working subject him/herself. Indeed, Tappe and Lindner accept that this focus on the culture of 'coolitude' is 'to promote a more self-conscious and affirmative stance towards this historically laden concept'.[43]

5 Butterfly Collecting

Dismissing what is termed 'standard definitions' of coerced labour as 'inconsistent', and because discussion of unfree relations is 'inevitably contentious', van der Linden asserts that consequently it is necessary 'to go beyond that' and look at all the empirical evidence – 'all forms of coerced labour' – in minute detail.[44] Tappe and Lindner similarly announce an intention to focus on 'diverse empirical cases' so as 'to avoid the dichotomy of free and unfree labour'.[45] Privileging empiricism in this manner, in the process downgrading or dispensing with theory, invites the same riposte as that made by the Thorners about the flawed methodology used by the First Agricultural Labour Enquiry in India, to the effect that 'if it is not clear what constitutes an attached labourer it does not matter whether [one] says that in a given state there are 1.3 per cent or 78 per cent of them.'[46]

In his well-known critique of the proliferating taxonomies that bedevilled anthropological theory, Edmund Leach termed this empiricist trend as 'butterfly collecting', a process having 'no logical limits', leading as it did to never-ending compilations of ever more patterns and sub-types.[47] According to Leach, therefore, what he described as a tendency to 'butterfly collecting' had become an end in itself, leading inevitably to the labelling of each particular instance as yet another ethnographic variant, different from all the rest in terms of inception, operation and effect. It is a critique that is particularly relevant to the attempt

---

43 Tappe and Lindner (2016: 25).
44 van der Linden (2016: 293–4).
45 Tappe and Lindner (2016: 10).
46 See Thorner and Thorner (1962: 187).
47 See Leach (1961: 2–4, 26), who concludes by noting 'the alarming proliferation of structuralist terminology [whereby] maximal, major and minimal lineages had been supplemented by medial, inner and nuclear lineages; effective lineages were distinguished from morphological lineages; social relations had acquired focal fields, vertebral principles and constellations of ties and cleavages'. What he objects to is not comparative analysis *per se*, a valuable and productive social scientific practice, but rather the elaboration of multiple sub-sets the distinctiveness of which turn out to be non-existent. As will be seen below, it is the latter which concerns us here.

by each of the approaches examined here to identify specific forms of bonded/coerced labour. For Tappe and Lindner, therefore, the object is to search out and catalogue 'historical variants of bonded labour', while van der Linden similarly dedicates himself to generating multiple taxonomies, in the process compiling numerous lists featuring many variables.[48]

Thus each of the 'three moments of coercion' pinpointed by van der Linden, consisting of entry-into, period-of, and exit-from work, subdivide into a plethora of mutant forms. Entry-into work gives rise to no less than ten, of which only one is 'actually voluntary'. Among the conditions leading to unfreedom, therefore, are: the hiring-out by an owner of slaves; self-sale or birth into slavery; debt, capture, and taxation. Once in work, a labourer toils according to 'compensation, conditional force and commitment'. Exit-from a work relation splits into seven variables, extending from obstacles imposed by an employer (debt repayment), via conditional discharge (age-related manumission), to unconditional cessation, such as casual work, flight (desertion) or death. The difficulty with these taxonomies is simply put: they are either factually incorrect or – as van der Linden himself agrees – overlapping.

Where casual workers are bonded labour because of loans taken from their employer, their capacity to exit from the production relation is conditional or blocked, and not unconditional, as categorized by van der Linden. Nor as he supposes is death 'the final and irrevocable termination of a labour relationship', since any outstanding debts owed by a deceased worker can be passed on to his kinfolk (sons, daughters) who then have to continue debt-servicing labour obligations. Almost immediately, moreover, van der Linden back-tracks, accepting that 'the distinction between these variants…is not always as clear-cut as it might seem', that there are 'many combinations and hybrid forms', and that 'my classification is more indicative than complete'.[49] Similarly, where the 'three moments of coercion' are concerned, he admits that the 'imprecise nature of our…classification is evident from the fact that, often, multiple combinations…are given the same label'.[50]

In the end, van der Linden concedes the fact that attempting to identify multiple variants always returns to a basic dichotomy – the free/unfree distinction – long known about and underlying the many forms composing his taxonomies.[51]

---

48 Tappe and Lindner (2016: 10–11); van der Linden (2016: 298ff.).
49 van der Linden (2016: 304–5).
50 van der Linden (2016: 314).
51 That he has not managed to transcend the way in which historically much political economy has conceptualized production relations as free or unfree is finally admitted by van der Linden (2016: 315) thus: 'I suspect that…entry and exit will prove to be of crucial

What matters in terms of definition, therefore, are not the variants themselves but the manner in which workers enter into and exit from production relations. Accordingly, generating multiple variants is at the root of his empiricist approach, itself a form of butterfly collecting. Acknowledging that his taxonomies are 'still rudimentary', van der Linden nevertheless asserts that 'coerced labour is a more complex phenomenon than is often thought', attempting thereby to justify the applicability of this empiricist methodology. What he fails to recognize is that 'still rudimentary' is *not* the problem, which is the attempt to see distinctions where none exist (along the lines of 'is a relation that is unfree at 9 in the morning still unfree at 9.05 am.'). From the viewpoint of political economy, both the definition and effects of the free/unfree dichotomy are *not* 'more complex than is often thought': much rather, the empiricist approach used by van der Linden runs the risk of attaching a different label to each specific instance of unfree labour encountered, the epitome of 'butterfly collecting'.

6   Conclusion

A common drawback encountered in social science disputes is the way earlier arguments are subsequently taken up in seemingly antithetical ways, combining a process of recycling with misinterpretation. Paradoxically, therefore, this kind of overlooking/misunderstanding – both of the debates themselves and their sources – can involve either taking for granted interpretations that have previously had to be fought for, alternatively downgrading their significance, or else ignoring them altogether. Where unfree production relations are concerned, discussion about their meaning, causes and systemic effects is of course necessary and continues, but this is not what each of these volumes does, adding not to existing interpretations and theory but only to the number of variants.

Ironically, therefore, and assertions by its exponents to the contrary notwithstanding, the empiricist categorization of production relations ends up conceding what it starts out by denying. Namely, that what structures both the definition and effects of all the variants identified is the simple polarity entry-into/exit-from the work arrangements concerned, a dichotomy which in turn informs the difference between labour-power that is free and that which

---

importance, while the way in which labour is extracted in the intervening period is of secondary importance and largely derived from these two elements. Of overriding importance [in determining the definition of unfreedom] is how labourers are recruited, and under what conditions they can leave.'

is unfree. Consequently, all attempts to define production relations in terms of multiple variants and causes in the end prove fruitless, and epistemologically fail to advance the debate about systemic change.

Part of the difficulty concerns the way unfree labour features in a wider paradigm shift, and how what is claimed to be new theories displace Marxist interpretation of the same relation. The fact that these had long epistemological lineages, firmly rooted in conservative discourse of the nineteenth century has not prevented their endorsement by many on the left, in the misplaced belief that such 'new' frameworks amounted to a more radical alternative to Marxism. Caught up in this paradigm shift was a debate to which Marxist theory has made substantial contributions: that about development in the so-called Third World, and in particular how production relations changed and what this presaged for revolutionary agency leading to a socialist transition. Among the results of an empiricist focus, therefore, is a failure to address is the negative impact on the existing working class – its formation, consciousness, struggle – of labour-power that is unfree.

Unfamiliarity with the debate about free/unfree labour has in turn led to raising as 'new' problems requiring explanation issues that have in fact been addressed previously and satisfactorily by Marxist and non-Marxist political economy alike. Linked to this are the burgeoning definitions of what constitutes unfree labour-power, unconnected with political economy, the resulting confusion licensing a proliferation of variants and theories. Hence the invocation of concepts such as 'subaltern' worker, the perception of rural families as composed of 'natural' peasants, and the labelling of unfreedom as a form of cultural 'otherness'. In short, all the tropes associated with the 'new' populist postmodernism, the epistemology is considered in the chapter which follows.

CHAPTER 7

Other Priorities, Other Identities: Unmasking the Subaltern

'We were now back in the pleasant high-class area. "That row of ten houses belongs to the Minister of Construction", she said. "They are let to different embassies at three thousand a year each". So what, I said within myself. Your accusation may be true but you've no right to make it. Leave it to us and don't contaminate our cause by espousing it'.

An unspoken exchange between an American woman in a fictional West African country, and an inhabitant of the latter, as outlined by Chinua Achebe.[1]

∴

1 Introduction: (Armchair) Generals Go to War

Where culture is concerned, many on the left have subscribed, wholesale, to an uncritically endorsing mode, adopting thereby a 'new' populist postmodern approach instead of – as argued by Marxism – one based on political economy. It was as a response to this specific cause that the critique of the Subaltern Studies project outlined below emerged. Among the reasons for this was the realization that many of the things which were being said about unfree labour in the Third World, notably that it corresponded to a benign relationship which had traditionally provided rural workers with a 'subsistence guarantee' and was thus empowering for the subject concerned, were also being said – in some cases by the same people – about the peasantry, agrarian change, and the dynamics of rural mobilization in less developed countries.[2]

Accordingly, a consideration of the influence exercised by the 'new' populist postmodernism on academic debates has throughout the preceding chapters been confined mainly to the way it structured interpretations of production relations in rural contexts, and more generally of the wider labour regime. The

---

1 Achebe (1966: 60).
2 This issue, which has been examined by me elsewhere in numerous publications (see, for example, Brass 2003), surfaces also in previous chapters.

focus in what follows shifts to a particular approach – the Subaltern Studies project – that shaped what its adherents maintained was a radical alternative to Marxist theory about peasant movements and society in Indian history. By promoting nationalism and quotidian resistance, the project contributed substantially to the banishment from leftist arguments of the twin Marxist concepts, revolution and socialism. Hence the view taken here, that the nationalist tone informing the Subaltern Studies project is incompatible with socialist internationalism, while its privileging of everyday-forms-of-resistance as the preferred (and most effective) form of 'from below' agency is similarly irreconcilable with the concept of revolutionary action.

However, the subsequent realisation by some adherents of the political direction taken by the 'cultural turn', and the consequent attempt to distance themselves from the Subaltern Studies project by claiming to have 'unmasked' its postmodern trajectory reveals the same difficulties – an intellectual trail exhibiting seemingly anomalous inconsistencies – that accompany the transfer of a radical Marxist critique from the margins to the academic mainstream.[3] This claim mimics what occurs after every great military victory in history, which is invariably followed by another, and usually fiercer, struggle (= the battle of the memoirs), this time between the generals on the winning side, in which each commander disputes the events and chronologies on the battlefield with the object of demonstrating that success was due to him alone. Perhaps the most famous historical example is the story told by Herodotus in Book Eight of *The Histories* of how, following the defeat by the Greeks of the Persian fleet at the battle of Salamis, in a ballot held by the triumphant commanders to decide which of them was responsible for the victory, each individual named himself first and Themistocles second, thereby unintentionally divulging the identity of the person actually responsible for the defeat of the Persians. Something akin to this is now happening in the academic world, where squabbles appear to be breaking out in recent anthologies and monographs over who can

---

3 Generally speaking, the margin/mainstream distinction is structured in the following way. The margins encompass contributors to the journal *Social Scientist*, the uncompromisingly Marxist approach of which generates discomfort among mainstream academics. Also on the margins, for much the same reason (on which see Brass, 2017b: 63–65), is one of those mistakenly categorized as belonging to the so-called new Cambridge School. In the academic mainstream, by contrast, are found the postmodern contributors to the Subaltern Studies project on the one hand, and on the other most of those thought to belong to the so-called new Cambridge School. Among the latter, it should be emphasized, are those – Bayley, O'Hanlon, and Washbrook – who, although part of the academic mainstream, have not drawn on concepts/ideas formulated on the margins.

rightly claim first to have identified the pre-figuring epistemology (and thus to have unmasked the politics) of the Subaltern Studies project.[4]

There are five reasons for commenting on the subsequent reaction to the debate about the Subaltern Studies project.[5] The first is that monographs by Sarkar and by Vanaik, and the collection edited by Chaturvedi, all represent an initial assessment of the political and theoretical impact of the project.

---

4 In the period following the original publication of the critique outlined in this chapter, yet more commentators have lain claim to the 'unmasking' of the Subaltern Studies project, in the process ignoring or overlooking those who had done this very thing much earlier. One such is Chibber (2013), another late-comer to the discussion, who – because in the words of a reviewer (Chowdhury, 2014: 547) he 'displays little interest in previous critical interrogations of the Subalterns' work [nor] does Chibber pay attention to previous Marxist criticisms of the Subaltern Studies project' – repeats many of the points raised by the preceding critique without adding much that is really new to the debate. A similar kind of objection – that Chibber provides 'a great deal of evidence and counter-argument [against the Subaltern Studies project], amplifying contentions found in others before him' – is made by Brennan (2014: 73). Another is Kaiwar (2015: 85 note 211) who – unlike Chibber – refers briefly to the Chaturvedi volume about the Subaltern Studies project, but – like Chibber – omits to mention the presence there of a prefiguring Marxist critique. Many of the arguments deployed by the latter – among them the populist nature of the project's anti-modern discourse ('post-colonial populism'), its perception of local agency and agrarian myth discourse ('archaic designations of the world') as empowering, and the fact that the project has 'Volkisch potentialities' – are found also in his analysis (Kaiwar, 2015: 128, 135, 147, 333, 365). These silences are curious, not least politically, since both Chibber and Kaiwar are described by Vanaik (2017: 17) as 'non-dogmatic Marxists'. The expectation is that the latter would, of course, not just be aware of but also make reference to earlier critiques by those espousing the same political approach.

5 Although this chapter draws on a critique that originally appeared in *The Journal of Peasant Studies* (28/1, 2000), a publication where much of the discussion about the project appeared, the points it made then are if anything more relevant now. Interestingly, in an updated edition of his original book, Vanaik (2017: 17) announces that he has removed the previous section on the Subaltern Studies project – the very portion criticized by me initially in the review of 2000 – because in his opinion Kaiwar and Chibber have covered all the issues ('the most powerful and scrupulously argued critique of those key theorists of the Subaltern Studies group ... has rendered further criticism otiose'). All the endorsing references to Sarkar found in the 1997 edition have vanished: in the 2017 edition, mention of his work – minus endorsements – has been relegated to a single footnote. Although Vanaik fails to mention the existence of that 2000 review, or indeed of the earlier Marxist critique by a member of the so-called second Cambridge School, and the fact that the same critique has appeared in many articles and books since then, it is clear that note has been taken of such earlier arguments. What has remained consistent throughout, however, is the continuing attempt by him at a nationalist appropriation of the critique: hence the silence about the objections to the Subaltern Studies project emanating initially from the so-called new Cambridge School (= 'the Western intelligentsia'), and the attribution of the same critique first to Sarkar and now to much later accounts by Chibber and Kaiwar.

The second is that, to some degree, each of the contending parties has written its rivals out of the despatches announcing victory, and it is to rectify this that a commentary is necessary. The third is that, because some of the claims to victory are framed in thinly-disguised nationalist terms, what follows is an attempt to restore the idea that the process of unmasking was – and could only ever have been – an international undertaking. The fourth is that the influence of the project has helped steer the object of development towards quotidian resistance in furtherance of empowering national/cultural/ethnic identity, and thus away from class formation/consciousness/struggle, and with it revolution aimed at a socialist transition. And fifth, the *volte face* on the part of one contributor to the Subaltern Studies project illustrates clearly the contradictions structuring an intellectual trajectory when a critique is transferred from the margins to the academic mainstream.

2 Subaltern Conquests

About the importance and global intellectual impact of the Subaltern Studies project itself, there is no disagreement whatsoever.[6] Associated most closely with the eponymous six volume series edited by Ranajit Guha that appeared over the 1982–89 period, it was an historiographical approach initially to South Asia, the focus of which was the interpretation (or re-interpretation) of grassroots agrarian mobilization and in particular the rural 'voice from below' during the colonial era.[7] Challenging the tendency to depict the peasantry as

---

6 The extensive bibliographies in all the texts considered here attest to the continuing sway exercised by the Subaltern Studies project. During the 1990s the latter ceased to be confined to the historiography of south Asia and was extended to include the study of Africa and Latin America (Latin American Subaltern Studies Group, 1993; Cooper, Mallon, Stern, Isaacman, and Roseberry, 1993; Prakash, 1994; Mallon, 1994; Cooper, 1994; Lowe and Lloyd, 1997; Joseph, LeGrand and Salvatore, 1998; Nugent, 1998). The reasons for the intellectual acceptability of the Subaltern Studies project to those in the academy are complex, and have to do with the rejection by many intellectuals/academics of universal categories associated historically with a progressive and forward-looking anti-capitalism, and a corresponding retreat into the national/regional/local/ethnic particularisms/identities that have long been the preserve of a backward-looking, romantic anti-capitalism (on which see Brass, 2000: Ch. 4; Brass, 2014b). In specifically institutional terms, this has been due partly to what Ahmad (1992) has termed the politics of migrancy, or the privileging of the migrant intellectual ('the figure of exile') whose discourse is actually nationalist, and partly to what Petras (1990) has identified as the recolonization of erstwhile organic intellectuals in the Third World by metropolitan capitalist funding and/or research agencies.

7 The first Subaltern Studies volume edited by Guha was published in 1982, and the last in 1989 (Guha, 1982–89). The series continues, but under a different editorship (Chatterjee and

passive and thus unquestioning accepters of its own subordination, the project sought to rescue and give an expression to this hitherto ignored form of ideological utterance. Among the easier academic conquests effected by the Subaltern Studies project were development theory and development studies, a rapid and largely unopposed occupation which took the specific form of the re-essentialization of the peasantry in postmodern analyses of the Third World.[8]

Neither is there much disagreement now as to the political direction taken by the Subaltern Studies project, a fact which emerges clearly from the approaches examined in this chapter. Opposed to Eurocentric metanarratives, which were equated with colonialism and thus also with the Enlightenment discourse of rationalism and progress, the Subaltern Studies project eschewed materialism and political economy: in terms of theoretical orientation, therefore, it was not just against class, Marxism, and internationalism, but – more significantly – its discourse also prefigured the specifically culturalist ideology that characterized the global rise of the 'new' populism, nationalism and conservatism which became prevalent from the 1980s onwards.[9] It was this

---

Pandey, 1992; Arnold and Hardiman, 1994; Amin and Chakrabarty, 1996; Bhadra, Prakash and Tharu, 1999; and Mayaram, Pandian, and Skaria, 2012). Among the more important monographs by contributors to the Subaltern Studies series are those by Guha (1974, 1983), Chatterjee (1986), Chakrabarty (1989), Pandey (1990), and Hardiman (1987; 1996). The kind of presentation undertaken by some of the contributors to the Subaltern Studies project has itself metamorphosed. Mimicking the guest appearance in the entertainments industry, a part of which they have now become, these interventions increasingly take the form either of celebrity interviews ('tell us once more Gayatri, just how wonderful you are ...') or celebrity forewords to collections by fawning admirers ('it gives me great pleasure to introduce yet another publication about everyday forms of resistance ...').

8 Now that the term 'a postmodern development theory' is at last being recognized by non-Marxists (and a few rather more shamefaced Marxists) as an oxymoron, a different process is unfolding. Some of its erstwhile exponents have changed their minds during the late 1990s, and have themselves begun to write critiques of postmodernism, recognizing rather late in the day a contradiction between it and the concept 'development'. Those who have done this include not just small fry – compare, for example, Corbridge (1990; 1994) with Corbridge (1998), and Lehmann (1990) with Lehmann (1997) – but also important and influential intellectuals such as Rorty, who espoused postmodernism yet accepted subsequently (Rorty, 1998) that a consequence is an inability to theorize about issues such as inequality, and Hobsbawm, who now finds it necessary to question his earlier views about the demise of class and class consciousness as neo-liberalism marched forward (see Chapter 9 below). In such later accounts, mention of the fact that other Marxists (and Trotskyists in particular) have been saying just this (postmodernism = depoliticization) for a very long time is made – if at all – only in footnote form.

9 For critiques of culturalist analyses of rural mobilizations in India, see the contributions in Brass (1994) and also the text by Sinha, Gururani and Greenberg (1997). The early defence by Chatterjee (1983: 64–65), an exponent of the project, against a non-existent accusation of

process of unmasking, of an epistemology the intellectual project shared with unconnected populist and/or conservative political mobilizations in India (the new farmers' movements, the Hindu chauvinist Bharatiya Janata Party) and elsewhere, which constituted the victory now claimed by rival generals.

What the disagreement is about, therefore, is which of the victorious generals, or contending parties, was responsible for this unmasking. The intellectual history of the Subaltern Studies project is already being rewritten, and a number of surprising candidates are being allocated (or are allocating themselves) a starring role in exposing its political lineage. Among the present claimants, three groups (some self-constituted, some not) in particular can be identified: accordingly, the process of unmasking is attributed, variously, to those outside India, in the form of the *New Left Review* and a second Cambridge school, while others maintain that the most effective critique involved scholars in India only, specifically an early critical reaction from the journal *Social Scientist*, while yet others argue that such a critique emanated from within the Subaltern Studies itself.

3   Nationalist Appropriation 1: Cambridge and England

Just as for some the demise of the Subaltern Studies project was a consequence of a twofold internal critique, within the Subaltern Studies itself and within India (see below), so an anthology edited by Chaturvedi identifies behind this same famous victory a different set of heroes. These, it is inferred, come from the *New Left Review* and also from a new Cambridge school of Indian historiography.[10] As someone who is identified as belonging to the latter, and who did indeed participate in the debate about the political antecedents and direction

---

  being a populist suggests that perhaps he was aware all along of the real nature of the discourse which structured Subaltern Studies.

10 These claims form the subtext of the introduction by Chaturvedi (2000) to the anthology. Hence the numerous references contained in the footnotes of the latter to those writing in or associated with the *New Left Review*, the inference being that much of what was said either by or about the Subaltern Studies project was prefigured there. For example, both the Gramscian influence and analogous debates within Marxism are traced to the *New Left Review*, which is then credited with discovering the same kinds of the transformations that were also taking place within the project (Chaturvedi, 2000: ix, xi, xvii note 34, xviii note 50, and xix note 52). Although Chaturvedi (2000: xviii note 43) concedes that '[s]cholars examining the international reception of Gramsci's writings were unaware of ... debates in India', the *New Left Review* itself is not blamed for a similar lack of awareness.

of the Subaltern Studies project, this comes as something of a surprise.¹¹ That either the *New Left Review* or a self-consciously new Cambridge historiography were by themselves solely responsible for the demise of the Subaltern Studies project is a claim that does not survive even a cursory inspection.

Not the least of the many ironies surrounding the role of the *New Left Review* are the following. First, it has been notably silent on the subject of the theoretical precursors, the political meaning and the implications of the Subaltern Studies project throughout the initial period of the debate about these issues. Consequently, a discussion about – let alone an engagement with – the issues raised by this debate have been largely absent from its pages.¹² And second, it was the *New Left Review* itself which was responsible originally for the introduction of much post-structuralist theory to an English-speaking audience, and thus also (and directly) for the academic rise both of postmodernism and – indirectly – of the Subaltern Studies project.

Hints about the existence of a second Cambridge school are equally misplaced. Itself a target of the Subaltern Studies discourse, the older Cambridge school was inculpated for categorizing colonialism as hegemonic, and thus ignoring or downgrading 'from below' resistance by the subaltern to colonial rule.¹³ Associated with the work of historians such as Anil Seal and Eric Stokes, the original Cambridge school was in the words of Ranajit Guha 'a strategy aimed at characterizing colonialism as hegemonic dominance'.¹⁴ Scholars in

---

11 Hence the view (Chaturvedi, 2000: xii, xviii note 47) that '[t]he most systematic engagement with the project came from scholars with ties to the University of Cambridge'. The latter are identified by Chaturvedi as C.A. Bayley, Tom Brass, Rajnarayan Chandavarkar, Rosalind O'Hanlon, and David Washbrook.

12 With the exception of Brennan (2014), the *New Left Review* has carried no detailed analysis of the Subaltern Studies project. Articles published in that journal during the 1980s that were specifically about political debate in India – for example by Vanaik (1986) – unaccountably made no mention of its existence. Things were little better in the 1990s, when only one article published in the *New Left Review*, about nationalism and communalism in India – again by Vanaik (1992: 46, note 3) – made any mention of Subaltern Studies, and even this was merely a passing and politically neutral reference to an early anthology.

13 In the light of this, the observation by one group of Indian scholars (Singh *et al.*, 1984: 5) is instructive: 'If Guha's [methodological] dictum is followed, the national movement vanishes and is replaced by so many struggles for local grievances. Methodologically there is little to distinguish this from the so-called "Cambridge School" with its search for caste, religion and factional identities which constitute the logic of peasant consciousness'.

14 See Guha (1989: 305ff.), who then proceeded to accuse all political viewpoints in the UK – even the socialist *History Workshop Journal* – of subscribing to the 'imperialist historiography' of the Cambridge School. While the latter claim is obviously incorrect, this view nevertheless demonstrates clearly the strength of feeling about the subject. The views of the original Cambridge School are to be found in Seal (1968), Stokes (1978), and the collections

India would rightly object to the suggestion that the political significance of the Subaltern Studies project eluded everyone until Cambridge pronounced on the topic; they would interpret this as an unjustified attempt not just at a nationalist appropriation but also – and perhaps more importantly – as merely the continuation of long discredited colonial attitudes.[15]

No second Cambridge school of Indian historiography exists.[16] Given the problematic status of one of its members, Raj Chandavarkar, as a contributor to the original critique of the Subaltern Studies project, the notion of a new Cambridge school becomes even less plausible.[17] For no intellectually justifiable reason, therefore, Chaturvedi reprints a text about Thompsonian influence on the Subaltern Studies project by Chandavarkar; not only is the latter a very latecomer indeed to the debate, but (perhaps because of this) he does not say anything that has not already been said before.[18] By positioning Chandavarkar's text early in the anthology (the contributions appear roughly in the order they were published), Chaturvedi compounds this difficulty, and inadvertently creates a doubly misleading impression: that Chandavarkar was not merely central to the debate (in the words of Chaturvedi, one of those who undertook '[t]he most systematic engagement with the project') but also that his was one of the initial critiques levelled at Subaltern Studies. The suspicion remains that the inclusion by Charturvedi of this superfluous text by Chandavarkar, at the expense of a single contribution from the earlier *Social Scientist*

---

edited both by Leach and Mukherjee (1970) and by Hasan and Gupta (1993). For a number of reasons, the elite/subaltern dichotomy, which structures the dispute between what are basically rival nationalist historiographies (the original Cambridge School, the Subaltern Studies project) is false. The objection, by exponents of the Subaltern Studies approach, that because the Cambridge School focused on elites it underestimated the existence/extent of 'from below' resistance to their rule, is correct; however, equally correct is the riposte from members of Cambridge School that the Subaltern Studies approach ignores the degree to which this 'from below' resistance was itself differentiated along class lines.

15 Such an interpretation is not dispelled by the inclusion in the anthology edited by Chaturvedi (2000: xiii) of not a single contribution from the *Social Scientist* discussion of the Subaltern Studies project.

16 For my part, I have never met O'Hanlon or Bayley, let alone discussed the Subaltern Studies project with them.

17 The text in question is Chandavarkar (1997). Given that the latter not only adds nothing new to earlier criticisms of the Subaltern Studies project, but was also published some fifteen years after the critique by the *Social Scientist* contributors and nearly a decade after that by other members of the so-called new Cambridge School, the intellectual reasons for its inclusion in the anthology edited by Chaturvedi are non-existent. When reference is made in this chapter to the critique by members of the so-called new Cambridge School, therefore, this designation does not include Chandavarkar.

18 The pre-figuring influence on the Subaltern Studies project of E.P.Thompson's 'history from below' – the subject covered by Chandavarkar – was noted by many of the early participants in the debate (see below).

OTHER PRIORITIES, OTHER IDENTITIES: UNMASKING THE SUBALTERN   161

discussion, is merely to bolster the inference about the (spurious) existence and role of a Cambridge connection.[19] It also constitutes an attempt to identify as a participant in a critique a contribution that does not fall within this category: in short, to a claim by a contributor from the academic mainstream to have been part of a critique that originated on the margins.

4   Nationalist Appropriation II: Delhi and India

If the claim that the Subaltern Studies project fell to non-Indian critiques emanating from the *New Left Review* or a second Cambridge School are mistaken, then so are a rival set of claims made by (or on behalf of) a different group of generals: namely, that the most effective critique was an internal one, emanating mainly (and perhaps even solely) from within India and the Subaltern Studies project itself. The nationalist subtext is that no one was aware of the political direction this discourse was following until the occurrence of an epistemological break in what was hitherto a progressive series, when an 'internal dissident' himself identified the problems and left the project. The latter is a view advanced by three commentators in particular, two of whom have written monographs considered here: Sumit Sarkar, Achin Vanaik and (to a lesser degree) T. V. Sathyamurthy.

The nationalist tone of the observations by Sathyamurthy, Sarkar and Vanaik is impossible to disguise, and takes a double form: downgrading, dismissing or simply ignoring earlier critiques which emanated either from non-Indian scholars or from outside India, and simultaneously privileging criticisms which were made only much later, and originated not just in India but emerged from within the Subaltern Studies project itself. Accordingly, Sathyamurthy defends the Subaltern Studies project against the critiques by Bayley – dismissed as 'slight and superficial' – and by O'Hanlon, who is accused of 'basic misunderstandings'.[20] He also endorses the defence mounted by its exponents against Marxist critiques, inaccurately describing the responses by Chatterjee and Chakrabarty as 'persuasive, lucid and undogmatic'.[21] That Sathyamurthy is engaged in a nationalist appropriation is evident not just from his endorsement of a national path of development but also from his insistence that 'the

---

19   That texts by those at Cambridge feature prominently among the commentaries on the Subalterns has more to do with the relative ease such academics have in publishing their work, due mainly to the way in which most journal editors evaluate submissions from this particular institution ('if *x* is at Cambridge, then it follows that what he/she writes must be good/sound', etc.).
20   See Sathyamurthy (1990: 139–40, note 1).
21   These references are to Chatterjee (1983) and Chakrabarty (1985).

most radical [and] major contradiction of the world' was between nationalism and imperialism and not capital and labour.²²

In much the same vein, Bayley's critique is located by Vanaik at 'the less generous end of the spectrum', and conflated with what is slightingly referred to as the reception of the project by 'American academia'.²³ The hostility to the latter implied in the comments by Vanaik, whose anti-Americanism remains latent, emerges into the open in those made by Sarkar, for whom the uncritical reception accorded the postmodernized project by those in 'the West' was determined by preference of 'the Western intelligentsia' for 'material [about South Asia] conveniently packaged [and] without too much detail or complexity'.²⁴ Not only does Sarkar fail to differentiate 'the West', therefore, but he adopts a nationalist discourse which, if it came from a member of 'the Western intelligentsia', he would be the first to label as 'Orientalist' or worse.

This nationalist appropriation is accordingly dependent on the invocation of an exclusionary discourse. Hence the inference that no one who is not an Indian national can possibly understand India, which is as a result intellectually accessible solely to those who reside there and correspondingly inaccessible to those whom Sarkar labels perjoratively as belonging to 'the West'. Noting that E.P.Thompson took a special interest in India, therefore, Sarkar commends him for his 'modest' approach when writing about 'a country and culture about which he [Thompson] knew little'.²⁵ In this respect, Sarkar continues, Thompson was 'very different from a growing number of academics

---

22 Hence the reference by Sathyamurthy (1998: 1448) to 'home-grown models' and 'home-grown modalities of change'.
23 See Vanaik (1997: 183, 227 note 117).
24 For his latent anti-Americanism, see Vanaik (1997: 183). In an attempt to explain why microstudies were superceded by postmodernism, Sarkar (1997: 95) comments: ' ... there was further the fact that this was emphatically not the kind of South Asian history that could win easy acclaim in the West, for its reading demanded, if not prior knowledge, at least the readiness to try to grasp unfamiliar and dense material, thick descriptions which were not at the same time exotic. One does get the strong impression that the majority among even the fairly small section of the Western intelligentsia interested in the Third World prefers its material conveniently packaged nowadays, without too much detail or complexity'. This is in every respect an astonishing, not to say outrageous, statement, a prime example of chauvinistic nonsense. To begin with, it was those connected with the Subaltern Studies, such as Sarkar, not 'the Western intelligentsia', who concocted and then presented to the world the image of India-as-exotic-'other'. As will be seen below, this was the view from which Sarkar himself did not dissent until very late, when – in conjunction with Indian scholars connected to *Social Scientist* – some members of this self-same reviled 'Western intelligentsia' (Inden, Bayley, O'Hanlon, and Brass) had already objected to this very process.
25 See Sarkar (1997: 62).

OTHER PRIORITIES, OTHER IDENTITIES: UNMASKING THE SUBALTERN 163

today who stride confidently across countries, continents and centuries, armed with the simple talismans of theory'. This nationalist subtext is reinforced by the claim, also by Sarkar, that the footnotes in the article by O'Hanlon 'clearly demonstrate that the initial debate around the [Subaltern Studies] project had been entirely within South Asia', the inference in this case being that she was merely passing on the critique embodied in the views of scholars in India.[26] The logical outcome of these exclusionary arguments is that the most successful critique of the Subaltern Studies series was an internal affair, located within India and the project itself.[27]

Among the more bizarre claims advanced in this connection, therefore, is one – made both by Sarkar and also by Vanaik – to the effect that the initial and most powerful critique of the Subaltern Studies project was the internal one mounted by Sarkar himself.[28] The latter now insists not just that there were 'the glimmerings of an alternative approach' within the Subaltern Studies project, but also that his own work ('an essay of mine') was part of this oppositional discourse.[29] For some unaccountable reason, Vanaik has adopted the role of cheerleader in making these claims on Sarkar's behalf: namely, that it was the latter who first identified the complicity between on the one hand anti-Enlightenment epistemology, the postmodern discourse of the Subaltern Studies, and an emphasis on cultural 'difference', and on the other the

---

26 See Sarkar (1997: 84 note 4).
27 Having invoked the existence of an earlier Indian critique of the Subaltern Studies project in order to lambast the 'Western intelligentsia', however, Sarkar then sidelines the former and passes quickly onto what for him is clearly the more significant dissenting voice in India – his own 'internal critique'.
28 These claims are set out in Sarkar (1997: 82ff.) and Vanaik (1997: 182, 224, note 106; 1998). 'Going against the views of my ex-colleagues in the Subaltern Studies editorial team', proclaims Sarkar (1997: 85), 'I intend to argue that the trajectory [of the project] has been debilitating in both academic and political terms'. The extent to which Vanaik relies on Sarkar's own account of the victorious battle waged against Subaltern Studies is evident from numerous references of the 'Sumit says ...' variety: for example, '[a]ccording to Sarkar ...', 'I have relied heavily here on S.Sarkar ...', '[m]any agree when Sarkar says ...', '[a]nyone familiar with Sarkar's various writings on this subject will recognize the measure of my indebtedness to him', 'Sumit Sarkar, the original and most important dissident ...', 'Sarkar points out ...', etc., etc., etc. (Vanaik, 1997: ix, 184, 185, 186, 224 note 106, 227 note 121, 228 notes 126 and 132). In what is a fulsome – and inaccurate – assessment, Vanaik (1997: 224 note 106) observes: 'Sumit Sarkar's various critiques of the Subaltern Studies School are simply the best and most comprehensive we have today. In addition to the logical force of his arguments, Sarkar's views have the additional authority of being the first and most sustained "internalist" critique'.
29 For this claim, see Sarkar (1997: 93).

rightwing/conservative Third World nationalism of the BJP/VHP/RSS.³⁰ It is to the sustainability (or otherwise) of such claims that we now turn.

Given the contending views about the unmasking of Subaltern Studies, it is necessary to ask about the kinds of reading undertaken by the three categories which commented on the project. With what aspects did each agree and disagree, and what passed unnoticed? In short, what in the Subaltern Studies did the first reception (within India, by the *Social Scientist*), the second (outside India, by members of the so-called Cambridge School), and the third (within and outside India, by Sarkar, Vanaik, Sathyamurthy) either condemn or endorse, and why? Although the element of chronology (the timing of the critique) is obviously important, it is argued here that political considerations (a perception of nationalism as 'progressive', a failure to identify postmodern discourse as reactionary) are more significant.

5   Critique of a Critique

The contributors to the initial discussion in India about the Subaltern Studies, which appeared in the CPI(M) linked journal *Social Scientist* during the early 1980s, all made valuable and significant observations.³¹ For example, Chopra rightly emphasized the importance of class collaboration by subalterns with elites, particularly where kinship/caste ties existed, while Alam questioned the nature of the peasant autonomy which Subaltern Studies claimed existed.³² In much the same vein, Singh and others accused the project of imbuing peasant rebellion with something akin to an a-historical Hegelian *geist*, a process whereby 'the development of history is the march towards the self-realization of this spirit'.³³ Similarly, in his wide-ranging review of comparative approaches to working class history, Bhattacharya issued a timely reminder that the historiography of the voice-from-below was neither new nor necessarily leftwing

---

30   Hence the claim made by Sarkar (1997: 44), a recent convert from the editorial team of the Subaltern Studies series, that 'I have argued ... that the shift towards criteria of indigenous "authenticity" and "community" can constitute, however, unwittingly, certain dangerous common discursive spaces, for already some of the more sophisticated ideologues of Hindutva have started using similar categories and arguments'.

31   Not only was the earlier interpretation by the contributors to the *Social Scientist* intellectually far more acute than that made subsequently by Sathyamurthy, Sarkar, and Vanaik, but – unlike the latter – no attempt was made to give this a nationalist tinge.

32   On these points, see Chopra (1982: 61) and Alam (1983: 47, 50ff.). The attempt by a Subaltern Studies contributor (Chatterjee, 1983, 1986) to rebut these criticisms was unpersuasive.

33   See Singh *et al.* (1984: 4). The methodological critique of Subaltern Studies undertaken by these contributors to the *Social Scientist* is particularly impressive.

in its political orientation.³⁴ These were serious criticisms, and indicate the extent to which the *Social Scientist* discussion – broadly speaking, on the margins of academia – accurately identified some of the basic flaws in the Subaltern Studies project.³⁵

The same can be said of the contributions which were published outside India later in the same decade. Although a consideration and assessment of the Subaltern Studies project outside India is widely regarded as having started with the texts by Bayley and O'Hanlon, both of which were published in 1988, this overlooks an earlier text on the subject by Inden, which arrived at roughly similar conclusions.³⁶ Examining the application specifically to India of Orientalist discourse, Inden argued rightly that at the centre of the latter was the essentialization of caste, which in turn led to a crisis of representation (of the Eastern/Other by the Western/Self). Consequently, Indology robbed India of human agency, by monopolizing representations of 'the Orient' and essentializing its inhabitants in terms of immutable defining characteristics and/ or institutions (caste, village, religion, family).³⁷ Both the overlap between the discourse of the Subaltern Studies and the new right was noted by Bayley, and also its potential appropriation by communalism.³⁸ Like Alam, Bayley also questioned the existence of an autonomous grassroots consciousness untainted by any 'from above' (= elite) political agendas, and argued that more emphasis should be put on the effects of peasant differentiation. Again like the *Social Scientist* reviewers, O'Hanlon equated the approach of Subaltern Studies with that of a Hegelian *geist*, and warned against the affinities such a discourse had with communal identity.³⁹

---

34 Bhattacharya (1983: 5).
35 It should be noted that there were some Indian scholars – for example, Gupta (1985) – not connected with the *Social Scientist* who also made interesting and valuable critical observations about the Subaltern Studies project at the same time as the *Social Scientist* discussants. Equally, there were others – for example, Ramachandra Guha (1989) – who uncritically endorsed the project at that same conjuncture.
36 Inden (1986). The latter is mentioned only in passing by most commentaries on the response outside India to the Subaltern Studies project.
37 For these points, see Inden (1986: 403, 428–29, 436, 440–41). 'Caste', he notes (Inden, 1986: 428), 'is assumed to be the "essence" of Indian civilization. People in India are not even partially autonomous agents. They do not shape and re-shape their world ... The people of India are not the makers of their own history. A hidden, substantialized agent, Caste, is the maker of it'.
38 See Bayley (1988: 113).
39 O'Hanlon (1988: 201–02, 210). In a subsequent text O'Hanlon (1993: 258–59) pinpoints different approaches to communalism as one of the issues which divides her and Bayley from the Subaltern Studies project. For one stalwart of the latter (Pandey, 1990), therefore, communalism is an effect largely of colonialism and the colonial state, whereas Bayley

These positive aspects in the critique of Subaltern Studies should not blind one to the presence of negative ones: specifically, what both the internal and external reception should have said but did not, and should not have said but did. The causes of symptomatic absences/silences on the part of the *Social Scientist* discussion are attributable not just to its earliness but also to its politics. Sections of the Left in India continued to believe, wrongly, both that capitalism was absent, and that 'progressive' elements of the national bourgeoisie should be supported. Because an indigenous bourgeoisie was opposed by international/monopoly capital, the argument went, the former could and should be won over in order to participate with workers in a national democratic state. For this reason, these same sections on the political left shared with Subaltern Studies an idealized view of nationalist discourse, in which the latter was perceived as actually/potentially politically 'progressive' on account of its opposition to pre-capitalist institutional forms, to imperialism and to Eurocentricity.[40] On account of their opposition to the latter, therefore both Chopra and Bhattacharya were among those contributing to the *Social Scientist* discussion who welcomed the appearance of the Subaltern Studies project.[41]

Hence the Indian bourgeoisie is categorized by Chopra as a subaltern class, and he accordingly suggests that there were two sets of exploiters: a reactionary elite, composed of landlords and external colonizers, and a progressive one, in which rich proprietors led peasants against planters and landlords.[42] This conceptual framework is reproduced by other contributors to the *Social Scientist* discussion, for whom the struggle is between a peasant/worker alliance on the

---

locates the seeds of communal discord much earlier, in the pre-colonial era. A denial of the latter, however, leads to the invocation of a pristine/'authentic' peasant selfhood which informs the pre-colonial golden age of the nationalist myth: namely, that until disrupted by colonialism, what existed in India was an harmonious rural idyll.

40   To categorize this opposition in terms of Europe versus the 'other' is not merely misplaced but also hints at the presence of a nationalist politics. In Europe, no less than in non-European contexts, this kind of thinly-veiled nationalism, masquerading as oppositional discourse, also occurs (on which see Brass, 2000; and Brass, 2014b). By labelling the 'other' discourse to which one is opposed as 'Eurocentric', however, it is possible to delineate the divide in terms of nationality and culture rather than class.

41   See Chopra (1982: 55) and Bhattacharya (1983: 16 note 23). If members of the so-called Cambridge school are open to the accusation from the Subaltern Studies and the Indian Left that they are 'soft' on colonialism (see above), then both the latter categories are vulnerable to the counter-accusation (from Bayley and O'Hanlon) that they, in turn, are 'soft' on nationalism. Although they agree with neither view, other kinds of Marxism are nevertheless located by the so-called new Cambridge School in the camp of the Subaltern Studies project, and *vice versa*.

42   See Chopra (1982: 62ff.), where the absence of capitalist development is attributed in turn to the continued existence in Indian agriculture of pre-capitalist relations of production, an argument which is central to the semi-feudal thesis.

one hand and colonialism and foreign capital on the other.⁴³ In a similar vein, Alam talks about incomplete transition to capitalism, and attributes the late colonial survival of the idea of peasant community to the fact that capitalism did not destroy pre-capitalist modes of exploitation.⁴⁴ Insofar as some Marxists continue to insist on the absence from agriculture of capitalism and the unbroken dominance of pre-capitalist (or semi-feudal) relations, therefore, capitalism must for them remain a politically progressive force; consequently, their oppositional discourse also remains trapped in nationalist ideology not so different from that of the Subaltern Studies project.

6   Difference and Sameness

The subsequent welcome extended by those outside India, by contrast, was due to the absence of a political framework. Having outlined and criticized the essentialist approach of Romantic Orientalism, Inden proceeded to endorse the Subaltern Studies project as the way forward, despite the fact that the latter is merely the latest manifestation of this same discursive tradition.⁴⁵ Like Inden, Bayley limited his analysis to Subalterns, broadly welcomed the project, and concluded on the optimistic note that if 'the great volume of good work ... can be ... reintegrated with other types of history, then something very interesting might well emerge'.⁴⁶ Much the same point was made by O'Hanlon.⁴⁷

---

43   See Singh *et al.* (1984: 18, 22, 25, 31). Ironically, given its opposition to the Indian left, the Subaltern Studies project is also structured by a similar distinction between a progressive and non-progressive nationalism. Having adopted the familiar elite/subaltern dichotomy, therefore, Hardiman (1981) then goes on to argue that, unlike that of its elite counterpart, peasant (= subaltern) nationalism was indeed progressive.
44   On this point, see Alam (1983: 51ff.). Most significantly, this view is also shared by exponents of the Subaltern Studies project, as one such admits (Chatterjee, 1983: 63).
45   See Inden (1986: 430ff.) for the description of what he refers to as 'Romantic Orientalism'. About the latter he observes: 'The romantics take those very features of Indian civilization which the utilitarian-minded criticize and see as worthless and find them worthy of study and even praise. The very ascetic practices, philosophies, cosmologies, customs, visual art forms, and myths which the utilitarian or materialist finds wasteful [or] deluded, the romantic idealist takes up with great fascination ... The romantic typically takes the stance not of a supporter of Western values and institutions, but of a critic of them ... there is a decided propensity on the part of the idealist to see internal *spiritual* factors as decisive' (original emphasis). All this, however, is followed by the view (Inden, 1986: 445) that 'Indians are, for perhaps the first time since colonization, showing sustained signs of reappropriating the capacity to represent themselves', in support of which he cites Subaltern Studies as an example.
46   See Bayley (1988: 120).
47   O'Hanlon (1988: 190).

Confronted with a seemingly novel approach to from below agency, but attempting to evaluate this without a politics, therefore, Inden, Bayley, and O'Hanlon could not but approve a seemingly progressive attempt to analyse grassroots mobilization.[48]

Unsurprisingly, this welcome extended to those epistemological elements subsequently identified as postmodern and/or populist. Accordingly, Chopra saw nothing wrong with a Gramscian analysis, despite its current appropriation by the political right.[49] While Chopra was correct to argue that in India communalism was a discourse imposed from above, he was wrong to conclude that it had no purchase on those below, on the 'organic solidarity of village community'.[50] In a similar vein, the *Social Scientist* review of the second volume was rather too optimistic politically when it suggested that a 'latent anti-imperialism [existed] within communal consciousness'.[51] Reviewing the second volume in the series, allegedly before postmodern theory colonized the project, commentators writing in *Social Scientist* nevertheless recommended French structuralism and the work of Foucault as offering 'meaningful insights' to those interested in a working class 'voice from below'.[52]

Much the same is true of O'Hanlon, who in a review of the first four volumes in the series insisted that Foucault's 'attack on humanism's subject ... has

---

48   This dilemma – how to evaluate Subaltern Studies while eschewing politics – is neatly captured by Inden. Having accepted the illegitimacy of the Orientalist claim to 'know' India and Indians better than they 'know' themselves (Inden, 1986: 408), he can then follow one of two paths: either invoke another 'external' framework (which is what Marxist political economy does), and risk being accused that he is still trying to 'know' India/Indians better than they 'know' themselves; or accept the self-definition of the rural grassroots. This same dilemma is subsequently addressed – but not solved – by O'Hanlon and Washbrook (1992).
49   On the Gramsciism of the political right, see among others Forgacs (1984), Levitas (1986) and Sunic (1990: 29ff.).
50   Chopra (1982: 59).
51   Singh *et al.* (1984: 21). Concepts such as class and class struggle are incompatible with a post-structuralist/postmodern celebration of grassroots empowerment. For Foucauldian postmodernism, class is doubly unacceptable: not merely is it equated with an Eurocentric metanarrative, but it also categorizes the subject as victim. In much of the development theory influenced by postmodernism (not just the subaltern, but also postcolonialism, everyday forms of resistance, eco-feminism), therefore, it is no longer possible to present the 'other' (= tribals, women, slaves, bonded labourers, ethnic groups) as victim, since this is perceived as demeaning and/or disempowering. Accordingly, as 'victimhood' is equated by postmodern development theory with passivity, and as self-empowerment on the part of the subject negates victimhood, the rejection of passivity through the devictimization of the subject entails among other things the abandonment of class identity.
52   See Singh *et al.* (1984: 28).

been extremely fruitful and liberating'.[53] In his review of the first four volumes, Bayley denied both that cultural essentialism was part of the Subaltern Studies project, and also that the latter possessed a theoretical framework (he was wrong on both these counts).[54] And although Bayley recognized the populist element, its connection with Gramscian, Maoist and French post-structuralist theory went unremarked.[55] Despite pointing out that Subaltern Studies shared a discourse with the political right, Bayley then *contrasted* subaltern struggles with the way in which the new right perceived such grassroots agency as religious and nationalist, whereas in fact the former are frequently about the latter. Inden went further, and professed that his own assessment of the project was actually influenced by the work of Gramsci, Foucault, and Derrida, a position which in effect precluded a critique of postmodernism.[56] Although in order to restore to the 'other' his/her agency, Inden proposed to de-essentialize caste, village, religion, family, he nevertheless failed to differentiate 'the other', who consequently remained monolithic and uniform, thereby reproducing the very stereotype that Inden himself criticized.[57]

Again like Inden, Bayley failed to see Subaltern Studies as part of a much broader, and politically less benign, trend both within and outside the academy: namely, the post-1968 re-emergence of conservatism in a neo-liberal guise, a process seemingly compatible with (even supportive of) grassroots choice of empowering culturalist and non-class identities, a populist approach combined with a simultaneous attack by postmodernism on enlightenment and development. These links were made during the early 1990s by Brass who, instead of regarding peasant essentialism, populism and postmodernism as theoretically anomalous, took a far more pessimistic view.[58] Linking not just

---

53 See O'Hanlon (1988: 208–09, 219–20). In keeping with this view, O'Hanlon (1988: 190–91) maintains both that the challenge posed to existing historiography by Subaltern Studies was unconnected with post-structuralism and, further, that the project has affinities with Marxist attempts to recuperate peasant consciousness.
54 Bayley (1988: 111).
55 Bayley (1988: 112).
56 For this point, see Inden (1986: 402, 410, 421).
57 See Inden (1986: 421). Ironically, he criticizes the theory of 'Oriental Despotism' for regarding self-sufficient villages composed of peasants as 'the distinctive economic (and social) institution of the East', and then goes on to endorse Subaltern Studies, many of whose exponents invoke the very same image of independent peasant smallholding as the distinctively economic 'other' of (western) capitalism, and hence by inference the authentically Indian rural 'self'.
58 See Brass (1991). The latter text argued that it was now possible to trace a common epistemological and politically conservative lineage from the new social movements and the Subaltern Studies project, both strongly influenced by postmodernism, back through the 'moral economy' argument, the middle peasant thesis, and 'resistance' theory, to neo-populist concepts which structure Chayanovian theory of peasant economy.

Subaltern Studies but also the 'new' social movements framework and resistance theory to populism and postmodernism, this argument was that such absences/presences were not accidental but symptomatic, and that what was on offer from this combined discourse was not a progressive but a reactionary form of anti-capitalism. Consequently the project could not be regarded as a welcome development.

This Marxist critique, which in certain crucial respects differed from that of the earlier *Social Scientist* contributors, rejected the inference that culture, ethnicity and 'difference' were somehow 'discovered' by the postmodernist 'new' populism, and were therefore concepts about which Marxism and Marxists had remained silent.[59] Marxism and Marxists, it was argued, had long pronounced on these issues, but – unlike postmodernism and the 'new' populists – had insisted that without reference to the class position of those involved, it was impossible either to understand different forms of 'difference', or to explain why culture took the form it did, or why some forms of identity but not others surfaced at particular moments. It was pointed out that to treat phenomena such as culture, ethnicity and 'difference' generally as innate, and thus as inexplicable in terms of relations beyond themselves, as postmodern 'new' populists seemed intent on doing, was to indulge in the most fundamental form of idealism, a procedure that forbade analysis and allowed only description.[60]

7 'A Reiteration of the Already Said'

Unlike those who took part in the earlier *Social Scientist* discussion, none of those who subsequently attempted a nationalist appropriation of the critique can claim that insufficient time had passed for a fundamental political appraisal of the Subaltern Studies project. In their initial enagement with the latter, therefore, Sathyamurthy, Sarkar, and Vanaik all omitted to criticize the emerging postmodern discourse. Since they all failed initially to spot the postmodern/populist trend, it is in a sense unsurprising that they now deny its presence when earlier they commented on or participated in the project. It is,

---

59 The existence of theoretical and political differences within Marxist reactions to the Subaltern Studies is something that most commentaries on the debate generated by the project have overlooked or ignored (e.g., Sivaramakrishnan, 1995: 421 note 13).

60 It is one thing to *describe* class as 'foundational', it is quite another to *demonstrate* that class is inapplicable. Since the latter is something 'new' populist postmodernism cannot do, because the analysis of class is so obviously central to any understanding of the development process, 'new' populist postmodernists are reduced to reciting meaningless mantras in the hope that this will be mistaken by the more gullible for theoretical analysis.

however, impossible to argue – as do Sathyamurthy, Sarkar, and Vanaik – that an epistemological break separates the early (= 'good') volumes in the Subaltern Studies series from the later (= 'bad') and postmodern ones.[61]

It is clear from what one exponent wrote in an early defence of the project that a postmodern epistemology (against universals, the idea of progress, and Enlightenment rationalism) was inscribed in Subaltern Studies from the very start.[62] As has already been noted, Vanaik failed to spot this trend in his contributions to the *New Left Review*, while the case of Sathyamurthy is even more problematic. His dismissive comments about the earlier analyses of Bayley and O'Hanlon notwithstanding, Sathyamurthy's own analytical judgement appears to be little better. Although he covered the first six volumes of the series, therefore, he made no reference to the influence – let alone the political implications – of postmodernism on the Subaltern Studies project.[63] The work of Spivak, for example, was noted without any mention of its postmodern framework, Sathyamurthy being content merely to describe her approach (inaccurately) as 'Marxist feminism'.[64]

Most problematic, however, is the case of Sumit Sarkar, a one-time contributor to and editor of the 'new' populist Subaltern Studies project, and the claims made (both by him and on his behalf) concerning the dissident nature of his role in the project. Accordingly, there are a number of reasons for questioning claims to the effect that he represented an 'alternative voice' within the Subaltern Studies project, and as such departed once the postmodern trend became

---

[61] Claims about the existence of an epistemological break separating the early/social-historical/'good' volumes in the series from the later/postmodern/'bad' ones take the form, for example, of the many references found in Sarkar (1997: 20, 41, 42, 45, 46, 88, 90, 93, 95, 98, 106, 107, 360) to a contrast between 'early Subaltern Studies' on the one hand and 'late Subalternism', 'recent Subaltern Studies', and 'today's Subaltern Studies'. 'The achievements of the early years of Subaltern Studies', the same source (Sarkar, 1997: 85) notes, 'need to be rescued', an unsurprising view given that it was in these 'early years' that his own work appeared in the series. Among those who subscribe to an early = good/late = bad view of the series is Vanaik (1997: 180ff.), who observes that 'the freshness and importance of Subaltern Studies as a different kind of Indian historiography was established in those early years'.

[62] Hence the following admission by Chatterjee (1983: 61): 'It is precisely this sort of framework, which the dominant strands of Marxist history-writing in India share with nationalist historiography, that Subaltern Studies has set out to criticize. One hardly needs to be apologetic if, at the fag end of the twentieth century, one find it difficult to subscribe to the ideas of "progress" or "reaction", those naive and unproblematic notions of universal history, born out of Enlightenment rationalism'.

[63] For the relevant section, see Sathyamurthy (1990: 131–39).

[64] See Sathyamurthy (1990: 132, 135).

manifest.⁶⁵ To begin with, Sarkar was a member of the editorial team (= someone who 'participated equally in every detail of planning and editing') from volume III up to and including volume VII of the series, long after the theoretical and political trends to which he now objects were already well-established.⁶⁶ Furthermore, his critique of the project emerged for the first time only in 1994, some while after the same objections had already been raised by a number of scholars outside the Subaltern Studies project.⁶⁷

Nor do Sarkar's claims to have been an early oppositional voice within the series withstand much scrutiny.⁶⁸ Despite an insistence that in his contribution to volume III he was challenging the elite/subaltern polarity and the search for 'subaltern autonomy' by 'arguing ... against over-rigid application of binary categories', therefore, the passage in question indicates clearly that Sarkar was *defending* and not attacking the concept 'subaltern'.⁶⁹ It is also

---

65   According to Sarkar (1997: 82), the epistemological break in the discourse of the project took place only after volumes VII and VIII, when in his view the series became too focussed on 'community consciousness' and religion.

66   Contributions by him appeared in volumes III and VI of the series (Sarkar, 1984; 1989), and Sarkar's active participation as a member of the editorial team is acknowledged in volume III (Guha, 1984), volume IV (Guha, 1985), volume V (Guha, 1987), volume VI (Guha, 1989), and volume VII (Chatterjee and Pandey, 1992). As an admirer of his work states (Vanaik, 1997: 224 note 106), '[h]e was one of the major figures ... of the editorial team'. Significantly, volumes IV and V, both of which Sarkar helped to edit, already carried symptomatically Foucauldian/postmodern contributions by Spivak; if he objected to the latter developments as strongly as he (and others) claims he did, why then did Sarkar not resign from the editorial team in 1985 or 1987, rather than when he did, only after the publication of volume VII in 1992?

67   For the date of his critique, see Sarkar (1997: ix, 44 note 89, 65 note 34).

68   Sarkar (1997: 104 note 58) does indeed give the impression of suffering from amnesia when he dismisses the Subaltern Studies project as 'a reiteration of the already said', claiming not only that a critical anti-colonial historiography long antedated the series but also referring the reader back to his own writings on the subject. This claim is repeated by Vanaik (1997: 182). Two questions immediately suggest themselves: first, why did he not point this out earlier, when quite happily subscribing to the discourse of the project? And second, this very point – about the long historiographical tradition preceding the Subaltern Studies – was indeed made earlier, but by Bhattacharya in the initial *Social Scientist* discussion (see above) and not Sarkar.

69   In support of his claim that he challenged the search for an autonomous subaltern and the elite/subaltern conceptualization, Sarkar (1997: 90 note 18) refers the reader to a section of his article in volume III of the series (Sarkar, 1984: 273–76). That he is not attacking but defending the concept 'subaltern' is evident from comments there to the effect that 'it does have the advantage however of emphasizing the fundamental relationships of power, of domination and subordination', and further that 'the subaltern concept [does not] exclude more rigorous class analysis where the subject or material permits it'. Clearly, Sarkar wished not merely to retain the concept but to allocate it epistemological primacy:

OTHER PRIORITIES, OTHER IDENTITIES: UNMASKING THE SUBALTERN 173

impossible for him to sustain the view that '"fragment" and "community" were important for these essays, but in ways utterly different from what has now become the dominant mode within Subaltern Studies', when a central argument in his current critique is precisely that 'fragment' and 'community' were essential components of postmodern discourse.[70] The non-dissenting nature of the contributions by Sarkar is reinforced by other evidence contained therein. Hence the fact that Sarkar eventually became highly critical of Foucault cannot disguise his earlier endorsement of this same theoretician.[71] Much the same is true of his attitude towards Ranajit Guha, where a similar dissonance exists between the initial supportive comments from Sarkar and his subsequent highly critical view.[72]

Of the many ironies structuring claims made by those forming the third reception of the Subaltern Studies project, three are worth mentioning. First, the kind of Marxism Sarkar now defends, the 'from-below' historiography of E.P.Thompson, is in many important respects no different from the postmodern 'new' populism informing the Subaltern Studies project.[73] Hence his view that '[t]he more essentialist aspects of the early Subaltern Studies actually

---

other concepts – such as class – were acceptable only insofar as they remained compatible with the 'subaltern'. In a revealing aside, Sarkar (1997: 90) observes in parentheses that, even when oppositional, 'I notice, for instance, that I had *quite inconsistently slipped* into the same language' as those to whom he was opposed (emphasis added). This is nothing more than a linguistically disingenuous attempt to put a positive spin on his epistemological complicity, by conveying the impression that his presence in the Subaltern Studies series/discourse was somehow anomalous/accidental (= 'quite inconsistently slipped'), and that in reality he was not actually part of the project.

70   On these points, see Sarkar (1997: 93–94). It is noteworthy that Sarkar (1997: 21, 98) now makes extensive reference to the historical exponents of rural 'community' (for example, Herder, the Narodniks, and the Slavophiles) without, however, providing any indication of what was said by them about the peasantry, where, when, and why.

71   Hence the contrast between current hostility towards Foucault (Sarkar, 1997: 67, 84, 91, 101, 105) and the earlier statements supportive of his views (Sarkar, 1989: 31).

72   Compare, for example, Sarkar (1989: 18 note 51) with Sarkar (1997: 85, 92). Sarkar (1997: 92) has the temerity now to criticize Guha's contribution to the first volume in the series as 'an *unnoticed* drift' (emphasis added) towards nationalism present at the start of the project. As has been argued above, it *was* noticed, and by virtually all the early commentators on the Subaltern Studies project – except Sarkar.

73   Hence the view (Sarkar, 1997: 51) that the relevance of E.P.Thompson 'continues, in some ways more than ever before, and that many moves away from "Thompsonian" social history [by the Subaltern Studies] have been simplistic and retrogressive'. For similar views, see also Sarkar (1997: 63, 79). Thompson's 'history from below' as a prefiguring discourse was noted right from the outset of the debate, in Indian and non-Indian contexts alike: by, among others, Bhattacharya (1983: 4–5, 13, 16 note 22) in his contribution to the *Social Scientist* discussion, as well as Bayley (1988: 113) and O'Hanlon (1988: 193 note 8, 198).

indicated moves away from the Marxian Worlds of Thompson and Gramsci', which suggests that both the latter are regarded by him as part of the solution, not the problem.[74] Sarkar's denial notwithstanding, Thompson's 'moral economy' framework is indeed a regressive and potentially reactionary form of anti-capitalism which romanticizes the pre-capitalist past.[75] Like the Subaltern Studies project itself, therefore, 'moral economy' allocates primacy to customs, traditions, culture and practices as these already exist within the peasantry and the working class, a view which contrasts with that of Marxists who have tended to emphasize the backward-looking, politically reactionary and historically transcendent role of much of what passes for resistance based on an already existing 'popular culture' (racism, nationalism, religion).[76]

The second irony concerns Vanaik, whose enthusiasm for Sarkar's warnings against the rise in India of the political right and the overlap between the discourse of the latter and the Subaltern Studies project contrasts markedly with his own earlier position on this subject.[77] Initially, therefore, it was Vanaik himself who decried a connection between European fascism and the Indian political right (BJP ≠ fascist), when some of those external critiques of the

---

74   Sarkar (1997: 88). For the difficulties with Gramscian theory, see above.
75   See Sarkar (1997: 61, 78) for an avowal that a Thompsonian framework is 'free from nostalgia', and a corresponding denial that it amounts to 'the romanticizing of the pre-modern'.
76   Other historians with strong links to the project (Hardiman, 1996: vii, 254, 261–62, 270) have found no difficulty in retaining Thompson's 'moral economy' framework within a Subaltern Studies discourse, alongside that of Gramsci and Foucault. Not the least problematic aspect of 'moral economy' is that it, too, depoliticizes the link between consciousness and action. Like postmodernism, it licenses the reification of every form of belief, which can then be subsumed within an all-embacing rubric of 'subaltern consciousness' (e.g., Hardiman, 1987). In contrast to Marxism, therefore, for which existing rural grassroots traditions/institutions generate the false consciousness (e.g., caste/community/religious solidarity) that misinforms/misleads/deflects 'from below' class struggle, both postmodernism and 'moral economy' recast these same non-class ideological forms in a positive light, and regard them as making a positive contribution to (non-class) grassroots agency. The falsity of consciousness applies not so much to perceptions of a problem (rural workers are indeed aware of the existence of oppression, injustice, etc.) as to perceptions of what can be done to remedy the situation. That is, the desirability/feasibility/possibility of specific political solutions (fascism, racism, and bourgeois democracy instead of socialism or communism) to the problem which exists and of which they are aware. The corollary of the view that there is no such thing as false consciousness is that all consciousness is true, a position akin to the neo-classical economic argument that individual 'choice'/'preference' is exercised on the basis of 'perfect knowledge', and about as convincing.
77   In keeping with his initial contribution to *New Left Review* (see above), therefore, in an earlier book Vanaik (1990) fails to consider the Subaltern Studies project in terms of the implications for political discourse in India of its postmodernism.

Subaltern Studies project were making precisely this point (BJP = fascist).[78] The final irony is that, nearly a decade later, although Sathyamurthy accepts that the Subaltern Studies project has been 'highjacked by rarefied postmodernist new-speak', he follows Sarkar and insists, wrongly, that such a description applied only to the later part of the series (in his case to volumes published after 1992).[79] Like postmodernism, moreover, Sathyamurthy attacks both the Enlightenment project and Marxism, and ends up advocating the framework of the Subaltern Studies project itself (the poor versus those-who-are-powerful) and also the 'new' populist agency of the new social movements.[80]

8 Conclusion

As in other cases examined in previous chapters, among the things the debate about the Subaltern Studies project illustrates is how a more radical theory formulated on the Marxist margins (by some connected either to the *Social Scientist* or to the so-called new Cambridge school) is subsequently transferred into the academic mainstream (postmodernists who belonged to the project), in the process accompanied by an incorrect assertion to have espoused such a view all along. Having subscribed to a 'new' populist postmodern approach, and then seeing it criticized effectively from those on the Marxist periphery, therefore, one particular contributor to the Subaltern Studies project attempted to draw back by claiming – wrongly – that he had been an early critic within the project itself.

This aspect helps explain why each of the approaches considered in this chapter is characterized by a curious set of absences/presences. Hence the bizarre nature of the multiple exclusions from the critique of the Subaltern Studies project. Most notably, of the *Social Scientist* contribution, by almost everyone: by Sarkar after a cursory reference, by Vanaik, and also by Chaturvedi. Similarly excluded (either largely or wholly) are the contributions by members of the so-called new Cambridge school, again by Vanaik and Sarkar. Equally bizarre, however, are the inclusions within the critique: on the one hand of Chandavarkar by Chaturvedi, and on the other of Sarkar, by Vanaik and also by Sarkar himself. The result is that – rather like the claims made by the victorious commanders about their role in the defeat of the Persians at Salamis – the

---

78 For his questioning of a fascist/BJP link, see Vanaik (1994).
79 For the claim that only from volume VII onwards did the Subaltern Studies series endorse postmodern theory, see Sathyamurthy (1998: 1451, note 3).
80 For these views, see Sathyamurthy (1998: 1448, 1449, 1450; 1999).

account of the unmasking of the Subaltern Studies project contained in each approach is correspondingly partial, in both senses of the term (incomplete and also onesided).

There is no Themistocles missing from the memoirs written by the generals who took part in this famous battle, and that is precisely the point. (If there was, it would most certainly be the ghost of Marx, hovering over the various stages of the debate).

Claims to the contrary notwithstanding, therefore, no single individual (or group of commanders) was responsible for unmasking the Subaltern Studies project; rather, it was from the beginning a collective and international effort, built on a cumulative critique to which the participants in the *Social Scientist* discussion within India and the members of the so-called new Cambridge school (and others) outside India all contributed. The problems at this stage derived from political considerations: an over-optimistic political assessment on the part of the critical reaction within India, and the absence of a politics in the case of the critique from outside India. Due to the anti-imperial/anti-colonial discourse of the project, and its focus on grassroots agency, therefore, both the Subaltern Studies series and also the postmodern epistemology were welcomed by some of the *Social Scientist* commentators and the so-called new Cambridge school, a critical reaction which stemmed from a common (and mistaken) perception of the voice-from-below as necessarily progressive.

This welcome by some participants notwithstanding, the various critiques published within and outside India from the early 1980s to the early 1990s nevertheless raised crucial questions concerning the epistemology and/or methodology of the Subaltern Studies project. In particular these focussed on the existence/efficacy of peasant autonomy, claims regarding the newness and politically progressive nature of the voice-from-below, and the class identity/collaboration of those in the subaltern category. The critical reaction at this conjuncture, mainly by the *Social Scientist* and also by the so-called new Cambridge school, also voiced warnings, against the populist and/or nationalist direction of grassroots mobilizations undertaken by the subaltern, as well as the dangers inherent in a discourse the latter shared with reactionary communal elements and those on the political right. The link between the latter and postmodern theory also emerged from this process, thereby offsetting (and atoning for) the unwarranted optimism.

By contrast, most – if not all – these issues were ignored initially by those who eventually composed the third, and much later, critique. Missing from these earlier analyses undertaken by those who commented on or remained within the Subaltern Studies series were precisely references to the anti-Enlightenment epistemology of postmodernism, and the fact that arguments about the cultural 'difference' of the 'other' at the centre of the project were difficult to distinguish from ultra-conservative forms of Third World populist and nationalist ideology. Having rectified this omission from the mid-1990s onwards, there followed a discernible myopia with regard to the fact that these same issues were pointed out in the early critiques, not least by those on the Marxist margins. Ironically, therefore, many of those who then stridently point to the presence of reactionary elements structuring the discourse of the Subaltern Studies, and unjustifiably condemn others for not noticing these, had themselves made precisely this same mistake earlier, when – as commentators on or participants in the project – they also failed to identify this same trend. Accordingly, those forming the much later critique not only 'reiterate the already said', but have also – and unfortunately – tended to downplay the international character of the critique (emphasizing instead its national origin or identity) as well as the important role in this of the initial Indian contribution.

PART 3

Alternatives to Revolution?

©ANNA LUISA BRASS

CHAPTER 8

Betraying Revolution (Again)

> 'We must begin with the mistake and transform it into what is true ... To convince someone of what is true, it is not enough to state it; we must find the *road* from error to truth'.
> An observation by LUDWIG WITTGENSTEIN.[1]

⁂

> '... it is not possible to write a good history of a revolution without understanding it, and, therefore, in some degree sympathizing with it – unless, of course, a revolution is regarded as a pathological or criminal phenomenon – which is not merely unhistorical but monstrously arrogant'.
> An observation by RAYMOND POSTGATE.[2]

∴

1   Introduction: Revolutionary Socialism as the Fifth Horseman

At times it seems there is little to separate the approaches considered in the previous part from that pursued by non- and anti-Marxist academics whose views are examined below in this chapter, with reference to the way the centenary of the 1917 Russian revolution has been marked in the media and popular culture of western capitalist nations. The unambiguous condemnations by these non- and anti-Marxist academics, not just of revolutionary agency designed to realize a socialist transition, but also of Marxist political theory generally, at least have the merit of being both explicit and consistent. No attempt is made by them to hide their contempt for Marxism, and their hostility both to socialism and to direct action undertaken by a working class intent on carrying out a systemic transcendence of capitalism.

Just as happened in the case of the 200th anniversary of the 1789 French revolution, so the centenary of the 1917 Russian revolution is being marked by

---

1 Wittgenstein (1979: 1, original emphasis).
2 Postgate (1920: vii).

publications depicting it in negative terms.³ Each of these two revolutionary episodes is presented by revisionism as a regrettable occurrence, a systemic anomaly of little meaningful historical significance beyond an unimportant *jacquerie*, generating no political or economic achievement of lasting worth.⁴ Opportunities have not be lost by revisionist texts to insert the events of 1917 into a wider and familiar narrative about what-a-dreadful-mistake-revolution-is: in the wake of established forms of counter-revolutionary demonization, long lines of academic grave-diggers-of-Marxist-theory have already queued up to reinforce this approach, condemning any/every form of socialism, and will doubtless continue to do so after the centenary has passed.⁵ Meanwhile, such views are accompanied in the real world by the continuing rise and rise of the far right populist mobilization associated with Le Pen, Farage, Trump *et al*.

Addressed here, therefore, is the following contradiction: between on the one hand the presence of auspicious conditions favouring 'going beyond' a neoliberal economy, yet on the other the seeming undesirability/impossibility

---

3   A brief note explaining why this chapter has the words 'Betraying Revolution' in the title is in order. Although it might be objected that the article has nothing to do with the 1920s Trotsky/Stalin debate, this would be akin to saying Isaac Deutscher ought not to have used the quotes from Machiavelli's *The Prince* as titles (*The Prophet Armed, The Prophet Unarmed, The Prophet Outcast*) for his Trotsky trilogy because the latter had nothing to do with the Medici, Savonarola, or 15th Century Florence. What the second part of the article title conveys is the discarding – and thus the conceptual betrayal – of revolution as part of leftist political agency, and as such is perfectly consistent with the use of the phrase by Trotsky (1937), whose critiques of Stalin included the fact that he discarded a central element of Marxist practice – the revolutionary seizure of the state by workers – in favour of reformist alliances with what he termed 'the progressive bourgeoisie'. The only difference between that use and the one here is the target: whereas Trotsky applied it to the state bureaucracy, it is used here to criticize trends mainly in academia. Both refer to what might be termed a process of institutional 'professionalization', one that involves political deradicalization. Indeed, it could be argued that the academic rise and consolidation of the 'new' populist postmodernism is not so dissimilar from the process of Thermidorian reaction identified by Trotsky in the case of the Soviet Union.

4   Whilst every mass grassroots uprising, from the 1871 Paris Commune to the 1959 Cuban revolution, has attracted its share of counter-revolutionary criticism, the exceptional levels of opprobrium visited on the revolutions in 1789 France and 1917 Russia is testimony both to their political importance and also to the fear they provoke – and continue to generate – among owners of means of production/distribution/exchange worldwide.

5   For examples of this kind of hostile approach, see among many others Pipes (1997; 2001), Figes (2014), McMeekin (2017), and Sebestyen (2017). In keeping with this, contributions to an establishment journal (*British Academy Review*, No. 29, January 2017, pp. 23, 31) merely add to the negative picture – 'I doubt we'll ever speak of the "achievements" of the Russian Revolution' – in which Marxism is compared to a clock that no longer works ('as lifeless as the idea of Leninism itself'). To mark the centenary, the 2014 book by Figes has been re-issued, now entitled *A People's Tragedy: The Russian Revolution (1891–1924), 100th Anniversary Edition*.

of this outcome ever taking the form of a socialist transition. At the heart of this paradox is the negative perception of revolutionary agency based on class. It is a truism nowadays that a political critique of accumulation premised on systemic transcendence – that is, a complete break with capitalism – has in effect been banished from the leftist political agenda. The reason for this, however, is still the subject of discussion, by no means confined to those on the political left. According to one interpretation, the capitalist system continues to reproduce itself because some of those at the grassroots benefit from this process, and thus deny support to political parties and/or mobilization advocating a transition to socialism. Others attribute this to widespread delusion arising from the end of actually existing socialism in 1989. Yet others insist that such delusion amounts to false consciousness which has its roots, partly, in the widespread academic challenges to socialism over the past quarter of a century.

Of these explanations it is the last one that is of particular interest, not least because received wisdom currently discounts the political efficacy and/ or role of academics. What is commonly referred to as a crisis of Marxism, a consequence it is usually said of an inability on the part of this theoretical framework to explain adequately current developments in the global capitalist system, has – it is argued here – more to do with changes in academia. Hence the significance of the role taken by intellectuals in advocating and pursuing a transition to socialism: as Lenin pointed out long ago, without a revolutionary theory, there can be no revolutionary practice.[6] The significance of the latter is that Marxist theory has been undermined as much from within as from without, an effect of being discarded either wholesale or piecemeal by many of those claiming to be socialists. Accordingly, the political legacy of 1917, and its negative reception, can be seen as having fallen victim to this wider process. The reasons for this, particularly the ideological shifts in academia over the last three decades, are the focus of the analysis which follows.[7]

---

6 Lenin (1961a: 369).
7 Whereas in Chapters 2 and 3 above, the emphasis is on the political and economic approach to revolution and socialism of Austro-Marxists and other kinds of revisionism, the focus of this chapter is specifically on the role their academic background played in such views, and the hostility expressed towards them by Bolsheviks and other Marxists on these very grounds. Broadly speaking, and as numerous instances – not least that of Austro-Marxism – underline, the latent fear of offending against the legal norms laid down by capitalism has always had a dampening effect on the kind of theory and/or political action advocated by many leftist intellectuals. In the case of 1930s Britain, therefore, a telling example is recounted in the introduction to a collection of writings by Jack Common (1980: 7), a working class writer: 'One December George Orwell decided to write an essay on "Christmas in prison". He planned to write an account from the inside, and this – of course – required an arrest. He talked with Jack Common about a scheme to light a bonfire in [London's] Trafalgar Square. He didn't get a sympathetic hearing. Common remembers

2 Peasants, Left and Right

Endorsements of an undifferentiated/a-historical peasantry initially as bearers of national identity and later as a cultural bastion against the spread of socialism, have been central to conservative discourse throughout German history. This was particularly true of the reaction against the 1789 French Revolution, when counter-revolutionary ideology took its lead from the pro-peasant discourse of a German Romanticism supportive of traditional rural economy and culture.[8] Thus, for example, the eighteenth century defence of rural tradition and hierarchy against the Enlightenment (*aufklarung*) undertaken by the conservative theoretician Justus Möser was coupled with admiration for what he regarded as the cultural 'otherness'/'difference' of peasant society, a golden age version of which in his view constituted the authentic and timeless embodiment of German national identity.[9]

Much the same was true of Johann Gottfried Herder, whose defence of pre-Enlightenment ideas at that same conjuncture generated a concept of national

---

how "I firmly held that if you were going to jail you might as well have something for it. My advice was 'take to theft; a bonfire simply suggests something undergraduate-like'". What this episode underlines is the unwillingness of Orwell, educated at an elite public school, to offend in a serious manner; for him opposition took the form of starting a bonfire, rather than theft, which – as a challenge to property relations – is a transgression that goes to the heart of capitalist society.

8 Godechot (1972). That the antagonism expressed by Cobban (1964: 91ff.) towards Marxist interpretations of the 1789 French Revolution is coupled with a defence of peasant proprietors underlines the degree to which pro-peasant ideology is a consistent aspect of anti-Marxist positions. Against the view that the revolution involved the overthrow of feudalism by the bourgeoisie, Cobban maintains that the conflict was centrally about countryside against the town, and that it was a struggle that Marxism overlooked. Not only do Marxists recognize the important role played by the rural/urban divide in the revolution, but – unlike Cobban – this distinction is seen by them as pitting a mainly urban bourgeoisie and rural non-bourgeois components against one another. Contrary to what he claims, therefore, the presence of this sectoral difference is supportive of, and thus does not invalidate, Marxist interpretations.

9 For details about Justus Möser (1720–94) see Epstein (1966: Ch. 6). Noting the prefiguring influence of Möser's views on German conservatives such as Adam Müller and Novalis, Epstein (1966: 324, 325) observes that his 'admiration for a society of peasants ... has a Jeffersonian flavour; it did not, however, imply any bias towards egalitarianism. On the contrary, Möser explicitly favoured a hierarchic order of society where everybody knew and kept his place ... Möser admired a society marked by a great diversity of status, where everybody was content to perform his traditional function for the common good. He looked upon inequality as a positive good, not a necessary evil ...'. For his view of a golden age, self-sufficient peasantry as the authentic representatives of German national identity, see Epstein (1966: 329).

identity based on an innate and enduring rural culture uniting king and peasant.[10] For Herder, therefore, the selfhood of national identity (cultural 'difference', 'otherness') was based on discourse of the agrarian myth. Every nation emerged from kinship groups, their place-specific environment, culture, religion and peasant farming; he reasserted the validity of these traditional identities against the universal categories of the Enlightenment. Any and all concepts of 'happiness' were – and could only be – realized in such national contexts, the inhabitants of which constituted themselves as a 'people'. Although the latter category subsumed monarch and peasant, Herder excluded from 'the people' the urban worker, 'the rabble' whose agency was for him synonymous with the 'mob in the streets'.

Before the 1914–18 war an undifferentiated peasantry continued to be regarded by conservatives as synonymous with Nature and the nation. Prince Bernard von Bülow, scion of the Junker landlord class, invoked what he claimed was an unbroken ancient rural lineage – composed of an unchanging/homogeneous peasantry (= a mythical ancestral being closer to Nature, and thus 'more natural') – as evidence for the existence of a pristine German nationalism, in terms which were no different from those used earlier by Möser and Herder.[11] Such pro-peasant views, it should be noted, are in many respects similar to those held not just by *Zemlya i Volya*, by the neo-populist Chayanov, and by Pan-Germanism, but also by Austro-Marxism and other revisionist Marxists at that same conjuncture.[12]

---

10   See Brass (2014b: Chapter 6). Among the exponents of German Romanticism opposed to enlightenment philosophy and 1789 French Revolution was Frederick von Schlegel (1772–1829). Like Justus Möser and Johann Gottfried Herder (1744–1803), therefore, Schlegel (1848: 248, 402, 450) blamed 'the empty philosophy of Rationalism' that emerged during 'the atheistic and revolutionary period of the French philosophy, immediately prior to the French Revolution' for what he saw as Enlightenment 'rationalist principles of freedom and equality'. Instead, he embraced an aesthetic philosophy of history that looked backwards to the Middle Ages, extolling an innate German character based on a 'love of nature' grounded in the landscape of Germany (Schlegel, 1849: 186, 193).

11   The argument of von Bülow (1915: 136–37) was that there existed in Germany a direct link between the peasantry, the Prussian landowning class, and the Kaiser, all united by a common bond of national identity, history, and – by inference – economic and political interest. Not only does von Bülow (1915: 233) point with satisfaction to the rising number of peasant smallholdings, which he claims increased by some 180,000 in the period 1895–1907 directly as a result of his 1902 Tariff Law protecting German agriculture, but he also makes clear the political advantage this process confers on Prussian landlordism: namely, to counter the dual political threat posed by a rapidly expanding and class conscious proletariat on the one hand, and the influence of the radical leftwing German Social Democrats on the other.

12   See below in Part I of this volume.

In the case of the Hapsburg empire, the ideological potency of claims to nationhood was founded on the longevity of an underlying ancient peasant culture, whether that of Austria or of Hungary.[13] That pristine cultural 'otherness', and its links both to Nature and to nationhood, were based epistemologically on what are interlocking essentialist concepts is evident from the attempt to connect them all in the person of the Hungarian peasant at the start of the twentieth century.[14] In this context, moreover, discourse about the countryside was informed by the familiar agrarian populist dichotomy (rural = good, urban = bad), with an added pathological inference of the urban/modern as 'unhealthy'.[15] Like the 'new' populist postmodernism now, the mere fact of Hungarian peasants having a culture was equated then with a situation of material well-being.

3 A Plan of Campaign?

A legitimate question to pose, therefore, is how these opposed positions in the debate about peasant economy and revolutionary change inform views about the legacy of the Russian revolution a century on. Broadly speaking, opposition expressed in bourgeois discourse to Marxism has on one particular issue remained constant: the fear of revolution. This concern underwrote popular and influential accounts, both by Burke in the late eighteenth century and by Carlyle in the nineteenth, of the 1789 French revolution.[16] Even before the 1917 revolution in Russia, British conservatives warned that 'Socialist leaders speak openly of revolution ... they turn to Paris and the barricades, and accept the historic methods of the Great French Revolution as illustrative

---

13   Nowhere is this view made more explicit than in the reasons advanced for the recuperation of peasant cultural 'otherness' in the Austro-Hungary at the beginning of the twentieth century (Holme, 1911: 30).
14   According to Holme (1911: 36), therefore, 'every one of us who travels through the country with open eyes feels convinced that there is a Hungarian national style, however much it may be furrowed and intersected by influences derived from other sources ... this elemental living spirit we discern everywhere in the peasant art of Hungary at the present day ...'
15   Hence the observation (Holme, 1911: 31) that '[t]he mountains of Transylvania keep watch over many a craft in which the genuine artistic impulse of a healthy, simple people can be seen at work, and which has nothing in common with the wholesale production of the modern factory system'.
16   See Burke (1790) and Carlyle (1902).

of what they have in their minds for the shaping of events in this country'.[17] Attacking a now-exiled Trotsky as part of a 'criminal class', Churchill objected to revolutionary agency in similar terms, observing during the 1930s that 'Communism is not only a creed. It is a plan of campaign. A Communist is not only the holder of certain opinions; he is the pledged adept of a well-thought-out means of enforcing them ... The method of enforcement is as much a part of the Communist faith as the doctrine itself'.[18] Although voicing similar concerns, at that same conjuncture Keynes nevertheless makes a different point, recognizing and indeed conceding both the logic and the necessity of direct action to Marxist theory ('Granted his assumptions, much of Trotsky's argument is, I think, unanswerable. Nothing can be sillier than to *play* at revolution').[19]

The same fear, more vehement but now tinged with relief at what is regarded as the passing of an historical threat, informs anti-Marxist accounts by revisionist academics and/or journalists currently writing about the centenary of the 1917 Russian revolution.[20] Dismissed in pathological terms by one such

---

17 London Municipal Society (1909: 109). The obverse of such warnings against the likelihood of revolutionary agency in pursuit of socialist aims was a complacent belief in national 'exceptionalism': that is, such political events which happened in other nations were impossible in England. Hence the dismissive attitude towards revolution by one high Tory, T.E. Utley, who in the 1950s rejected this kind of systemic overturning in the following terms (Moore and Heffer, 1989: 298): '...the English are very good at not quarrelling bitterly when they have nothing of substance to quarrel about; they are very good at avoiding quarrels; and the chief characteristic of their genius for conducting them consists in their instinctive perception of when to stop and the shortness of their memories when they have stopped. There is really nothing much to be done even by immortal youth when confronted with the simple arithmetical calculation of the number of our revolutions compared with other people's'.
18 Churchill (1937: 199).
19 Keynes (1933: 90, original emphasis).
20 Among the many examples of journalistic attempts to discredit socialism, the hostile sentiments expressed in the following leader article of a major Sunday newspaper is not untypical: 'Why doesn't the very memory of communism fill the hard Left with revulsion?... There is in fact nothing good to say about communism. Nothing it accomplished economically or socially wasn't achieved in the free world – and with far greater success and without the bloodshed ... Given these indisputable facts [*sic*], why do some on the Left continue to make the case for communism or insist upon applying a ridiculous veneer of objectivity when discussing its history?... Vanishingly few who lived under communism want it back. On the contrary, they have enthusiastically embraced democracy and Nato, and got rich on capitalism – the only real means of progress'. See 'Why does the Left still love communism?', *The Sunday Telegraph* (London), 18 February 2018. Apart from the fact that every single claim it makes against socialism is wrong – that the interventions of the

narrative, as a 'state-dominated tyranny' guided by nothing more than Lenin's 'strident demands' and 'bullying' tactics, the 'totalitarian communism' of the Bolsheviks is blamed for the rise of fascism, the 1939–45 war and the Cold War.[21] The 1917 revolution is banished as 'one of history's great dead ends, like the Inca Empire', Lenin is equated with Hitler and Mussolini, and Bolshevism is likened not just to 'plague' but also to ISIS ('the revolutionary movement itself can only be compared in fanaticism and propensity to the violence of today's extreme Islamists'.). Conceding that an attempt to locate 'a number of moments during the revolution when things might have gone differently' (no sealed train, had Lenin been assassinated, etc.) amounts to counterfactual history that has been described as 'right-wing wishful thinking', the object of this revisionist approach is to argue for the existence of a non-revolutionary, 'moderate' liberal political alternative to tsarism. In keeping with this, the collapse of the USSR in 1991 is compared favourably with 1917, since 'not the least of the lessons of the Russian Revolution is that [economically] the market works much better than the state'.

So as to illustrate this claim about the economic superiority of the market, revisionism turns to the agrarian policies of the 1920s, in the process attributing to Trotsky the view that it was necessary to abandon the Bolshevik 'obsession' with class struggle waged by the state against kulaks, and focus instead on market-friendly appeals to peasant smallholders.[22] For a number of reasons, however, it is impossible to sustain this attempt to portray Trotsky as an advocate of pro-peasant free market policies. To begin with, the assertion that there were actually no rich peasants, not least because '[w]ho was a kulak and who was not was clear to no one, and there were neither customary understandings nor legal definitions that enjoyed authority, either before the revolution or after' is quite simply incorrect. Like other Bolsheviks, Trotsky was clear not only about the

---

'free world' throughout the globe have been done 'without bloodshed' is a risible statement that would rightly be greeted with guffaws of laughter in every corner of the earth – the description of present-day capitalism, crisis-ridden as it now is, as 'the only real means of progress' is quite simply nonsense.

21 These descriptions and those outlined in the paragraph that follows, are by Brenton (2016a, 2016b). Contributors to the volume he edits (Brenton, 2016c) include Orlando Figes and Richard Pipes, revisionist academics hostile to Bolshevism and Marxist political economy. Brenton himself is a retired diplomat.

22 For these claims, see Landis (2016: 220, 229–30, 231). Blaming the grain procurement policy for famine, the same source (Landis, 2016: 239–40, 241) maintains that 'the decision [was] to begin decriminalizing the market, a necessary component that helped to provide agricultural producers with an outlet for the sale of surplus (after tax) grain and, as Trotsky ... had emphasized, incentives to improve production'.

existence and the socio-economic characteristics of rich peasants but also the threat they posed to a socialist programme, consolidating rural property at the expense of poor peasants and collective enterprises, selling produce on the black market, and acquiring/cheapening labour-power by means of money-lending.[23] Having depicted Trotsky as a supporter of peasant economy and free market policies, revisionism admits that actually he espoused neither of these positions ('Trotsky ... did not speak openly of the market, nor [was he] in truth, "pro-peasant" in his political outlook'.).

Turning to the way other kinds of (notionally non-revisionist) discourse are marking the 1917 centenary, the message projected by the commentary accompanying an exhibition at the Royal Academy in London, *Revolution: Russian Art 1917–1932* (11 February – 17 April 2017) is unambiguous: aesthetically, the revolution was a success, but in terms of politics and economics, it was a failure.[24] This distinction emerged most clearly in two of the exhibition rooms, one dealing with the peasantry and the other with nationalism. Implied in the commentary appearing in the first of these two rooms was that it was the Bolsheviks themselves who were to blame for all the agrarian problems: their political duplicity towards smallholders ('they promised the peasantry ownership of land, a pledge they had no intention of keeping') leading inevitably to a catastrophic economic decline in agricultural production ('undermined by hunger and empty fields').[25] Art displayed in the second room, the focus of which – under the rubric 'Eternal Russia' – was on national identity, was explained in terms similarly hostile to Bolshevism. Here the commentary effected a

---

23 On these points, see previous chapter, and also Trotsky (1937: 32ff.) and Kritsman (1984). Analogous attempts by rich peasants to undermine socialist planning, pricing systems and production targets occurred in the cooperative or collective agrarian units of 1970s Chile and 1980s Cuba.

24 A similar emphasis on the aesthetic informs another exhibition marking the centenary, that in the British Library (28 April – 29 August 2017) entitled *Russian Revolution: Hope, Tragedy, Myths*. This emphasis is also apparent in the publications accompanying each exhibition (The Royal Academy of Arts, 2017; Rogatchev, 2017). The mood informing this kind of approach can be gauged from the festivities accompanying the Royal Academy exhibition, announcing: 'The dress code is Soviet for this night of drinking, dancing and revolutionary art. Tickets cost £35 [*sic*] including a themed cocktail and entry into the *Revolution: Russian Art 1917–1932* exhibition'. Similar in tone were advertisements proclaiming a 'Revolution meal deal'.

25 The title, painted in large letters on the wall of the room containing art work addressing the impact of the revolution on rural society, was 'Fate of the Peasants'. Underneath it was written the following: 'When the Bolsheviks came to power in 1917, they promised the peasantry ownership of land, a pledge they had no intention of keeping ... agriculture was undermined by hunger and empty fields'.

contrast between the agency of plebeian barbarians driving the revolutionary process ('the boots of the proletarian masses', 'State nationalization and confiscation of private and ecclesiastical property') and the destruction of what is presented as a benign pre-revolutionary Tsarist social order ('the beauty and charm of the old Russia', 'the preservation of churches and the traditional peasant culture').[26] A similar antagonism informed other exhibitions, despite the fact that these were not explicitly about the revolution.[27]

This damning-with-faint-praise approach to the 1917 Russian revolution, discarding as worthless everything but its aesthetic dimension, is consistent with the way adherents of the 'new' populist postmodernism express hostility towards a regime disapproved of by privileging only culture. Thus, for example, a 2018 attempt to update and revise the presentation by Kenneth

---

26 Hence the view: 'Even in revolutionary times, the traditional images of Tsarist Russia such as birch forests and colourful onion-shaped domes, persisted as signs of national identity. Many Russian artists, philosophers and writers were nostalgic for the beauty and charm of the old Russia, rapidly disappearing under the boots of the proletarian masses. During this era of State nationalization and confiscation of private and ecclesiastical property, they pleaded for the retention of the Orthodox faith and argued for the preservation of churches and the traditional peasant culture threatened by collectivization ... artists expressed their longing for a country that no longer existed'.

27 Although not specifically marking the centenary, another exhibition at the Victoria and Albert Museum in London during the same year, *Opera: Passion, Power and Politics* (30 September 2017 to 25 February 2018) the focus of which was on the connection between this art form and politics, engaged in a similar process of Soviet-bashing. Covering operas such as Monteverdi's *L'incoronazione di Poppea*, Handel's *Rinaldo*, Mozart's *The Marriage of Figaro*, Verdi's *Nabucco*, and *Salome* by Richard Strauss, it eschewed the politically significant *Fidelio* by Beethoven and Brecht's *The Threepenny Opera* and *The Rise and Fall of the City of Mahagonny*, opting instead to end with the reception of Shostakovich's *Lady Macbeth of Mtsensk*. Music in the Soviet Union is accordingly presented within the Stalinist framework, thereby equating revolution and socialism negatively with censorship. Interestingly, Shostakovich's *Lady Macbeth* barely features in an earlier and still important analysis of the link between Opera and politics (Arblaster, 1992), which contains a more measured assessment of music in the Soviet Union at that conjuncture. Arblaster (1992: 210) notes, not uncritically: 'The word "Stalinist" is widely and loosely used, and almost always as a term of abuse; so I may be misunderstood if I describe [Prokofiev's] *War and Peace* as a Stalinist opera. But there is an innocuous sense in which it undoubtedly is. Soviet audiences at least could hardly help equating the French invasion of 1812 with the German invasion of 1941, or seeing in Marshal Kutuzov an historically disguised, and of course idealized, portrait of Marshal Stalin, the farseeing patriotic leader who saves his country at a time of terrible danger. The portrait is a flattering one, and its relation to reality is questionable, since Stalin's war leadership was probably not the triumph of the military genius that official Soviet propaganda proclaimed it to be. But that is really beside the point. For Russians the 1941–45 war was a war of national survival, and Stalin played the same symbolic leadership role in that struggle as Churchill did for the British'.

Clark of his 1969 BBC television documentary series, *Civilization: A Personal View*, is focused largely on cultural difference.[28] Although Clark stressed the importance of European culture, yet he expressed concern at the lack of attention the series paid to its non-European equivalent.[29] The current series by contrast lionizes non-European societies, invoking comparisons only of culture, reducing thereby the difference between colonizer/colonized simply to one of aesthetics so as to emphasize the parity – not to say the superiority – of achievements by 'other' civilizations. In doing so, what it in effect champions is not just 'other' culture but also – and most problematically – the pre-capitalist social order that gave rise to these 'other' aesthetics. Restricting a critique of colonization to questions of culture licenses a false comparison, especially when it fails to address crucial political, ideological and economic issues; hence a Marxist critique of imperial conquest is mainly about system and class, not only national or ethnic identity. Implicitly, therefore, a post-colonial defence of non-European civilization along aesthetic lines amounts, in the end, also to a defence of the kinds of society and social hierarchy that preceded colonization.

In keeping with the depiction of 1917 Russia in mainly aesthetic terms is the emphasis placed on the role of Bolshevik literary taste. Lenin, argues Tariq Ali, 'found it difficult to make any accommodations to modernism in Russia or elsewhere', and conveys the impression that he championed the literary work of the populist Chernyshevsky, adding that the latter 'was the writer who had perhaps the strongest impact on Lenin'.[30] However, Lenin was certainly not influenced by him politically, dismissing Chernyshevsky's interpretation of

---

28 See in particular the post-colonial approach informing one contribution to the present series (Olusoga, 2018), similar in many respects to that of the Subaltern Studies (on which see above, Chapter 7). Its object appears to be to combine unstinting praise for the cultures of conquered populations – along the lines of how 'Benin was a complex and sophisticated civilization capable of creating wondrous art', and how the Spanish were 'wilfully blind to the resourcefulness [of] the Aztecs' who possessed a 'highly sophisticated aesthetic tradition', corresponding to 'an intricate civilization of rich artistic output' (Olusoga, 2018: 30, 51, 56, 57) – with denigration not of imperial conquest *per se* but rather of Europeans. The latter, we are told (Olusoga, 2018: 37, 38, 81), were not only dependent on the colonized and non-colonized 'other' for many of their cultural and technical achievements (the Portuguese 'adopted new navigation knowledge gleaned from Islamic sailors', the late fifteenth century voyages of discovery being 'achieved with the assistance of an Arab navigator'), but were also perceived by this same 'other' as 'barbarians' on account of a lack in personal hygiene, etiquette and table manners.
29 For all his political shortcomings – highlighted by John Berger (see below, Chapter 10) – Clark did at least make a connection between the philosophy that emerged from the Age of Enlightenment and the revolutionary politics at the end of the eighteenth century.
30 See 'Reading from the front', *The Guardian* (London), 25 March 2017.

history as 'naïve'.³¹ Moreover, noting that Trotsky held the same negative view about plebeian cultural forms as Lenin, Ali nevertheless fails to point out the *political* reason for this: namely, and as Marxists have frequently pointed out, first-hand accounts of peasant/village life emanating from the rural grassroots are usually beset by two kinds of bias; such discourse is not only penetrated by landlord ideology but also localized and parochial in scope. It was this absence of the bigger picture – life beyond the village, in other words – that Trotsky found problematic in accounts of village life written by organic intellectuals.³² Ironically, the more 'authentic' such literary accounts were, the less they could be said to address the problems of the wider society.

Even leftists ostensibly sympathetic to the aims of 1917, such as the novelist China Miéville, are ambivalent as to the current necessity for and efficacy of revolutionary agency.³³ This is evident from his confessed vacillation when called upon to defend the revolution, along the lines of 'when I am asked why it still matters, what comes to me first is hesitation. A silence'. It is also there in his conclusion that 'one occasionally sees a foolish kind of [mimicry] in the desire to treat Lenin's party of 1917 as a paradigm for today ... No such special pleading or fawning re-enactment is necessary'. Like Ali, Miéville places a similar – and of itself unproblematic – emphasis on the cultural achievements of the 1917 Russian Revolution, pointing out that its 'influence is incalculable ... [we] can trace the revolution in cinema and sociology, theatre and theology, realpolitik and fashion [so] of course the revolution matters'. Yet like Ali, he notes the influence on Lenin of Chernyshevsky, but – as problematically – fails to mention the critical *political* attitude Lenin had towards the populist views of Chernyshevsky.

---

31 Writing in 1910, Lenin (1961b: 530–31) observed: 'It follows from Chernyshevsky that in history vice is always punished as it deserves. In reality ... the facts known to us do not at all warrant this view, which may be comforting but is certainly naïve'.

32 Strongly opposed to attempts by Russian populists to romanticize village life, Trotsky (1925: 72–73) acknowledged that Ivanov, an organic intellectual of the peasantry, 'knows and understands the Siberian peasant, the Cossack, the Khirgiz', but was nevertheless critical of him, observing that 'whether Ivanov wants it or not, he shows that the peasant uprisings in "peasant" Russia are not yet revolution. The peasant revolt bursts forth suddenly ... and no one sees why it flared up or whither it leads'.

33 See 'You say you want a revolution', *The Guardian* (London), 6 May 2017. Where the ambivalence of China Miéville is concerned, I am unfortunately in a very small way to blame. In an email to me of 15 March 2002, he stated 'although there is no reason you should remember me, you lectured me on "The Politics of Food" in Cambridge in 1993–4, and I badgered you with questions many times. Those lectures and discussions were enormously influential on me, and formative in my becoming a Marxist, and I'd like – very belatedly – to thank you'. Clearly, I did not manage to communicate to him the centrality of revolution to Marxist theory, a grievous shortcoming on my part.

Significantly, perhaps, Ali is also a contributor to a current attempt to formulate a radical leftist programme for the UK. The diminished state of what passes for current progressive opposition to conservatism in Britain is nowhere so evident as in the responses of what are termed 'writers and thinkers' to an invitation to outline a modern version of the 1960s May Day Manifesto.[34] Whereas the earlier version argued for 'a socialist alternative ... in the fight against capitalism', the current one makes no mention either of socialism as a desirable objective, the need to transcend capitalism in order to realize even a minimal reformist programme, or of the effects of the wholesale embrace by many in academia of postmodernism. At best, therefore, it advocates a programme to be realized within a reformed (= 'kinder'/'caring') capitalism; at worst, it unwittingly supports policies that are central to class struggle waged 'from above' by producers – such as expanding the industrial reserve army of labour – which strengthen the accumulation process.[35] Elsewhere in the same newspaper one of the contributors to the updated manifesto reveals not just his vehemently anti-socialist politics but also his anti-intellectualism, declaring '[l]ife is ... still way too short to spend any time reading theoretical gibberish concocted by superannuated Marxists that purports to still further stretch this ideological corpse like Procrustes on the rack of contemporary events'.

In terms of popular culture, the centenary of 1917 is commemorated on film and television by inserting it into the familiar tragedy/farce dichotomy that informs discourse hostile to this episode. One example is the film *The Death of Stalin* (2017), directed by Armando Iannuci. Subtitled 'A Comedy of Terrors', it reduces everything about the Russian Revolution to a version of Carry On Up the Kremlin, whereby members of the Politbureau are depicted as no more than an inept collection of opportunist spivs/gangsters (along the lines of 'In the Kremlin, no one can hear you scheme', 'It's every comrade for himself') jockeying for political power. In order to succeed the now-dead Stalin, therefore, they are shown as prepared to do/say anything; the humour deriving from the latter manoeuvres projects revolutionary incompetence, while darker images involving not just betrayal but also scenes of torture and execution convey revolutionary terror. In the process the events of 1953 become a metaphor for 1917, as the narrative presents bungling/uselessness and horror as failings innate

---

34 For the updated manifesto, see *The Guardian* (London) 29 April 2017.Contributors to the initial May Day Manifesto (Williams, 1968b) included among their number E.P. Thompson and Raymond Williams, leftists who knew about both socialism and Marxist theory. By contrast, contributors to the 2017 version are for the most part academics and journalists who lack any understanding either of socialism or of Marxism.

35 In political terms, such advocacy of a 'kinder'/'caring' capitalism is no different from the plea by Breman for the 'patronage' of the neoliberal state (see below, Chapter 5).

to and the inevitable results of any/every 'from below' attempt to break with the capitalist system. All revolutions and attempts to achieve socialism, it is inferred, necessarily end like this, combining ineptitude with terror, a negative assessment the effect of which is to condemn both leftist political theory and radical struggle/agency in furtherance of this.

A similar kind of approach informed two BBC television programmes entitled *Tunes for Tyrants: Music and Power* (2017) presented by Suzy Klein, the focus of which was on the role of music in consolidating/mobilising political support. Invoking an equivalence between the function of music in the Russian Revolution and the rise to power of Nazism in Germany, her programme maintained – much like the film *The Death of Stalin* – that all forms of radical challenge to the status quo end in tragedy, and are thus by inference politically illegitimate. She concluded optimistically by pointing to the enthusiasm with which in the period immediately after 1945 musicians/composers in Germany played tunes forbidden by the Nazi regime, and argued – wrongly – it was evidence for the triumph of liberal democracy.[36] In keeping with this kind of approach, at the beginning of November 2017, the time of the anniversary itself, BBC Radio 3 broadcast a series of programmes the declared aim of which was to demonstrate how the Russian revolution influenced culture. Again, the narrative encountered is one that focuses on the aesthetic, not political, lessons of 1917.

4 Power Wanting, But Wanting Power?

How is one to explain the revisionist project, based on the rejection of Marxist approaches to revolution and peasant economy?[37] That is, one that replaced a

---

36 The enthusiasm displayed by musicians/composers for music banned by the Nazis had little or nothing to do with an endorsement by them of liberal democracy. A very different explanation was given me by my father, Denis Brass, who was the British Council music officer in Vienna at that same immediate post-war conjuncture: during the late 1940s and early 1950s, he got to know many of the leading musicians there, including those such as Furtwangler, who were busily befriending anyone connected with the British and American occupying powers in order to distance themselves from their own earlier links to the Nazi regime. It was this desire to be on the side of the victors, whoever these might be, not any supposed enthusiasm for liberal democracy, that determined their actions, musical and otherwise.

37 The title of this section indicates the presence of two interrelated processes. First, a desire to find an alternative to neoliberalism, seen as having failed politically and economically ('Power Wanting'). And second, the conceptual jettisoning of revolutionary agency designed to realize socialism ('Wanting Power?'), a form of direct action which used to be

hitherto dominant Marxist conceptual framework – structured by class formation/struggle, modernity, working class internationalism and a revolutionary transition to socialism – with nationalism and a concept of an undifferentiated peasant as an 'authentic' but unheard indigenous voice. In part, the institutional locus of this project, and the transformation of consciousness from the sameness of class, via the tacit acceptance both of national/ethnic difference and of some form of capitalism, to the abandonment of revolutionary transformation and seizure of the State as a necessary objective, was a product of the intelligentsia in academia.

In a sense, it is – or should be – unsurprising that the academy as a bourgeois ideological institution should be the prime target of Marxist critiques.[38] Historically, those against whom Marxists have argued most strongly have been academics, seen rightly as the ideological defenders of the existing social order. For this reason, the most common arguments deployed by Marxism against those in the academy have been twofold. First, that they are part of a university system which – in a capitalist context – is innately hostile to socialist ideas and practice. Second, even where socialists are employed by the academy, they are necessarily subject to institutional pressures that prevent or pre-empt a genuine commitment to revolution and/or systemic transformation.[39]

Among most European socialists in the late nineteenth and early twentieth century – not just Marx himself but also Engels, Lenin, Kautsky, and Trotsky – there was a deep suspicion of combined with uniform hostility towards academia in general.[40] This antagonism derived principally from the deleterious

---

    a central tenet of Marxism. As in other sections throughout this chapter, this title refers back to another sort of overturning, in the sense that these days Marxism appears to have shifted from the streets into the academy ('Betraying Revolution'), in the process metamorphosing from a theory involving direct action to one requiring largely or only study.

38   For details, see Brass (2017b: Ch. 18).

39   Needless to say, this institutional pressure extends also to the form (= 'tone') in which disagreement is expressed. Lenin himself was subject to its exercise whilst exiled in France at the start of the twentieth century, as the following account by Trotsky (1930: 130) illustrates: 'Pressed by the Marxist sections of students, Lenin agreed to give three lectures on the agrarian question at the Higher School organized in Paris by professors expelled from Russian universities. The liberal professors asked the undesirable lecturer to refrain from polemics as far as possible. But Lenin made no promise on this score, and began his first lecture with the statement that Marxism is a revolutionary theory, and therefore fundamentally polemical'.

40   It must be stressed that such hostility on the part of early Marxists was most emphatically *not* to the fact of intellectual practice, but rather to its confinement to and control by academia. This view does not constitute anti-intellectualism, which objects to intellectual activity *per se*, and is a form of ideological 'primitivism' that has been the historical preserve of those on the political right.

impact on revolutionary theory and practice of the reformism advocated by self-proclaimed socialists holding senior teaching posts in the bourgeois university system at that conjuncture, a political group belonging to what was identified as *katheder*-socialism. Significantly, neither Lenin nor Trotsky was an academic, unlike Bauer, Sombart and the Austro-Marxists.[41]

In the late 1870s, therefore, Marx expressed strong opposition to the increasing influence on leftist politics in Germany of *katheder*-socialism, describing its exponents as 'counter-revolutionary windbags' composed of 'nonentities in theory and useless in practice [who] want to draw the teeth of socialism (which they have fixed up in accordance with the university recipes)' in order to 'make the [Social Democratic] Party respectable in the eyes of the petty bourgeoisie'.[42] Engels took a similarly critical approach, noting in a letter to August Bebel (20 January 1886) that during the mid-1880s universities in France and England were increasingly appointing *katheder*-socialists in an attempt to rescue capitalism from its contradictions, notwithstanding the 'rubbish' propagated by such academic 'socialists'.

Lenin, too, was critical of the deleterious influence exercised on the working class movement by the reformist line advocated by *katheder*-socialism, dismissed by him as 'professorial socialism'. When considering 'the turn of progressive public opinion towards Marxism' in Russia at the end of the nineteenth century, moreover, Lenin clearly delineated the element of opportunism – 'jumping on the bandwaggon' – at work among the exponents of *katheder*-socialism.[43] He was not for a minute taken in by this political 'conversion', however, accurately identifying its objective as being to dilute the element of struggle, turning thereby 'the nascent working class movement into an appendage of the liberals'.[44]

---

41 A footnote in Luxemburg (2014: 507) contains the following apposite observation: 'In [Rosa] Luxemburg's era it was virtually unheard of for a revolutionary socialist or a Marxist to have a position at a German university'.

42 These critical views about *katheder*-socialism, expressed by Marx in his correspondence, are cited approvingly by Lenin (1962: 366–67). In the early 1890s, (Tudor and Tudor, 1988: 9) 'Bernstein was indeed becoming increasingly academic in his approach ... [he] was more than ever inclined to see the element of truth on both sides of the question, and his political utterances were increasingly couched in the language of scholarly caution'.

43 Lenin (1961a: 360). About *katheder*-socialism, Rosa Luxemburg (2014: 507) noted that 'all of them are professors [and it has] been absorbed into the camp of the employers. One of these professors even voted for the anti-socialist laws'.

44 Taking issue with the attempts by *katheder*-socialism to find common ground – and thus form political alliances – with the bourgeoisie, Lenin (1961a: 362–63) observed: 'But an essential condition for such an alliance must be the full opportunity for the socialists to reveal to the working class that its interests are diametrically opposed to the interests of

A similar disdain for 'professorial socialism' was exhibited by Kautsky, who noted that 'the academics are those among us who are least friendly to the idea of revolution'.[45] Describing them as 'parlour socialists', he regarded academics as 'a very unreliable ally', due principally to their being members of a 'new middle class' located between 'the proletariat and the ruling class'. Although such elements were aware of the problems with capitalism, and consequently on occasion sympathetic towards working class objectives, when it came to agency based on this, observed Kautsky, academics 'seek to throw discredit on the idea of revolution, and to represent it as a useless means'.[46]

A deep suspicion of academia generally, and in particular of the true commitment of *katheder*-socialism to the transcendence of a socio-economic order at the apex of which they themselves were positioned, also informed most of what Trotsky said about those for and against Marxist theory/practice. In his survey of the pre-revolutionary social forces in Russia during 1905, for example, he presciently noted that intellectuals were only fair-weather friends who at the first sign of crisis would reveal their authentic political allegiance.[47] That is, not to the transcendence of capitalism, let alone to its revolutionary overthrow, but rather to the preservation of the existing socio-economic order.

This opinion did not change, as is clear from the view about Austro-Marxism he took when looking back on his life once in exile. Categorizing academic Marxists in 1907 Vienna 'as far from revolutionary dialectics as the most conservative

---

the bourgeoisie. However, the Bernsteinian and "critical" trend, to which the majority of the legal Marxists turned, deprived the socialists of this opportunity and demoralised the socialist consciousness by vulgarizing Marxism, by advocating the theory of the blunting of social contradictions, by declaring the idea of the social revolution and of the dictatorship of the proletariat to be absurd, by reducing the working class movement and the class struggle to narrow trade unionism and to a "realistic" struggle for petty, gradual reforms ... in practice it meant a striving to convert the nascent working class movement into an appendage of the liberals'.

45   Kautsky (1916: 4, 45–46).
46   Accepting that 'professional scholars' who have 'a continually increasing sympathy for the proletariat' are consequently 'easiest won for our party', Kautsky (1916: 46–47) notes that 'friendship for labour becomes popular among the cultured classes, until there is scarcely a parlour in which one does not stumble over one or more "Socialists"'. However, he continues that (Kautsky, 1916: 48–49) 'Socialism has become a fad. It no longer demands any especial energy, and no break with capitalist society to assume the name of Socialist. It is no wonder then that more and more these new Socialists remain entangled in their previous manner of thought and feeling ... They declare themselves ready to grant the proletariat their moral support, but only on condition that it renounces the idea of the application of force, and this not simply where force is hopeless – there the proletariat has already renounced it – but also in those places where it is still full of possibilities'.
47   Trotsky (1972a: 53).

Egyptian pharaoh', Trotsky continued: 'The psychological type of Marxist can develop only in an epoch of social cataclysms, of a revolutionary break with traditions and habits; whereas an Austrian Marxist too often revealed himself a philistine who had learned certain parts of Marx's theory as one might study law, and had lived on the interest that *Das Kapital* yielded him'.[48]

5   Resistance, Not Revolution

During the first half of the twentieth century, when Marxist theory had an impact on the grassroots even in Britain, this occurred – significantly – outside the university system. Because academics were regarded by many on the left as hostile to a labour movement objective of socialism, therefore, workers' education was perceived as correspondingly incompatible with a capitalist university system. Over the latter part of the twentieth century, however, orthodox leftist views about the role of academic institutions underwent something of a reversal. Rather than being seen as bastions of bourgeois thought the main objective of which was to defend capitalism, universities were perceived as places from which to mount an ideological attack on the capitalist system. In an important sense, the expansion of higher education in the 1960s channelled this process into the university system, by creating additional (and salaried) employment opportunities for intellectuals who would otherwise have remained outside academia.

Once socialists were installed as lecturers, so the argument went, the teaching and thus the influence of universities would undergo a radical transformation. What actually happened was predictably different: in order to become and remain part of the academy, socialists were required to water down or even discard their political principles. By the 1980s many of them had metamorphosed into the 'new' populist postmodernists, who mobilized discourse about peasant/nation/Nature that historically has been the domain of conservatives and the political right in order to challenge neoliberalism. Nowhere was this more evident than in the epistemological recuperation of a specifically cultural dimension of 'peasant-ness', a discourse associated most powerfully with the Subaltern Studies project, formulated initially in the context of Asian historiography and latterly with regard to Latin American history.[49] Reinstatement of the peasant voice as an undifferentiated/pristine subaltern

---

48   Trotsky (1930: 180–81).
49   For subaltern approaches to Asian historiography, see Chapter 7 and also Guha (1982–89); for the same approach to Latin American history, see Beverley and Oviedo (1993).

'other', tainted neither by class, by economic development nor by the wider capitalist system, was licensed by the dematerialization of discourse, itself an effect of postmodern deconstruction.

Postmodernists such as Beverley compare the nationalist discourse featuring subaltern identity to that developed in the first decade of the twentieth century by Bauer.[50] This, it is suggested by Beverley, is the way forward politically, and hence the model that the left should incorporate into its theory and practice because, in the present stage of capitalism, national difference and not class antagonism is the main contradiction. Against this, the crucial distinction informing the Marxist position on nationalism is best summed up by Lenin: 'Combat all national oppression? Yes, of course! Fight *for* any kind of national development, *for* "national culture" in general? – Of course not'.[51] By contrast, and like the prefiguring discourse of Bauer, exponents of the subaltern studies project eschew this distinction. Consequently, they do indeed end up supporting 'the [f]ight *for* any kind of national development, *for* "national culture" in general'. All of them – Bauer then and postmodernists now – regard indigenous peasant nationalism (= 'the unheard voice from below') as a politically desirable goal and historically innate, and as such a positive and an empowering identity.

For the 'new' populist postmodernists, the construction of 'civil society' replaced the capture of State power. Similarly, preserving grassroots culture became an alternative to (and substitute for) economic development, an epistemological stance that entailed, among other things, the defence of 'civil society' composed of all those traditional institutions that socialist theory usually criticizes and opposes. In the analytical framework of the 'new' postmodern populism, therefore, the meaning and object of contemporary rural grassroots agency has changed. Instead of attempting to realize the economic fruits and benefits of development by capturing and exercising control of the State

---

50   *Pace* Beverley (2004: 272ff.), in Austria a consequence of Bauer's Popular Front reformist politics during the late 1920s and early 1930s was not to strengthen but to *demobilize* working class opposition to fascism, and thus in effect to make easier the taking of power by the far right, on which see Chapter 3 above and also Kitchen (1987).

51   See Lenin (1964b: 35, original emphasis) and also Trotsky (1934: 908ff.). Earlier, Marx warned that a working class divided along national and/or ethnic lines undermined the solidarity necessary for revolutionary agency. In the late 1860s and early 1870s he (Marx, 1973: 166–71) argued that in Britain 'antagonism [between English and Irish industrial workers] is artificially sustained and intensified by the press, the pulpit, the comic papers, in short, by all the means at the disposal of the ruling classes'. Much the same point was made subsequently by Luxemburg (1976) with regard to peasants and agricultural workers in eastern Europe, and by Shachtman (2003) in the case of small farmers, tenants, and agricultural workers in the Southern US.

apparatus (as Marxists argue), poor peasants and workers in India and Latin America eschew revolutionary agency.[52] Rather, they are said to struggle on a quotidian basis, as subalterns engaged in resistance, and generally only at a local level, merely to retain their existing cultural identity (= 'difference').[53] It is the latter process and objective, and not class or economic development, which empowers the rural 'other', insists postmodern theory.[54]

The irony is unmistakable. Over the past twenty-five years, many academics – especially those in the social sciences – writing about the undesirability of further economic development where peasant smallholders are concerned have done so from a 'new' populist postmodern theoretical framework.[55] In support of this view, they not only invoked the right of the rural 'other' to his/

---

52 As noted in previous chapters, Marxism confers political legitimacy only on revolutionary struggles for political power undertaken by class categories (a nascent bourgeoisie in the case of a dominant feudalism, a proletariat in the case of a dominant capitalism). Marxists argue that because the peasantry is not homogeneous, consequently resistance by rich, middle and poor peasants has a different class basis, meaning and objective. It is the exponents of postmodernism who maintain the fiction of an homogeneous peasantry confronting a non-class specific state (a binary opposition which structures the discourse not of Marxism but of populism, the 'other' of Marxism). And again as is outlined in previous chapters, and also elsewhere (Brass, 2017b: Ch. 12, especially 152–56), the impact beyond academia of views supportive of the 'cultural turn' extends to the 'new' postmodern populists advocating resistance instead of revolution. Hence the overlap between on the one hand resistance taking a 'spatial' form, so as to bolster a case for the existence in Asia of a space called 'Zomia', and on the other the location of an analogous space called 'Eurasia', the context and history of which have become central to Russian nationalist discourse.

53 For quotidian 'everyday forms of resistance', see Scott (1985).

54 The reason for this fusion between the subaltern/resistance framework on the one hand and the 'new' populist right on the other is not difficult to discern. In the epistemology shared by the latter, any/every form of resistance is declared to be legitimate (landlords as well as tenants, the rich as well as the poor). The difficulty with concepts such as 'resistance' and 'power' as deployed by the subaltern framework, therefore, is not so much its ubiquity as its politics. By eschewing a politics, resistance theory not only makes no distinction between resistance (by socialists) against fascism and (by fascists) against socialism but also – with typical postmodern aporia – denies the necessity any longer to have to make such a distinction.

55 For evidence of the way this has affected what is currently published in academic journals, see Brass (2015). Typical of the vehemence with which Marxist approaches are dismissed by populists (Hall, Edelman, Borras, Scoones, White & Wolford, 2015: 469–70) is the following: 'numerous lamentations about "false consciousness", "hegemony" or failure to recognize the collective's "true" … interests … The Marxists' bemoaning of "false consciousness"… Peasants' "failure" (for many Marxists)…to transcend "defensive" local struggles (for social movements theorists), became just one more indication of their atavistic politics and culture'. This is followed by a classic populist statement asserting peasant essentialism, and its political efficacy: 'When struggles for land are seen in their own

her own culture, but declared the latter identity innate and thus the ideological and organizational basis for the construction of a local 'civil' society outside and against the neoliberal State. In essence, this is consistent with the perception encountered currently, that the only worthwhile legacy of the 1917 Russian revolution is an aesthetic one. Accordingly, from the 1980s onwards 'new' populist postmodernism unknowingly deployed the very same arguments against further economic development in the Third World countryside as had reformists and conservatives earlier in the case of Europe.

Not the least problematic aspect of the 'new' postmodern populism, therefore, is that its endorsement of 'difference'/'diversity' fails to differentiate between two antithetical forms of anti-capitalism: one emanating from the political left and another that has its origins in the discourse of the political right. Whereas the former posits socialism as the transcendent 'other' of capitalism, revisionists invoke a pre-capitalist rural order in which landlord and peasant (= 'the people') live in harmony. The centrality to the latter discourse of notions of cultural innateness rooted in nationhood is a matter of record, as is the fact that such epistemology is the same across time and space, to the degree that its core assumptions reappears everywhere and consistently in the ideas of and claims made historically by conservatism.

6 Conclusion

Considered here are both the fact of and the reasons for the current disappearance of revolutionary agency from leftist theory/practice. In the centenary year of the 1917 Russian revolution, this process of vanishing, not just of direct action designed to capture state power but also of socialism itself, is traced from the advocacy of evolution and latterly resistance to – but not transcendence of – capitalism. This reformist trend is linked in turn to changes in academia, and in particular the rise there of the 'new' postmodernism. The latter has resulted on the one hand in the championing both of peasant economy/culture and of non-class identities, thereby returning to earlier views held by revisionism; and on the other a consequent abandonment of class analysis, socialist politics, revolutionary agency, and allied concepts of progress, modernity and development.

Contrary to idealized images depicting the pre-revolutionary Russian countryside as one of arcadian tranquillity, a pastoral inhabited by landlords

---

terms [sic], however, it is obvious that claiming land or defending the land one has often reflects clear class consciousness, albeit of a smallholding peasant ...'

co-existing happily with an unchanging/undifferentiated and subsistence-oriented peasantry, evidence suggests it was context both of acute class struggle and where capitalist farmers, buying/leasing rural property from landlords, had already emerged from among the rich peasant stratum. As noted in Section 1, Marxist theory about the connection between agrarian struggle and systemic transition, formulated by – among many others – Lenin, Trotsky, Luxemburg and Preobrashensky, warned against the folly of regarding the peasantry as undifferentiated in class terms, since this would hide within its ranks a powerful rich stratum, which would oppose all attempts to collectivize agricultural production, to introduce or consolidate redistributive taxation, and any further socialisation of landholdings.

When marking – not celebrating – the 1917 Russian revolution, therefore, it is in a sense unsurprising that conservatives have been and are vehemently opposed to the advocacy by leftists of revolutionary agency: what is surprising, however, is that among progressives and some leftists this kind of direct action is also viewed negatively, and dismissed as unfeasible. Such an approach emerges currently in the tendency to perceive the Russian revolution as mainly or only as a cultural phenomenon. The issue is not that to regard culture as a positive outcome of the revolution – which it undoubtedly was – but rather to see it as the only worthwhile legacy of 1917, almost a way of avoiding other equally important aspects of the revolutionary process, especially politics. It is difficult not to see this as a method of political deradicalization, a process in which some on the contemporary left have unwittingly participated, and in some instances even supported. Part of the reason for this, it is suggested here, has to do with the fact that critiques of capitalism entailing a socialist transition were replaced in post-1980s academia by endorsements of the 'new' populist postmodernism, a form of anti-capitalism which eschews systemic transcendence, and is thus politically less threatening. The role of Eric Hobsbawm in this process is exasmined in the next chapter.

CHAPTER 9

Viva La Revolución? Eric Hobsbawm on Peasants

'Lucky are the men who write few books, they have no time to give themselves away...'
A Diary entry on 4 December 1944 by PIERRE DRIEU LA ROCHELLE.[1]

∴

1 Introduction: A Time There Was ...

The publication of yet another volume containing articles written by the late Eric Hobsbawm (1917–2012), this time about Latin America in general, and its agrarian structures and rural mobilizations in particular, is perhaps a good time to reassess, from an anthropological point of view, his somewhat overblown reputation as a commentator on peasants, their interests and agency.[2] It might be objected that, although Hobsbawm was not an anthropologist, his analyses of Latin American peasant movements are nevertheless those of an accomplished Marxist historian, and should be judged simply as conforming to this kind of approach. In short, outlining how class formation and struggle leads to revolutionary socialist transition.[3] Assessed in terms of Marxist theory,

---

1 Drieu la Rochelle (1973: 45).
2 His views about the peasantry of Latin America and elsewhere remain influential, and have been cited extensively in the literature on agrarian movements and rural development (see, for example, Huizer, 1973: 73–83, 168; Paige, 1975: 176–77; Florescano, 1975: 43, 346ff.; Pearse, 1975: 165–67; Newby, 1978; Foweraker, 1981; Bethell, 1991: 394ff., 826).
3 The general ambivalence of Hobsbawm towards prospects for revolutionary agency is clear. Hence the following (Hobsbawm, 1973a: 14–15): 'The trouble about the revolutionary left in stable industrial societies is not that its opportunities never come, but that the normal conditions in which it must operate prevent it from developing the movements likely to seize the rare moments when they are called upon to behave as revolutionaries ... Being a revolutionary in countries such as ours just happens to be difficult. There is no reason to believe that it will be less difficult in future than is has been in the past'. Written originally at t end of the 1960s development decade, this perception that conditions necessary for a revolutionary transcendence of capitalism are absent is not only indistinguishable from that expressed by bourgeois modernization theory, but has, it seems, continued to inform his ideas ever since.

however, it is argued here the analyses by Hobsbawm were faulty to the degree that, in retrospect, they cannot be said to be as significant a contribution to our understanding of rural Latin America as was once thought to be the case.

The nearest Hobsbawm got to producing an ethnographic analysis was his influential account of the agrarian structure on the large estates (*haciendas*) in the Province of La Convención, located in the Department of Cusco on the sub-tropical eastern slopes of the Peruvian Andes.[4] This was an area where commercial agriculture had developed, and in the early 1960s was the location of an important peasant movement, based on the formation of peasant unions, and leading to the expropriation of the landlord class. In the agrarian reforms which followed, tenants and sub-tenants acquired property rights to holdings they had previously leased, and by the 1970s estates had become agrarian cooperatives. Analysing the causes and effects of these events, Hobsbawm misinterprets the kind of transformation taking place, a problem which stems in a large part from a corresponding misunderstanding of the way in which unfree production relations were – and are – central to the accumulation process. Passing references to the presence of *kulaks* notwithstanding, he omitted to differentiate peasants in terms of class. Consequently, Hobsbawm missed the significance of the role unfree labour played in the class struggle, and that in Peru such relational forms continued to be used by rich peasant ex-tenants who benefited from the agrarian reform programmes following the expropriation of landlords.

Among other things, the path he followed, and – in terms of Marxism – its political inconsistency, bears out the concerns expressed historically by socialists about the ambivalent role of academics in relation to transcending capitalism.[5] As such it serves to remind the present generation studying development of two things. Not just the continuing relevance of old debates about the reasons for and the desirability of socio-economic transformation, but also the political efficacy and/or role in such discussion of academics. It is a truism nowadays that a critique of accumulation premised on systemic transcendence – that is, a break with capitalism *tout court* – has all but vanished from the social sciences in general, and especially from the agenda of development studies. What is commonly referred to as a crisis of Marxism, a consequence it is usually said of an inability on the part of this theoretical framework to

---

4   This account, originally published in 1969, is reproduced in Hobsbawm (2016: 109–129). Elsewhere he maintains (MARHO, 1983: 30–31) that he had originally intended to study 'the agrarian problem in North Africa', since 'it was a very interesting problem'.
5   See below (Parts I and 2, plus Chapter 8) for details, and also Brass (2017b: Ch. 18).

explain current development adequately, has – it is suggested here – more to do with those who profess to be socialists.

Hence the significance of the role taken by intellectuals in advocating and pursuing a transition to socialism: as Lenin pointed out long ago, without a revolutionary theory, there can be no revolutionary practice. Appearances to the contrary notwithstanding, the attack on Marxist theory of development has been as much an internal as an external phenomenon. Over past decades, therefore, this decline has to a large extent been a result of the abandonment by many socialists in academia of the basic tenets of Marxism. Significantly, the effect of this attack on Marxist theory has not been confined to Marxism: it has had a deleterious impact on the social sciences generally, and on theory about Third World development in particular. Hence the unravelling has not merely undermined socialism as a desirable objective of the development process, but also contributed to a wider disillusion with the very concept of development itself. In this process the role of Hobsbawm has not been negligible, not least because of his capacity to bridge academia and popular culture.

Of the six sections which follow, the first draws a methodological contrast between the level at which Hobsbawm engaged with Latin America, and the rural institutions on which his studies focused. The resulting shortcomings are linked also to his espousal of the prevailing development discourse associating rural Latin America with feudalism, a problem addressed in the second section, while the third considers the institutional framework on the *hacienda* system that anthropological research might have uncovered. Attempts by Hobsbawm to qualify his earlier analysis by admitting the presence of an external capitalism are examined in the fourth, and the broader issues raised by his problems with theory are the focus of the fifth. The final section assesses the extent to which these difficulties are anomalies (linked specifically to his engagement with rural Latin America) or much rather symptomatic (connected more broadly to his political approach). Taken together, these difficulties illustrate how and why revolution and socialism can be – and have been – banished from the political agenda of the left.

2   Big in Brazil

Edited and introduced by Leslie Bethell, an historian of Latin America and a close friend of Hobsbawm, for whom the latter is always and only 'Eric', the articles in this collection unwittingly chronicle the extent of analytical shortcomings and political misdiagnoses.[6] Hence the introduction inadvertently reveals both the level and the form of Hobsbawm's engagement with Latin America, as well as his constant references to the influence and importance of his own views and writings. Despite his claim that rural Latin America was a context 'which he felt he knew well', therefore, Hobsbawm forwent long stays in fieldwork locations, preferring instead to meet the great and the good (President Fernando Enrique Cardoso, Lula), and attend conferences which 'brought together several international stars, the greatest of them [being] the historian Eric Hobsbawm'.[7] The introduction recounts how Hobsbawm 'found [himself] not surprised to meet presidents, past, present and future', noting that '[t]he bookshops of São Paulo and Rio de Janeiro were, and are, full of his books, which are virtually all best-sellers', as a consequence of which '"I'm big in Brazil", he would say'.[8]

Although such statements can be dismissed as an understandable and harmless form of auto-felicitation, they nevertheless hint at a potential difficulty: namely, a mismatch between the claims themselves, and the ethnography on which they are based. Unlike an anthropologist, for whom fieldwork involves a sustained process of participant/observation conducted at the rural grass-roots, Hobsbawm admits that his 'own research has been superficial', and that where peasant movements are concerned this is 'far from sufficient to make the study a serious one'.[9] This absence of a sustained period of fieldwork would itself not be so problematic, were it not for the fact that the objects of his Latin American research are precisely those elements – peasant economy, forms of tenure, production relations, the agrarian structure – the minutiae of which are usually accessible only as a result of close and prolonged engagement with the context where they occur. As the introduction by Bethell makes clear,

---

6 Bethell (2016: 1–25).
7 See Bethell (2016: 1, 16, 17). Much of this engagement took the form of many visits during the early 1960s, to Cuba, Brazil, Argentina, Chile, Peru, Bolivia, and Colombia. In fact, Hobsbawm (Bethell, 2016: 14) 'claimed to have visited every country in the region except Venezuela and Guyana'.
8 Bethell (2016: 15, 17). Worsley (2008: 211) describes an encounter with Hobsbawm on a beach in Brazil, newspapers having announced where one should go 'if you wanted to see the celebrated English historian, Prof. Eric Hobsbawm', and that 'I looked up, and there indeed was Eric [who] had his swimming trunks on already, underneath his street clothes'.
9 Hobsbawm (2016: 181–82). It is a mistake to regard anthropology, as does Hobsbawm, as being concerned solely with the study of 'archaic' or 'pre-capitalist' social and economic organizational forms. Thus, for example, an ethnography by Manning Nash (1958), which predated by some five years the visit by Hobsbawm to La Convención, was a comparative analysis of the indigenous population in Central America employed both in agriculture and in industry.

however, what Hobsbawm did methodologically was to apply to Latin America the same approach as he had done earlier in the case of Europe, the main distinction being that the usual secondary historiographical sources (books, articles) were in the case of Latin America supplemented by discussions with academic colleagues.[10]

Not the least difficulty faced by the way his contributions appear in this volume is that, for reasons of space, many of the article footnotes identifying references, publications and quotations are excluded.[11] Absent from the book version, therefore, are most of the sources on which Hobsbawm draws, inadvertently boosting not just the originality of his findings, but also the view that they are based on participant observation. Although not normally a problem, this lacuna is rendered problematic by claims Hobsbawm himself makes. Hence the assertion that his account of the peasant movement in La Convención is the earliest to have been written by an outsider is quite simply incorrect.[12] Furthermore, other and similarly earlier accounts of the same peasant movement – by Villanueva, and more generally by Cuadros about

---

10 'As a professional historian', notes Bethell (2016: 19, emphasis added), 'Eric was mainly interested in modern Europe. But, from his *extensive reading* and his *conversations* with academic and intellectual friends and colleagues, he accumulated an astonishing knowledge of the history of the rest of the world, especially the Third World ...' In an earlier collection of essays, Hobsbawm himself makes the same point: 'Much of what I know', he accepts (Hobsbawm, 1973a: vii–viii), 'comes from the authors reviewed here. Little is based on first-hand research. The most I can claim is to have kept my eyes open during the past decades as a modest participant, or what the anthropologists call a "participant observer", to have listened to friends in numerous countries who know a great deal more than I, and to have had at least a tourist's view of some of the activities with which these essays deal'. Even these concessions with regard to methodology are problematic: his claim to have undertaken 'participant observation' associated with anthropological fieldwork is – certainly in the case of La Convención – open to question, while 'friends in numerous countries' appear to have been, for the most part, the kind of people (= the great and the good) who would provide a 'from above' view about what was happening at the rural grassroots.
11 Thus, for example, the original article by Hobsbawm (1969a) about the agrarian structure of La Convención in Peru had 39 footnotes and five Tables, whereas the version reproduced in the book has only five footnotes and no Tables. It should be emphasized most strongly that there is absolutely no suggestion a deliberate attempt has been made to hide these published sources; as anyone responsible for putting together a volume of collected essays will attest, the issue of space – the single criterion determining what is and what is not to be left out – is invariably the only and paramount consideration driving the editing process.
12 Hobsbawm (2016: 436). At least three accounts (Craig, 1967, 1969; Bourricaud, 1970: 127ff., 332, 334), all by an 'outsider', preceded his own. The volume by Bourricaud was published first in French during 1967, and then translated for the later English edition.

the tenure structure of La Convención – make precisely the case about a link between European feudalism and the *hacienda* system in the province that subsequently resurfaces in the original article by Hobsbawm.[13] The overlap between them suggests that it is largely from these sources, and not from any Marxist theory, that he drew the argument about La Convención being a case of 'neo-feudalism'.

3   Hobsbawm and Feudalism

In order to understand the reason for and the difficulties confronting Hobsbawm's views about rural Latin America, it is necessary to contextualize them in terms of academic debates taking place after the 1939–45 war about the desirability of economic development in the Third World. His interest in the peasantry coincided with and was part of this wider discussion, the object of which was to identify and eliminate obstacles to economic growth, since these were regarded by planners and academics as the principal cause of underdevelopment, and consequently for a corresponding weakness (or absence) of a domestic bourgeoisie in what were mainly Third World nations. Over the following three decades, therefore, there existed unanimity between Marxist and non-Marxist development theory about two things: the need both for economic growth, and for the elimination of institutional obstacles to its achievement.

Throughout the 1950s the development debate was conducted mainly by historians, with reference to case-studies of transition long past.[14] Examining how and why feudalism in Europe and Japan had been replaced by capitalism, a discussion that focussed on the relative importance to these transitions of trade and class. Although the parameters were defined by historical materials, some – such as Hobsbawm – who participated in the debate about historical transitions also took part in subsequent discussions about economic growth in the Third World. Debate about development (and thus transition) underwent a twofold shift, both in terms of emphasis and the kind of case-studies involved. Instead of being concerned with specifically historical instances of transition

---

13   Compare Hobsbawm (1969a) with Villanueva (1967: 19–32) and Cuadros (1964: 15): the influence of the latter on the subject of tenure relations is acknowledged by Hobsbawm (2016: 116).

14   Published originally in the Marxist journal *Science & Society*, the 1950s debate included contributions by historians such as Maurice Dobb, Rodney Hilton, Christopher Hill, Georges Lefebvre, and Kohachiro Takahashi, as well as Hobsbawm; it was eventually collected in a single volume edited by Hilton (1976).

from feudalism to capitalism, therefore, it was conducted now largely within the domain of the social sciences, and focused on current obstacles to economic growth in underdeveloped nations.[15]

The epistemological confluence became more marked from the 1960s onwards, as development strategy for Latin America – and also Asia – was premised on the extension of the internal market so as to raise consumer demand for industrial products, thereby generating capitalist investment. Central to this strategy was a process of institutional reform. To generate economic growth, therefore, it became important to identify those components of the agrarian sector in less developed countries which – because they were thought to hinder productive efficiency – blocked investment and planning. Since economic growth was regarded by many economists as incompatible with feudal *latifundia*, a characteristic of which was unfree labour, the presence of the latter relation prevented a transition to capitalism. Along with the unreformed land tenure system, controlled by a traditional landowning class, the power of the latter was based on labour-rent coercively extracted from tenants, unfree relations of production were as a consequence equated solely with landlord/ tenant relations.

Throughout this period, development theory was guided by the orthodox view that a relation should be categorized as feudal because it prevents accumulation from taking hold, and is thus an obstacle to economic development, a process interpreted historically as the retardation of agricultural production.[16] Such relations are seen as part of the way in which a landlord class exercises and reproduces its monopoly over land, thereby depriving economically more efficient peasant cultivators from putting this resource to productive and

---

15   From the viewpoint of bourgeois economic theory, this debate, which continued throughout the 1950s, into the 1960s (the development decade) and beyond, possessed an explicit political objective. Peasants in the so-called Third World were the object of much development theory aimed at eliminating rural poverty by modernizing agriculture and making it more efficient, again to prevent socialism gaining a foothold in underdeveloped countries. The logic was simple: take land away from unproductive landlords, redistribute it to landless or land-poor peasants, who would as a result be converted into productive smallholders. As such, they would not only grow crops to feed the cities, but also consume the products produced by domestic capitalists. This, many development theorists argued, would kill four birds with one stone (agrarian reform). It would prevent the expenditure of foreign exchange on food imports, and enable the state to invest this instead on infrastructural improvements; it would combat inflationary pressures in the economy; it would form a market for domestic capitalists; and it would prevent socialism from establishing a foothold.

16   For the centrality of economic retardation to the analysis of agricultural backwardness during the feudal system in European history, see Blum (1978: Ch. 6).

better use. Deemed feudal, since they involve the presence of relational forms that are both an obstacle to economic efficiency and antagonistic to the market, therefore, unfree working arrangements such as serfdom, debt peonage, bonded labour, and the *enganche* system, represent the way the non-market power of the landlord blocks the entry into the market of smallholding peasants. Employers are dissuaded from using more flexible forms of working arrangements, such as free wage labour which can be hired and fired as and when this is necessary.

This is a crucial aspect of the claim that, where unfree 'neo-feudal' or 'semi-feudal' relations still exist, they have to be eliminated for capitalist production in the countryside to establish itself and flourish. Those holding this view, which argued that the retardation (or economic backwardness) of agriculture in the Third World was due to the continuing presence there of unfree production relations, were exponents of the semi-feudal thesis, influential in the study of agrarian development from the 1960s onwards, not just in Latin America but also in India.[17] During the following two decades, the prevailing Marxist orthodoxy advanced by exponents of the semi-feudal thesis was that unfree production relations in agriculture were an obstacle to economic growth in the Third World.[18] Since they were thought to impede productive efficiency, and thus hindered accumulation by a domestic bourgeoisie, the eradication of what were defined as pre-capitalist relational forms, and their replacement with free wage labour was central to the development theory and practice of the period. In keeping with this orthodoxy, Hobsbawm equated the Latin American form of bonded labour (the *enganche* system) with feudalism, and

---

17 For the influence on the development debate from the 1960s onwards of the semi-feudal thesis, see below Chapter 4 and also Brass (1995; 2002). Among its many exponents at that conjuncture were Pradhan Prasad, Utsa Patnaik, Terry Byres, Jan Breman, Amartya Sen, Jairus Banaji and Amit Bhaduri. Some continued to hold this view, whilst others abandoned the semi-feudal thesis when it was subject to criticism.

18 The difficulty with this interpretation is that it departs from what Marx himself said. It is clear that Marx subscribed to the view that owners of American slave plantations were capitalists, thereby confirming that in his view accumulation could occur on the basis of unfree labour. An observation about the way in which this argument by Marx has been misinterpreted deserves citing in full (Assies, 2003: 124, note 21, original emphasis): 'Note that I do not follow ... Eric Hobsbawm's edition of the *Formen* ... [where the] translation states: "If we now talk of plantation-owners in America as capitalists, if they *are* capitalists ..." The German text, however, is quite clearly affirmative: "sondern daß sie es *sind* ..." A more accurate translation might have saved a lot of ink and paper'. The updated translation that appears in the English version of the collected works (Marx, 1986: 436, original emphasis) is unambiguous on this point: 'That we now not only describe the plantation-owners as capitalists, but that they *are* capitalists ...'.

consequently saw a decline in one as evidence for a corresponding decline in the other.

As has already been noted above in Chapter 6, the Marxist view that unfree labour was an obstacle to the development of agrarian capitalism, to be eliminated and replaced by workers who were free, was challenged in the 1980s by an alternative Marxist interpretation. Much rather the opposite was the case, in that bonded labour was coercive, unsought by workers, and reproduced by capitalism due to the acute nature of the class struggle. Agribusiness enterprises, commercial farmers and rich peasants reproduced, introduced or reintroduced unfree relations because, contrary to the view of those adhering to the semi-feudal thesis, unfree workers are cheaper to employ and also more efficient.[19] Labelled deproletarianization, this was a process of workforce decomposition/recomposition frequently resorted to by employers in their conflict with rural labour.[20] The twofold object was, first, to discipline and cheapen labour-power, an undeniable economic advantage in a global context where agricultural producers had to become increasingly cost-conscious in order to remain competitive. And second, to pre-empt or block the emergence or consolidation of a consciousness of class, in the process undermining workers' solidarity and making a transition to socialism all the more difficult.

4   Hobsbawm and the *Hacienda* System

The limited engagement with the rural context in La Convención meant that Hobsbawm either missed or misinterpreted the significance of crucial aspects in the organization and reproduction of the *hacienda* system and its form of tenure. He maintains, incorrectly, that although tenancies paid for in labour services are usually defined by 'the name of *pongaje* ... this term is not used in La

---

19   In the case of labour-service obligations on the pre-reform estate system of Peru, therefore, work is undertaken not by an individual tenant but by all the members of the household, and for this reason the wage covers not one but a number of labourers. Accordingly, non-disaggregated wage levels hide the fact that they are not for individuals so much as for family groups. Rather than benefiting the rural household, therefore, unfree production relations enable a landholder to obtain the labour-power of its separate members at a far cheaper rate than he would have to pay them individually as free wage labour.

20   On the concept deproletarianization, and its challenge to earlier interpretations concerning the capitalism/unfreedom link, see Chapter 4 above. Breaking with the prevailing 'whips and chains' concept – whereby the presence/absence of unfreedom was associated simply with visual images of physical oppression – Marxist contributions to the debate restored the sale/purchase of labour-power to definitions of work arrangements that were not free.

Convención, where the labour tenants are known as *arrendires*.[21] Hobsbawm confuses the term for tenant (*arrendire*), which refers to the tenure form indicated in the landlord contract, with *ponguaje*, a term most certainly used by the rural population in the *hacienda* system of the province, which refers to a form of rental payment due as a result of entering into a tenure contract.[22] An initial observation to the effect that smallholders in the province were unable to speak Spanish is later contradicted, when noting that these same peasants 'rapidly learned to understand or even speak Spanish'.[23]

Also misrecognized was the link between peasant mobilization and religion, a result of overestimating the influence in the province of Evangelical Protestantism.[24] Similarly mistaken was his view that 'if the immigrants into the valleys had brought their communal institutions with them, the agrarian structure of La Convención would have been quite different'.[25] In fact, peasants from highland areas who migrated to lowland Amazonia and became tenants on the *hacienda* system did indeed bring their institutions with them, as the presence there of the fiesta system, fictive kinship, and exchange labour all attest. Among the things anthropological fieldwork might have revealed, therefore, was the role of the fiesta system as a form of landlord appropriation; the compatibility between accumulation, fictive kinship and exchange labour relations; and how such 'archaic'/'traditional' institutions continued to function in the post-reform era after the demise of the landlord class.

In the pre-reform era, sponsoring the annual fiesta on the hacienda system of the province entailed considerable expenditure on the part of the religious officeholder (*carguyoj*) appointed to this post by the landlord.[26] Those chosen to fulfil this economically onerous task were the better-off tenants, who regarded it as a form of labour-service, since refusal to undertake this carried the sanction of eviction from their tenant holding. Along with labour-rent, therefore, fiesta sponsorship was structured by a discourse which contributed to the notion of an intra-estate community as perceived by (and reflecting the interests of) the landlord class. Significantly, this religious institution ceased

---

21 Hobsbawm (2016: 116).
22 On this point see Fioravanti (1974: 76–77) and Brass (1999: 48). The seminal analysis of *ponguaje* as imposed on *hacienda* tenants throughout the Andean region is by Reyeros (1949).
23 Cf. Hobsbawm (2016: 38, 121).
24 See Hobsbawm (2016: 123, 192), whose interpretation about the influence of Protestantism has been challenged by Fioravanti (1974: 180–81).
25 Hobsbawm (2016: 127).
26 For the economic and ideological role of the fiesta system in pre- and post-reform La Convención, see Brass (1986a).

to be celebrated with the rise of tenant unionization, and when it was revived by the peasant membership (*socios*) of the agrarian cooperatives that came into being as a result of the land reform programme, the cost of sponsorship – undertaken by rich peasants and merchants – had diminished, declining to virtually nothing. About this institutional form, its role and transformation, Hobsbawm remains silent.

Traditional work arrangements, mistakenly idealized by Hobsbawm as 'reciprocal' and seen by 'those below' as 'legitimate', were in La Convención anything but. Usually presented in terms of equal – and therefore non-exploitative – exchanges between smallholders, the institution of fictive kinship (*compadrazgo*) was used by rich peasants in La Convención to discipline and maintain control over the labour-power of poor peasant co-parents (*compadres*) and/or godchildren (*ahijados*).[27] Forms of exchange labour (*ayni, mink'a*) were also used in much the same way by rich peasants, who exchanged not personal labour with one another but rather the labour-power of debt bonded poor peasants and agricultural workers who – in the company of their own household labour – undertook such tasks in order to repay money borrowed from better-off proprietors.[28]

---

27   For details, see Brass (1986b). Elsewhere there is a reference by Hobsbawm (1973b: 7–8) to the presence of fictive kinship, but he makes no mention of its use by capitalist rich tenants to exercise control over their unfree workforce within the *hacienda* system of La Convención. This relatively late recognition on his part may have been prompted by the work of an anthropologist (Meillassoux, 1973) who drew attention to the important economic role in peasant society of such institutions. That analyses of fictive kinship that idealize the latter in ways similar to Hobsbawm persist is clear, for example, from an account by Winchell (2018) of these links involving erstwhile tenants and landlords on the post-reform hacienda system in Bolivia. She depicts them in the same benign fashion – as the continuation of what in her view is historically a 'reciprocal' form of patronage, whereby material resources were redistributed by a 'kind' landowner as 'aid' to peasant households on the estate. No attempt is made by the case study in question to differentiate the peasantry in terms of class, let alone to analyse exchange relations as forms of surplus extraction, which suggests a return to the kind of conceptual apparatus criticized both by Marxists and by exponents of 1960s bourgeois modernisation theory (see above, Chapter 2 in this volume).

28   Hobsbawm is not alone in missing the significance of traditional work arrangements involving exchanges of labour-power between kin or fictive kin. Because many anthropologists – and others (see, for example, the attempts to redefine coercion examined in Chapter 6 above) – interpret the peasant family farm in terms of unit where the social relations are those of kinship, overlooked as a result is the extent to which such links are also ones of class. The different components within such units stand in relation of ownership of and separation from means of production belonging not just to their own household but also other ones. The fact that members of a peasant family work for and sell their own labour-power both to their own household head and also to other similar units in the

In keeping with this is the kinship dimension to subletting by rich peasants, an aspect also missing from the analysis by Hobsbawm. In order to meet labour-rent obligations to the landlord, tenants in La Convención leased out portions of their land to sub-tenants, who not only worked on behalf of the tenant on the demesne land but also on the holding operated by the tenant. Only the first kind of labour provision, by a tenant's sub-tenant to the landlord, is considered by Hobsbawm, who perceives this working arrangement simply as one arising from tenure.[29] However, the term for sub-tenant, *allegado*, also means kinsman, and indeed this kind of intra-kin-group leasing was common in pre-reform La Convención.

When Hobsbawm observes that labour-service entailed 'the obligation to work [for the landlord] a certain number of days ... with all the tenant's dependants', therefore, it was kinsfolk drawn from the peasant household who not only met the rental payments of the *arrendire*, but were also the ones evicted from their small plots when rich peasant ex-tenants reabsorbed sub-tenancies within their own holdings once they had become proprietors of land previously leased from the *hacendado*.[30] Not the least important outcome is the fact that tenure relations which additionally involved kinship recast conflict within the peasant family as that of class, a production relation that in La Convención transected rural households. The presence of this structural feature questions the validity of the assertion by Hobsbawm that 'the divisions at the heart of the peasantry were largely neutralized by ... bonds of solidarity'.[31]

---

vicinity is for this kind of anthropology nothing more than proof for the economic dynamism/adaptability/flexibility of peasant economy. Thus the purchase and sale of peasant family labour-power inside a cooperative structure, which for anthropology is evidence of the viability of smallholding agriculture, is for Marxism an indication of the socio-economic differentiation of the peasantry. Class divisions within the peasantry not only surface inside the agrarian cooperative structure, therefore, but also define its accumulation project. The economic direction followed is accordingly determined in a large part by a struggle – involving peasants, the state and agricultural workers – for control over the labour-power of non-owning kinsfolk resident on peasant family farms. Consequently, an ability to maintain control over this particular economic resource by means of the debt bondage mechanism – that is, the *enganche* system – plays an important role in deciding the economic reproduction of the agrarian cooperative.

29 Hobsbawm (2016: 119).
30 Hobsbawm (2016: 117, 119).
31 Hobsbawm (2016: 182). In the course of an interview I conducted on an ex-estate – now an agrarian cooperative – in La Convención during 1974, an agricultural labourer who was himself the son of an ex-tenant characterized pre-reform tenants as small landlords who leased tiny plots of land to sub-tenants in order to secure labour-power. This was confirmed by a poor peasant who, describing the tenant as a landlord in his own right, explained that in the pre-reform era it was necessary to work six days per month on his

5 Hobsbawm and Capitalism

During the early 1960s, when he visited La Convención, Hobsbawm was categorically of the view that its estate system – like much of the rest of rural Latin America – was quite simply feudal.[32] That the latter was the system that existed there was in his opinion due to a specific combination of economic backwardness + serfdom + non-monetary exchange + dependence on landlords.[33] It was, in short, a context where 'the oligarchies of landowners … stand in the way of industrial development'. Where feudalism was concerned, obstacles to further economic development were twofold: on the one hand the inefficiency of unfree production relations (serfdom), and on the other the fact that prestige and not wealth was the object of landownership.[34] For these two reasons, Hobsbawm argued, 'haciendas might be within or on the margins of a capitalist economy, but were not necessarily capitalist enterprises'.[35]

Not the least of the many difficulties confronting Hobsbawm, therefore, is that having dismissed the applicability of European concepts and political

---

tenant's land, and then to undertake a further six day's work for the landlord on behalf of the former, describing the tenant as a similar kind of exploiter/oppressor (*Gamonal era, pues, el arrendire*).

32 Noting 'the virtual exclusion of impoverished and marginalized peasant masses from the modern economy' in Latin America, elsewhere Hobsbawm (2011: 355, emphasis added) nevertheless maintained that during the development decade and after, '[f] or orthodox communists … the struggle for an immediate socialist transformation of these countries was not on the agenda, *as indeed it was not*'. As has been indicated above in previous chapters, this is precisely the case made by exponents of the semi-feudal thesis for the view that transition in Third World nations would be to capitalism, not socialism.

33 According to Hobsbawm (2016: 53–54), therefore, '[t]o call much of rural Latin America medieval is not a metaphor but the strict truth; for in many cases there is still substantially the mental world of the European middle ages … it is hardly misleading to call a society medieval in which feudal lords run ramshackle estates, often cultivated by serfs doing labour service … often hardly using money, linked together by feudal dependence'.

34 In La Convención, therefore, 'the choice of a *corvée* system has a tendency to restrict the contacts of a permanently large part of agricultural production … with the market', as a result of which Hobsbawm (2016: 90, 126) maintained that 'we may therefore conclude – and this is not surprising – that neo-feudalism seems to be a rather inefficient way of expanding agricultural output in frontier areas'. Equally, for Hobsbawm (2016: 96) a *hacendado* exhibited 'the quasi-feudal attitude of a man who cared not so much about the wealth his land procured, as about the prestige of owning large territories and the control over large numbers of people living on them'.

35 Similarly, and as already noted above, Hobsbawm (2016: 93) did not regard the cotton plantation in the American south as a capitalist enterprise because 'though a plantation owner evidently had to make economic calculations similar to those of any other producer for a world market, he cannot be identified with a capitalist entrepreneur, either economically or socially'.

theory to an understanding of rural Latin America, he then proceeds to explain the agrarian structure of La Convención in terms of 'medieval' European feudalism.[36] This despite the fact that, as Hobsbawm accepts, the main characteristics of feudalism – the exercise by landlords of 'independent politico-military power', their acquisition of aristocratic status, and property inheritance spanning generations – were clearly absent from La Convención.[37] Much rather, landowners produced for the market, and consequently for profit, while their estates were not inherited by other members of the same family but bought and sold. By 1976, Hobsbawm appeared to be rowing back somewhat on his earlier pronouncements about feudalism, qualifying them to the extent that, although the *hacienda* was perceived by him as internally still feudal, it was now regarded as externally 'part of a generally capitalist market or a capitalist world economy, *and subordinate to it*'.[38]

Ironically, almost a decade earlier the same combination – feudal units within the capitalist system – had been dismissed by Gunder Frank as an intellectually unsatisfactory fudge ('I can no longer recommend this distinction'); because they not only produced for the market, but were also reproduced systemically by a wider accumulation process, he consequently redefined the *hacienda* system and its relational forms as capitalist.[39] The latter interpretation is upheld by those who undertook subsequent research in La Convención; among the reasons for this view are the transformation of its peasantry from subsistence to surplus producers, the increasingly monetized economy, the reinvestment of profits, infrastructural improvements, and peasant differentiation, all processes that had been developing and/or consolidating there since the 1940s.[40]

---

36   For the inapplicability to Latin America of European political concepts, see Hobsbawm (2016: 46–47, 51).
37   Hobsbawm (2016: 94, 96–97).
38   Hobsbawm (2016: 92, 94, emphasis added). This modification stemmed, perhaps, from issues raised at a conference about 'Landlord and Peasant in Latin America and the Caribbean', held in 1972, which Hobsbawm attended. Most of the conference papers were later published in a volume edited by Duncan, Rutledge and Harding (1977).
39   Gunder Frank (1967).
40   See, for example, Fioravanti (1974: 113, original emphasis), who states that in the period before the peasant movement the mode of production in the province was already capitalist (*'En definitiva, podemos caracterizar al modo de producción dominante, en La Convención-Lares antes del levantamiento campesino, como **capitalista** ...'*).

6   Hobsbawm and Marxism

Turning to an assessment of the extent to which the analytical framework deployed by Hobsbawm is consistent with Marxist theory and historiography, broadly defined, here too there is evidence of shortcomings. To begin with, his claim that '[c]ommunism first and foremost represents a demand for human rights' is quite simply wrong.[41] What Marxism advocates is not human rights, a very general and non-class-specific political objective that can be invoked and realized by all class elements defensively within capitalism, but rather control of the state in order to achieve working class hegemony (= dictatorship of the proletariat) prior to establishing socialism.[42] Equally problematic is the characterization of feudal landlordism in terms of consumption. Thus the *hacendado* is labelled by Hobsbawm a 'traditional feudal lord' not on account of production (as would an approach that was Marxist), but rather because of the consumption patterns exhibited by those belonging to this class, which ignores the fact that currently the rich do indeed consume luxuriously, but only because they have resources to do so.[43] They are no less capitalists for that, a proportion of their surpluses being used for reinvestment.

As well as mistakenly regarding unfreedom as a characteristic only of precapitalist production relations, and consequently as evidence for the presence of feudalism, Hobsbawm perceives the *enganche* system of bonded labour as benign, again a surprising view for a Marxist historian to hold.[44] Doubting its

---

41 Hobsbawm (2016: 195).
42 Elsewhere and later, Hobsbawm (1984: 311) appeared to recognize this, when stating that 'the language of human rights was and is unsuited ... to the struggle for the achievement of the economic and social changes to which labour movements were dedicated: whether reforms within existing society or gradual changes, or revolutionary transformations of the social and economic order'.
43 According to Hobsbawm (2016: 121), therefore, '[t]he only limits to the hacendado's prosperity were those of the traditional feudal lord: managerial and financial incompetence and a tendency to throw money out of the window for purposes of luxury or status-competition'. Conspicuous consumption of surpluses is not indicative solely of pre-capitalist ('feudal' or 'neo-feudal') elites: it is very much a characteristic of present-day capitalists, as underlined by the purchase by Russian oligarchs and Asian billionaires of yachts, luxury homes, rural properties, football clubs and vast art collections. Hence the consumption patterns of Roman Abramovitch would come as no surprise to the Visconti family which ruled Milan during the medieval era. This is just the way very rich businessmen use (not just spend) their surpluses.
44 See Hobsbawm (2016: 101–02), whose views about the nature of the *enganche* may have been influenced by the revisionist interpretation of Arnold Bauer (1975), who argued that production relations on the the Chilean hacienda system were essentially benign.

efficacy where the recruitment/controlling of workers on the hacienda system in La Convención is involved, he interprets cash advances made by labour contractors as 'a sufficient incentive to make people migrate', thereby adhering to the positive way the *enganche* is viewed not by Marxists (who see it negatively, as coercive and involuntary) but rather by neoclassical economists (for whom it is a voluntary arrangement, and thus an indication of its actually being free labour). That such relations continued to be used by capitalist rich peasants during the post-reform era undermines the view linking it to feudalism, and thus decoupling the *enganche* system from the accumulation process.

His approach to the peasant movement in La Convención was similarly influenced by a perception of grassroots agency as essentially a type of *jacquerie*, a rural uprising consistent with earlier forms of 'archaic' rebellion or resistance encountered in other contexts, rather than what it was: a movement led by capitalist rich tenants, and representing their *class* interests.[45] When considering the peasant unionization in La Convención, therefore, Hobsbawm attributes the split that occurred in the Provincial Federation of Peasant Unions (*Federación Provincial de Campesinos de La Convención y Lares*) simply to different forms of mobilization, between the more radical line pursued by FIR (*Frente de la Izquierza Revolucionaria*), led by Hugo Blanco who advocated direct action (land occupations, strikes), while the reformist PCP (*Partido Comunista Peruano*) was content to operate politically within the existing legal framework. Because he omitted conceptually to differentiate the peasantry on the estate system, as Marxist historiography requires, Hobsbawm missed the significance of this split: it was class struggle arising from the class distinctions

---

The latter interpretation, subsequently extended by Bauer (1979) to the whole of rural Latin America, suggested that debt peonage was not coercive, a claim that was itself challenged (Brass, 1990). In a later publication, Bauer (2004) conceded that he may have overestimated the extent to which in Chile relations between landowners and their workforce were harmonious.

45 For his view that peasant uprisings were simply forms of 'archaic' rebellion, see Hobsbawm (1959). The genesis of the latter text is referred to by Hobsbawm in an interview (MARHO, 1983: 32–33, 36–37) where he describes *Primitive Rebels* as being about 'non-political protest movement[s]', adding that '[w]hen I wrote *Primitive Rebels* it was quite clear that this type of phenomenon was much more important in the Third World than it was in Europe'. That he eschews the possibility such mobilizations are led by and represent the interests of capitalist rich peasants – as in La Convención – is clear from his view that the 'whole question of primitive rebellion is one that arises because of the transition from precapitalist or preindustrial societies to capitalist societies'. In short, Hobsbawm's expectation is that resistance comes simply from petty commodity producers opposed to capitalist penetration of agriculture, not from commercial producers engaged in an already-established process of accumulation.

transecting the Federation of Peasant Unions.[46] Ironically, it was better-off tenants who joined FIR, which enabled them both to cease labour-service obligations to the landlord and to take possession of their own holdings, while the struggle for property rights conducted by economically more vulnerable poor peasant sub-tenants – represented by the PCP – remained within the law.[47]

7   Outside Latin America

It might be thought that the difficulties encountered by Hobsbawm when applying Marxist theory to his analysis of peasants in La Convención, are an anomaly, and specific to his limited engagement with the rural grassroots in Latin America. However, that does not seem to be the case, since the shortcomings evident in his Latin American materials – breaking with a Marxist approach, underestimating the significance of class, and thus also of class struggle – are replicated elsewhere. During the early 1980s, therefore, claims made by Hobsbawm about the decline of the working class as the subject of history were firmly in step with the fashionable anti-Marxist views of the time, and in fact no different from – and thus epistemologically supportive of – those made at the same conjuncture by many who were (or became) postmodernists.[48] He was in the vanguard of the move by those associated with 'New Times' – which heralded both the rightwards drift of 'New Labour', and the championing of identity politics which informed the 'cultural turn' – to replace working class mobilization with a populist multi-class alliance.[49]

---

46   See Blanco (1972), Alfaro and Ore (n.d.) and Fioravanti (1974: 5), who notes that Hobsbawm failed to analyse the peasant movement inn terms of class struggle (*'Para Hobsbawm, por tanto, el movimiento tenía por objectivo eliminar la "superestructura parásita" de la hacienda que contenía formas precapitalistas de producción. Su análisis, sin embargo, carece de dinamismo. No presenta el problema desde el punto de vista de la lucha de classes'*).
47   On this point, see Brass (1989).
48   One wonders whether this episode is among the things Hobsbawm had in mind when observing (Snowman, 2007: 40) that he 'worries about the incursions of postmodernism into the writing of history, the moral and even factual relativism of some historical writing ... [t]he business of the historian ... is to remember what others forget'. Others do indeed remember what Hobsbawm seems to have forgotten: his complicity with 1980s anti-foundational views that were in step with the then-emerging postmodernism that he subsequently condemned.
49   Hobsbawm confesses as much when endorsing the ideas of Gramsci, whose concept 'hegemony' epistemologically underwrote the 'cultural turn'. About Gramsci, therefore, Hobsbawm has observed (MARHO, 1983: 38): 'He's got an enormous amount of very

For those movements, the object was to emulate Thatcher, so as to become as popular as her, and the result we know: embrace the market, and see virtue in 'popular capitalism'.[50] In answer to the question about a future political direction, Hobsbawn argued that 'it has to be done by parties that have moved forward not only as class parties ... but as "people's parties" ... as spokesmen for the nation in time of crisis'.[51] This means, he elaborated, 'a broad party leading a broad movement', embodying the diversity of classes and other groups of the population', one in which 'both left and right, however embattled, have a right to be there'. In other words, a multi-class alliance uniting everyone from left to right under a nationalist banner – the very essence not just of Tony Blair's 'New Labour' but also David Cameron's 'Big Society'. Echoing Thatcher's infamous dictum TINA, Hobsbawm subsequently maintained that, in the end, there is no alternative to capitalism.[52] It is not difficult to understand why Hobsbawm became the capitalist media's 'favourite Marxist'.

In keeping with this was the criticism directed at Hobsbawm for an idealized view of rural banditry in Latin America and elsewhere as a form of social protest – an approach prefiguring the postmodern recasting of any/every 'from below' agency as progressive in political terms, simply because it was 'from below' agency.[53] This problem (as with his approach to La Convención)

---

beautiful things to say about the history of the subaltern classes, as he calls it, that I've certainly benefited greatly from'.

50   Seemingly unaware of the irony, in his autobiography Hobsbawm (2002: 273) maintains that the 'success [of *Marxism Today*] was overwhelmingly due to ... the decision to open its pages to writers far from the [CPGB] Party line, and the orthodoxies of the old socialists', in the process celebrating the fact that among its contributors were 'eminent Conservative politicians'. With a certain amount of pride, Hobsbawm (2002: 268ff.) also recounts how he intervened on behalf of those who wanted to oppose a more radical left-turn in the Labour Party, a role he discharged by criticizing the far left from a (supposedly) leftist position. Among those he opposed was Tony Benn, who in his view (Hobsbawm, 2002: 271, 275) 'was totally unsuited for the job' of Labour Party leader, and the Miners' Union during the 1984–5 strike, a struggle dismissed by him as 'the delusions of an extremist leadership'.

51   Hobsbawn (1981: 179).

52   Echoing the view of the revisionist Austro Marxist Otto Bauer (on which see Part I above), who maintained in the late 1920s that in Austria 'capitalist and socialist elements will coexist with each other' (Blum and Smaldone, 2016: 346), Hobsbawm wrote the following in an article published in *The Guardian* (London) on 20 April, 2009: 'The future, like the present and the past, belongs to mixed economies in which the public and private are braided together in one way or another'. In short, nothing to do with Marxism or socialism, but – again – the very essence of Blairite 'New Labour'.

53   For his view about bandits, see Hobsbawm (1969b). An early analysis of rural banditry in the Peruvian Andes is by López Albújar (1933). The problem with focusing on grassroots agency, and concluding that it corresponds to a form of empowerment simply

was rooted in his reliance on literary sources, which romanticized bandits as opponents of the social system, rather than its upholders. Similarly, in an essay written in 1966, Hobsbawm made a prognosis about Yugoslavia that turned out to be rather wide of the mark. Hence the problematic nature of his confident prediction that 'Belgian capitalism or Yugoslav socialism may well change, perhaps fundamentally; but both are obviously far less likely to collapse at slight provocation than the complex ad hoc administrative formulae for ensuring the coexistence of Flemings and Walloons, or of various mutually suspicious Balkan nationalities'.[54]

Regarding the transfer of a more radical critique from the margins to the academic mainstream – he was nothing if not academically mainstream, notwithstanding protests to the contrary and his position in the domain of popular culture – around the late 1990s Hobsbawm was beginning (finally) to realize the political difficulties connected with the 'new' populist postmodernism, long after these problems had been highlighted by others. Disregarding the fact that his own approach had helped lay the ground for the 'cultural turn', he began to express concerns about its influence and impact on the writing of history, declaring that an essay by him 'takes issue with the relativism of some current ("postmodern") intellectual fashions'.[55] As with other issues Hobsbawm addressed, therefore, the pervasive trend to replace Marxist concepts such as class with the academically fashionable approach of identity politics was something he seemed willing to criticize only once it was intellectually 'safe' to

---

because it occurs, is accurately summed up by Blok (1988: 99–100): 'What seems wrong with Hobsbawm's perception of brigandage is that it pays too much attention to the peasants and the bandits themselves. We must, however, look as well at the larger society in which peasant communities are contained. Without taking into account these higher levels, which include the landed gentry and the formal authorities, brigandage cannot be fully understood, for many particular characteristics of peasant communities are dependent upon or a reflex of the impact of the larger society. Given the specific conditions of outlawry, bandits had to rely strongly on other people ... all outlaws and robbers required protection in order to operate and to survive at all ... Protectors of bandits [include] powerful politicians: those who held formal office as well as grass-roots politicians. Protection thus involved the presence of a power domain'.

54 Hobsbawm (1973a: 71).
55 See Hobsbawm (1997: 266, 271), where he confesses: 'History as fiction has ... received an academic reinforcement from an unexpected quarter: the "growing scepticism concerning the Enlightenment project of rationality". The fashion for what (at least in Anglo-Saxon academic discourse) is known by the vague term "postmodernism" has fortunately not gained as much ground among historians as among literary and cultural theorists and social anthropologists ... It is profoundly relativist ... But it is wrong'. That he was taken by surprise is hinted at by the term 'unexpected', a revealing admission for a mainstream academic to have to make.

do so – when others on the margins had, so to speak, already done the heavy lifting. Moreover, such criticism made no mention of his earlier complicity with the approach he now deemed wanting.

Under the guise of 'dialogue with non-Marxists', therefore, some of the difficulties faced by Hobsbawm stem from a preparedness on his part to incorporate within his own mainstream analyses arguments originating on the margins of academia.[56] Not only was he willing to accept rather too uncritically concepts and arguments outside Marxist theory the anti-Marxist lineage and epistemology of which Hobsbawm seemed unaware, but he joined the (mainly Marxist) voices raised against the latter when their disapproval became impossible to ignore. This suggests that he transferred what was in effect a more radical critique from the margins to the mainstream – twice: first, in the form of the hostility expressed towards Marxism by the 'new' populist postmodern populism; and second, when Marxists on the margins in turn mounted a critique aimed at the 'cultural turn', which in the interim had become an academically entrenched orthodoxy.

8   Conclusion

The rarefied level of his engagement with rural Latin America meant that Hobsbawm either missed the presence of crucial institutional forms (the fiesta system, fictive kinship, exchange labour) or else misrecognized the role of those he deemed feudal (the *enganche* system). As a participant in debates during the 1950s about historical instances of feudalism, and then in the 1960s about the desirability of economic development in the Third World, Hobsbawm can be said to have approached the combined issues of agrarian

---

56   In the decade after the end of the 1939–45 war, the Communist Party Historians' Group, according to Hobsbawm (MARHO, 1983: 33) had 'above all ... been encouraged to, and had ourselves taken the initiative in, establishing dialogue with non-Marxists. We were always ... instinctively "popular frontiers"'. He then elaborates (MARHO, 1983: 39): 'What is important is that there should be such a dialogue. Marxism has become so central that a great many of the non-Marxists accept far more of the Marxist problematic than they ever did. It is impossible for them to get away without considering either Marx or a good many of the subjects raised by Marx'. When asked, finally, 'What do you think are the most fruitful areas that Marxist historians ... should undertake?', Hobsbawm (MARHO, 1983: 40–41) referred among other topics to 'the discussion of the peasantry, peasant economics and so on, where once again it seems to me, the work done by radical and Marxist historians is crucial'. While the work of Marxists on peasant economics and society is indeed crucial, what Hobsbawm missed was the extent to which it has been the object of unrelenting attacks from the 'new' populist postmodernism.

structure, landlordism, and peasant agency in Latin America with already formed ideas as to what he would encounter there. Where *haciendas* in the eastern lowlands of Peru were concerned, therefore, he saw what an historian of pre-capitalist Europe might have expected to see: landlord and tenant connected by non-market relations in an archaic, economically backward agrarian structure redolent of an earlier feudal system.

However, because the agrarian structure of La Convención was not feudal or neo-feudal but capitalist, the kinds of unfree labour Hobsbawm associated simply with landlordism, and thus in his view ended with the 1960s agrarian reform programmes, continued beyond that point, when these same production relations were used in the post-reform era but now by rich peasants. Since he ignored class struggle, and in particular its role in reproducing debt bondage, Hobsbawm failed to spot this. Differentiating the peasantry would have shown that it was (and is) not a uniformly non-market category; as both Marxist theory and anthropological research underline, its distinct rural strata participate in the market in opposing ways. In the Peruvian location where he conducted research, therefore, rich peasants employed the unfree labour-power of poor peasants, their family members and kinsfolk, in order to accumulate capital.

Moreover, the problems Hobsbawm had in analysing rural Latin America were not anomalous, in that similar kinds of difficulties are evident in his approach to issues of class and class struggle elsewhere. Of the two contrasting images – on the one hand the clenched fist on the front cover of the book *Viva La Revolución*, signifying revolutionary solidarity and fervour, and on the other the notorious photo of the author kneeling in front of the Queen to receive his decoration (the Companion of Honour, an establishment bauble) – it is perhaps the latter that is the more apposite, symbolizing as it does the political trajectory followed by Eric Hobsbawm. When all the dots are joined up, therefore, what emerges is an undeniable connection between two things. On the one hand the seeming acceptability of his views to those with socio-economic power/authority: and on the other his perception of the *hacienda* system in La Convención as feudal (making the next step a transition not to socialism but to capitalism); his opposition both to a more radical Labour politics and to the 1984–5 miners strike; his advocacy of class collaboration; and his opinion that – ultimately – the capitalist system itself cannot be transcended.

CHAPTER 10

Marxism, or Postmodern Precursor? John Berger on Peasants

> 'I was a literary radical, indifferent to economics, suspicious of organization, planning, Marxist solemnity and intellectual system-building; it was the rebels of literature, the great wrestlers-with-God, Thor with his mighty hammer, the poets of unlimited spiritual freedom, whom I loved – Blake, Emerson, Whitman, Nietzsche, Lawrence … I thought of socialism simply as a moral idea, an invocation of History in all its righteous sweep'.
>
>> A self-description of his own 1930s politics by ALFRED KAZIN that could equally apply to the same kind of radical opposition to modern capitalism on the part of the 'new' populist postmodernists.[1]

∴

> "'Do you know … what the trees say when the axe comes to the forest?… When the axe comes to the forest, the trees say: Look! The handle is one of us!'"
>
>> An observation by a peasant recounted in Berger that could equally describe the welcome extended by many on the left to the 'new' populist postmodernism.[2]

∴

1   Introduction: Holy Humble Peasants?

Any interpretation of the way in which John Berger (1926–2017) – Marxist, art critic/historian, poet, novelist and artist – writes about the peasantry must itself be aware of two things: first, not at issue are his views about art and art history, which fall outside the analysis that follows; and second, his views about peasants merit examination precisely because of the preeminent role Berger occupied in popular culture. Two further reasons why such views matter are: first, the rising tide of populism currently in metropolitan capitalist nations

---

1   Kazin (1966: 5, 6).
2   Berger (1992: 239).

(Europe, the United States), and specifically its rural component; and second, the need to understand how and why populism differs from Marxism, and what this distinction entails politically. This divergence has not always been recognized on the left today, where it is still possible to encounter arguments that fail to distinguish between Marxist theory and populist approaches.[3] Nowhere is this conflation more evident than in the way peasants are conceptualized, as a sociological category (bearers of an economic, ideological and cultural identity) and in relation to socialist politics (agency generated by such identity).

The 1980s, when Berger was writing his trilogy about the peasantry, was also a decade characterized by a number of interrelated transformations: on the one hand the academic decline of development theory itself, and in particular those approaches – such as modernization and Marxism – which adhered to notions of 'progress'; and on the other, the simultaneous rise of neoliberalism and postmodernism. Critiques of capitalism underwent a corresponding shift, away from political economy and towards culture/aesthetics, and increasingly took the form of opposition to the impact of accumulation on grassroots rural farming/tradition/culture/ethnicity. In keeping with this, class as an analytical concept was downgraded and/or replaced by non-class identity; modernity, revolution, and socialism as desirable objectives gave way to tradition, resistance, and a benign (= 'nicer') capitalism.

It is argued here that the approach of Berger to peasant society neatly reflects this shift: not only was he by profession an art critic/historian, where aesthetic issues are important considerations, but his interest in 'the rural' emerged from a concern that outmigration to 'the urban' undermined custom, tradition, culture, community, and subsistence cultivation at the level of the village.[4] The epistemological and political shifts taking place at that conjuncture are significant, moreover, in that the literary depiction by Berger of peasant society constitutes an influential link in the domain of popular culture between similar epistemologies spanning two distinct conjunctures: it both harks back to pre-1939 concepts of village life as portrayed historically by populists or ethnographers, and simultaneously prefigures the way petty commodity producers were to be recuperated as pristine 'cultural subjects' in the emerging 'new' populist postmodern analyses (Subaltern Studies, eco-feminism, post-colonialism, post-structuralism, post-development).

---

3   This is an issue that surfaces and is explored in previous chapters of this volume.
4   That aesthetic considerations structured the way rural society was perceived by Berger is clear from the attention (Mohr and Berger, 1979: 153) he drew to a photograph of 'a young Polish peasant girl...totally uninfluenced and untouched by sexist consumerist glamour', thereby underlining the contrast between peasant = rural = pristine = culturally authentic before the contamination by its 'other', the 'urban'.

In the early 1960s Berger left Britain for Europe, settling in a French village in Haut-Savoie during the mid-1970s.[5] His experiences there form the subject matter of the *Into Their Labours* trilogy that appeared in the course of the 1980s, consisting of three books: *Pig Earth* (1979), *Once in Europa* (1987), and *Lilac and Flag* (1990).[6] This experience is itself supplemented by material contained in his archive – the John Berger Manuscripts, British Library (Add. Ms. 8864) – which consists for the most part of unpaginated notes. The latter reveal the full extent of his background research for the trilogy, extending from monographs/ articles (written by, among others, Malcom Caldwell, Foucault, Shanin, Chayanov, Eric Wolf, F.G. Bailey, Fanon, René Dumont, Samir Amin, Trotsky, Marx and Engels) to French history and ethnographies about Haut Savoié (van Gennep, Amelie Gex). Accordingly, there can be no doubt either about the depth and impressiveness of this preparation, or indeed about the quality of his writing, neither of which are questioned here.

Broadly speaking, as the trilogy proceeds the narrative mood becomes progressively darker: the first book is mainly about 'the rural', and in effect largely a celebration of peasant life, albeit an existence structured by hardship and misfortune; the second charts the incursion of 'the urban' into 'the rural', bringing with it destruction of petty commodity production, the corrupting influence of the city leading increasingly to outmigration; the events of the final book are located in 'the urban', portrayed in images that are unambiguously dystopian as erstwhile peasants – now displaced/alienated migrants – struggle unsuccessfully to survive, all the while wanting to return 'home' to village life (which they are no longer able to do). Of interest politically is that the critical discourse of Berger is aimed not so much at capitalism as a socio-economic system that transects the urban/rural sectoral divide as at 'the urban' itself, and in his view

---

5 The description by Caute (1971, 68, 75, original emphasis) of the political 'awakening' by Sartre – when long-held ideas call forth action – might apply just as well to one of the reasons why Berger settled in a French village: '[T]he writer shares with other members of the intelligentsia an acute sense of guilt, and therefore of responsibility, in the face of the prehistoric peasant poverty ... The masses, the poor, the proletariat, the oppressed, about whom Sartre had written so much, and whose cause he had championed *on paper*, suddenly declare their absolute reality. Their cries, their songs, their stench, their marching feet invade his study; they move towards him accusingly, challenging his right to turn them into figments of his imagination'.

6 All references here are to the single-volume edition (Berger, 1992), containing each book in the trilogy: *Pig Earth* (Berger, 1992: 1–179), *Once in Europa* (Berger, 1992: 181–342), and *Lilac and Flag* (Berger, 1992: 343–513). The volume also contains a non-fictional account by Berger outlining his views about the peasantry: originally appearing as a postscript to *Pig Earth*, it is placed as the Introduction (Berger, 1992: xiii–xxix) to the single-volume edition.

its alienating/corrupting/destructive impact on what for him is its pristine 'other': the rural generally, village life, and especially the peasant family farm.

A crucial and twofold background to what Berger thought and wrote about peasant society was on the one hand longstanding debates between Marxism and populism and the future role of peasant economy, and on the other how the latter was addressed politically during the development decade of the 1960s. Because of this, and also because of the position Berger occupies in popular culture, his views about peasant society, how it is transformed and what kinds of political outcome are as a result desirable/feasible, all merit closer examination in terms of discussions about capitalism, socialism, development, and 'progress' taking place at that conjuncture. At a time when 'progress' and 'development' were perceived as desirable and feasible goals (both at home and abroad), therefore, he was one of those writers – others included V.S. Naipaul and John Fowles – who combined anti-modern, anti-urban views with a championing of 'the rural'.[7]

Early on in the development decade Berger declared his opposition to all forms of modernisation theory ('unpolitical realists today'), not just bourgeois variants but also Marxist ones: at that same conjuncture, moreover, he also recognized a commitment to 'the truth of the peasant driven by the seasons' in effect broke with socialist theory.[8] The strength both of this commitment, and of the corresponding rejection of development-as-modernisation as applied

---

7   On the pro-rural/anti-urban discourse of Naipaul, see Brass (2014b: 309ff.). The same combination pervades the journals kept by Fowles (2003, 2006). In 1968, therefore, he (Fowles, 2006: 50) declares 'my love of this countryside very strongly. I do not want to live anywhere else in the world. I never want to live for more than a few days at a time in London again', while in 1971 Fowles (2006: 106–07, original emphasis) writes that 'I become progressively ... more deeply involved in the natural process – in *Mother* Nature, to use the old term'. Twenty years later the same theme is reiterated (Fowles, 2006: 375, 386), but now more pessimistically: 'Nature now becomes the past, in the sense of what-is-going rather than what-is-gone ... This is why so much in modern life (and modern London) alienates me, why I have such doubts about the political left; that is, my token "socialism" of the last twenty or thirty years ...' and 'I have always been "for" conservation, the protection of nature and all the rest of it ...'.

8   Invoking the images of 'holy humble peasants' found in the art of Millet, Berger (1960: 189, 190–91) observed that the artist 'chose to paint peasants because he was one, and because – under a somewhat similar influence to the unpolitical realists today – he instinctively hated the false elegance of the beau monde'. The same essay continues: 'When [Millet] was accused of being a socialist, he denied it ... because socialism seemed to him to have nothing to do with the truth he had experienced and expressed: the truth of the peasant driven by the seasons: the truth so dominating that it made it absolutely impossible for him to conceive of any other life for a peasant'. The latter sentiment, as will be seen below, encapsulates Berger's own approach to the peasantry.

to petty commodity production, was confirmed subsequently when castigating planners in Europe 'who do not use the word *elimination* but the word *modernisation*. Modernisation entails the disappearance of the small peasants (the majority) and the transformation of the remaining minority into totally different social and economic beings'.[9] In short, both capitalism and socialism are politically unacceptable because each is equally culpable of advocating a 'progress' which threatens, finally, to eradicate the peasant family farm.[10] Like populists, therefore, Berger lamented the process of depeasantsation linked to development-as-modernization, and – unlike Marxism – sought to reverse this by defending/protecting/re-establishing a subsistence-oriented peasantry cultivating its own family farm.

2   No Country for Old Peasants

Over the three books of the trilogy a discourse-for and a discourse-against composed by Berger emerges unmistakeably. Endorsed by the discourse-for is what he regards as positive aspects, voiced either by a narrator or by characters in the stories. These include Nature, rural-based small-scale economic activity (peasant family farming, handicrafts) and culture (religious/regional/family identities derived from Nature). Arraigned against the latter, and depicted negatively, are the elements which constitute the discourse-against: urban-based large-scale economic activity, consisting of industrialisation, finance capital, the city, manufacturing, technology, and money, all of which are imposed on rural inhabitants and result in the erosion of a hitherto pristine local culture, traditions, and values. In keeping with this duality, Berger portrays not only folk remedies – an anthropological trope – positively, but also equates Nature with 'natural' peasant farming, describing Nature/agriculture in terms of an eternal/unchanging rhythm that 'resists change', like peasants.[11] 'I would like to

---

9   Berger (1992: xxv).
10 'The peasant suspicion of "progress"', writes Berger (1992: xxviii, emphasis added), 'as it has finally been imposed by the global history of corporate capitalism and by the power of this history even over *those seeking an alternative to it*, is not altogether misplaced or groundless'. Notes in the archive (Add. Ms. 8864/1/30) expand on this, observing that peasants 'are never *within* the plans of progress[,] always on the margins, ignored or seen as an obstacle which the plans must overcome. They are never the subjects of history according to those who make it but an object: an object to be circumscribed or transformed. History therefore tends to become for them a force to be either ignored or resisted' (original emphasis).
11 Berger (1992: 26–27, 47, 48). The harshness of Nature is described (Add. Ms. 8864/1/30) thus: 'Nobody in the mountains can be blind to the fact that nature is pitiless. Or, more

know what life was like ten thousand years ago', a peasant says, 'Nature would have been the same. The same trees, the same earth ... People exaggerate the changes in nature', 'Nature resists change'.

Accounts of birth and slaughter of animals convey the 'naturalness' of the life cycle in the countryside, in which livestock, peasant, and nature itself are depicted by Berger as indistinguishable and interchangeable.[12] Violent death is an ever-present event in the trilogy, a recurring theme underlining what for him is in one sense the overlap in terms of signification: nature = farming = peasant = animal = death.[13] Hence the parallel between two kinds of loss experienced by the peasant farm of family members, due both to violent deaths (war, avalanches) and to emigration (abandoning the rural): for this reason, where the family farm is concerned, migration is merely additional form of death.[14] In another and opposite sense, it marks the rebirth of the peasantry, since it is only when dead that rural smallholders are able to exercise the autonomy they desire and seek – but are prevented from realizing – in life.[15]

Hence the antithetical and doubly symbolic aspect – (on earth) peasant family farming dies, (in heaven) peasant family farming lives – that Berger ascribes to death, a twofold view consistent with the claims of religion. However, he denies that the cycle of birth/life/death as conceived by the peasant, although it accounts for the importance of religious belief, is the same as that of priests and rulers.[16] This is because what the peasant wants is 'to return to a

---

accurately, that its scale of action, re-action and recurrence takes no account of a single life. There are places on the plains ... where the idea of an appeal to nature does not seem a total absurdity. Among the mountains, beneath the crags, beside the fallen boulders, along the stones of the rivers, such an idea cannot occur: nothing suggests that any appeal could be heard, let alone considered. We are without resort to rights, or any appeal. At the same time the fineness and variety of what grows between the rocks ... the intricacy of what lives cannot be explained by brute chance. This is why we are metaphysicians of one kind or another'.

12 Berger (1992: 3–6, 10–14, 42, 66, 110, 153, 262, 315).
13 Berger (1992: 26, 152, 153, 405–16, 488–500).
14 Berger (1992: 214). A variation on this kind of concern – not so much Nature = death as the death of Nature itself – occupied Fowles (2006: 411), who attributed his unhappiness to the fact, as he saw it, that 'Nature will shortly cease to exist', adding: 'Crystal-clear what is wrong, and equally clear that as a species we cannot face doing anything about it. We are now far too many, beyond restraint, and multiplying like an uncontrolled virus'.
15 Conceptually differentiating the term 'survivor' between on the one hand someone who survives an ordeal, and on the other 'a person who has continued to live when others disappeared or perished', Berger (1992: xvi) indicates that it is in the second sense that he uses the term. The latter meaning is consistent with the interpretation of death-as-rebirth, or the fact that peasants survive even when dead.
16 Berger (1992: xvii).

life that is not handicapped [by taxes, rent]. His ideals are located in the past'. Hence the belief that '[a]fter his death [the peasant] will not be transported into the future – his notion of immortality is different: he will return to the past'. For smallholders, therefore, death also opens the door to a desirable – yet in life unobtainable – golden age in the pre-capitalist era, when they were able to reproduce themselves economically as 'pure' subsistence farmers, not subordinated to more powerful social forces (landlord, capitalist).[17]

Much the same is true of those who migrate to the city, for whom death is also the only way to escape from the alienation that is the urban. Thus the final story of the trilogy recounts how all the dead are now on a white ship, a 'floating palace' on which the homeless/exiles – the migrants – had 'rooms of their dreams': these cabins are in fact their tombs, and the dead occupants are returning 'to the village, my father's village'.[18] In the majority of instances, peasants want migrants to return – or stay – so that the family farm can survive, but migrants refuse to comply. Yet the latter accept that they fail to benefit from migration, and regret their quest for income that urban employment brings, dismissing it as 'avarice' or a desire to consume which in turn fuels the necessity for money. In other narratives, however, migrants who either feel alienated or else fail to find employment in the city all express a desire to return to the rural, one such advising his son to '[g]o back to the village, that's what I'd like to do'.[19]

Accordingly, the rural is presented by Berger as the embodiment of all that is 'good', and counterposed as such to the urban, indicted as the locus of all that is 'bad'. In doing so, he reasserts during the 1980s both the approach to and concepts about petty commodity production which 1960s modernization theory and Marxism had challenged as obstacles to development, among them fatalism. The latter is a recurring trope in the trilogy, extending from the view that for peasants '[l]ife has always been a struggle. Do you think it can ever be anything else?' to a reply by a female peasant when informed by a male communist worker that '[t]hings can't go on as they are', when she says: 'They do go on ... every hour ... till one day each of us dies'.[20] He, a communist worker, believes in progress, in change for the better as something possible; she, by contrast, a peasant (from a farming background) is fatalistic – things can't be

---

17 'The peasant imagines an unhandicapped life', writes Berger (1992: xviii), as 'a life in which he is not first forced to produce a surplus before feeding himself and his family, as a primal state of being which existed before the advent of injustice'. It is in this sense, therefore, that peasants only come alive when in fact they are dead.
18 Berger (1992: 501–11).
19 Berger (1992: 381, 414, 416, 436, 449–50, 494, 499).
20 Berger (1992: 77, 326–27).

changed, won't ever change. Peasant acceptance of misfortune (= passivity/ fatalistic) is itself another anthropological trope.[21]

Indeed, at times it seems that Berger is intent on reinserting many of the concepts deployed by earlier anthropological discourse into the debate about rural development and the place within this of peasant farming. Significantly, perhaps, his methodology – long-term participant/observation – was not so different from ethnographic practice, although this alone would not explain the reappearance of anthropological tropes.[22] Alongside a broadly positive view about the nature of peasant society, therefore, he chronicles a process of rural decay, a smallholding agriculture marked by a steady decline.[23] For Berger, therefore, all peasants are merely 'survivors'.[24] Even for those who manage to do well – pay off debts, build up a large herd – there is no guarantee of survival, since outmigration (and related processes) deprives them of the workforce to ensure the continuity of the rural economy.[25] As will be seen below, this epistemological restoration has political consequences, not least in anticipating (and helping to create) the ideological space subsequently filled by the 'new' populist postmodernism.

3   Migrants, Gender, Money

Turning to the discourse-against as depicted in the trilogy, the decline both of peasant family farming and with it peasant society is due to a combination of external threats: outmigration, money, technology, and – more generally – the impact on all things rural of the urban.[26] Of these, by far the most

---

21   Passivity/fatalism attributed by Berger (1992: 17–21, 33) to smallholders is illustrated by the way in which a rockfall that destroyed a rural dwelling is perceived, or the utterance by a peasant that he had 'always expected little'.
22   Whereas Berger can justifiably be regarded as having engaged methodologically with the rural grassroots, and thus to have undertaken a long-term process of participant/observation, the same cannot be said of Hobsbawm (see above, previous chapter).
23   Berger (1992: 244).
24   Berger (1992: 52–64, 114ff.).
25   Berger (1992: 244ff.).
26   Fowles (2003: 616–17) also depicts the urban as despoiler of all things rural, and – like Berger in the case of France – equates this process with national decline: 'But the country dies hard. Billhooks and rabbit snares in an ironmonger's; and out of the towns the emptiness of the countryside is extraordinary ... I think this is owed to modern agriculture. There have never been fewer farm-workers; and those that remain fight a sort of rear-guard action against the town. But we are the last generation to know this old England. The population of 2064, with their three-car families and their autostradas and helicopters, will kill the England I love beyond all hope'.

destructive process is outmigration, which itself possesses a gender-specific dimension. Throughout the trilogy, therefore, main antagonism expressed by Berger is towards the deleterious effect of an increasingly significant pattern of rural-to-urban migration, which threatens what he maintains is the stability of the family farm, and thus of peasant society itself.[27] Hence the loss of a cow is a metaphor for the loss to peasant economy of family members – either male or female – who migrate to the city.[28] Those who leave the land for the city are for the most part family members: neighbours, brothers, sisters, or adult children of the peasant farmer who remains.[29] This rural predicament is not entirely gender-specific, in that peasant-as-victim as depicted by Berger can be either male or female, notwithstanding the similarity of their fate (oppression, misfortune, loss of land/livestock, death).[30] Neither are their exploiters gender-specific, having in common only the identity of coming from the town/city and possessing money.

One narrative concerns an old peasant woman who never married because men left the valley, due to insufficient land to persuade them to remain, while others involve male peasant farmers also ageing and unmarried who either remain so – because it is women who outmigrate – or are seduced/misled by urbane females.[31] This negative image of urban-woman-as-predator reproduces not only the familiar opposition rural=good/urban=bad that structures agrarian myth discourse, therefore, but also the way females are depicted in film *noir*.[32] The latter portrays the city woman as dangerous/temptress/seducer/whore, who is characterized as the unnatural 'other' of the rural woman, depicted as the virtuous/safe/mother who is both the provider of family subsistence and the guardian of nature itself. Since the labour-power of females is a crucial element that enables the peasant family farm to reproduce itself economically, its loss due to outmigration cannot but undermine petty commodity production.[33] When a village school recommends that the daughter of a peasant farmer be sent to continue her studies in town, enabling her

---

27 Berger (1992: 36).
28 Berger (1992: 52ff.). A consequence of rural outmigration by women is that '[n]obody wants to marry a peasant today' (Berger, 1992: 193).
29 Berger (1992: 248).
30 Berger (1992: 95–152, 184–212).
31 For these narratives, see Berger (1992: 23–33, 248, 262, 267–68, 184–212, 213–43).
32 As has been argued elsewhere (Brass, 2000: Ch. 7), the opposition between rural/good and urban/bad that structures populism and agrarian myth discourse is also central to the film *noir* genre.
33 So important to the survival of peasant economy are women that Berger (1992: 207) equates them with Nature ('Women are stronger [than men], they merge with the weather ...').

to train to be a teacher, the father objects that 'she'll never be a teacher ... [s]he's too close to the ground'.³⁴ In his eyes, therefore, her destiny is to remain on the farm, marry and have children, thereby ensuring the continuity (= survival) of smallholding cultivation, as against becoming part of the urban economy (study, teaching) and leaving agriculture.

Where the stability of the peasant family farm is concerned, it is not just out-migration but also immigration that is depicted as having a negative impact on the smallholding economy. Thus a successful but unmarried livestock farmer loses the affections of a village woman who is attracted to a young immigrant undertaking seasonal labour in the locality, eventually marrying him and moving to a town on the other side of the frontier.³⁵ Accordingly, 'foreigners' (from Italy) are responsible for a threefold depletion of nature: they not only succeed in drawing women (= nature) away from the land (= nature), but by cutting down the forest with chainsaws are engaged in destroying Nature for commercial gain (= money). The latter is seen by Berger as one of the principal forms in which the city comes to – and corrupts – the countryside.

Money is the embodiment of urban 'otherness', to be contrasted as such with a peasantry that eschews economic transactions. Hence the 'lasting impression [of a peasant woman who did menial work in Paris] was one of money continually changing hands. There, without money, you could literally do nothing ... with money you could do anything', a view echoed by another peasant woman, who says 'money changes everything'.³⁶ Similarly, another smallholder refuses to sell his farm to the factory, which increasingly surrounded it physically, despite being offered large sums (= to a peasant money is not important), proclaiming '[m]y patrimony is not for sale'.³⁷ In the city, a migrant is informed by a tramp that 'with no money there's little left on the surface of the earth ... [i]n dreams money's abolished. Everywhere'. This reiterates two claims made by Berger: not just the view of a pre-capitalist golden age where subsistence farmers have no need of money, but also that it is only in dreams that money – and capitalism – can be eradicated. The inference is that any attempt – by, for example, revolutionary agency – to transcend the economic system is (and always will be) a chimera, a pessimistic view that is consistent with the way Berger conceptualizes the city as an unmitigated dystopia. Nothing can be done is the political message, except to return to peasant farming in the countryside.

---

34   Berger (1992: 280–82).
35   Berger (1992: 256ff.).
36   Berger (1992: 25, 127, 255–56).
37   Berger (1992: 277).

Penetration of the rural subsistence economy by money licenses the introduction of yet another destructive (= negative) element. That technology is perceived by Berger as the negative urban 'other', not just of the rural and Nature but also of gender is evident from the way it features throughout the trilogy. Along the lines of 'bad things happen to those who abandon farming', therefore, one migrant to the city is badly burned by a faulty television set (= technology), and dies as a result.[38] In another narrative a peasant whose family incurred debts and lost land but then became a successful livestock farmer, married a wife because she could milk cows, and when she died young bought a milking machine.[39] Set in the early 1960s, the same account – the title of which is *The Time of the Cosmonauts* – underlines the contrast between the traditional forms of subsistence cultivation in 'the rural' and scientific advances in 'the urban'. When Gagarin circled the earth, therefore, technology made this possible, whereas in the countryside down on earth peasants were unable to survive, grinding out a living.

Each of these negative elements – outmigration, money, technology – symbolize for Berger the power of the urban, a theme that grows in importance across the first two books of the trilogy. A local factory is the described as the 'enemy' of the farm, while a peasant whose two sons worked in a local factory opposed this, saying: 'First, they try to take our land, then they want our children. What for? To produce their manganese. What use is their manganese to us?'.[40] This sectoral divide separating city from countryside is emphasized by a contrast between factory/urban/industry as 'dead' ('inert, barren'), poisoning the land, the forest, livestock, and peasant/farming/agriculture/Nature as alive, living.[41]

It is in the third book of the trilogy, however, that negative views about urban society proliferate and become more pronounced, as Berger outlines the lives of those who have migrated from the rural. The city is depicted by him as confused and confusing, a prison located in an unknown/unknowable context possessing names drawn from different geographies and histories (Troy, Swansea, Champ-de-Mars, Escorial).[42] Urban identities are in constant flux, unfixed, and always changing; the city even consumes its inhabitants ('eat me for ever and ever') who barely get by in the informal economy. Unsure of their identities, both the city and its inhabitants form the dystopic 'other' of

---

38   Berger (1992: 374, 378, 384).
39   Berger (1992: 244–71).
40   Berger (1992: 274, 307).
41   Berger (1992: 311, 321, 435).
42   Berger (1992: 347–65).

the village, where money is unimportant and peasants know who they are and what they need to do.[43]

Sectoral duality (urban = nasty, rural = nice) extends to the contrast between the city police station – a menacing place – and its cosy rural counterpart 'where there are curtains in the windows, wives upstairs, and sometimes even the smell of cooking'.[44] Informed as it is by the sectoral dichotomy urban = bad and rural = good, Berger continuously underscores this dissimilarity, painting the city – to which 'countless men have migrated' as a place where only a downward spiral awaits those who leave the land.[45] Having left the village, therefore, 'there is nothing in the world they can trust or depend upon' in an urban dog-eat-dog setting where money is everything; this is to be distinguished from the rural, where according to Berger there is little or no money, and certainly no accumulation process, and consequently no similar dog-eat-dog competition.[46]

4 Different Stories, Same Themes

All these themes pervade one of the longer stories, *The Value of Money*, where the demise of the peasant family farm is blamed on outmigration, technology, and the state.[47] Sons refuse to follow the father as peasants, preferring instead to get better-paid urban employment. Consequently, the farm becomes unviable as an economic unit. The purchase of a tractor indicates the way – debt, consumption – in which smallholders will be separated from their means of production, and with this their form of existence. Significantly, this development is initiated and paid for with gains from fraudulent deals in the city by the youngest son, who expresses contempt for his father's occupation and 'antique' farming methods, and goes ahead with the purchase despite resistance from the latter to tractorization. As a result of installing modern technology, the peasant proprietor falls into debt and is unable to meet tax

---

43 Even the way the dead are remembered is for Berger (1992: 386) sectorally distinct. Hence those who die in the village have memorials, and are in some sense fixed in the physicality of the rural itself, whereas in the city the dead are 'forgotten more quickly', and only the rich/famous are remembered by having streets named for them (= power of money). In the city, therefore, remembering the dead is part of unsuccessfully trying to recall who one is – in other words, the fate of any migrant who abandons farming for city life.
44 Berger (1992: 405).
45 Berger (1992: 462).
46 Berger (1992: 462–71).
47 Berger (1992: 66–92).

payments due to the state. He kidnaps the tax inspectors, then releases them, but is arrested and imprisoned.

In what amounts to a morality tale, therefore, Berger links the demise of a positive institutional form (subsistence farming = virtuous/good/authentic) to a series of negative consequences (= corrupting/bad/inauthentic): outmigration generates money from urban employment, which in turn licenses the consumption of technology ('he bought [the tractor] because he can't help buying') that starts the whole process of decline, whereby the peasant loses both land and liberty.[48] Betraying his father in multiple ways, the son refuses to continue farming, migrates to the city, finally invoking modernity and installing machinery, all of which undermine the viability of the family smallholding. Observing that '[t]he world has left the earth behind it', the father accuses the son of abandoning the earth, and asks: 'Do you know what those machines [tractors] are for?... There's one job they all do ... Their job is to wipe us [= peasant family farmers] out'. He concludes that '[o]n the plains there will be no more peasants'.

Many of the same themes inform the next three stories, where Berger traces what he terms the three lives of a peasant woman. The first of these recounts how males (the narrator; and her brothers) migrate to the city, she is depicted as an 'authentic peasant', the embodiment of rural virtues who works hard to keep the farm going, event to the extent of seducing the narrator in an unsuccessful attempt to keep him on the farm.[49] Like the son in the preceding story, he is the antithesis of the 'authentic peasant', and eschews agriculture in favour of urban work, migrating to Latin America and then Canada in search of work. This story also replicates the theme of migration-as-betrayal, a negative image juxtaposed with a positive one of peasant-as-backbone-of-the-nation, the latter a familiar claim made in populist discourse. When in 1944 resistance fighters against the Germans come to the farm, it is the two brothers (= migrants) who betray them, causing their deaths. By contrast, she helps and protects them, and – learning of the betrayal – refuses ever again to work for her brothers.

The second part of this narrative takes place in 1967, and pursues these events in terms of outcome and implications.[50] Disinherited by her brothers, and landless, the now aged peasant woman is described by Berger as 'a child of the earth' and a 'patriot'; she reproaches the narrator for his lack of patriotism (abroad when needed at home) and labels her brothers 'traitors' for having

---

48   The archive (Add. Ms. 8864/1/33) makes it clear that consumerism is the 'other' of subsistence.
49   Berger (1992: 95–122).
50   Berger (1992: 123–52).

betrayed the resistance fighters some two decades earlier. A 'survivor', the peasant woman becomes a petty trader and smuggler, so as 'to move back to the village'. Rumoured to have a hidden fortune, she is murdered by an unknown assailant searching for it, emphasizing the link between money and death. For Berger, therefore, peasants defend the nation, while migrants are portrayed as doubly disloyal: to the countryside and to the country. Nevertheless, the fate of the peasant woman – like that of all peasants – is landlessness and suffering.

The third story in this series begins with the funeral of the murdered peasant woman, and continues by focussing on her thoughts/actions in the afterlife.[51] Now dead, she addresses the still-living narrator, whom she wanted to marry, and chides him for refusing her.[52] The aged narrator, a widely travelled migrant, expresses regret for his wasted existence ('Where had my life gone? I asked myself'.), lamenting both that he should have married her and remained in the village, and that '[a]varice is an excessive longing for the good things of life and particularly money'. All those who have died violently – including the resistance fighters – live on in the forest, where they build a chalet for the peasant woman and the narrator to occupy, once married. Only when they are dead and in the forest do peasants own everything and have no need of money.[53]

At the beginning of the second book in the trilogy a long story once again highlights the impact on the peasant family farm of all the negative characteristics attributed by Berger to the urban.[54] Although the protagonist – a young but gullible peasant proprietor – imagines himself to be doing well economically, what he owns is in the process of being taken from him by a combination of urban 'others': his desire for money and a blonde female from the city. Encountering a visiting couple from the city looking for a place in the countryside, he begins an affair with the woman. For his part, the peasant proprietor is physically strong and a hard worker, but easily deceived: he thinks she loves him, and wants to have his children, thereby continuing the line of those who cultivate the land and thus ensure the survival of the smallholding. He ignores advice from a local shepherd that 'she is from the city [and] city women are not the same [as rural females]' because they 'calculate everything for money',

---

51   Berger (1992: 153–78).
52   There are further instances throughout the trilogy of the narrator and/or others being addressed by peasants now dead (Berger, 1992: 200, 216–17).
53   The link between the dual themes of money and death, and the absence of the former once peasants are dead/reborn is expressed in the archive (Add. Ms. 8864/1/33) thus: 'What is the story really about? ABOUT MONEY. *It's about a preparation for a life to come*' (original emphases).
54   Berger (1992: 213–43).

and the warning to '[b]e careful, your blonde will strip you of everything. Then she'll throw you aside like a plucked chicken'.

Sure enough, the young peasant proprietor begins along the path of decline, in the course of which core elements of rural identity are betrayed: he neglects his livestock, is interested only in money, and openly conducts an affair with a woman from the city. In order that they can marry (= rural + urban) and have room for their children (= continuity of peasant farming), the peasant proprietor makes her a gift of his village house. When he loses much of his livestock to a lightning strike in a big storm, therefore, villagers interpret this as the revenge of nature for his neglect/abandonment of rural values in favour of urban ones ('Providence [= nature] was delivering him a warning'). He sells what remains of his livestock to a cattle dealer, and plans to use the money to go to Canada with the blonde. Despite the fact that the peasant proprietor thinks, amidst 'inhospitality of life on this earth', that he has found a 'shelter' in the shape of someone who 'was like a place ... where the law of inhospitality did not apply', she refuses to migrate and soon leaves him. Alone, he pines away and dies.[55]

Notwithstanding the portrayal of the urban as the source of multiple exactions/temptations/deceits, leading to the loss of resources and rural livelihood, and the complicity of the peasant proprietor with this process, he is depicted by Berger as victim. What is to be refuted by this particular narrative, therefore, is agency, and with it culpability for decline; the view, namely, that the peasant proprietor was himself responsible for his own death, and the decline/demise of his farm and livestock: for Berger, he wasn't. The peasant farmer was led on by and stripped of his material assets by a rapacious set of 'others': money (the desire for), the urban (exploits the rural), and the woman (who symbolizes the preceding two processes and locale). It is all the latter which put the survival of the peasant proprietor – and more generally the peasant family farm – at issue. Among other things, this depicts the peasant as a passive subject, a trope associated with the anthropological studies criticized by modernization theory and Marxism.

---

55   In many ways, this narrative resembles Hogarth's *The Rake's Progress*, which similarly chronicles the financial ruin of a young man who squanders an inherited fortune. As an art historian, Berger would have been aware of this early eighteenth century parallel, not least because of his admiration for Frederick Antal (Berger, 2016a: 33–35) who himself produced an important analysis of Hogarth (Antal, 1962). The main difference is that for Antal the subject of *The Rake's Progress* is a bourgeois mimicking aristocratic behaviour, whilst for Berger it is a peasant corrupted simply by urban values. What for Antal – a Marxist art historian – is a class distinction, is for Berger largely one of sectoral difference.

5 Looking, But Seeing?

In part, the origin of views Berger expressed about the importance and nature of peasant society can be traced to his previous writings, both fictional and non-fiction. The protagonist of the 1960s novel *Corker's Freedom* adheres to the notion that one cannot be free unless everyone else is also free, identifying what for Berger was a concept of solidarity (Pan-Europa = 'Unity in essentials, liberty in inessentials, charity in all') he later extended to a defence of the right of peasant family farming to survive, to remain what it had always had been.[56] A decade later descriptions of urban-as-dystopia accompanied the argument that European art depicted the way Nature is appropriated ('predestined for man's use'), in the process de-essentializing it by rendering it explicable and unmysterious.[57] Objectifying Nature in this manner, European ruling classes paid for an art which 'rearranged life to frame their own image', thereby altering the 'naturalness' of the rural and excluding other and different perceptions of Nature.[58] What Berger opposed at this earlier conjuncture, therefore, was how the artistic meaning of the rural and Nature itself were appropriated by 'those above', in defiance of the way they might have been conceptualized by 'those below' – that is to say, peasants who lived and worked in the same countryside. In support of the view that where landscape was concerned '[a]ny peasant born in a village knows it a thousand times better', he concluded that '[t]oday to hold a mirror to nature is only to diminish the world'.[59]

Similar themes can also be glimpsed in the publication accompanying his widely-acclaimed and justly-celebrated BBC television series *Ways of Seeing*.[60] Despite the application of market value to pictures, in effect corrupting art by

---

56 Berger (1964). This broad and in class terms undifferentiated concept of solidarity also surfaces in a 1976 essay about Jean-François Millet, where Berger (1980: 72, emphasis added) considers why the artist painted scenes from peasant life: 'His view of history was too passive and too pessimistic to allow him any strong political convictions. Yet the years of 1848 to 1851, the hopes they raised and suppressed, established for him, as for many others, the claim of democracy: not so much in a parliamentary sense, as in *the sense of the rights of man being universally applicable*'.
57 Berger (1972a: 19–27). Hence the view (Berger, 1972b: 214, 215) that 'European means of representation refer to the experience of taking possession ... Painting becomes the metaphorical act of appropriation', therby making '[t]he workings of Nature, however complicated, ... mechanically explicable and unmysterious'.
58 See Berger (1972b: 219), who earlier (1972b: 176) in the same text explained what art ought to be in the following terms: 'The process of painting is the process of trying to re-achieve at a higher level of complexity a previous unity which had been lost'.
59 Berger (1972a: 172, 174).
60 Berger (1972b).

money, he insisted that '[p]ainting maintains its own authority', occupying as it does a specific time and space: it is still a thing-in-itself, regardless of how it is reproduced by film, camera, press or television.[61] All the latter, however, correspond to technological de-essentialization, which contributes to a process whereby 'each image reproduced has become part of an argument which has little or nothing to do with the painting's original independent meaning'.[62] Anticipating the postmodern argument about decentering/fragmentation of discourse, therefore, Berger maintained that an effect of the way a camera reproduced images was that representation itself becomes unfixed and 'multiplies and fragments into many meanings'.[63]

---

61   See Berger (1972b: 23, 26). He (Berger, 1972b: 90) is quite specific about the corrupting power of money – as has been argued above, seen by him as an important element in the decline of the peasant family farm – in the modern era: 'Works of art in earlier traditions celebrated wealth. But wealth was then a symbol of a fixed social or divine order. Oil painting celebrated a new kind of wealth – which was dynamic and which found its only sanction in the supreme buying power of money'. In keeping with this, Berger (1972b: 131, 143) equates money with unnecessary consumption ('buying something more') – also a cause of rural decline – arguing: 'Money is life. Not in the sense that without money you starve. Not in the sense that capital gives one class power over the lives of another class. But in the sense that money is the token of, and the key to, every human capacity. The power to spend money is the power to live. According to the legends of publicity, those who lack the power to spend money become literally faceless'. The latter designation is one which, as has been seen, he applied to peasants and migrants, ex-peasants in urban contexts.

62   Berger (1972b: 28).

63   Berger (1972b: 19). The way meaning fragments – 'it contains another view of the scene' – as a result of unfixed images is hinted at by Berger elsewhere. His archive (Add. Ms. 8864/1/33) contains a section entitled 'Passing Event' that was intended for the Introduction to the trilogy, but which in the end did not appear in the published version: 'I want to consider a new kind of relation. Essentially it relates to tourism. It consists of no more than a very temporary form of confrontation. Yet to consider it, may illuminate something else. It is the relation between foreigners in a car and peasants working in the fields which border the road. The "foreigners" may be of another nationality or from cities in another part of the same country. Most of those in the cars are either on holiday or out for a drive; a few may be travelling in connection with their work. The peasants, of whom I am thinking, work their own land: they are not *kulaks* but nor are they desperate. The plight of a rural population who have nothing with which to work, who listlessly watch the world go by (and this can happen in Calabria or Turkey as well as in Latin America) is something different. The peasants working and the motorists. How do they see each other? Each perceives the other as a passing event. Those in the car may not be looking out. (Some ride in cars as if they were in fact air-liners). Equally if the traffic is continuous, the peasant will not notice single vehicles, but will occasionally stop to look at the stream of them he sees, not envy, but a way of life, not events but a process. First and very simply the passing event is a pretext for stopping work for a moment. A pause. A straightening of the back. The car changes the scene. Not by its colour or noise. But by the fact that it contains another view of the scene. The car crosses the landscape like a gaze. When that view has passed, the scene reverts to normal, and the job being done is part of the normalcy'.

Later that same decade a similarly influential analysis of migration by Berger and Mohr focused on two negative aspects of this process: both the plight of the immigrant in the urban context itself, and the impact that outmigration had on the sending nation.[64] Since migration was regarded as a temporary work arrangement, migrants were conceptualized as essentially peasants and migration as a 'disruption' of rural society in southern Europe.[65] At that conjuncture, just after the development decade, the principal concern of Berger was that outmigration would have a deleterious effect on the European rural periphery. It was from this initial focus on the plight of the migrant worker employed in European industry, therefore, that led Berger back to the locus of outmigration, the village community, and subsequently to the predicament facing the peasant family farm there, specifically in France but also more generally throughout Europe and beyond. From this concern with the continuing viability of rural society in the villages migrants left behind, a view he had addressed hitherto in non-fictional form, Berger turned to a fictional representation of the problem: since migrants came from peasant families, the trilogy would in the decade that followed trace back to the rural economy the reasons why outmigration occurred, and the effect of the latter process both on subsistence cultivation by and on the lives of smallholding proprietors.

There are two main contexts into which Berger inserts his views about the peasantry: the nation (France) and theories about rural society (Marxism, modernization, populism, and postmodernism). To begin with, it is clear that his views about petty commodity production depart substantially from the way other Marxists have interpreted the French countryside, in terms of grassroots politics and – more recently – encounters with modernity. Thus, for example, Trotsky outlined how in 1930s France the populist discourse of the far right sought to mobilize rural discontent by ignoring class differences within the peasantry, on the one hand upholding idealizing notions of the small-scale (locality, tradition, village, smallholding agriculture) whilst on the other opposing the large-scale (foreign monopoly capital, finance capital, the state).[66] Some three decades later, Morin who conducted research in a village in rural Brittany during the mid-1960s pointed out that: 'The nineteenth century has no defenders in Plodémet ... Among the peasants, craftsmen,

---

64 Berger and Mohr (1975).
65 For the view that migrants are essentially peasants, see Berger and Mohr (1975: 90, 107–08).
66 Hence the view (Trotsky, 1959: 75) that '[r]egionalism is a response to the diversity of agrarian conditions in France. The provincial fascist and pre-fascist programmes will be varied and contradictory as are the interests of the different categories – the vine growers, truck gardeners, wheat growers – as well as the different social strata of the peasantry. But all these programmes will have in common their hatred of the bank, the treasury, the trust and the legislators'.

tradesmen, and seamen, there is no wish to rehabilitate the past. Young people do not dream of a bucolic world where man lived in harmony with nature; the experience of the old is still present to remind them that the past meant poverty, ignorance, and subjection. Only a few formerly large landowners are wistful about the past'.[67]

This is confirmed by much of what Weber documents in his analysis of the way rural France was transformed over the latter part of the nineteenth century, an era which 'saw the wholesale destruction of traditional ways', adding that it 'is no coincidence … that this period saw a great spurt of interest in folklore studies'.[68] The latter approach, as Weber makes clear, represented the views and interests not of French peasants but rather of the bourgeoisie, and intellectuals in particular: although '[m]any grieved over the death of yesterday … few who grieved were peasants'.[69] Although the transformations of the French countryside that Weber outlines – specifically the penetration of capital accumulation ('the logic of the money economy') and its attendant cultural dislocation – are no different from those charted by Berger, the former – unlike the latter – indicates that such changes were perceived by many rural inhabitants as 'emancipations', not least because these modern developments were seen as part of an unfolding historical process.[70] In short, 'old ways died unlamented', while 'new ways that had once seemed objectionable were now deliberately pursued and assimilated'.

Turning to the way Berger's views fit in or depart from theories about rural society, it is also clear from the trilogy that he regards any leftist project in rural contexts as ineffectual and consequently doomed to failure, an approach underlined by the way he represents political struggle, both in the countryside

---

67 Morin (1970: 212ff.).
68 Weber (1976: 471–72), whose description of this approach could be applied to that of Berger himself: 'Peasants were studied as a vanishing breed; their culture was dissected and their sentimental value grew … writers took up the noble peasant as an earlier century had taken up the noble savage. Sets of picture postcards featured scenes that had scarcely been worth notice before: thatched cottages, farmers pitching hay, harvest feasts, peasants in regional costumes'. Significantly, however, Weber continues: 'But for all those who rued the loss of the olden ways and sought to record and preserve their memory, many others rejoiced at their passing and did all they could to speed it'.
69 See Weber (1976: 478), who adds: 'This helps explain the extraordinary difference between the intellectual despair and decadence of the *fin-de-siècle* elite and the optimism, hope, and sense of progress so evident among the masses. To be sure, elite intellectuals and reformers had seen that the new panaceas – democracy, education – did not bring the betterment they had once seemed to promise [but] "the world we have lost" was no loss to those who had lived in it, or so at least the evidence suggests'.
70 In France, notes Weber (1976: 492), 'traditional culture was itself a mass of assimilations, the traditional way of life a series of adjustments … the changes modernity brought were often emancipations, and were frequently recognized as such'.

and in the city. Hence conflict involving farm and factory has as its subtext competition for the allegiance of the peasantry (a female smallholder) between two characters (both male) symbolizing communism and anarchism, and how each of her suitors is in turn crippled or killed.[71] She eventually settles down with the communist, now disabled as a result of an industrial accident, who can – it is inferred – do little to stop/prevent the onward march of the factory (= capitalism/urban/largescale) and its undermining/destruction of all that is 'the rural' (agriculture, peasant farming, the forest, the river, village society, smallscale, Nature). Looked at from a Marxist perspective, this amounts to a counsel of despair – a form of anti-capitalism without knowing quite what to do about it.[72]

Much the same negative case disparaging leftist politics informs the final story in the second book, about an encounter involving a peasant visiting a city as a member of a village band to perform in a communist-organized festival, and a young urbane female who belongs to the party.[73] That the city in question is Venice, the epitome of urban civilization/culture, highlights the contrast structuring the resulting 'duel' between them: on the one hand a female/urban/worker/communist and on the other a male/rural/peasant/cultivator. He is depicted as a 'realist', interested only in making a living (higher milk prices), not theory, while she is presented as an utopian idealist, concerned only with 'unreal' theory. Symbolically, their encounter in Venice occurs under a large portrait of Marx, where the communist female chides the visiting peasant about the reactionary political allegiances of smallholders. They make love in a gondola, after which she invites him to live and work in the urban, but he refuses and returns with the band to his village.

As is clear from this particular narrative, therefore, the rural is vindicated, successfully resisting the (unreal) blandishments of the urban. For her part, the communist woman is the voice of the urban left: that is, portrayed by Berger negatively, because she is the embodiment of political 'otherness' where a rural inhabitant is concerned, in terms both of form (as talking down to him, because of his supposed rustic ignorance) and also content (an unrealistic belief in progress and a classless society, and an equally misplaced insistence that all petty commodity producers 'will disappear').[74] For his part, the

---

71 Berger (1992: 272–332).
72 The same kind of pessimistic view pervades a more recent text by Berger (2016b).
73 Berger (1992: 333–41).
74 The belief voiced by a communist that peasants 'will disappear' is also voiced subsequently (Berger, 1992: 428) by another equally negative character, an urban criminal ('Peasants! I'm talking about the twenty-first century, about today and tomorrow'). Clearly, the argument that peasants are destined to vanish because they belong to the past, and are no longer relevant to current society is a view with which Berger strongly disagrees.

peasant farmer dismisses her opinions, because she is from Venice ('a place of water and islands') where 'there is no earth at all', and thus not rooted in the soil and its lived experience.[75]

In the city itself, moreover, the leftist project as described by Berger also falters, as migrants from the village are either interested only in their own personal advancement within the urban system as it is or attempt unsuccessfully to organize as workers.[76] On a building site, therefore, a discussion between migrants about justice which at one point advocates 'taking what belongs to us [workers]' only elicits the reply '[n]othing belongs to us'. Significantly, the migrant who promotes the idea of worker organization is himself injured in an industrial accident and ends up a cripple, selling leftist newspapers on the street (headline: 'Trojan Workers Refuse Intimidation!').[77] The only feasible alternative is presented as being money-making criminal activity (theft, selling drugs, scams), a bleak option expressed by a migrant as 'we're outside the law and whatever we do, we break it'.[78] Central to migrant existence in the urban, therefore, is the element of deceit (≠ authenticity, trust, virtue), since there survival is based on each individual taking advantage of all others, which undermines leftist politics arising from – and requiring – solidarity and collective organization/mobilization.[79]

6   Too Much History, Too Many Lives

Observing that peasant economics 'are not those of … Marxist political economy', Berger endorses views about peasant farming held not by Marxism but rather by neo-populists such as Shanin and Chayanov.[80] Like them, Berger not only regards the peasantry as an undifferentiated category, as forming a class, but also considers 'peasant economy [as] an economy within an economy', all concepts that are central to populism. He maintains that, whereas bourgeois and Marxist ideals of equality are based on economic models of plenty, to be constructed and/or redistributed in a situation of scientific progress, the peasant by contrast thinks of equality as occurring in a world of scarcity ('a just

---

75 If it is Berger's contention that Venice lacks a rural dimension, then this is incorrect, as shown in Brass (2014b: Ch. 8).
76 Berger (1992: 388–404, 418, 421–22).
77 For the industrial accident that befalls the migrant worker, see Berger (1992: 423–24, 468). The migrant shares thereby the same kind of fate as other leftist characters appearing in the trilogy.
78 Berger (1992: 407, 428, 434–61, 472–77).
79 Berger (1992: 462–71).
80 Berger (1992: xiii–xxix).

sharing of what work produces'). Not only does this avoid defining what is 'just' – will, for example, peasant proprietors agree to pay taxes in order to provide for the urban poor – but notions of an eternal scarcity correspond to rural beliefs about 'fatalism' and 'limited good' the efficacy of which were challenged earlier by Marxism and modernization theory.

Accordingly, petty commodity production is for Berger – as it is for Shanin and Chayanov – nothing more than subsistence cultivation, an economic activity carried out wholly or mainly by family members on the smallholding. Having as a consequence defined peasants as just engaged in 'survival', he laments that 'the class of survivors may not survive', without asking why it is desirable that such a category ought to 'survive'. The nearest he comes to this is the argument that peasants deserve to survive into the present because 'to dismiss the peasant experience as belonging only to the past, as having no relevance to modern life ... is to deny the value of too much history and too many lives'. Avoiding thereby arguments found in political economy, this view amounts to the problematic sentiment that, because they have existed throughout history, this of itself validates the right of the peasantry to be conserved as such, almost as a rural theme park of the kinds which are now ubiquitous.

His view reproduces the classic populist trope, whereby capital is always an external phenomenon, a process that operates outside the smallholding itself, whereas Marxists see accumulation as penetrating and remaining within the agrarian sector and differentiating rural producers into rich, middle and poor peasant farmers. Rather than supporting Marxist theory about the desirability of progress as the motor of historical development, therefore, Berger argues that, where peasant economy is concerned, progress is undesirable and unrealizable.[81] Instead of 'cultures of progress [which] envisage future expansion', he endorses 'a culture of survival' central to which is tradition, thereby creating the ideological space that was eventually occupied by postmodern theory.

Unsurprisingly, this approach leads to a defence of peasant conservatism, based on an attempt to reinterpret its meaning. Hence the assertion by Berger that Marxism – equated by him with a specifically urban political and social theory – is wrong to call peasants conservative, since small peasants defend richer counterparts because of a commonality of 'generations threatened by ... change'.[82] The difficulty with this is that better-off producers benefit from

---

81   Berger (1992: xx).
82   Berger (1992: xxv). That he nevertheless remains ambivalent about this characterization of peasant conservatism is evident from an observation in his archive (Add. Ms. 8864/1/33): 'It would be possible to take many other examples of misinterpreted peasant attitudes and, by relating them to the sum of peasant experience to interpret them more correctly. Yet to do this in the abstract would become a schematic exercise. Having established the

accumulation, and for this reason have no cause to object to the development process; where they do, and seek alliances with middle and/or poor peasants, the object is to oppose not capitalism *per se* but only competition from more powerful and economically successful rural enterprises (agribusiness, commercial farmers, large merchants). Similarly partial is grassroots rural suspicion of and/or objection to money; where the latter occurs, it is to the way money is used by others (e.g. merchants, traders), not as gained by their own efforts. As presented by Berger, however, peasants are opposed to money *tout court*, a view consistent with his idealised view of peasants as subsistence producers, nothing more. Neither is it the case that peasant subjectivity 'has been left out of social theory', nor that 'revolutionaries, even those who are concerned with the popular classes, have mostly misunderstood the experience of peasants'.[83]

Among his more problematic arguments, therefore, is that '[p]easant conservatism scarcely defends any privilege', a view that ignores counter-revolutionary agrarian movements such as the Vendée in France during 1793, and the Cristeros and Sinarquistas in Mexico during the 1920s and 1930s.[84] Having indicted both left and right for their respective adherence to a concept of 'progress' that entailed the disappearance of the peasant, the 'conservatism' of the latter is characterized by Berger not merely as a refusal of this outcome but also as entirely justified in the face of this double threat.[85] In doing so, he overlooks the way the right actually *privileges* the peasantry, to the extent of advocating its reproduction *as a peasantry*. This is bound up with the concept of the nation (*not* the state) held by the right, and the important role of the peasantry in its defence and culture (peasant = backbone-of-the-nation), being the bearers of an 'authentic' (because of longstanding) national identity based on rural tradition (language, customs, dress, rituals, etc.).

Even modern capitalist forms of political reaction, such as Nazism in Germany, promoted the idea of peasant family farming as central to their own version of national culture/economy, and indeed fashioned the ideology of *lebensraum* to accommodate this. Nor is it the case that 'the peasant is unprotected', since historically tenants on large rural estates owned by landlords

---

       principle, the only way to go further is to enter into the contradictions and wholeness of particular cases. And for this the imagination of the story-teller is necessary. An imagination which, incidentally, is highly familiar to peasants. All villages tell stories. And those stories are distinct from urban stories in two ways: in their facticity – the result of observation and of what is wrongly termed gossip – and in their tolerance'.

83   Mohr and Berger (1979: 158).
84   Berger (1992: xxv).
85   Berger (1992: xxi).

were regarded by the latter as 'protected': it was precisely this claim that constituted the *raison d'être* of landownership, taking the form of 'we provide protection' when you need it, in return for the surplus we get from you (rent, labour obligations).[86] The 'subsistence guarantee' argument fitted into this discourse about reciprocity, notwithstanding the fact that when needed it was not forthcoming.

Elsewhere Berger has argued that 'never again will a single story be told as though it were the only one', a claim that is no different from postmodern aporia, and its insistence on undecidability.[87] Dismissing the possibility even of there being a single story which is in fact accurate, he seems to ally himself with the postmodern claim that none ever are, or indeed can be deemed to be so. In subscribing to this view, Berger – like postmodernists – confuses material reality (= objective existence) with ideology (= subjective interpretations of what material reality is), and reifies the latter, maintaining subjectivity and not the objective determines 'what is'. Materially, 'what is' is not variable in essence, unlike opinions about and perceptions of 'what is'. In short, there is an 'out there' material reality, a point conceded by Berger when he observes that 'if one remembers that the first, the basic, purpose of painting is to conjure up the presence of something which is not there'.[88] Precisely so: namely, to construct or create (= 'conjure up the presence') a perception of reality that is not of itself immediately discernable ('something which is not there'). Furthermore, the 'resistance theory' of Scott – who has provided the 'new' populist postmodernism with its specific form of rural agency – surfaces as part of the justification advanced by Berger for rural stasis (= peasant 'survival').[89]

That a concept of an undifferentiated peasantry engaged in resisting modernity/progress is central to a postmodern approach to development theory is in fact conceded by one of its high priests. Wrongly castigating Marxism (and bourgeois economics) for failing to notice that peasants have not disappeared, therefore, Escobar – like Berger at an earlier conjuncture – objects to development *per se*, on the grounds that it is an inappropriate foundational/ Eurocentric imposition on Third World nations.[90] Maintaining inaccurately that 'one never finds in these [developmentalist] accounts ... how the peasants'

---

86 Berger (1992: xxiii).
87 Berger (2015: iv).
88 Berger (2015: 284).
89 Scott (1985), Berger (1992: xxiv).
90 Escobar (1995: 106). Needless to say, such an objection ignores the view of Kautsky (1984) who pointed out that peasant survival is an effect neither of its supposed economic efficiency nor of the desire of smallholders themselves, but rather of the need on the part

world may contain a different way of seeing problems and life', he proceeds – again like Berger earlier – to endorse what is an unambiguously populist view of the peasantry – labelled by him 'post-development' – as an alternative to capitalism.[91] Development is in his view nothing more than a failed attempt to apply Enlightenment values to Asia, Africa, and Latin America, since '[i]n the Third World, modernity is not "an unfinished project of the Enlightenment"'. Much rather, instead of development linked to the Enlightenment, Escobar invokes 'grassroots movements, local knowledge and popular power', citing as an example the capacity of smallholders in Peru to 'reinvent ... elements of longstanding peasant culture'. The resulting 'culture-specific productive strategy' is categorized by him as alternative to capitalism grounded in 'the sheer fact of cultural difference'.

When Berger talks about how capitalism destroys history, therefore, like Escobar and other postmodernists he means both the social existence and the 'otherness' of peasant culture/economy.[92] However, there is another meaning to this which for obvious reasons Berger misses: capitalism does indeed destroy history, but not quite in the way he imagines. This it does by generating the very force – postmodernism – which denies not just the efficacy but the desirability of history-as-process/'progress', an epistemology which emerges in opposition to capitalism, certainly, but which is populist and thus a *conservative* form of anti-capitalism.[93] Berger fails to spot this because he, too, is opposed to 'progress' – an indictment he levels not just at capitalism but also at socialism and Marxism. As his discourse-for and discourse-against about the peasantry suggests, Berger's political affinity was much rather with the 'new' populist postmodernism, of which he was a precursor.

---

        of agribusiness enterprises and/or rich peasant farmers to have continuing access to the labour-power on the peasant family farm.

91   Escobar (1995: 111). For the claims which follow, see Escobar (1995: 205, 215, 219, 221, 225). Contrary to what he thinks – that development theory in general and its Marxist variant in particular has somehow overlooked the fact that peasants have 'a different way of seeing problems and life' – no theory of development ignores the presence, the content and the distinctiveness of rural opinion. The problem is that the latter is not uniform, and consequently economic and political interests diverge, for the simple reason that different class elements at the rural grassroots (rich peasants, poor peasants, agricultural labourers) hold opposed views about crucial issues such as the role of the state, land reform, property redistribution, wage levels, etc.

92   Berger (1992: xxviii).

93   Details as to why this is so are outlined elsewhere (Brass, 2000, 2014b).

7 Conclusion

In making this critique one point has to be emphasized most strongly: unlike some currently who write about peasants, John Berger – besides being a very fine writer – clearly researched his subject, read widely about the issues involved, and was knowledgeable about the kinds of questions to be asked. In short, as a veritable Renaissance person he was rather obviously neither ignorant nor was his approach that of a dilettante. In a sense this makes his interpretation and its politics all the more problematic: the view to which he adhered was one he *chose* to espouse, a conscious act taken in the light of evidence he himself had assembled. That is, in political terms, he took a specific position – more anti-urban than anti-capital – on the subject he was writing about in the trilogy: not so much with regard to what was actually happening in the countryside as on what was desirable in terms of a solution to the plight faced by its rural inhabitants.

At the time Berger was writing, each of the dominant approaches to development theory was promoting radical change in the countryside. Whereas bourgeois modernization theory sought to better the lot of smallholders within capitalism, Marxists by contrast maintained this was impossible, since accumulation could not but undermine petty commodity production. For this reason, Marxists envisaged a different kind of characterization and transformation, involving the dissolution of peasant economy along class lines, and consequently the pursuit by its distinct components of radically different political and systemic outcomes. Rejecting both these arguments, Berger instead recuperated a view deployed by populists and/or ethnographers of undifferentiated peasant family farmers engaged in subsistence cultivation.

This same view resurfaced subsequently as the 'cultural turn', which similarly championed rural petty commodity producers as 'eternal'/'authentic'/'natural' subaltern identities, in the process abandoning not just class analysis and socialist politics but also notions of development/progress/modernity as desirable in village communities inhabited by an homogenous peasantry. For this reason, it has been argued here that the future trajectory of peasant society as envisaged by Berger not merely departed from Marxism but has more in common with – and thus prefigured the way in which it was perceived by – the 'new' populist postmodernism.

Conclusion

The case made here is simply put; against the usual argument heard most frequently on the left, that there is no subject for a radical politics together with its form of political mobilization, there is – but in the absence of a radical leftist project, this subject has in the past transferred, and in many instances is still transferring, his/her support to the radical politics on offer from the other end of the ideological spectrum. Hence the combination of on the one hand a globally expanding industrial reserve army, generating ever more intense competition in the labour markets of capitalism, and on the other the endorsement by many on the left not of class but rather of non-class identities espoused by the 'new' populist postmodernism, has fuelled what can only be described as a perfect storm, politically speaking. That is to say, a relay-in-statement whereby the conceptual absence from leftist agendas of revolution and socialism + little or no leftist opposition to an expanding industrial reserve + intense ethnic/national rivalry in labour markets + espousal on the left of identity politics in preference to that of class = an increasingly disempowered leftist project + an increasingly empowered rightist one.

Consequently, arguing for the conceptual reinstatement of revolutionary agency and socialism necessarily involves accounting for the disappearance of such theory/practice from the political agenda of the left. On the centenary anniversary of the 1917 Russian revolution, it seems that the latter has been stripped of its politics, and is an episode marked largely in terms of aesthetics. The process of vanishing, not just of direct action designed to capture state power but also of socialism itself, is traced from the advocacy of evolution of and latterly resistance to – but not a transcendence of – capitalism. This politically reformist trend is linked in turn to changes in academia, and in particular the rise there of postmodernism. The latter has resulted on the one hand in the championing both of peasant economy/culture and of non-class identities, thereby returning to earlier views held by revisionism; and on the other a consequent abandonment of class analysis, socialist politics and allied concepts of progress, modernity and development. The price of this vanishing is equally clear.

The current alternative proposed by such reformism – resistance against globalization – is not new, but much rather a familiar and very old argument. It is a populism informed by nationalist ideology, a combination that has a very long history in Europe, North America and Russia and also in Third World countries. What such populism attempts to do is to unite the different class interests within a given nation – a domestic bourgeoisie and petty bourgeoisie no less than urban workers plus rural labour and peasant smallholders – in a common form of resistance against capital that is international (= 'foreign'). This is does, moreover, by avoiding potentially divisive class distinctions within the nation thus mobilized, and focusing instead on what it categorizes as an externally-driven process of cultural erosion, conceptualized as a denial of national selfhood. Ironically, this kind of position is one that the anti-globalization movement shares not only with postmodern and post-colonial theory, but also with much of the political right in Europe and elsewhere.

The disappearance of revolutionary theory/practice from the leftist agenda and its replacement with parliamentary reformism has in the past created a space filled by the direct action of the political right. In terms of agency, therefore, the parliamentary road in defence of bourgeois democratic reform followed by socialism (Austro-Marxism) and its enemies (Pan-Germanism) led to each of these political approaches being outflanked at either end of the spectrum: on the left by the Bolsheviks in Russia, and on the right by National Socialists in Germany. Ironically, many of the identities that historically have been the way in which the counter-revolution mobilized are now invoked by those who still regard themselves – and are regarded by many others – as leftists. The latter suggests that the old – very old – trope of using Stalinism and the gulags to discredit both the necessity for and the fact of revolutionary agency generally, never mind the 1917 uprising in Russia, is only the most obvious form of antagonism expressed by those opposed to Marxism, revolution, and socialism.

A crucial aspect of the revolutionary drive, and thus also of the transition to socialism, is the dynamic of class formation/consciousness/struggle. The subject of the historical process is for Marxism the proletariat, the identity of which is based on class, and the struggle derived from this entails the revolutionary transcendence of the capitalist system. All Marxists regard the peasantry as a socio-economic form that fragments into a rural bourgeoisie and a rural proletariat, and for this reason does not of itself form a class but is internally differentiated along class lines. Capitalist penetration of agriculture generates division into rich, middle and poor peasant strata; some middle peasants join rich counterparts and become agrarian capitalists, while the majority join the poor peasantry to become agricultural workers. In this regard, and their shared commitment to direct action notwithstanding, both populism and neo-populism are the mirror image of Marxism.

For populists, by contrast, the historical subject is an homogenous peasantry, the economic identity of which is linked to small-scale family farming in the village community. The non-economic identity of populist/neo-populist theory is mainly ethnic/cultural/national/regional, and currently – but not historically – its agency takes the form of resistance not designed to achieve systemic transformation. Although the Will of the People shares with the 'new' populist postmodernism a desire to empower the peasantry by reinstating/protecting individual proprietorship in the countryside, therefore, it parts company with those such as Scott over the method of achieving this. The Will of the People is still committed to an individualistic variant of radical agency the object of which is to overthrow the state; modern resistance theory, by contrast, avoids confronting the state, which it has no intention of capturing, and eschews revolution, its preferred form of agency being quotidian resistance at the rural grassroots. In this way, current populism, in the shape of contemporary resistance theory, has discarded the most radical aspect of its populist precursor.

That the primary object of revolution is to secure a transition which in the end is the only form of action capable of addressing issues of oppression/exploitation affecting the working class – the very point made by Lenin in his analysis of the limits posed by 'spontaneity' – can be illustrated with reference to recent changes in the capitalist labour regime. When confronted with increasing levels of unfree labour deployed by agribusiness enterprises and sweatshop production world-wide, critical analysis emanating from leftist theory espousing the modern equivalent of 'spontaneity' appeals to the state, calling simply for nothing more than improved working conditions and/or higher wages. As is clear from the debate about the use by capitalists of labour-power that is unfree in preference to free variants, ending the resort by employers to unfree production relations is an objective that can be achieved only in the course of a transition to socialism, and not – as advocates of 'patronage' or human rights wrongly maintain – within the confines of a system that remains capitalist.

It was for this reason that Bolshevism was critical of the undue focus by fellow leftists merely on exposing factory conditions, rather than overturn the system that gives rise to such conditions in the first place. Exactly the same problem faces the left now, with the difference that the lessons from the start of the twentieth century still have not been learned: many socialists have been absorbed into academia, from the secure portals of which are undertaken anti-capitalist pronouncements bereft of effect and outcome. Hence the continuing relevance of the critique made by Lenin a century ago, that in the end merely engaging in – or simply advocating – trade-union work (= 'spontaneity') fails to address the systemic issue, that of capitalism itself, if (and how) it is to be transcended, and what is to replace it. Merely to advocate a return to a 'nicer'/'kinder' form of accumulation solves nothing, since this is not going to happen, and even if it did, a *laissez-faire* project would soon emerge, because this is the way capitalism necessarily develops. At present the latter takes the form of restructuring the labour process, involving decomposition of the existing workforce and then its recomposition on less favourable pay/conditions, a procedure licensed by a globally expanding industrial reserve army: class struggle waged 'from above', in other words. That such is the trajectory pursued by capital is ignored or downplayed by those who appeal to a moral order which neoliberalism clearly lacks, their pleas lamenting the 'uncaring' nature of the capitalist state destined as a consequence to fall on deaf ears.

Apart from those who accept the existence of the state, and thus leave unchallenged its claim to political legitimacy, there are at least three ways in which this institution is open to challenge. First, and in a sense the most radical confrontation, is to destroy the state: consequently, it ceases to function. This is the approach of those who advocated the kind of direct action associated with anarchism, the Will of the People, and populists in late nineteenth century Russia. A second way, and one that is fashionable in much current development theory, takes the form of either resistance to or avoidance of the state. The latter institution continues to function as before, and may – or may not – leave those who resist or avoid it alone. Unlike revolution, therefore, which entails mass organization/mobilization, resistance/avoidance informing the theory of 'new' populist postmodernism involves no more that small-scale quotidian agency (= 'everyday-forms-of-resistance') conducted mainly at village level by individual petty commodity producers. The third form entails state capture, the object of which is to take it over and put this institution to the same or a different use. Significantly, this kind of action can be undertaken by those at each end of the political spectrum. Just as Bolsheviks advocated capture of the state, an end to be realized by a working class taking mass action on the streets, so too did the far right in Austria and Germany. Ironically, nowadays there has indeed been a process of state capture, but this has been done not 'from below' by workers or peasants but rather 'from above' by capital (with not a little assistance from its media representatives).

Since the history of class struggle indicates that at no conjuncture and in no context have capitalists voluntarily surrendered their wealth and power to a workers' government, this of itself underlines the need for revolutionary agency as the only method of obtaining economic and political resources necessary for carrying out a socialist programme. This was the view advanced by Trotsky, who championed permanent revolution, in his debate with Kautsky, who followed a democratic path, about how to implement socialism. Among the other reasons why revolution is deemed by Marxism to be necessary is the unwillingness of a bourgeoisie to put in place all the progressive advances usually associated by bourgeois ideology with economic development (political democracy, welfare provision, full employment, higher wages and better work conditions). These advances fall instead to the proletariat, which must therefore undertake revolutionary agency, seize power and carry out such tasks on its own, in a socialist context.

For its part, the bourgeoisie tends to oppose much of what is recognizable as progressive advance, since realization of the latter at some point will pose a threat to and thus potentially endanger its own accumulation project. This is because to proceed with a programme that empowers workers would bring into being a proletariat that is politically conscious, well organized and confident. Since the political consolidation of a powerful working class brought (and brings) with it the possibility of revolution and consequently a challenge to existing property rights, the link between a class-in-itself and a class-for-itself is never entirely absent from ruling class consciousness, ideology and politics. Thus the objection to seemingly unimportant but incremental political advances made by workers and their organizations is underwritten by a fear of potential revolutionary action as the outcome of 'from below' class struggle. Accordingly, it is not so much inability as unwillingness to put in place a genuine democratic project that structures bourgeois ideology.

This problem – the contradiction between the class interests of the bourgeoisie and those of workers, and the limits posed as a result on political and economic progress – is one that can be traced back to the very different kinds of practice involved. Along with Lenin, Rosa Luxemburg, Karl Leibknecht, and Victor Serge, Trotsky belonged to that group of Marxists (Bolsheviks and others) for whom engagement meant politicization/organization – much of it clandestine – conducted at the rural (and urban) grassroots, running numerous risks thereby. It is necessary merely to be aware of the fate (execution, imprisonment, exile) of those who at the end of the nineteenth century 'went to the people' – no matter how much one disagrees with populism, the personal courage and dedication of its adherents were not characteristics they lacked – to understand how different the level of political commitment and engagement was then when compared with what passes for this now. Comfort and safety were for them never going to be part of this process. Revolution was seen by all as something feasible, and if socialism was itself not imminent, then such agency was regarded as a worthwhile form of struggle in furtherance of this systemic objective, to be pursued with vigour in the present.

Nowadays, by contrast, the discourse remains to some degree radical, but the practice is wholly different. At best, what is promoted currently by many on the left is creating the conditions for revolution, not revolution itself. And since these same leftist elements are the ones who define when, where, and whether the conditions licensing revolutionary action have been met, that point recedes continuously into a distant future, never in fact to be reached at all. Evidence of this is the pervasive and baleful influence of the semi-feudal thesis, which seeks to promote a transition not to socialism but to capitalism, insisting that the latter is not mature enough to permit one to contemplate a revolutionary transition. As was observed during the 1960s development debate, this amounts in effect to postponing socialism until the Greek Calends (there were no Greek Calends). In part, this was an effect of the fact that from that conjuncture onwards Marxism vanished from the streets and resurfaced in the academy, where it has taken on a very different (= depoliticized) role, akin to that undertaken much earlier by Austro-Marxist *katheder*socialists. Significantly, in both eras – as indeed is the case at present – reformism is linked to discourses that emerged from academia.

Unlike the Bolsheviks and the Will of the People, Austro-Marxist theory and practice was characterized by an inability or unwillingness to move beyond stasis, a situation of parliamentary reformism described by Bauer as a 'balance' of power, or an 'equilibrium' between the classes. In the end, this ostensibly transitory 'balance' took on a permanency that defied transcendence, and this in turn conveyed to workers the message that they should look elsewhere for the necessary political support in their struggles to prevent labour market competition. Applying concepts such as 'equilibrium', 'balance', 'co-determination', and 'organic democracy' as did Austro-Marxism to what are in fact antagonistic relations between classes, is rather like the now-familiar tropes of the 'new' populist postmodernism, whereby those engaged in what is clearly a fierce struggle – between nations or classes – are said to be engaged merely in a 'negotiation'. One is tempted to observe that, framed in this way, the 1939–45 conflict might be depicted as no more than a 'negotiation' between fascist and non-fascist ideologies.

The problem faced by the Austro-Marxists highlights a contemporary difficulty. In Europe today, populations from adjacent nations are migrating to places where economic development occurs, and jobs are – comparatively speaking – relatively well paid. In doing so, they seen as being competitors in the same labour market as existing workers. Populists take advantage of this to garner political support. Simply to decry this, as many on the left currently do, arguing that politically this ought not to be allowed to happen, is fatuous, in that it fails to address why it occurs. Where labour market competition involves ethnic rivalry, and is taken advantage of by capitalist producers who want to keep wages/conditions low, populism has – so to speak – a 'natural' advantage, particularly when the left eschews political economy, and instead adopts a moral discourse that – like its populist counterparts – privileges ethnic/national 'otherness'.

Discarding or limiting the scope of action based on class identity/struggle not only makes systemic transcendence of any kind more or less impossible, but also has a long history. In a number of ways, the epistemology informing 1960s modernisation theory – and especially that of Rostow – is no different from that of eighteenth and nineteenth century liberals such as Turgot, Saint-Simon, Dunoyer, for whom class struggle is waged only against feudalism, not bourgeois accumulation. For them all, 'pure' capitalism entails harmony not class struggle; according to this kind of interpretation, therefore, class struggle ceases with the expropriation of non-capitalist landowners. Systemic transcendence was not on their agenda, except insofar as it applied to a landlord class emblematic of feudalism. Marxists who shared much of this approach include exponents of the semi-feudal thesis and Hobsbawm; by eschewing revolution and postponing a socialist transition, they in effect reproduced many of the same assumptions as liberal theory and the modernisation approach regarding the structure and dynamic of the accumulation process.

Conceptually, stages theory rests centrally on the premise that modes of production are defined by work arrangements specific to them, and that historical progress entails passing from one stage, with a given set of production relations, to another, with a different, more advanced and equally specific relational form. In this model, the presence or absence of capitalism is as a consequence determined by whether or not the unfree worker – categorized as subordinated by what is a feudal or pre-capitalist relation – has been replaced with free wage labour. When and where it has, capitalism is declared to be present; when/where it hasn't, capitalism is deemed to be absent, or insufficiently developed. For this reason, political alliances between workers and a national bourgeoisie are thought to be appropriate, in order to usher in a proper accumulation project. Those holding such a view, influential in the study of agrarian development in India and Latin America from the 1960s onwards, include exponents of the semi-feudal thesis.

Since the 1980s, the arguments of the semi-feudal thesis – and by implication the stages framework more generally – have been challenged by developments in the way global capitalism operates. Rather than being a pre-capitalist remnant, therefore, in many contexts unfree production relations have been introduced, reintroduced, or simply reproduced by employers, and as such form part of the way class struggle is waged 'from above'. Along with downsizing/outsourcing, this is a method whereby nowadays capital restructures its labour process, cutting costs so as to maintain/enhance profitability. An expanding industrial reserve army makes this kind of restructuring not just possible but also necessary, enabling rich peasants and commercial farmers to compete with agribusiness enterprises. Whereas in the past the colonial state in India attempted to eliminate debt bondage and similar unfree working arrangements there, because they were thought to be obstacles to economic development, currently the neoliberal state (lip-service apart) is content to see them continue – and even flourish – as they contribute to profitability.

If unfree labour is not a pre-capitalist remnant but in many cases a relation of choice where capital is concerned, used as much by a national bourgeoisie as by a foreign one, then it is difficult to see how entering alliances with the employing/owning class within the nation to further the cause of capitalist development there is still on the political agenda of workers' organizations. This suggests that it is socialism, not a progressive form of capitalism, which should be the objective of any 'from below' political mobilization and programme. Furthermore, the use of these kinds of unfree production relation tends to hinder and/or undermine the formation of class consciousness among labour, particularly when they involve the recruitment of migrants (who are unfree and thus cheaper to employ) in order to displace unionized and politically militant workers (who are free and thus more costly to employ).

Liberal theorists such as Turgot, Saint-Simon and Dunoyer, all saw the attainment of freedom – to produce, sell and trade in commodities – as part of the class struggle only against feudalism, so as to *promote* capitalism. This is in keeping with their more general view of class struggle as a conflict designed to eliminate nothing more than the monopoly power (exerted via the state) of landowners. Once established, industrial capitalism in its most 'pure' systemic form – *laissez-faire*, in short – class struggle ceases because the state, the principal locus of conflict and exploitation, is no longer under the control of feudal landowners. This is no different from the agenda of the semi-feudal thesis, exponents of which similarly look backwards and focus on what they take to be the tenacity of pre-capitalist relations. Until the latter have been replaced by wage-labour that is free, capitalism is declared by exponents of the semi-feudal thesis to be either absent or not yet fully developed. Having pronounced a 'fully functioning' capitalism absent, exponents of the semi-feudal thesis advocate a reformist politics based on the existence of a 'progressive national bourgeoisie' that would usher in capitalism, democracy and free labour. Marxism, by contrast, sees these same unfree relational forms both as compatible with the accumulation process and as an obstacle to the realization not of capitalism but rather of socialism.

For both *laissez-faire* and the semi-feudal thesis, therefore, class struggle is aimed at what each perceives as pre-capitalist landowners: economic efficiency is counterposed to social privilege, in the process abolishing unfree relations (labour-rent, feudal dues) that permit exactions from petty commodity producers. Freed from landowner control and exactions, better-off peasants are consequently able to invest in agricultural improvements, thereby enhancing economic growth. By contrast, poor peasants are free to make their labour-power available to employers engaged in capital accumulation. Encouraging the creation/operation of buying/selling produce and labour-power leads in turn to an expansion of the market, thereby licensing accumulation and the process of capitalist development.

The similarity between on the one hand the semi-feudal thesis and on the other the reformist approach of both Austro-Marxism and bourgeois modernization can be gauged from the shared epistemology where their discourse-for and discourse-against are concerned. Each of them depicts as positive a number of issues, of which the most important is that the object of 'from below' struggle is to realize bourgeois democracy, not socialism. Consequently, all privilege national identity, as distinct from class, and thus promote the formation of class alliances (workers + bourgeois) so as to deepen bourgeois democracy. Since for them all capitalism is – and for the foreseeable future will remain – insufficiently developed, what is on the economic agenda is yet more efficient (= 'pure') accumulation. To this end, exponents of both the semi-feudal thesis and bourgeois modernisation – like Austro-Marxists before them – argue that in the interim peasant family farming has to be assisted economically.

Equally similar are the issues to which they each object. All banish revolutionary agency, unsurprisingly in the case of bourgeois modernisation but rather more surprisingly in the case of those approaches that are supposedly leftist (Austro-Marxism, semi-feudalism). None of them equate rich peasants with capitalism, and all deny that a class of capitalist farmers has emerged from the ranks of better-off peasant proprietors. All regard landlords as feudal, unproductive and thus preventing economic development from establishing itself or consolidating its position in the agrarian sector, which ignores the fact that some landowners are capitalist producers. This is consistent with the target of expropriation being only unproductive landlords, not landlordism *per se*, nor – especially – landlords that are capitalist. For this reason, too, each of them perceives unfree labour simply as a feudal or pre-capitalist relation, and thus as an obstacle to accumulation, and consequently the cause of an inability to realize industrialization (= 'pure' capitalism). In what is a circular argument, therefore, the current presence of unfree production relations is then deployed in order to cast doubt on the capitalist nature of contemporary economic development, a categorical assertion that engagement with current Marxist debate – about why accumulation replaces free with unfree production relations – would render problematic.

Among the many ways of avoiding a transition to socialism, and with it revolutionary action, are a number of familiar ones deployed by academics whose studies of rural development have tackled and continue to address change at the rural grassroots, especially as this entails contemporary forms of social mobilization. For supporters of liberal political economic theory, who advocate a market operating along pure *laissez faire* lines, the twin issues of socialism and revolution simply do not arise, since everyone is perceived as benefitting from this 'pure' form of capitalism. Those who do not share this optimistic interpretation, but nevertheless baulk at the prospect of revolution and socialism, are compelled to invoke a variety of avoidance mechanisms. These range from arguments that, as what exists now is an economic system which is not properly capitalist, neither revolution nor socialism is consequently on the political agenda; that the conditions necessary for such a transformation no longer obtain (historically in the case of revisionism, or currently in the case of the semi-feudal thesis); that economic development, poverty, and unfreedom, are problems that can be solved in ways that do not require a transcendence of the capitalist system (a retreat either into empiricism or advocating the patronage of an 'uncaring' neoliberal state); or that concepts like socialism and revolution are simply dismissed because each is inappropriate to Third World conditions (the 'new' populist postmodernism).

Many of the analyses criticized throughout this volume adhere to one – and in some instances to more than one – of these positions. Deploying instead terms such as 'subaltern'/'multitude', therefore, the 'new' populist postmodernism invokes all the usual tropes generated by an anti-capitalist discourse that is nevertheless antagonistic to socialism. These include the unheard rural voice-from-below, peasant essentialism, unfreedom-as-cultural-empowerment, hostility towards (and rejection of) Marxism as a 'master narrative' amounting to merely one more kind of Eurocentric foundationalism imposed on but inappropriate for understanding the rural 'other' in the Third World. Not surprisingly, therefore, 'new' populist postmodernists quickly labelled theories (like socialism) and practices (like revolution) designed to secure economic and social development as inappropriate Eurocentric impositions based on outmoded Enlightenment grand narratives, and as such demeaning to a rural grassroots already (and sufficiently) empowered by its own existing cultural practices.

Most of those who initially signed up uncritically to a nationalist/populist/postmodern critique of neoliberalism were unaware of its reactionary roots, and the fact that the political right also has an anti-capitalist discourse. Much development theory – including the 'everyday forms of resistance' framework and the Subaltern Studies project – which are influential where the study of Asia is concerned, is informed by this kind of 'new' populist postmodernism. Unsurprisingly, the belated recognition on the part of the academic mainstream of the fact that the postmodern 'cultural turn' shared epistemological underpinnings with conservatism and the far right led in a number of instances to a backtracking process, incorporating more radical political arguments found on the intellectual periphery. As in the case of the unfreedom/capitalism link, this entailed a transfer from the margins, where a particular radical argument originates, to the academic mainstream, where the same argument is deradicalized and then recycled.

The chronology is significant, in that radical argument surfaces in the academic mainstream (but now in an altered form) always after – never before – it appears at the margins. Common to this kind of procedure is an unacknowledged debt to earlier Marxist analyses, deriving in some instances from misinterpreting or overlooking the presence of this political approach. It was Marxism in general, and the deproletarianisation framework in particular, that from the 1980s onwards refocused the issue on metropolitan capitalism, pointing out that as a result of class struggle unfree production relations were found at home, and thus as much a feature of advanced capitalist economies as they were once thought to be a characteristic of economically underdeveloped nations in the so-called Third World.

Apart from academic fashion and the institutional advantages this confers on its followers, quite why postmodernism is – or should be – viewed sympathetically by leftists is unclear. In the case of development studies, therefore, the impact of postmodern theory has been negative, in that the 'cultural turn' set out to deprivilege socialism, materialism and class as illegitimate Enlightenment/Eurocentric forms of 'foundationalism' inapplicable to the Third World. Quotidian resistance by (undifferentiated) peasants in defence of indigenous culture and tradition is instead seen as a legitimate part of the struggle against capitalism, a result being that rural struggle is no longer about class but identity politics. That the latter structures the view of Berger about village society is confirmation of its reach outside academia, in the wider domain of popular culture. This recuperation by postmodernism of an essentialist peasant culture/economy leaves intact the existing class structure, and reproduces the populist mobilizing discourse associated historically with the political right. It is, in short, a 'new' populist form of anti-capitalism, the most influential example of which in the recent past has been – and to a large degree remains – the Subaltern Studies project.

Symptomatically, for the 'new' populist postmodernism the central epistemological problem is to construct a model that subsumes all kinds/forms of narrative, a framework that accounts merely for the fact of narrative, not its purpose. No significance is attached to the link between language and the material conditions that give rise to or sustain a particular narrative. Indeed, it is a link the very existence – let alone the efficacy – of which postmodern theory denies. This means that there is no longer a necessary relation between ideological practice and infrastructure, a non-determinate view that postmodernism inherited from structuralism. Nor is there any form of consciousness that – from the point of view of a particular class – can be categorized as false. In ignoring both the fact and effect of the presence of class *within* the ranks of those opposed to colonialism, therefore, the Subaltern Studies framework overlooked also the degree to which anti-colonial discourse/mobilization was that of small capitalist producers and rich peasants as much as that of poor peasants and agricultural workers. This is among the more damaging Marxist accusations levelled against postmodernism.

The political implications of the postmodern 'cultural turn' for Marxist theory/practice in the academy are not difficult to discern. To begin with, those on the left who abandoned Marxism for the 'new' populist postmodernism ended up fighting the wrong battle: for ethnic 'otherness' and national culture, rather than for class and internationalism. Consequently, populism become the theoretically dominant framework in the social sciences, and its counterpart – 'resistance' by individuals or by 'new' social movements – replaced revolution as the radical practice of choice. Hence the depoliticization of political discourse within the university system as a result of what might be termed the institutional 'domestication' of Marxist theory and practice. Accordingly, the situation is not so much an abandonment of first principles as not knowing any longer what these are or might be. The resulting focus on non-class identities (age, gender, religion, sexuality, ethnicity, nationality) as 'subversive' *foci* of resistance by 'new' social movements overlooks two crucial points. Where these contribute to the accumulation process, both resistance and empowerment based on identities other than class have been and are encouraged by capital. Consequently, in most instances empowerment/emancipation linked to non-class identity can be achieved as much under capitalism as under socialism.

More worryingly, the influence of the 'cultural turn' now extends well beyond academics debating rural development in Third World countries, and currently has an impact on politics in metropolitan capitalist Europe and America. Insofar as it privileges cultural identity as empowering, therefore, postmodern theory is complicit with the kind of nationalist ideology represented by populists such as Farage, Le Pen and Trump. All the latter feed off *laissez-faire* accumulation where economic crisis – generating both an expanding industrial reserve army of migrant labour and also more intense competition, between capitalists themselves and between workers seeking employment – results inexorably in political crisis.

By limiting their engagement to the economic struggle – that is, trade union activity which seeks improvements within capitalism, and not its transcendence – workers necessarily avoid confronting (and cannot eradicate) the systemic causes that led them to undertake struggle in the first place. Hence the importance attached by Lenin and Bolshevism generally to the necessity of bringing ideas about class, its formation and consciousness, to workers from the outside: that is, from beyond the confines not just of the economic struggle, but also limited to the purview of worker/employer relations and conflict. What has to be addressed, and can only be done from the outside, is the *totality* of 'relationships of *all* classes and strata and government', plus 'the interrelations between *all* classes'.

This critique, and its resolution by Lenin, underlines the error of 'new' populist postmodernists – not just Scott, Negri and Hardt, but also others, such as Berger – who privilege what they term 'everyday-forms-of-resistance' conducted at the rural grassroots by those opposed to capital, epistemologically and politically limiting empowerment to what occurs at village level. Quotidian agency of this kind corresponds to avoidance of the state, not its capture, and as such leaves intact in the hands of agribusiness enterprises, corporations, banks, and employers generally, a powerful capitalist institution which can – and will – be used in any class struggle waged 'from above'. Similarly indicted by this Bolshevik critique are the plaintive appeals by those such as Breman to an 'uncaring' state which ignores the plight of workers and poor peasants: this weak sort of argument – based on a non-existent capitalist morality – stems from an inability to locate economic development within an accumulation project structured by an industrial reserve army that is global in scope. In short, the capitalist state no longer has to 'care' about workers, because the latter are all replaceable, and indeed no longer simply workers of a specific nation and its state.

It was perhaps because of this background – rival ethnic groups competing within the same labour market of the nation state – that Austro-Marxism sought legal protection for and thus privileged the reproduction of cultural 'otherness' generally. In an important sense, therefore, this procedure contributed to the very problem it was designed to solve: namely, the segmentation of the labour market along ethnic/national lines, enabling capital to drive a wedge into what it might otherwise face as a united working class. In these situations, moreover, appeals to the democratic principle of self-determination amount in effect to valorising ethnic selfhood, both of those already in the labour market and of those entering it. That counter-revolutionary ideology and agency thrive on precisely this invocation of a broadly encompassing non-class 'difference' (Pan-Germanism, Pan-Slavism) is clear from the way Schönerer, Lueger and Hitler benefited from discourse championing specific 'indigenous' ethnic/national selfhoods (Germans, Austrians) all of which were then contrasted with 'other' identities (Jews, Slavs) present both in the nation state itself and/or in its labour market.

Against what it categorizes as the 'alien' internationalism of the left (proletariat, class structure, class struggle, socialism), both conservatism and the far right counterpose their own 'authentic' form of internationalism: namely, the global existence of peasant economy and culture – the embodiment of ethnic identity, nationhood, and the repository of cherished rural tradition – threatened with destruction by finance capital and depeasantization. This in turn confers legitimacy on historical and contemporary forms of grassroots resistance conducted by peasant cultivators and farmers in defence of their private property against any ('redistributive') State attempting to change existing social relations of production and thus disrupt what conservatives maintain are organic and 'natural' rural communities/traditions/hierarchy.

Like the Russian populists belonging to the Will of the People, therefore, advocates of counter-revolutionary agency in Austria at the same conjuncture sought to harness – and thus to act upon – traditional discourses as these already circulated at the grassroots, which in the Austrian case at the end of the nineteenth century included pervasive forms of racism: anti-semitism in rural areas and opposition to Slav immigrants searching for work in urban contexts. Where and when the left fails to address – let alone deal with – the issue of the industrial reserve army of labour, workers will seek out and increasingly turn to the remedies on offer from parties or movements of the populist far right, the mobilising discourse of which frames the opposition between self-as-victim and other-as-exploiter simply in non-economic terms, as an effect of ethnic and/or national identity.

Once again, this has lessons for the left in present-day capitalist nations, where implementation of the same kind of policy has much the same effect. When confronted with such competition in the labour market, therefore, workers are encouraged by populists to experience this as an effect of non-class identity. Acting in keeping with the latter is precisely what licenses the emergence of or reinforces an already-existing far-right narrative which in turn facilitates counter-revolutionary agency. Simply to say that such division ought not to happen, and to challenge this far-right ideology when it has already emerged or established itself, is to avoid the central issue of why it does when it does. In much the same way as their Austro-Marxist precursors, therefore, the academic left is culpable for the timidity of its response to this problem: discarding socialism as a desirable/feasible objective, consequently abandoning revolutionary agency as a method of realizing this, and instead privileging a theoretical framework (= the 'new' populist postmodernism) that seeks grassroots empowerment in ways that are little different from those sought historically and currently by conservatism and the far right.

Bibliography

Achebe, Chinua, 1966, *A Man of the People*, London: Heinemann.
Adams, Douglas, 1985, *The Hitch-Hiker's Guide to the Galaxy: The Original Radio Scripts*, London and Sydney: Pan Books.
Ahmad, Aijaz, 1992, *In Theory: Classes, Nations, Literatures*, London: Verso.
Alam, Javeed, 1983, 'Peasantry, Politics and Historiography: Critique of New Trend in Relation to Marxism', *Social Scientist*, No.117.
Alfaro, Julio, and Teresa Ore, n.d., circa 1974, *El desarrollo del capitalismo en La Convención y los nuevos movimientos políticos de campesinos con tierra 1963–1973*, Lima: Memoria de Bachiller, Universidad Católica del Peru.
Amin, Shahid, and Dipesh Chakrabarty (Eds.), 1996, *Subaltern Studies IX: Writings on South Asian History and Society*, Delhi: Oxford University Press.
Annan, Lord [Noel], 1966, *The Disintegration of an Old Culture* (The Romanes Lecture delivered in The Sheldonian Theatre 16 November 1965), Oxford: The Clarendon Press.
Antal, Frederick, 1962, *Hogarth and his place in European Art*, London: Routledge & Kegan Paul.
Anti-Slavery Reporter, 1833, *Abstract of the Report of the Lords' Committees on the Condition and Treatment of the Colonial Slaves, and of the Evidence taken by them on that subject*, Vol. V, No. 14, London: The London Society for the Abolition of Slavery throughout the British Dominions.
Arblaster, Anthony, 1992, *Viva la Libertà! Politics in Opera*, London: Verso.
Arnold, David, and David Hardiman (Eds.), 1994, *Subaltern Studies VIII: Essays in Honour of Ranajit Guha*, Delhi: Oxford University Press.
Aron, Raymond, 1967, *18 Lectures on Industrial Society*, London: Weidenfeld & Nicolson.
Ashcroft, Bill, Gareth Griffiths, and Helen Tiffin (Eds.), 1995, *The Post-Colonial Studies Reader*, London and New York: Routledge.
Assies, Willem, 2003, 'From Rubber Estate to Simple Commodity Production: Agrarian Struggles in the Northern Bolivian Amazon', in Tom Brass (ed.), *Latin American Peasants*, London and Portland, OR: Frank Cass Publishers.
Badiou, Alain, 2010, *The Communist Hypothesis*, London: Verso.
Barrientos, Stephanie, Uma Kothari, and Nicola Phillips, 2013, 'Dynamics of Unfree Labour in the Contemporary Global Economy', *The Journal of Development Studies*, Vol. 49, No. 8.
Bauer, Arnold J., 1975, *Chilean Rural Society from the Spanish Conquest to 1930*, Cambridge: Cambridge University Press.
Bauer, Arnold J., 1979, 'Rural Workers in Spanish America: Problems of Peonage and Oppression', *Hispanic American Historical Review*, Vol. 59, No. 1.

Bauer, Arnold J., 2004, *Chile y algo más: Estudios de historia Latinoamérica*, Santiago, Chile: Instituto de Historia, Universidad Católica.
Bauer, Otto, 1919, *El camino hacia el Socialismo*, Madrid: Editorial América.
Bauer, Otto, 1925, *The Austrian Revolution* (Translated by H.J. Stenning), London: Leonard Parsons.
Bauer, Otto, 2000 [1907], *The Question of Nationalities and Social Democracy* (Translated by Joseph O'Donnell), Minneapolis, MN: University of Minnesota Press.
Bax, E. Belfort, 1899, *The Peasants War in Germany 1525–1526*, London: Swan Sonnenschein & Co., Ltd.
Bayley, C.A., 1988, 'Rallying Around the Subaltern' *The Journal of Peasant Studies*, Vol.16, No.1 (also in Vinayak Chaturvedi (ed.) [2000]).
Bensaïd, Daniel, 2002, *Marx for Our Times*, London and New York: Verso.
Berger, John, 1960, *Permanent Red: Essays in Seeing*, London: Methuen & Co. Ltd.
Berger, John, 1964, *Corker's Freedom*, London: Methuen & Co.
Berger, John, 1972a, *Selected Essays and Articles: The Look of Things* (Edited with an Introduction by Nikos Stangos), Harmondsworth: Penguin Books.
Berger, John, 1972b, *Ways of Seeing*, London: The British Broadcasting Corporation & Penguin Books.
Berger, John, 1980, *About Looking*, London: Readers and Writers Publishing Cooperative.
Berger, John, 1992, *Into Their Labours (Pig Earth, Once in Europa, Lilac and Flag): A Trilogy*, New York: Pantheon Books.
Berger, John, 2015, *Portraits: John Berger on Artists* (Edited by Tom Overton), London: Verso.
Berger, John, 2016a, *Landscapes: John Berger on Art* (Edited with an Introduction by Tom Overton), London: Verso.
Berger, John, 2016b, *Confabulations*, London: Penguin Books.
Berger, John, and Jean Mohr, 1975, *A Seventh Man: The story of a migrant worker in Europe*, London: Penguin Books.
Bernstein, Eduard, 1961, *Evolutionary Socialism: A Criticism and Affirmation* [1899], New York: Schocken Books.
Bethell, Leslie, 2016, 'Introduction: Eric and Latin America', in J. Eric Hobsbawm [2016].
Bethell, Leslie (ed.), 1991, *The Cambridge History of Latin America – Volume VIII: 1930 to the Present*, Cambridge: Cambridge University Press.
Beverley, John, and José Oviedo (eds.), 1993, *The Postmodernism Debate in Latin America*, Durham, NC: Duke University Press.
Beverley, John, 2004, 'Subaltern Resistance in Latin America: A Reply to Tom Brass', *The Journal of Peasant Studies*, Vol. 31, No. 2.
Bhadra, Gautam, Gyan Prakash, and Susie Tharu (eds.), 1999, *Subaltern Studies X: Writings on South Asian History and Society*, Delhi: Oxford University Press.
Bhattacharya, Sabyasach, 1983, '"History from Below"', *Social Scientist*, No.119.

Blanco, Hugo, 1972, *Land or Death: The Peasant Struggle in Peru*, New York: Pathfinder Press.

Blok, Anton, 1988 [1974], *The Mafia of a Sicilian Village 1860–1960: A Study of Violent Peasant Entrepreneurs*, Cambridge: Polity Press.

Blum, Jerome, 1978, *The End of the Old Order in Rural Europe*, Princeton, NJ: Princeton University Press.

Blum, Mark E., and William Smaldone (eds.), 2016, *Austro-Marxism: The Ideology of Unity – Volume I: Austro-Marxist Theory and Strategy*, Chicago, IL: Haymarket Press.

Blum, Mark E., and William Smaldone (eds.), 2017, *Austro-Marxism: The Ideology of Unity – Volume II: Changing the World – The Politics of Austro-Marxism*, Leiden and Boston, MA: Brill.

Borkenau, Franz, 1938, *Austria and After*, London: Faber and Faber.

Bose, S.K., 1954, *Capital and Labour in the Indian Tea Industry*, Bombay: All-India Trade Union Congress.

Bottomore, Tom, and Patrick Goode (eds.), 1978, *Austro-Marxism*, Oxford: Clarendon Press.

Bourdieu, Pierre, 1990, *In Other Words: Essays Towards a Reflexive Sociology*, Stanford, CA: Stanford University Press.

Bourricaud, François, 1970 [1967], *Power and Society in Contemporary Peru* (translated by Paul Stevenson), London: Faber and Faber.

Bradby, Barbara, 1982, '"Resistance to Capitalism" in the Peruvian Andes', in D. Lehmann (ed.), *Ecology and Exchange in the Andes*, Cambridge: Cambridge University Press.

Brass, Tom, 1986a, 'Cargos and Conflicts: The Fiesta System and Capitalist Development in Eastern Peru', *The Journal of Peasant Studies*, Vol. 13, No. 2.

Brass, Tom, 1986b, 'The Elementary Strictures of Kinship: Unfree Relations and the Production of Commodities', *Social Analysis*, No. 20.

Brass, Tom, 1989, 'Trotskyism, Hugo Blanco and the Ideology of a Peruvian Peasant Movement', *The Journal of Peasant Studies*, Vol. 16, No. 2.

Brass, Tom, 1990, 'The Latin American *Enganche* System: Some Revisionist Reinterpretations Revisited', *Slavery & Abolition*, Vol. 11, No. 1.

Brass, Tom, 1991, 'Moral Economists, Subalterns, New Social Movements, and the (Re-) Emergence of a (Post-) Modernised (Middle) Peasant', *The Journal of Peasant Studies*, Vol.18, No.2 (also in Vinayak Chaturvedi (ed.) [2000]).

Brass, Tom, 1995, 'Reply to Utsa Patnaik: If the Cap Fits...', *International Review of Social History*, Vol. 40, No. 1.

Brass, Tom, 1999, *Towards a Comparative Political Economy of Unfree Labour: Case Studies and Debates*, London: Frank Cass Publishers.

Brass, Tom, 2000, *Peasants, Populism and Postmodernism: The Return of the Agrarian Myth*, London: Frank Cass.

Brass, Tom, 2002, 'Rural Labour in Agrarian Transitions: The Semi-Feudal Thesis Revisited', *The Journal of Contemporary Asia*, Vol. 32, No. 4.

Brass, Tom, 2003a, 'On Which Side of What Barricade? Subaltern Resistance in Latin America and Elsewhere', in Tom Brass (ed.) [2003].

Brass, Tom (ed.), 2003b, *Latin American Peasants*, London & Portland, OR: Frank Cass Publishers.

Brass, Tom, 2007, 'How Agrarian Cooperatives Fail: Lessons from 1970s Peru', *The Journal of Peasant Studies*, Vol. 34, No. 2.

Brass, Tom, 2010, 'Capitalism, Primitive Accumulation and Unfree Labour', in H. Veltmeyer (ed.), *Imperialism, Crisis and Class Struggle: The Enduring Verities of Capitalism – Essays Presented to James Petras*, Leiden & Boston, MA: Brill.

Brass, Tom, 2011, *Labour Regime Change in the Twenty-First Century*, Leiden: Brill.

Brass, Tom, 2012, 'Scott's "Zomia", or a Populist Postmodern History of Nowhere', *The Journal of Contemporary Asia*, Vol. 42, No. 1.

Brass, Tom, 2014a, 'Modern Capitalism and Unfree Labor: The Unsaying of Marxism', *Science & Society*, Vol. 78, No. 3.

Brass, Tom, 2014b, *Class, Culture and the Agrarian Myth*, Leiden: Brill.

Brass, Tom, 2015, 'Peasants, academics, populists: Forward to the past?', *Critique of Anthropology*, Vol. 35, No. 2.

Brass, Tom, 2017a, 'Who These Days is Not a Subaltern? The Populist Drift of Global Labour History', *Science & Society*, Vol. 81, No. 1.

Brass, Tom, 2017b, *Labour Markets, Identities, Controversies: Reviews and Essays 1982–2016*, Leiden: Brill.

Brass, Tom (ed.), 1994, *New Farmers Movements in India*, London and Portland, OR: Frank Cass Publishers.

Breman, Jan, 1974, *Patronage and Exploitation*, Berkeley, CA: University of California Press.

Breman, Jan, 1985, *Of Peasants, Migrants and Paupers*, Delhi: Oxford University Press.

Breman, Jan, 1993, *Beyond Patronage and Exploitation*, Delhi: Oxford University Press.

Breman, Jan, 1996, *Footloose Labour*, Cambridge: Cambridge University Press.

Breman, Jan, 2016, *On Pauperism in Present and Past*, New Delhi: Oxford University Press.

Brennan, Timothy, 2014, 'Subaltern Stakes', *New Left Review*, 89.

Brenton, Tony, 2016a, 'Introduction', in Tony Brenton (ed.) [2016c].

Brenton, Tony, 2016b, 'Lenin and yesterday's Utopia', in Tony Brenton (ed.) [2016c].

Brenton, Tony (ed.), 2016c, *Historically Inevitable? Turning Points of the Russian Revolution*, London: Profile Books.

Bukey, Evan Burr, 2000, *Hitler's Austria: Popular Sentiment in the Nazi Era, 1938–1945*, Chapel Hill, NC: The University of North Carolina.

Burke, Edmund, 1790, *Reflections on the Revolution in France* (3rd edition), London: J. Dodsley, Pall Mall.

Byres, Terence J., 1996, *Capitalism from Above and Capitalism from Below: An Essay in Comparative Political Economy*, London: Macmillan.

Carlyle, Thomas, 1902, *The French Revolution: A History*. Volumes I–III (Introduction, Notes and Appendices by John Holland Rose), London: George Bell & Sons.

Carsten, Francis L., 1977, *Fascist Movements in Austria: From Schönerer to Hitler*, London: Sage Publications.

Caudwell, Christopher, 1938, *Studies in a Dying Culture* (with an Introduction by John Strachey), London: John Lane The Bodley Head.

Caute, David, 1971, *The Illusion: An Essay on Politics, Theatre and the Novel*, London: Andre Deutsch.

Chakrabarty, Dipesh, 1985, 'Invitation to a Dialogue', in Ranajit Guha (ed.) [1985].

Chakrabarty, Dipesh, 1989, *Rethinking Working-Class History: Bengal 1890–1940*, Princeton, NJ: Princeton University Press.

Chandavarkar, Rajnarayan, 1997, '"The Making of the Working Class": E.P.Thompson and Indian History', *History Workshop Journal*, 43 (also in Vinayak Chaturvedi (ed.) [2000]).

Chatterjee, Partha, 1983, 'Peasantry, Politics and Historiography: A Response', *Social Scientist*, No.120.

Chatterjee, Partha, 1986, *Nationalist Thought and the Colonial World: A Derivative Discourse?* Delhi: Oxford University Press.

Chatterjee, Partha, and Gyanendra Pandey (eds.), 1992, *Subaltern Studies VII: Writings on South Asian History and Society*, Delhi: Oxford University Press.

Chaturvedi, Vinayak (ed.), 2000a, Mapping Subaltern Studies and the Postcolonial, London: Verso.

Chaturvedi, Vinayak, 2000b, 'Introduction', to Vinayak Chaturvedi (ed.) [2000].

Chibber, Vivek, 2013, *Postcolonial Theory and the Specter of Capital*, London: Verso.

Chopra, Suneet, 1982, 'Missing Correct Perspective', *Social Scientist*, No.111.

Chowdhury, Kanishka, 2014, 'Review of Chibber, Postcolonial Theory and the Specter of Capital', *Science & Society*, Vol. 78, No. 4.

Churchill, Winston S., 1937, *Great Contemporaries*, London: Thornton Butterworth Ltd.

Clover, Charles, 2016, *Black Wind, White Snow: The Rise of Russia's New Nationalism*, New Haven, CT: Yale University Press.

Cobban, Alfred, 1964, *The Social Interpretation of the French Revolution*, London: Cambridge University Press.

Common, Jack, 1980, *Revolt against an 'Age of Plenty'* (edited by Huw Beynon and Colin Hutchinson), Rochdale: Rochdale Alternative Press Ltd.

Cooper, Frederick, 1994, 'Conflict and Connection: Rethinking Colonial African History', *The American Historical Review*, Vol.99, No.5.

Cooper, Frederick, Florencia E. Mallon, Steven J. Stern, Allen F. Isaacman, and William Roseberry, 1993, *Confronting Historical Paradigms: Peasants, Labor, and the Capitalist World System in Africa and Latin America*, Madison, WI: The University of Wisconsin Press.

Corbridge, Stuart, 1990, 'Post-Marxism and Development Studies: Beyond the Impasse', *World Development*, Vol.18, No.5.

Corbridge, Stuart, 1994, 'Post-Marxism and Post-Colonialism: The Needs and Rights of Distant Strangers', in David Booth (ed.), *Rethinking Social Development*, Harlow: Longman Scientific & Technical.

Corbridge, Stuart, 1998, '"Beneath the Pavement Only Soil": The Poverty of Post-Development', *Journal of Development Studies*, Vol.34, No.6.

Craig, Wesley W., 1967, *From Hacienda to Community: An Analysis of Solidarity and Social Change in Peru*, Latin American Program Dissertation Series No. 6, Cornell University.

Craig, Wesley W., 1969, 'Peru: The Peasant Movement of La Convención', in Henry A. Landsberger (ed.), *Latin American Peasant Movements*, Ithaca, NY: Cornell University Press.

Crouch, Colin, and Alessandro Pizzorno (eds.), 1978a, *The Resurgence of Class Conflict in Western Europe since 1968 – Volume 1: National Studies*, London: The Macmillan Press Ltd.

Crouch, Colin, and Alessandro Pizzorno (eds.), 1978b, *The Resurgence of Class Conflict in Western Europe since 1968 – Volume 2: Comparative Analyses*, London: The Macmillan Press Ltd.

Cuadros, Carlos Ferdinand, 1964, *Principios jurídicos de la reforma agraria*, Cuzco: Ediciones del Centro de Estudios Jurídicos No. 17.

D'Eramo, Marco, 2013, 'Populism and the New Oligarchy', *New Left Review* 82.

Dahrendorf, Ralf, 1975, *The New Liberty: Survival and Justice in a Changing World* (The Reith Lectures), London: Routledge & Kegan Paul.

Damir-Geilsdorf, Sabine, Ulrike Lindner, Gersine Müller, Oliver Tappe, and Michael Zeuske (eds.), 2016, *Bonded Labour: Global and Comparative Perspectives (18th-21st Century)*, Bielefeld: Transcript Verlag.

Das, Raju J., 2014, *A Contribution to the Critique of Contemporary Capitalism: Theoretical and International Perspectives*, New York, NY: Nova Publishers.

Das, Raju J., 2017, *Marxist Class Theory for a Skeptical World*, Leiden & Boston, MA: Brill Publishers.

Davies, Robert H., 1979, *Capital, State and White Labour in South Africa 1900–1960: An Historical Materialist Analysis of Class Formation and Class Relations*, Brighton: Harvester Press.

de Maistre, Joseph, 1974 [1797], *Considerations on France* (translated by Richard A. Lebrun), Montreal and London: McGill-Queen's University Press.

Dew, C.B., 1966, *Ironmaker to the Confederacy: Joseph R. Anderson and the Tredegar Iron Works*, New Haven, CT: Yale University Press.

Dominick, Raymond H., 1982, *Wilhelm Liebknecht and the founding of the German Social Democratic Party*, Chapel Hill, NC: The University of North Carolina Press.

Drieu la Rochelle, Pierre, 1973, *Secret Journal and other writings* (translated and introduced by Alastair Hamilton), Cambridge: Rivers Press.

Duncan, Kenneth, Ian Rutledge, and Colin Harding (eds.), 1977, *Land and Labour in Latin America: Essays on the development of agrarian capitalism in the nineteenth and twentieth centuries*, Cambridge: Cambridge University Press.

Dunoyer, Carlo, 1859, *Della libertà del lavoro, o semplice esposizione delle condizioni nelle quali le forze umane si esercitano con maggiore potenza*, Torino: Stamperia dell'unione tipografico-editrice.

Eliade, Mircea, 1963, *Myth and Reality*, New York: Harper & Row, Publishers.

Elliott, E.N. (ed.), 1860, *Cotton is King and Pro-Slavery Arguments*, Augusta, GA: Pritchard, Abbott & Loomis.

Elmhirst, L.K. (ed.), 1939, *Proceedings of the Fifth International Conference of Agricultural Economists (held at Macdonald College, Canada, 21–28 August 1938)*, London: Oxford University Press.

Epstein, Klaus, 1966, *The Genesis of German Conservatism*, Princeton, NJ: Princeton University Press.

Escobar, Arturo, 1995, *Encountering Development: The Making and Unmaking of the Third World*, Princeton, NJ: Princeton University Press.

Ferrara, Francesco, 1859, 'Introduzione', in Carlo Dunoyer [1859].

Figes, Orlando, 2014, *A People's Tragedy: The Russian Revolution*, London: Bodley Head.

Figner, Vera, circa 1927, *Memoirs of a Revolutionist*, London: Martin Lawrence Limited.

Fioravanti, Eduardo, 1974, *Latifundio y sindicalismo agrario en el Peru: El caso de los valles de La Convención y Lares (1958–1964)*, Lima: Instituto de Estudios Peruanos.

Fischer, Conan, 1983, *Stormtroopers: A Social, Economic and Ideological Analysis, 1929–35*, London: George Allen & Unwin (Publishers) Ltd.

Fitzhugh, George, 1960 [1854–57], *Antebellum*, London: H. Jonas & Co.

Florescano, Enrique (ed.), 1975, *Haciendas, latifundios y plantaciones en América Latina*, México, DF: Siglo Veintiuno Editores, s.a.

Fogel, Robert W., and Stanley W. Engerman, 1974, *Time on the Cross: Volume I – The Economics of American Negro Slavery*, London: Wildwood House.

Forgacs, David, 1984, 'National-popular: genealogy of a concept', in Formations Editorial Collective (eds.), *Formations: Of Nations and Peoples*, London: Routledge & Kegan Paul.

Foweraker, Joe, 1981, *The Struggle for Land: A Political Economy of the Pioneer Frontier in Brazil from 1930 to the Present Day*, Cambridge: Cambridge University Press.

Fowles, John, 2003, *The Journals – Volume 1: 1949–1965* (Edited with an Introduction by Charles Drazin), London: Jonathan Cape.

Fowles, John, 2006, *The Journals – Volume 2: 1966–1990* (Edited with an Introduction by Charles Drazin), New York: Alfred A. Knopf.

Furet, François, 1981, *Interpreting the French Revolution*, London: Cambridge University Press.

Furet, François, 1998, 'The French Revolution Revisited', in Gary Kates (ed.), *The French Revolution: Recent Debates and New Controversies*, London: Routledge.

Galbraith, John Kenneth, 1977, *The Age of Uncertainty*, London: André Deutsch Ltd., and The British Broadcasting Corporation.

Gay, Peter, 1952, *The Dilemma of Democratic Socialism: Eduard Bernstein's Challenge to Marx*, New York: Columbia University Press.

Gay, Peter, 1966, *The Enlightenment: An Interpretation – Volume I: The Rise of Modern Paganism*, New York: Alfred A. Knopf.

Gay, Peter, 1969, *The Enlightenment: An Interpretation – Volume II: The Science of Freedom*, New York: Alfred A. Knopf.

Ghosh, Kaushik, 1999, 'A Market for Aboriginality: Primitivism and Race Classification in the Indentured Labour Market of Colonial India', in Prakash Bhadra and Tharu (eds.) [1999].

Ginsborg, Paul, 2008, *Democracy: Crisis and Renewal*, London: Profile Books.

Glyn, Andrew, 2006a, *Capitalism Unleashed*, Oxford: Oxford University Press.

Glyn, Andrew, 2006b, 'Will Marx be proved right?', *Oxonomics*, Vol. 1.

Godechot, Jacques, 1972, *The Counter-Revolution: Doctrine and Action, 1789–1804*, London: Routledge & Kegan Paul.

Gracián, Baltasar, 1953 [1647], *The Oracle: A Manual of the Art of Discretion (Oráculo manual y arte de prudencia)* (Translated by L.B. Walton), London: J.M. Dent.

Graeber, David, 2011, *Debt: The First 5,000 Years*, New York, NY: Melville House Publishing.

Guérin, Daniel, 1977, *Class Struggle in the First French Republic: Bourgeois and Bras Nu 1793–1795*, London: Pluto Press.

Guha, Ramachandra, 1989a, 'Sociology in India: Some elective affinities', *Contributions to Indian Sociology*, Vol.23, No. 2.

Guha, Ranajit (ed.), 1989b, *Subaltern Studies VI*, Delhi: Oxford University Press.

Guha, Ranajit, 1989c, 'Dominance Without Hegemony and Its Historiography', in Ranajit Guha (ed.) [1989].

Guha, Ranajit (ed.), 1982a, *Subaltern Studies I*, Delhi: Oxford University Press.

Guha, Ranajit, 1982b, 'On Some Aspects of the Historiography of Colonial India', in Ranajit Guha (ed.) [1982].

Guha, Ranajit (ed.), 1983a, *Subaltern Studies II*, Delhi: Oxford University Press.

Guha, Ranajit, 1983b, *Elementary Aspects of Peasant Insurgency in Colonial India*, Delhi: Oxford University Press.

Guha, Ranajit (ed.), 1984, *Subaltern Studies III*, Delhi: Oxford University Press.

Guha, Ranajit (ed.), 1985, *Subaltern Studies IV*, Delhi: Oxford University Press.

Guha, Ranajit (ed.), 1987, *Subaltern Studies V*, Delhi: Oxford University Press.

Guha, Ranajit, 1974, 'Neel-Darpan: The Image of a Peasant Revolt in a Liberal Mirror', *The Journal of Peasant Studies*, Vol.2, No.1.

Gunder Frank, André, 1967, *Capitalism and Underdevelopment in Latin America*, New York: Monthly Review Press.

Gupta, D., 1985, 'On Altering the Ego in Peasant History: Paradoxes of the Ethnic Option', *Peasant Studies*, Vol.13, No.4.

Hall, Ruth, Marc Edelman, Saturnino Borras, Ian Scoones, Ben White and Wendy Wolford, 2015, 'Resistance, acquiescence or incorporation? An introduction to land grabbing and political reactions "from below"', *The Journal of Peasant Studies*, Vol. 42, Nos. 3–4.

Halpern, Joel M., 1967, *The Changing Village Community*, Englewood Cliffs, NJ: Prentice-Hall, Inc.

Hardiman, David, 1981, *Peasant Nationalists of Gujarat: Kheda District, 1917–1934*, Delhi: Oxford University Press.

Hardiman, David, 1987, *The Coming of the Devi: Adivasi Assertion in Western India*, Delhi: Oxford University Press.

Hardiman, David, 1996, *Feeding the Baniya: Peasants and Usurers in Western India*, Delhi: Oxford University Press.

Hart, David Mercer, 1997, *Class Analysis, Slavery and the Industrialist Theory of History in French Liberal Thought, 1814–1830: The Radical Liberalism of Charles Comte and Charles Dunoyer*, Unpublished PhD dissertation, University of Cambridge.

Hasan, Mushirul, and Narayani Gupta (eds.), 1993, *India's Colonial Encounters: Essays in Memory of Eric Stokes*, New Delhi: Manohar.

Hilton, Rodney (ed.), 1976, *The Transition from Feudalism to Capitalism*, London: New Left Books.

Hitler, Adolf, 1939, *Mein Kampf* (Translated and introduced by James Murphy), London: Hurst and Blackett Ltd., Publishers.

Hobsbawm, Eric J., 1959, *Primitive Rebels: Studies in archaic forms of social movements in the 19th and 20th centuries*, Manchester: Manchester University Press.

Hobsbawm, Eric J., 1969a, 'A Case of Neo-Feudalism: La Convención, Peru', *Journal of Latin American Studies*, Vol. 1, No. 1.

Hobsbawm, Eric J., 1969b, *Bandits*, London: Weidenfeld & Nicolson.

Hobsbawm, Eric J., 1973a, *Revolutionaries: Contemporary Essays*, London: Weidenfeld and Nicolson.

Hobsbawm, Eric J., 1973b, 'Peasants and Politics', *The Journal of Peasant Studies*, Vol.1, No.1.

Hobsbawm, Eric J., 1981, 'The Forward March of Labour Halted?', and 'Observations on the Debate', in Martin Jacques and Francis Mulhern (eds.), *The Forward March of Labour Halted?* London: Verso.

Hobsbawm, Eric J., 1984, *Worlds of Labour: Further studies in the history of labour*, London: Weidenfeld & Nicolson.

Hobsbawm, Eric J., 1997, *On History*, London: Weidenfeld & Nicolson.
Hobsbawm, Eric J., 2002, *Interesting Times: A Twentieth-Century Life*, London: Allen Lane, The Penguin Press.
Hobsbawm, Eric J., 2011, *How to Change the World: Tales of Marx and Marxism*, London: Abacus Books.
Hobsbawm, Eric J., 2016, *Viva la Revolución: Eric Hobsbawm on Latin America*, London: Little, Brown.
Hochschild, Adam, 1999, *King Leopold's Ghost: A Story of Greed, Terror, and Heroism in Colonial Africa*, London: Macmillan.
Holme, Charles (ed.), 1911, *Peasant Art in Austria and Hungary*, London, Paris, New York: The Studio, Ltd.
Hoppe, Hans-Hermann, 2012, 'Marxist and Austrian Class Analysis', in Yuri N. Maltsev (ed.), *Requiem for Marx*, Alabama: Ludwig von Mises Institute.
Howe, Irving, 1964, 'Introduction', in *The Basic Writings of Trotsky* (Edited and Introduced by Irving Howe), London: Secker & Warburg.
Huizer, Gerrit, 1973, *Peasant Rebellion in Latin America*, Harmondsworth: Penguin Books.
Hussain, Athar, and Keith Tribe (eds.), 1984, *Paths of Development in Capitalist Agriculture: Readings from German Social Democracy, 1891–99*, London: Macmillan.
Huws, Ursula, 2013, 'The underpinnings of class in the digital age: living, labour and value', in Leo Panitch et al. (eds), *Socialist Register 2014 – Registering Class*, London: The Merlin Press.
Inden, Ronald, 1986, 'Orientalist Constructions of India', *Modern Asian Studies*, Vol.20, No.3.
Jeffery, Charlie, 1995, *Social Democracy in the Austrian Provinces, 1918–1934: Beyond Red Vienna*, London: Leicester University Press.
Johnson, Douglas (ed.), 1976, *French Society and the Revolution*, Cambridge: Cambridge University Press.
Jones, Andy, 2014, 'UKIP and immigration', *International Socialism*, No. 143.
Joseph, Gilbert M., Catherine C. LeGrand, and Ricardo D. Salvatore (eds.), 1998, *Close Encounters of Empire: Writing the Cultural History of US-Latin American Relations*, Durham, NC: Duke University Press.
Kaiwar, Vasant, 2015, *The Postcolonial Orient: The Politics of Difference and the Project of Provincialising Europe*, Chicago, IL: Haymarket.
Kaufman, Allen, 1982, *Capitalism, Slavery, and Republican Values: American Political Economists, 1819–1848*, Austin, TX: University of Texas Press.
Kautsky, Karl, 1916, *The Social Revolution*, Chicago, IL: Charles H. Kerr & Co.
Kautsky, Karl, 1920, *Terror and Communism: A Contribution to the Natural History of Revolution* (Translated by W.H. Kerridge), London: George Allen & Unwin Ltd.
Kautsky, Karl, 1984 [1894/95], 'The Competitive Capacity of Small-scale Enterprise in Agriculture', in Athar Hussain and Keith Tribe (eds.), *Paths of Development in Capitalist Agriculture*, London: Macmillan.

Kautsky, Karl, 1988, *The Agrarian Question* [1899], 2 Volumes, London: Zwan Publications.

Kazin, Alfred, 1966, *Starting Out in the Thirties*, London: Secker & Warburg.

Keynes, John Maynard, 1933, *Essays in Biography*, London: Macmillan & Co., Limited.

King-Hall, Stephen, 1938, *K-H News-Letter Service: Volume Four, letters 79–104 [5.1.38 to 1.7.38]*, London: Cresswell Place.

Kitchen, Martin, 1987, 'The Austrian Left and the Popular Front', in Helen Graham and Paul Preston (eds.), *The Popular Front in Europe*, London: Macmillan Press.

Kohl, Johann Georg, 1843, *Austria: Vienna, Prague, Hungary, Bohemia and the Danube, &etc.*, London: Chapman and Hall, 186 Strand.

Kritsman, L.N., 1984, 'Class Stratification of the Soviet Countryside', in Terry Cox and Gary Littlejohn (eds.), *Kritsman and the Agrarian Marxists*, London: Frank Cass Publishers.

Lacey, Marian, 1981, *Working for Boroko: The Origins of a Coercive Labour System in South Africa*, Johannesburg: Ravan Press.

Laibman, David, 2015, *Passion and Patience: Society, History, and Revolutionary Vision*, New York, NY: International Publishers.

Landis, Erik C., 2016, 'The fate of the Soviet countryside', in Tony Brenton (ed.) [2016c].

Latin American Subaltern Studies Group, 1993, 'Founding Statement', in Beverley, John and José Oviedo (eds.) [1993].

Leach, Edmund R., 1961, *Rethinking Anthropology*, London: The Athlone Press.

Leach, Edmund R., and S.N. Mukherjee (eds.), 1970, *Elites in South Asia*, Cambridge: Cambridge University Press.

LeBaron, Genevieve, and Nicola Phillips, 2018, 'States and the Political Economy of Unfree Labour', *New Political Economy*, DOI: 10.1080/13563467.2017.1420642.

Lehmann, David A., 1990, *Democracy and Development in Latin America*, Cambridge: Polity Press.

Lehmann, David A., 1997, 'An Opportunity Lost: Escobar's Deconstruction of Development', *Journal of Development Studies*, Vol.33, No.4.

Lenin, V.I., 1961a, 'What Is To Be Done [1902]?', *Collected Works*, Volume 5, Moscow: Progress Publishers.

Lenin, V.I., 1961b, 'Philosophical Notebooks', *Collected Works*, Volume 38, Moscow: Foreign Languages Publishing House.

Lenin, V.I., 1962, 'Preface [1907]', *Collected Works*, Volume 12, Moscow: Progress Publishers.

Lenin, V.I., 1964a, 'The Development of Capitalism in Russia [1899]', *Collected Works*, Volume 3, Moscow: Foreign Languages Publishing House.

Lenin, V.I., 1964b, 'Critical Remarks on the National Question [1913]', *Collected Works*, Volume 20, Moscow: Progress Publishers.

Lenin, V.I., 1965, 'A Publicist's Notes [1920]', *Collected Works*, Volume 30, Moscow: Progress Publishers.

Leroux, Robert, and David Hart (eds.), 2012, *French Liberalism in the 19th Century: An Anthology*, London: Routledge.

Levitas, Ruth (ed.), 1986, *The Ideology of the New Right*, Cambridge: Polity Press.

Lichtenstein, Alex, 1996, *Twice the Work of Free Labor: The Political Economy of Convict Labor in the New South*, London: Verso.

Liebknecht, Karl, 1973 [1907], *Militarism and Anti-Militarism* (translated with an introduction by Grahame Lock), Cambridge: Rivers Press.

Liggio, Leonard P., 1977, 'Charles Dunoyer and French Classical Liberalism', *Journal of Libertarian Studies*, Vol. 1, No. 3.

Lochore, R.A., 1935, *History of the Idea of Civilization in France (1830–1870)*, Bonn: Ludwig Röhrscheid Verlag.

Loew, Raimund, 1979, 'The Politics of Austro-Marxism', *New Left Review*, 118.

London Municipal Society, 1909, *The Case Against Socialism: A Handbook for [Conservative] Speakers and Candidates*, London: George Allen & Sons.

López Albújar, Enrique, 1933, *Los Caballeros del Delito*, Lima: Compañia de Impresiones y Publicidad.

Lowe, Lisa, and David Lloyd (eds.), 1997, *The Politics of Culture in the Shadow of Capital*, Durham, NC: Duke University Press.

Luxemburg, Rosa, 1961, *The Russian Revolution and Leninism or Marxism?* Ann Arbor, MI: University of Michigan Press.

Luxemburg, Rosa, 1976, *The National Question*, New York and London: Monthly Review Press.

Luxemburg, Rosa, 2014, *The Complete Works: Volume I, Economic Writings 1* (edited by Peter Hudis; Translated by David Fernbach, Joseph Fracchia and George Shriver), London and New York: Verso.

Machiavelli, Nicolò, 1938 [1513], *The Prince*, London: J.M.Dent & Sons, Ltd.

Mallon, Florencia, 1994, 'The Promise and Dilemma of Subaltern Studies: Perspectives from Latin American History', *The American Historical Review*, Vol.99, No.5.

Manuel, Frank E., 1956, *The New World of Henri Saint-Simon*, Cambridge, MA: Harvard University Press.

Marchal, Jules, 2008, *Lord Leverhulme's Ghosts: Colonial Exploitation in the Congo* (Translated by Martin Thom, Introduced by Adam Hochschild), London: Verso.

MARHO (The Radical Historians Organization), 1983, *Visions of History* (Interviews with E.P. Thompson, Eric Hobsbawm, *et al.*), Manchester: Manchester University Press.

Markham, F.M.H. (ed.), 1952, *Henri Comte de Saint-Simon (1760–1825): Selected Writings*, Oxford: Basil Blackwell.

Marx, Karl, 1973, *The First International and After*, London: Penguin Books.

Marx, Karl, 1986, 'Economic Manuscripts of 1857–58', in Karl Marx Frederick Engels, *Collected Works*, Volume 28, London: Lawrence & Wishart.

Marx, Karl, and Frederick Engels, 1934, *Correspondence 1846–1895*, London: Martin Lawrence Ltd.

Marx, Karl, and Frederick Engels, 1978 [1850], 'Review of Latter-Day Pamphlets by Thomas Carlyle', in Karl Marx Frederick Engels, *Collected Works*, Volume 10, London: Lawrence & Wishart.

Mattick, Paul, 1967, 'The Limits of Integration', in Kurt H. Wolff and Barrington Moore Jr. (eds.), *The Critical Spirit: Essays in Honor of Herbert Marcuse*, Boston, MA: Beacon Press.

Mayaram, Shail, M.S.S. Pandian, and Ajay Skaria (eds.), 2012, *Subaltern Studies xii: Muslims, Dalits, and the Fabrications of History*, New Delhi: Permanent Black.

McCarthy, Mary, 1953, *The Groves of Academe*, London: William Heinemann Ltd.

McMeekin, Sean, 2017, *The Russian Revolution: A New History*, London: Profile Books.

Mead, Margaret, 1956, *New Lives for Old: Cultural Transformation – Manus, 1928–1953*, New York: William Morrow and Company.

Meek, Ronald L. (ed.), 1973, *Turgot on Progress, Sociology and Economics*, London: Cambridge University Press.

Meillassoux, Claude, 1973, 'The Social Organization of the Peasantry: The Economic Basis of Kinship', *The Journal of Peasant Studies*, Vol. 1, No. 1, 81–90.

Miller, Norman N. (ed.), 1969, *Research in Rural Africa*, East Lansing, MI: African Studies Center, Michigan State University.

Mitrany, David, 1951, *Marx Against the Peasant*, Chapel Hill, NC: University of North Carolina Press.

Mohr, Jean, and John Berger, 1979, 'Discussion at the BSA Conference, April 1978', in Terry Dennett and Jo Spence (eds.), *Photography/Politics One*, London: Photography Workshop.

Moore, Charles, and Simon Heffer (eds.), 1989, *A Tory Seer: The Selected Journalism of T.E. Utley* (Foreword by Margaret Thatcher, Introduction by Enoch Powell), London: Hamish Hamilton.

Morin, Edgar, 1970, *The Red and the White: Report from a French Village*, New York: Pantheon Books.

Müller, Gersine, and Johanna Abel, 2016, 'Cultural Forms of Representation of "Coolies": Khal Torabully and his concept of Coolitude', in Damir-Geilsdorf *et al.* (eds.) [2016].

Mukhtyar, G.C., 1930, *Life and Labour in a South Gujarat Village*, Calcutta: Longmans, Green.

Munck, Ronaldo, 2009, 'Globalization, Governance and Migration: an introduction', in Ronaldo Munck (ed.), *Globalization and Migration: New Issues, New Politics*, Abingdon: Routledge.

Nash, Manning, 1958, *Machine Age Maya: The industrialization of a Guatemalan Community*, Chicago: The American Anthropological Association Memoir No. 87.

Naumann, Friedrich, 1916, *Central Europe* (Translated by Christabel M. Meredith, with an Introduction by W.J. Ashley), London: P.S. King & Son, Limited.
Newby, Howard (ed.), 1978, *International Perspectives in Rural Sociology*, Chichester: John Wiley & Sons.
Nugent, Daniel (ed.), 1998, *Rural Revolt in Mexico: US Intervention and the Domain of Subaltern Politics*, Durham, NC: Duke University Press.
O'Hanlon, Rosalind, 1988, 'Recovering the Subject: Subaltern Studies and Histories of Resistance in Colonial South Asia', *Modern Asian Studies*, Vol.22, No.1 (also in Vinayak Chaturvedi (ed.) [2000]).
O'Hanlon, Rosalind, 1993, 'Historical approaches to communalism: perspectives from Western India', in Peter Robb (ed.), *Society and Ideology: Essays in South Asian History*, Delhi: Oxford University Press.
O'Hanlon, Rosalind, and David Washbrook, 1992, 'After Orientalism: Culture, Criticism, and Politics in the Third World', *Comparative Studies in Society and History*, Vol.34, No.1 (also in Vinayak Chaturvedi (ed.) [2000]).
Olusoga, David, 2018, *Civilizations: First Contact – The Cult of Progress*, London: Profile Books Ltd.
Orwell, George, 1965, *Decline of the English Murder and other essays*, Harmondsworth: Penguin Books.
Ovid [P. Ovidius Naso], 1955, *The Metamorphoses* (translated by Mary M. Innes), Harmondsworth: Penguin Books.
Oxaal, Ivar, Michael Pollak, and Gerhard Botz (eds.), 1987, *Jews, Antisemitism and Culture in Vienna*, London and New York: Routledge & Kegan Paul.
Page, Thomas Nelson, 1919 [1892], *The Old South*, New York: The Chautauqua Press.
Paige, Jeffrey M., 1975, *Agrarian Revolution*, New York: The Free Press.
Pandey, Gyanendra, 1990, *The Construction of Communalism in Colonial North India*, Delhi: Oxford University Press.
Panitch, Leo, and Greg Albo (eds.), 2016, *Socialist Register 2017: Rethinking Revolution*, London: The Merlin Press.
Patel, Sujata (ed.), 2008, *The Jan Breman Omnibus*, New Delhi: Oxford University Press.
Patnaik, Utsa (ed.), 1990, *Agrarian Relations and Accumulation*, New Delhi: Oxford University Press.
Patnaik, Utsa, 1999, *The Long Transition: Essays on Political Economy*, New Delhi: Tulika.
Patnaik, Utsa, 2007, *The Republic of Hunger*, Monmouth: The Merlin Press.
Patnaik, Utsa, and Manjari Dingwaney (eds.), 1985, *Chains of Servitude: Bondage and Slavery in India*, Madras: Sangam Books.
Pearse, Andrew, 1975, *The Latin American Peasant*, London: Frank Cass.
Petras, James, 1990, 'Retreat of the Intellectuals', *Economic and Political Weekly*, VOL.XXV, No.38.
Pipes, Richard, 1997, *The Russian Revolution, 1899–1919*, London: Harvill.
Pipes, Richard, 2001, *Communism: A Brief History*, London: Weidenfeld & Nicolson.

Pollock, Frederick, 1984, 'Socialism and Agriculture [1932]', in Athar Hussain and Keith Tribe (Eds.), *Paths of Development in Capitalist Agriculture: Readings from German Social Democracy, 1891–99*, London: Macmillan.
Postgate, Raymond (ed.), 1920, *Revolution from 1789 to 1906*, London: Grant Richards Ltd.
Postgate, Raymond, 1934, *How to Make a Revolution*, London: The Hogarth Press.
Pozzolini, Alberto, 1970, *Antonio Gramsci: An introduction to his thought*, London: Pluto Press.
Prakash, Gyan, 1994, 'Subaltern Studies as Postcolonial Criticism', *The American Historical Review*, Vol.99, No.5, 1475–1490.
Preobrazhensky, Evgeny A., 1980, *The Crisis of Soviet Industrialization: Selected Essays*, London: Macmillan.
Raico, Ralph, 2012 [1993], 'Classical Liberal Roots of the Marxist Doctrine of Classes', in Yuri N. Maltsev (ed.), *Requiem for Marx*, Alabama: Ludwig von Mises Institute.
Reed, John, 1926, *Ten Days that Shook the World*, London: The Communist Party of Great Britain.
Renner, Karl, 1949, *The Institutions of Private Law and their Social Functions* (Edited, with an Introduction and Notes, by O. Kahn-Freund), London: Routledge & Kegan Paul Limited.
Reyeros, Rafael, 1949, *El Pongueaje: La Servidumbre Personal de los Indios Bolivianos*, La Paz: Empresa Editora Universo.
Rhys Williams, Albert, 1929, *The Russian Land*, London: Geoffrey Bles, Suffolk Street, Pall Mall.
Rodríguez García, Magaly, 2016, 'On the Legal Boundaries of Coerced Labour', in Marcel van der Linden and Magaly Rodríguez García (eds.) [2016].
Rogatchev, Ekaterina (ed.), 2017, *Russian Revolution: Hope, Tragedy, Myths*, London: The British Library.
Rogers, Everett M., 1970, 'Motivations, Values and Attitudes of Subsistence Farmers: Toward a Subculture of Peasantry', in Clifton R. Wharton, Jr. (ed.), *Subsistence Agriculture and Economic Development*, London: Frank Cass & Co. Ltd.
Rogers, Everett M., 1976, 'Communication and Development: The Passing of the Dominant Paradigm', in Everett M. Rogers (ed.), *Communication and Development: Critical Perspectives*, London: Sage Publications.
Rogger, Hans, and Eugene Weber (eds.), 1965, *The European Right: A Historical Profile*, London: Weidenfeld & Nicolson.
Rorty, Richard, 1998, *Achieving Our Country: Leftist Thought in Twentieth Century America*, Cambridge, MA: Harvard University Press.
Roseberry, William, 1993, 'Beyond the Agrarian Question in Latin America', in Cooper et al. [1993].
Rostow, Walt W., 1960, *The Stages of Economic Growth: A Non-Communist Manifesto*, London & New York: Cambridge University Press.

Roth, Karl-Heinz, and Marcel van der Linden, 2014, 'Results and Prospects', in Marcel van der Linden and Karl-Heinz Roth (eds.), *Beyond Marx: Theorizing the Global Labour Relations of the Twenty-First Century*, Leiden: Brill.
Rothbard, Murray N., 1995, *Austrian Perspective on the History of Economic Thought*, Volume 2, Cheltenham: Edward Elgar Publishing.
Rudé, George, 1959, *The Crowd in the French Revolution*, Oxford: Clarendon Press.
Rudra, Ashok, et al., 1978, *Studies in the Development of Capitalism in India*, Lahore: Vanguard Press.
Saith, Ashwani, 2016, 'A Defiant Sociologist and His Craft: Jan Breman – An Appreciation and a Conversation', *Development and Change*, Vol. 47, No. 4.
Salvadori, Massimo, 1979, *Karl Kautsky and the Socialist Revolution 1880–1938*, London: New Left Books.
Sánchez, Rodrigo, 1977, 'The Model of Verticality in the Andean Economy: A Critical Reconsideration', *Bulletin of the Society for Latin American Studies*, No. 2.
Sánchez, Rodrigo, 1982, 'The Andean Economic System and Capitalism', in D. Lehmann (ed.), *Ecology and Exchange in the Andes*, Cambridge: Cambridge University Press.
Sarkar, Sumit, 1984, 'The Conditions and Nature of Subaltern Militancy: Bengal from Swadeshi to Non-Cooperation, c.1905–22', in Ranajit Guha (ed.) [1984].
Sarkar, Sumit, 1989, 'The Kalki-Avatar of Bikrampur: A Village Scandal in Early Twentieth Century Bengal', in Ranajit Guha (ed.) [1989].
Sarkar, Sumit, 1997, *Writing Social History*, Calcutta: Oxford University Press.
Sathyamurthy, T.V., 1990, 'Indian Peasant Historiography: A Critical Perspective on Ranajit Guha's Work', *The Journal of Peasant Studies*, Vol.18, No.1.
Sathyamurthy, T.V., 1998, 'Labour of Sisyphus, Feast of the Barmecide: The Sentence and the Promise in Development Studies', *Economic and Political Weekly*, Vol.XXXIII, No.24.
Sathyamurthy, T.V., 1999, 'South Asia: Fifty years after Independence', *Soundings*, No.11.
Schlegel, Frederick von, 1848, *The Philosophy of History, in a Course of Lectures delivered at Vienna 1829*, London: Henry G. Bohn.
Schlegel, Frederick von, 1849, *Aesthetic and Miscellaneous Works (1794–1808)*, London: Henry G. Bohn.
Schorske, Carl E., 1980, *Fin-de-Siècle Vienna: Politics and Culture*, London: Weidenfeld and Nicolson.
Scott, James C., 1985, *Weapons of the Weak: Everyday Forms of Peasant Resistance*, New Haven, CT: Yale University Press.
Seal, Anil, 1968, *The Emergence of Indian Nationalism: Competition and Collaboration in the Later Nineteenth Century*, Cambridge: Cambridge University Press.
Sebestyen, Victor, 2017, *Lenin the Dictator*, London: Weidenfeld & Nicolson.
Second Congress of the Communist International, 1977, *Minutes of the Proceedings (1921) – Volume 1*, London: New Park Publications Ltd.
Serge, Victor, 2012 [1963], *Memoirs of a Revolutionary* (Translated by Peter Sedgwick and George Paizis), New York: New York Review of Books.
Shachtman, Max, 2003, *Race and Revolution*, London and New York: Verso.

Shukla, J.B., 1937, *Life and Labour in a Gujarat Taluka*, Calcutta: Longmans, Green.
Singh, Sangeeta, et al., 1984, 'Subaltern Studies II: A Review Article', *Social Scientist*, No.137.
Sinha, Subir, Shubhra Gururani, and Brian Greenberg, 1997, 'The "New Traditionalist" Discourse of Indian Environmentalism', *The Journal of Peasant Studies*, Vol.24, No.3.
Sivaramakrishnan, K., 1995, 'Situating the Subaltern: History and Anthropology in the Subaltern Studies Project', *Journal of Historical Sociology*, Vol.8, No.4.
Snowman, Daniel, 2007, *Historians*, Basingstoke: Palgrave Macmillan.
Sombart, Werner, 1909, *Socialism and the Social Movement*, London: J.M. Dent & Co.
Sombart, Werner, 1937, *A New Social Philosophy*, Princeton, NJ: Princeton University Press.
Spencer, Herbert, 1881, *Man versus the State*, London: Williams and Norgate.
Stalin, Joseph, 1928, *Leninism*, London: George Allen & Unwin Ltd.
Stelzer, Irwin (ed.), 2005, *Neoconservatism*, London: Atlantic Books.
Stephens, W. Walker (ed.), 1895, *The Life and Writings of Turgot, Comptroller-General of France 1774–6*, London: Longmans, Green and Co.
Stokes, Eric, 1978, *The Peasant and the Raj: Studies in agrarian society and peasant rebellion in colonial India*, Cambridge: Cambridge University Press.
Sumner, William Graham, 1959 [1906], *Folkways*, New York: Dover Publications, Inc.
Sunic, Tomislav, 1990, *Against Democracy and Equality: The European New Right*, New York: Peter Lang.
Tappe, Oliver, 2016, 'Coolie chains: global commodities, colonialism and the question of labour', *Die Erde – Journal of the Geographical Society of Berlin*, Vol. 147, No. 3.
Tappe, Oliver, and Ulrike Lindner, 2016, 'Introduction: Global Variants of Bonded Labour', in Damir-Geilsdorf et al. (eds.) [2016].
The Royal Academy of Arts, 2017, *Revolution: Russian Art 1917–1932*, London: Royal Academy of Arts.
Thorner, Alice, 1982, 'Semi-feudalism or Capitalism? Contemporary Debate on Classes and Modes of Production in India', *Economic and Political Weekly* XVII, Nos. 49–51.
Thorner, Daniel, 1964, *Agricultural Cooperatives in India: A Field Report*, Asia Publishing House, New York.
Thorner, Daniel, and Alice Thorner, 1962, *Land and Labour in India*, New Delhi: Asia Publishing House.
Tilly, Charles, 1964, *The Vendee*, London: Edward Arnold (Publishers) Ltd.
Tise, Larry E., 1987, *Proslavery: A History of the Defense of Slavery in America, 1701–1840*, Athens, GA: The University of Georgia Press.
Toynbee, Arnold J., 1928, *The Conduct of British Empire Foreign Relations since the Peace Settlement*, London: Oxford University Press.
Trotsky, Leon, 1925, *Literature and Revolution*, London: George Allen & Unwin Ltd.
Trotsky, Leon, 1930, *My Life*, London: Thornton Butterworth Limited.
Trotsky, Leon, 1934, *The History of the Russian Revolution*, London: Victor Gollancz Ltd.
Trotsky, Leon, 1935 [1921], *The Defence of Terrorism: Terrorism and Communism – A Reply to Karl Kautsky*, London: George Allen & Unwin Ltd.

Trotsky, Leon, 1936 [1928], *The Third International After Lenin*, New York: Pioneer Publishers.
Trotsky, Leon, 1937, *The Revolution Betrayed*, London: Faber and Faber.
Trotsky, Leon, 1940, *The Living Thoughts of Karl Marx, based on Capital: A Critique of Political Economy*, London: Cassell and Company, Ltd.
Trotsky, Leon, 1953, *The First Five Years of the Communist International*, Volume II, New York: Pioneer Publishers.
Trotsky, Leon, 1956 [1943], *The New Course*, London: New Park Publications Ltd.
Trotsky, Leon, 1959, *Trotsky's Diary in Exile 1935*, London: Faber and Faber.
Trotsky, Leon, 1962, *The Permanent Revolution and Results and Prospects*, London: New Park Publications.
Trotsky, Leon, 1969, 'The Three Conceptions of the Russian Revolution', *Writings 1938–39*, New York: Merit Publishers.
Trotsky, Leon, 1972a, *1905* (Translated by Anya Bostock), London: Allen Lane, The Penguin Press.
Trotsky, Leon, 1972b, *Writings 1932–33*, New York: Pathfinder Press, Inc.
Trotsky, Leon, 1973a, *Writings 1930–31*, New York: Pathfinder Press, Inc.
Trotsky, Leon, 1973b, *The Spanish Revolution (1931–39)*, New York: Pathfinder Press.
Trotsky, Leon, 1979, *Writings 1929–33 (Supplement)*, New York: Pathfinder Press, Inc.
Tudor, H., and J.M. Tudor (eds.), 1988, *Marxism and Social Democracy: The Revisionist Debate 1896–1898*, Cambridge: Cambridge University Press.
United States Senate Commission, 1913, *Agricultural Cooperation and Rural Credit in Europe*, Washington, DC: Government Printing Office.
van der Linden, Marcel, 2016, 'Dissecting Coerced Labour', in Marcel van der Linden and Magaly Rodríguez García (eds.) [2016].
van der Linden, Marcel, and Magaly Rodríguez García, 2016a, 'Introduction', in Marcel van der Linden and Magaly Rodríguez García (eds.) [2016].
van der Linden, Marcel, and Magaly Rodríguez García (eds.), 2016b, *On Coerced Labor: Work and Compulsion after Chattel Slavery*, Leiden: Brill.
van Melkebeke, Sven, 2016, 'Coerced Coffee Cultivation and Rural Agency: The Plantation Economy of Kivu (1918–1940)', in Marcel van der Linden and Magaly Rodríguez García (eds.) [2016].
Vanaik, Achin, 1986, 'The Indian Left', *New Left Review*, No.159.
Vanaik, Achin, 1990, *The Painful Transition: Bourgeois Democracy in India*, London: Verso.
Vanaik, Achin, 1992, 'Reflections on Communalism and Nationalism in India', *New Left Review*, No.196.
Vanaik, Achin, 1994, 'Situating the Threat of Hindu Nationalism - Problems with Fascist Paradigm', *Economic and Political Weekly*, Vol. XXIX, No.28.
Vanaik, Achin, 1997, *The Furies of Indian Communalism: Religion, Modernity and Secularization*. London: Verso.

Vanaik, Achin, 1998, 'Marxist-Thompsonian History', *Economic and Political Weekly*, Vol. XXXIII, No.21.
Vanaik, Achin, 2017, *The Rise of Hindu Authoritarianism*, London: Verso.
Villanueva, Victor, 1967, *Hugo Blanco y la rebelión campesina*, Lima: Libreria-Editorial Juan Mejia Baca.
von Bülow, Prince Bernard, 1915, *Imperial Germany*, Cassell & Co., Ltd, London.
von Mises, Ludwig, 1966 [1949], *Human Action: A Treatise on Economics*, Chicago, IL: Henry Regnery Company.
Vyas, V.S., 1964, 'Agricultural Labour in Four Villages', in V.S. Vyas (ed.), *Agricultural Labour in Four Indian Villages*, Vallabhvidyanager: Sardar Vallabhbhai Vidyapeeth.
Weber, Eugen, 1976, *Peasants into Frenchmen: The Modernization of Rural France 1870–1914*, Stanford, CA: Stanford University Press.
Weiner, Myron (Ed.), 1966, *Modernization: The Dynamics of Growth*, Washington, D.C.: Voice of America Forum Lectures.
Weiss, John, 1977, *Conservatism in Europe 1770–1945: Traditionalism, Reaction, and Counter-Revolution*, London: Thames and Hudson.
Wertheimer, Mildred S., 1924, *The Pan-German League 1890–1914*, New York and London: Longmans Green & Co., P.S.King & Son, Ltd.
Whiteside, Andrew Gadding, 1962, *Austrian National Socialism before 1918*, The Hague: Martinus Nijhoff.
Whiteside, Andrew Gadding, 1975, *The Socialism of Fools: Georg Ritter von Schönerer and Austrian Pan-Germanism*, Berkeley, CA: University of California Press.
Williams, Gwyn A., 1968a, *Artisans and Sans-Culottes: Popular Movements in France and Britain during the French Revolution*, London: Edward Arnold.
Williams, Raymond (ed.), 1968b, *May Day Manifesto 1968*, Harmondsworth: Penguin Books.
Winchell, Mareike, 2018, 'After Servitude: bonded histories and the encumbrances of exchange in indigenizing Bolivia', *The Journal of Peasant Studies*, DOI:10.1080/0306 6150.2016.1229309.
Wittgenstein, Ludwig,1979, *Remarks on Frazer's Golden Bough*, Retford, Nottinghamshire: The Brynmill Press Limited.
Worsley, Peter, 2008, *An Academic Skating on Thin Ice*, Oxford and New York: Berghahn Books.
Wright, Erik Olin, 2010, *Envisioning Real Utopias*, London: Verso.
Wunderlich, Frieda, 1961, *Farm Labour in Germany 1810–1945*, Princeton, NJ: Princeton University Press.
Zeuske, Michael, 2016, 'Coolies – Asiáticos and Chinos: Global Dimensions of Second Slavery', in Damir-Geilsdorf *et al.* (eds.) [2016].
Žižek, Slavoj, 2010, *Living in the End of Times*, London: Verso.
Žižek, Slavoj, 2016, *Against the Double Blackmail: Refugees, Terror and Other Troubles with the Neighbours*, London: Penguin Random House.

Author Index

Abel, J.   148
Achebe, C.   153
Adams, D.   133
Alam, J.   164, 165, 167
Alavi, H.   28
Albo, G.   3
Alfaro, J.   219
Amin, Samir   226
Amin, Shahid   157
Annan, N.   83
Antal, F.   238
Anti-Slavery Reporter   123
Arblaster, A.   190
Arnold, D.   157
Aron, R.   61
Ashcroft, B.   147
Assies, W.   210

Badiou, A.   3
Bailey, F.G.   226
Banaji, J.   210
Banfield, E.C.   58
Barrientos, S.   138, 141–2
Bauer, A.   139, 217ff.
Bauer, O.   44, 46 passim, 69 passim, 89, 130, 196, 199, 220, 255
Bax, E.B.   13
Bayley, C.A.   154, 159 passim, 171, 173
Bensaïd, D.   3
Berger, J.   19, 20, 39, 58, 191, 224 passim, 231 passim, 242 passim, 260, 262
Bernstein, E.   5, 32, 44ff., 50, 53, 196–7
Bethell, L.   203, 205ff.
Beverley, J.   198ff.
Bhadra, G.   157
Bhaduri, A.   210
Bhattacharya, S.   164ff., 172–3
Blanco, H.   218–19
Blok, A.   221
Blum, J.   209
Blum, M.E.   46–7, 69 passim
Borkenau, F.   67, 69, 79
Borras, S.   200
Bose, S.K.   148
Bottomore, T.   71–2

Botz, G.   81
Bourdieu, P.   40
Bourricaud, F.   207
Bradby, B.   124
Brass, T.   10ff., 28, 31, 45, 61, 88, 97, 100, 108, 112, 123, 126, 138, 141 passim, 153 passim, 162, 166, 169, 185, 195, 200, 204, 210, 212–13, 218–19, 227, 232, 244, 248
Breman, J.   37, 98, 117 passim, 127 passim, 135, 138, 193, 210, 262
Brennan, T.   155, 159
Brenton, T.   188
Bukey, E.B.   70
Burke, E.   186
Byres, T.J.   6, 105ff., 135, 210

Caldwell, M.   226
Carlyle, T.   30, 186
Carsten, F.L.   67–8
Caudwell, C.   95
Caute, D.   61, 226
Chakrabarty, D.   157, 161
Chandavarkar, R.   159ff., 175
Chatterjee, P.   156ff., 164, 167, 171–2
Chaturvedi, V.   155, 158ff., 175
Chayanov, A.V.   42, 47, 169, 185, 226, 244–5
Chibber, V.   155
Chopra, S.   164, 166, 168
Chowdhury, K.   155
Churchill, W.S.   187, 190
Clover, C.   11
Cobban, A.   96, 184
Cohn, B.   60
Common, J.   183
Cooper, F.   156
Corbridge, S.   157
Craig, W.W.   207
Crouch, C.   84
Cuadros, C.F.   207–8

D'Eramo, M.   144
Dahrendorf, R.   84–5
Damir-Geilsdorf, S.   141
Das, R.J.   134, 142
Davies, R.H.   142

AUTHOR INDEX

de Maistre, J.   23
Derrida, J.   169
Deutscher, I.   182
Dew, C.B.   4
Dingwaney, M.   105
Dobb, M.   61, 208
Dominick, R.H.   32
Drieu la Rochelle, P.   203
Dumont, R.   226
Duncan, K.   216
Dunoyer, C.   96 passim, 110, 111, 114, 256–7

Edelman, M.   200
Eliade, M.   59
Elliott, E.N.   122
Elmhirst, L.K.   49
Engels, F.   30, 35, 89, 104–5, 112, 195–6, 226
Engerman, S.W.   105, 122–3, 140
Epstein, K.   184
Escobar, A.   247–8

Fanon, F.   226
Ferrara, F.   96
Figes, O.   182, 188
Figner, V.   24 passim, 90
Fioravanti, E.   212, 216, 219
Fischer, C.   78
Fitzhugh, G.   122
Florescano, E.   203
Fogel, R.W.   105, 122–3, 140
Forgacs, D.   168
Foster, G.M.   58
Foucault, M.   168–9, 173–4, 226
Foweraker, J.   203
Fowles, J.   227, 229, 231
Furet, F.   96

Galbraith, J.K.   13
Gay, P.   45, 57
Gex, A.   226
Ghosh, K.   148
Ginsborg, P.   3
Glyn, A.   10, 83 passim
Godechot, J.   96, 184
Goode, P.   71–2
Gracián, B.   14
Graeber, D.   6, 141
Gramsci, A.   51

Greenberg, B.   157
Griffiths, G.   147
Guérin, D.   96
Guha, Ramachandra   165
Guha, Ranajit   144, 156ff., 172–3, 198
Gunder Frank, A.   216
Gupta, D.   165
Gupta, N.   160
Gururani, S.   157

Hall, R.   200
Halpern, J.M.   58
Hardiman, D.   157, 167, 174
Harding, C.   216
Hart, D.M.   96, 100ff.
Hasan, M.   160
Heffer, S.   52, 187
Hill, C.   208
Hilton, R.   208
Hitler, A.   67, 68, 78, 81
Hobsbawm, E.J.   19, 20, 84, 157, 202, 203
  passim, 208 passim, 215 passim, 231, 256
Hochschild, A.   142
Holme, C.   186
Hoppe, H.-H.   104
Howe, I.   56
Huizer, G.   203
Hussain, A.   44
Huws, U.   138

Inden, R.   162, 165, 167ff.
Isaacman, A.F.   156

Jeffery, C.   78
Johnson, D.   96
Jones, A.   88
Joseph, G.M.   156

Kaiwar, V.   155
Kalecki, M.   5–6, 86
Kaufman, A.   4
Kautsky, K.   3, 5, 41, 50 passim, 62, 129–30,
  195ff., 247, 253
Kazin, A.   224
Keynes, J.M.   10, 61, 135, 187
King-Hall, S.   23
Kitchen, M.   199
Kohl, J.G.   48

Kothari, U.   138, 141–2
Kritsman, L.N.   189

Lacey, M.   142
Laibman, D.   135
Landis, E.C.   188
Latin American Subaltern Studies
    Group   156
Leach, E.R.   149, 160
LeBaron, G.   141ff.
Lefebvre, G.   208
LeGrand, C.C.   156
Lehmann, A.D.   157
Lenin, V.I.   2, 4, 9, 15, 24, 30 *passim*, 43–44,
    46, 51, 53, 61, 72, 74, 89, 90, 112, 182–3,
    188, 191ff., 195–6, 199, 202, 205, 252,
    261–2
Leroux, R.   100
Levitas, R.   168
Lewis, O.   58
Lichtenstein, A.   142
Liebknecht, K.   254
Liggio, L.P.   103
Lindner, U.   135, 140–41, 148ff.
Lloyd, D.   156
Lochore, R.A.   96, 103
Loew, R.   72
Löhr, L.   49
London Municipal Society   187
López Albújar, E.   220
Lowe, L.   156
Luxemburg, R.   44, 51, 113, 196, 199, 202, 254

Machiavelli, N.   14, 182
Mallon, F.E.   156
Manuel, F.E.   96, 99, 101ff.
Marchal, J.   142
MARHO   204, 218ff.
Markham, F.M.H.   96, 99, 103
Marx, K.   29, 30, 89, 104, 196, 199, 210
Mattick, P.   5–6, 10
Mayaram, S.   157
McCarthy, M.   14
McMeekin, S.   182
Mead, M.   59
Meek, R.L.   96, 101
Meillassoux, C.   213
Miller, N.N.   58–59

Mitrany, D.   47
Mohr, J.   225, 241, 246
Moore, Charles   52, 187
Moore, Clive   140
Morin, E.   241–2
Müller, G.   148
Mukherjee, S.N.   160
Mukhtyar, G.C.   123
Munck, R.   137
Munro, D.   140
Murra, J.V.   124

Naipaul, V.S.   227
Nash, M.   206
Naumann, F.   12
Newby, H.   203
Nugent, D.   156

O'Hanlon, R.   154, 159 *passim*, 173
Olusoga, D.   191
Ore, T.   219
Orwell, G.   116, 128, 183–4
Ovid [P. Ovidius Naso]   1
Oviedo, J.   198
Oxaal, I.   81

Page, T.N.   122
Paige, J.M.   203
Pandey, G.   157, 165, 172
Pandian, M.S.S.   157
Panitch, L.   3
Patel, S.   119, 121, 127
Patnaik, U.   6, 105–6, 135, 210
Pearse, A.   203
Petras, J.F.   156
Phillips, N.   138, 141–3
Pipes, R.   182, 188
Pizzorno, A.   84
Pollak, M.   81
Pollock, F.   46
Postgate, R.   65, 181
Pozzolini, A.   51
Prakash, G.   147–8, 156
Prasad, P.   210
Preobrazhensky, E.A.   43

Raico, R.   103–4
Redfield, R.   58

AUTHOR INDEX

Reed, J. 2
Renner, K. 70, 74, 90
Reyeros, R. 212
Rhys Williams, A. 2
Rodríguez García, M. 134–5, 139ff., 146–7
Rogatchev, E. 189
Rogers, E.M. 7, 58, 60
Rogger, H. 67, 68, 81–2
Rorty, R. 157
Roseberry, W. 156
Rostow, W.W. 7, 10, 58ff., 255
Roth, K.-H. 144
Rothbard, M.N. 104
Rudé, G. 96
Rudra, A. 105
Rutledge, I. 216

Saith, A. 117
Sallnow, M. 124
Salvadori, M. 44
Salvatore, R.D. 156
Sánchez, R. 124
Sarkar, S. 155, 161ff., 170ff.
Sathyamurthy, T.V. 161ff., 170–71, 175
Schlegel, F. von 185
Schlomowitz, R. 140
Schorske, C.E. 67, 81
Scoones, I. 200
Scott, J.C. 9, 35, 200, 247, 252, 262
Seal, A. 159
Sebestyen, V. 182
Second Congress of the Communist International 50
Sen, A. 210
Serge, V. 29, 254
Shachtman, M. 199
Shanin, T. 226, 244–5
Shukla, J.B. 123
Singer, M. 60
Singh, S. 159, 164, 167–8
Sinha, S. 157
Sivaramakrishnan, K. 170
Skaria, A. 157
Smaldone, W. 46–7, 69 *passim*
Snowman, D. 219
Sombart, W. 5, 44–5, 50, 53, 130, 196
Spencer, H. 101
Srinivas, M.N. 60

Stalin, J. 109, 182, 190, 193–4, 251
Stelzer, I. 128
Stephens, W.W. 96, 98ff., 107
Stern, S.J. 156
Stokes, E. 159
Sumner, W.G. 122
Sunic, T. 168

Takahashi, K. 208
Tappe, O. 135, 140–41, 148ff.
Taussig, M. 147
Tharu, S. 157
The Royal Academy of Arts 189
Thompson, E.P. 160, 162, 173–4, 193
Thorner, A. 105, 149
Thorner, D. 45, 149
Tiffin, H. 147
Tilly, C. 96
Tise, L.E. 122, 123
Toynbee, A.J. 129
Tribe, K. 44
Trotsky, L.D. 4, 9, 10, 30, 40 *passim*, 51 *passim*, 62, 109ff., 130–31, 136, 157, 182, 187ff., 195ff., 202, 226, 241, 253–4
Tudor, H. 50, 196
Tudor, J.M. 50, 196

United States Senate Commission 49
Utley, T.E. 52, 187

van der Linden, M. 134ff., 140 *passim*
van Gennep, A. 226
van Melkebeke, S. 134ff., 143ff.
Vanaik, A. 155, 159 *passim*, 170ff.
Villanueva, V. 207–8
von Bülow, Prince B. 185
von Mises, L. 104
Vyas, V.S. 122

Washbrook, D. 154, 159, 168
Weber, E. 67, 68, 81–2, 242
Weiner, M. 7, 58, 60
Weiss, J. 67, 81
Wertheimer, M.S. 69
White, B. 200
Whiteside, A.G. 67ff., 78ff.
Williams, G.A. 96
Williams, R. 193

Winchell, M.   124, 213
Wittgenstein, L.   181
Wolf, E.R.   58, 226
Wolford, W.   200
Worsley, P.   206
Wright, E.O.   3

Wunderlich, F.   50

Zeuske, M.   140ff.
Žižek, S.   3, 141

Subject Index

academia   xiii, 11, 12, 14, 16, 19, 20, 44, 116, 133,
   162, 165, 182, 183, 193, 195, 197, 198, 200,
   201, 202, 205, 222, 250, 252, 255, 260
   American   162
   Cambridge University   5, 154–55, 158ff.,
      164, 166, 175–6, 192
   katheder-socialism   3, 15, 29, 32, 69–70,
      130, 196–7, 255
   margin/mainstream   11ff., 18ff., 47, 70,
      116–17, 131ff., 154, 156, 161, 165, 175, 177,
      221–22, 228, 260
   Zurich University   26
Adler, Max   72
Adler, Victor   73, 90
Africa   16, 58, 59, 134, 142, 145, 153, 156, 204,
   248
agency
   economism   16, 37
   exposure literature   35
   mob-in-the-streets   1, 79
   radical/non-radical   2, 3, 4, 5, 14, 17, 18, 19,
      24, 31, 34, 37, 38, 41, 65, 66, 69, 71, 78, 80,
      81, 82, 83, 84–5, 90, 96, 117, 182, 194, 198,
      218, 249, 250, 252, 253, 259, 261
   spontaneity   16, 32, 33, 34, 35, 37, 39, 252
   (*See also* class, counter-revolution,
      reformism, resistance, revolution)
agrarian question
   (*See* class formation, depeasantisation/
      repeasantization, democracy,
      deproletarianization, Marxism,
      proletarianization)
agrarian reform   4, 7, 20, 44, 60, 204, 209, 223
Ali, Tariq   191ff.
anarchism   30, 243, 253
anthropology   57, 58, 60, 117, 119, 124, 149,
   203, 205, 206, 207, 212, 213–14, 221, 223,
   228, 231, 238
   fieldwork   60, 118, 119, 124, 147, 206, 207,
      212
   participant/observation   20, 119, 206,
      207, 231
Argentina   206
Asia   16, 58, 86, 134, 135, 140, 156, 162, 163, 198,
   200, 209, 217, 248, 259
   Eurasia   200

Zomia   200
Augustine, Saint   xii
Austria   17, 24, 46ff., 66 *passim*, 77ff., 87,
   89ff., 186, 198–99, 220, 253, 262–3
   Habsburgs   68, 80
   Vienna   68, 78–9, 80, 194
   (*See also* Hungary)
Austro-Marxism   xi, 15, 17, 24, 32, 41, 44, 46,
   49, 62, 65 *passim*, 78, 85, 89ff., 130, 133,
   183, 185, 196–7, 251, 255, 258, 262, 263
   co-determination   69, 74, 90, 255
   equilibrium/balance   69, 71 *passim*, 90,
      255
   interval in history   69, 71ff.
   organic democracy   69, 74, 103, 168, 255,
      263
   (*See also* Max Adler, Victor Adler, Otto
      Bauer, *katheder*-socialism, reformism,
      Karl Renner)

Bauer, Otto   44, 46ff., 69, 71 *passim*, 90, 130,
   196, 199, 220, 255
Belgium   221
Berger, John   19, 20, 39, 58, 191, 224 *passim*,
   231 *passim*, 242 *passim*, 260, 262
Bernstein, Eduard   5, 32, 44–5, 49–50, 53,
   196–7
Blanco, Hugo   218–19
Bolivia   124, 206, 213
Bolsheviks   1, 2–3, 15, 16–17, 24, 31 *passim*, 40,
   42ff., 50, 55–56, 70, 90, 133, 183, 188ff.,
   191, 251, 253, 254, 255, 262
   Mensheviks   55, 56
   (*See also* class, Lenin, Marxism, revolution,
      Russia, Trotsky, socialism)
bourgeoisie
   'progressive' national   98, 107, 136, 167,
      257
   (*See* class consciousness, class formation,
      class struggle, democracy, Marxism,
      semi-feudalism)
Brass, Denis   194
Brazil   205–6
Britain   53, 129, 183, 193, 198, 199, 226
   Benn, Tony   220
   Blair, Tony   220

Britain (*cont.*)
  Cameron, David 220
  House of Lords 123
  Labour Party 65, 88, 220
  New Labour 219–20
  New Times 219
  Thatcher, Margaret 220
  United Kingdom Independence Party (UKIP) 88–89
Burke, Edmund 186

Canada 236, 238
capitalism
  anarcho- 101
  financial 46, 48, 103, 108, 145, 228, 241, 263
  industrial 5, 6, 7, 10, 18, 42, 46, 50, 60, 61, 67, 71, 81, 83, 86, 87, 100 *passim*, 110, 114, 129, 203, 209, 215, 228, 257, 258
  kinder/caring 3, 12, 117, 128, 132, 193, 225, 252
  laissez-faire 18, 79, 96 *passim*, 108, 110, 111, 113ff., 133, 143, 252, 257, 261
  moral discourse of 113, 255
  not-yet-proper 6, 8, 110, 259
  pure xi, 18, 95, 96, 97, 101, 103 *passim*, 114, 256, 257, 258, 259
  (*See also* class, conservatism, counter-revolution, democracy, development, imperialism, labour, labour-power, liberalism, Marxism, neo-liberalism, populism, reserve army, revolution, transition)
capitalist abundance 5, 6
capitalist competition 13, 17, 48, 49, 55–6, 61 *passim*, 80ff., 87ff., 99–100, 129, 143, 145, 147, 235, 246, 250, 255, 261, 263
capitalist financialisation 6
Cardoso, Fernando Enrique 206
Caribbean 134, 216
Carlyle, Thomas 30, 186
Chayanov, A.V. 42, 46, 169, 185, 226, 244–5
Chernyshevsky, N.G. 191–2
Chile 4, 57, 189, 206, 217–18
China 58, 86, 88, 109, 134
Churchill, Winston S. 187, 190
citizenship 53–4, 57, 84, 85
Clark, Kenneth 190–91
class

(*See also* agency, capitalism, counter-revolution, development, labour, labour-power, Lenin, Marxism, migration, peasantry, proletariat, revolution, state, transition, Trotsky)
class consciousness xii, 2, 6, 9, 16, 25, 31, 32, 33, 34, 36, 37, 38, 40, 62, 80, 87, 131, 132, 145, 152, 156, 157, 174, 185, 195, 197, 200, 201, 211, 251, 254, 257, 260–61, 262
class and depeasantisation 5, 17, 20, 41, 42, 54, 62, 228, 263
class formation xii, 5, 17, 18, 36, 40, 45, 62, 111, 112, 113, 152, 156, 195, 203, 251, 262
class in-itself/for-itself 3, 5, 132, 254
class struggle xii, 2, 5, 6, 8, 9, 12, 17, 18, 32 *passim*, 40, 45, 51–2, 55, 60ff., 65 *passim*, 77, 79, 82 *passim*, 96 *passim*, 110 *passim*, 117, 125 *passim*, 136ff., 141, 144, 147, 152, 156, 168, 174, 188, 193 *passim*, 211, 214ff., 220, 223, 251, 253 *passim*
Colombia 206
colonialism xii, 28, 64, 118, 123, 134–5, 142, 143, 147–8, 155 *passim*, 172, 176, 191, 256, 261
communism 4, 43, 46, 50, 56, 76, 77, 78, 174, 187–88, 215, 222, 230, 243
Congo 145–6
conservatism xi, xiii, 2, 8, 15, 19, 40, 43, 52, 55, 59, 67, 78, 85, 89, 90, 103, 117, 128, 152, 157, 158, 164, 169, 177, 184ff., 193, 197–8, 201, 202, 220, 245ff., 248, 259, 262–3
  (*See also* capitalism, class consciousness, class struggle, counter-revolution, landlords, T.E.Utley)
counter-revolution 1, 2, 8, 17–18, 23–4, 41, 43, 50, 65 *passim*, 75, 78, 80, 84 *passim*, 182, 184, 196, 246, 251, 262, 263
  Brownshirts (SA or *Sturmabteilung*) 78
  Christian Social movement 47, 79, 80
  fascism 4, 7, 24, 53, 65, 68, 71, 78, 81, 82, 90, 91, 174–5, 188, 199, 200, 241, 251, 255
  Nazism/ National Socialist Movement 7, 53, 78, 194, 245
  Pan-Germanism 24, 47, 68, 78, 80ff., 185, 251, 262
  (*See also* Austria, conservatism, counter-revolution, French liberalism, Hitler, Nazism, peasant movements, populism, von Schönerer)

crops
  cereal   49
  coffee   145
  cotton   105, 215
Cuba   57, 182, 189, 206
culture
  art   101, 186, 189, 190, 191, 224, 227, 239–40, 247
  as empowerment   7, 65 passim, 91, 148, 155, 156, 169, 199, 200, 259, 261
  as tradition   2, 17, 33, 34, 58 passim, 79ff., 118, 153, 174, 184–5, 190–91, 198, 199, 212, 213, 225, 228, 242, 245–6, 260, 263
  music   19, 190, 194
  popular   1, 16, 19, 134, 174, 181, 193, 205, 221, 224, 225, 227, 260
  (See also conservatism, counter-revolution, development, ethnicity, historiography, intellecuals, methodology, modernisation, nationalism, Nature, non-class identities, peasantry, populism, postmodernism, religion, Subaltern Studies)

Dahrendorf, Ralf   84–5
David, Eduard   5, 44
democracy
  bourgeois   xi, 17, 52, 57, 61–2, 82, 89, 131, 174, 258
  choice   12, 33, 55–6, 139, 169, 174
  civil society   8, 43, 199, 201
  humanity   55, 102
  liberty   55, 80, 84, 85, 100, 103, 108, 236, 239
  parliamentary   xi, 17, 23, 32, 41, 48 passim, 62, 65, 66, 69 passim, 81, 89ff., 116, 239, 251, 255
depeasantisation/repeasantization   17, 20, 41, 42, 44, 54, 263
  (See also class consciousness, class formation, class struggle, counter-revolution, Marxism, populism, postmodernism, resistance, revolution, transition)
deproletarianization   12, 111, 112, 114, 125, 126, 127, 131, 132, 136, 137, 138, 141, 144, 147, 211, 260
  decommodification and   137

downsizing and   xi, 7, 86, 256
outsourcing and   xi, 7, 86, 109, 112, 146, 256
restructuring and   xii, 63, 66, 107, 112, 136, 137, 252, 256
  (See also capitalism, class struggle, depeasantisation, Marxism, proletarianisation)
Derrida, Jacques   169
Deutscher, Isaac   182
development
  as-modernization   7, 10, 20, 41, 42, 57 passim, 87, 203, 225, 228, 230, 238, 241, 245, 249, 258
  as-progress   xi, xii, 2, 9, 15, 16, 17, 20, 30, 47, 57, 58, 59, 61, 62, 63, 74, 82, 84, 85, 96, 98, 100, 103, 106, 107, 108, 109, 117, 128, 130, 137, 144, 156, 157, 164, 166, 167, 170–71, 176, 182, 187, 188, 193, 196, 201, 202, 220, 225, 227, 228, 230, 242 passim, 250, 253, 254, 256, 257
  combined and uneven   109, 137
  decade (1960s)   63, 107, 203, 209, 215, 227, 241
  Keynesian   10, 61, 135
  mercantilism   103
  neoclassical economic   105, 122, 139, 140, 218
  physiocratic   99
  qualitative improvement   84
  quantitative expansion   84
  (See also capitalism, class, depeasantsation, Enlightenment, Marxism, modernisation, socialism, transition)
Dickens, Charles   116, 128
Dobb, Maurice   61, 208
Dunoyer, Charles   96 passim, 110, 114, 256–7

Egypt   56, 57, 197–8
employment full   xi, 5–6, 8, 10, 49, 52, 61, 63, 67, 81, 82ff., 86–7, 129, 145–6, 198, 253
Enlightenment   7, 57, 147, 157, 163, 169, 171, 175, 176, 184ff., 191, 221, 248, 259, 260
environment   26, 185
  (See also Nature, peasant economy)
ethnicity
  Czech   67ff., 73, 78, 82, 90

ethnicity (*cont.*)
  German   7, 68ff., 78, 80ff., 89ff., 184, 246, 251, 262
  Jewish   78, 79, 80, 81, 262
  (*See also* conservatism, counter-revolution, development, migration, nationalism)
  Europe   16, 18, 28, 39, 45, 50, 58, 61, 66, 67, 84, 86, 91, 100, 129, 134, 135, 142, 166, 174, 191, 195, 199, 201, 207ff., 215–6, 218, 223, 225, 226, 228, 239, 241, 250, 251, 255, 261

famine   98–99, 188
food security   106
feudalism   2, 4, 6, 17, 42, 46, 53, 70, 76, 95 *passim*, 106, 108, 113ff., 121, 131–2, 136, 184, 200, 205, 208 *passim*, 222–3, 256, 257, 258
  (*See also* capitalism, semi-feudalism, socialism, transition)
Figner, Vera   24 *passim*, 90
film directors
  Eisenstein, Sergei   1
  Feyder, Jacques   1
  Iannuci, Armando   193
  Lean, David   1
  Mann, Anthony   2
  Schaffner, Franklin   1
  (*See also* films)
films
  Doctor Zhivago (1965)   1
  Inside Job (2010)   13
  Knight Without Armour (1937)   1
  Nicholas and Alexandra (1971)   1
  October (1927)   1
  The Battleship Potemkin (1925)   1
  The Death of Stalin (2017)   193
  The Fall of the Roman Empire (1964)   2
  (*See also* film directors)
Florence   182
Foucault, Michel   168–9, 173–4, 226
Fowles, John   227, 229, 231
France   98, 101, 103, 106, 131, 134, 182, 195–6, 231, 241 *passim*
  Brittany   241
  Haut-Savoie   226
  Limoges   99
  (*See also* counter-revolution, John Berger, revolution, Anne-Robert-Jacques

Turgot)

gender   8, 25, 231 *passim*, 261
  eco-feminism   168, 225
Germany   7, 12, 13, 23, 24, 47, 50, 53, 67 *passim*, 78, 80ff., 89–90, 142, 184–5, 190, 194, 196, 210, 236, 246, 251, 253, 262
Gramsci, Antonio   51, 158, 168–9, 174, 219–20
Guatemala   57, 206
Guha, Ranajit   144, 156ff., 172–3, 198
Gunder Frank, André   216
Guyana

Hall, Stuart   61
Hegel, G.W.F.   102, 164–5
Herder, Johann Gottfried von   7, 173, 184–5
historiography   19, 30, 100, 118, 123, 134, 140, 148, 156, 158, 159, 160, 164, 169, 171, 172, 173, 198, 207, 217, 218
  anti-colonial   172, 176, 261
  cliometric   100, 123, 140, 148
  Communist Party Historians' Group   222
  imperialist   xii, 145, 159
  nationalist   19, 106, 154, 155, 156, 158ff., 161ff., 164, 166, 167, 170, 171, 177, 199, 200, 259
  new Cambridge School   154, 155, 158, 159ff., 164, 166, 175, 176
  orientalist   162, 165, 167, 168, 169
Hitler, Adolf   67, 68, 78, 81, 188, 262
Hobsbawm, Eric J.   19, 20, 84, 157, 202, 203 *passim*, 208 *passim*, 215 *passim*, 231, 256
human rights   8, 34, 57, 146, 147, 217, 252
Hungary   48, 68, 186

identity, non-class   xi, 3, 7, 8, 9, 10, 11, 18, 38, 39, 134, 147, 169, 174, 201, 225, 250, 261, 262
  caste   60, 159, 164, 165, 169, 174
  communalism   159, 165, 168
  sectoral (rural/urban)   3, 39, 184, 226, 234, 235, 238
  (*See also* counter-revolution, ethnicity, gender, nationalism, populism, postmodernism, resistance, Subaltern Studies)
imperialism   9, 46, 57, 71, 73, 89, 147, 162, 166, 168
Inca   188

SUBJECT INDEX   293

India   19, 33, 45, 58, 60, 86, 105, 110, 118
    passim, 134ff., 142–3, 146ff., 154, 157
    passim, 167 passim, 200, 210, 256
    Bharatiya Janata Party (BJP)   158, 164,
      174–5
    Gujarat   118 passim, 138
Indonesia   57
intellectuals   3, 11, 13, 14, 15, 32, 36, 37, 40, 52,
    76, 100, 102, 103, 156, 157, 158, 183, 192,
    193, 197, 198, 205, 207, 242
    migrant   156
    organic   156, 192
    Western   59, 155, 162, 163
    (See also academia, Austro-Marxism,
      katheder-socialism, 'new' populist
      postmodernism, reformism, Subaltern
      Studies)
Ireland   89
Italy   53, 233

Japan   86, 134, 208
journals
    History Workshop Journal   159
    Journal of Pacific Studies   140
    Journal of Peasant Studies   11, 155
    Marxism Today   220
    New Left Review   158–9, 161, 171, 174
    Science & Society   208
    Slavery & Abolition   140
    Social Scientist   154, 158, 160, 162, 164
      passim, 172ff.

Kalecki, Michael   5, 86
Kautsky, Karl   3, 5, 41, 50ff., 55, 57, 62, 129,
    130, 195, 197, 247, 253
Keynes, John Maynard   10, 61, 135, 187
Korea   86

labour
    aristocracy   72
    attached   122, 123, 125, 134, 149
    bonded   18, 95, 106, 107, 112, 113, 117, 120,
      122, 123, 124, 125, 126, 129, 132, 139, 142,
      150, 168, 210–11, 213, 217
    coercion   64, 100, 105, 112, 120, 121, 126, 133
      passim, 143 passim, 151, 209, 211, 213, 218
    corvée   97, 99, 101, 106, 107, 215
    debt peonage   101, 106, 134, 148, 210, 218
    division of   10, 86, 87
    enganche   139, 210, 214, 217, 218, 222

    exchange/reciprocal   121, 212, 213, 222
    gender/age-specific   68, 83, 89, 140, 213,
      232, 233, 234, 237, 238, 243
    hali   120, 121, 122
    ponguaje   212
    productive/unproductive   100, 101, 103,
      104, 105, 107, 108ff., 114, 127, 209, 210, 258
    rent   99, 145, 209, 212, 214, 257
    subcontracted   112
    sweatshop   112, 146, 252
    trafficking   146
labour-power
    as property   35, 62, 102, 112, 138, 140–1
    free   12, 18, 86, 98, 102, 106, 113, 114, 122,
      126, 136, 137, 138, 142, 146, 148, 149, 152,
      218, 257
    'neo-bondage' and   126, 127, 138
    'survivals'   136
    unfree   xi, 6, 12, 18ff., 40, 50, 56, 63–4,
      76, 86, 95, 97 passim, 105 passim, 117
      passim, 125ff., 131 passim, 139 passim,
      151ff., 204, 209ff., 215, 217, 223, 252, 256,
      257, 258, 259–60
land tenure
    collective   4, 30, 31, 41, 44, 46, 47, 110, 189,
      190, 200, 202
    co-operative   45, 46, 47, 189, 204, 213, 214
    estate   1, 2, 4, 24, 25, 43, 47, 79, 108, 123,
      124, 204, 211 passim, 246
    plantation   105, 140, 145, 210, 215
    sharecropping   30, 134
    smallholding   5, 7, 16, 26, 27, 30, 31, 38, 39,
      41 passim, 50, 53, 58, 59, 62, 81, 99, 105,
      106, 126, 145, 169, 185, 188, 189, 200–201,
      209ff., 229 passim, 243, 245, 247ff.
    sub-tenant   204, 214, 219
    tenant   25, 30, 124, 145, 199, 200, 204, 209,
      212ff.
landlords
    feudal   132, 217
    Junker   142, 185
    rentier   99
Latin America   16, 20, 45, 58, 105, 136, 139,
    140, 142, 147–8, 156, 198, 200, 203 passim,
    215 passim, 236, 240, 248, 256
legislation   33, 34, 47, 48, 54, 70, 77, 79, 83,
    101, 114, 116, 142, 143, 146, 147, 185, 196,
    198, 219, 241, 244
Lenin, V.I.   2, 4, 9, 15, 24, 30 passim, 43–44,
    46, 51, 53, 61, 72, 74, 89, 90, 112, 182–3,

188, 191–2, 195–6, 199, 202, 205, 252, 254, 261, 262
liberalism   13, 14, 18, 32, 56, 70, 78, 79–80, 84, 85, 95, 96, 100, 104, 105, 110, 114, 122, 188, 194, 195, 196, 197, 256, 257, 258
  French   84, 95, 115
  (*See also* capitalism, Charles Dunoyer, the market, neo-liberal capitalism, Henri Saint-Simon, Anne-Robert-Jacques Turgot)
Liebknecht, Wilhelm   254
Lueger, Karl   67, 79ff., 90, 262
Lula   206
Luxemburg, Rosa   44, 51, 113, 196, 199, 202, 254

MacDonald, Ramsay   65
Machiavelli, Niccolò   14, 182
Mao Zedong   xiii, 169
Marcuse, Herbert   5–6, 10
market, the   xi, 2, 6, 10, 17, 44, 46, 48, 49, 55–6, 60, 61, 64 *passim*, 79, 83, 84, 86, 87, 88, 90, 91, 95 *passim*, 108 *passim*, 126, 128, 129, 136, 143, 145, 188, 189, 209, 210, 215, 216, 220, 223, 239, 250, 255, 258, 262
  (*See also* capitalism, liberalism, neo-liberalism)
Marx, Karl   xi, 6, 29, 30, 45, 59, 61, 72, 74, 85, 86, 89, 97, 102ff., 112, 114, 137ff., 141, 143, 147, 176, 195–6, 198–99, 210, 222, 226, 243
Marxism   xiff., 2 *passim*, 14 *passim*, 24, 27, 30, 32, 34, 35, 38, 41, 44ff., 50, 51, 58, 59, 61, 62, 64, 66, 70, 72, 74, 80, 85, 87, 95ff., 104–5, 110 *passim*, 125, 131, 132, 136, 138, 141 *passim*, 153 *passim*, 166 *passim*, 181 *passim*, 191 *passim*, 202, 203, 205, 208, 210, 211, 213, 217ff., 220ff., 224, 230, 238, 241, 243, 244, 247ff., 251, 253, 255, 256, 257, 258, 259, 260, 261
  'foundational'/'Eurocentric'   39, 147, 148, 157, 166, 170, 219, 247, 259, 260
  (*See also* agency, Bolsheviks, capitalism, class, depeasantisation, deproletarianisation, development, historiography, intellectuals, labour, labour-power, Lenin, Marx, proletariat, revisionism, revolution, socialism, transition, Trotsky)
Mead, Margaret   59
methodology   13, 17, 48, 60, 113, 119, 124, 149, 151, 159, 164, 176, 205, 207, 231
  'butterfly collecting'   149ff.
  (*See also* anthropology, social sciences)
Mexico   246
Middle East   134
Miéville, China   192
migration   49, 66, 67, 82, 83, 86ff., 109, 113, 118–19, 123, 129, 225, 226, 229 *passim*, 241
  Czech   67, 68ff., 90
  Irish   89, 199
  Pacific Island   140
  Polish   68
  (*See also* capitalism, class, counter-revolution, deproletarianisation, development, employment, ethnicity, identity, labour, market, Marxism, modernisation, nationalism, neo-liberalism, populism, reserve army)
modernisation   7, 10, 17, 20, 41, 57 *passim*, 78 *passim*, 191, 195, 201, 203, 209, 213, 225, 227, 228, 230, 236, 238, 241, 242, 245, 247, 248, 249, 250, 255, 256, 258
  (*See also* capitalism, class, democracy, development, full employment, industrial reserve, labour, Marxism, transition)
Möser, Justus   2, 184–5
multitude   7, 8, 54, 259
myth
  agrarian   30, 59, 155, 166, 167, 185, 232
  (*See also* anthropology, counter-revolution, culture, historiography, identity, nationalism, peasant movements, peasantry, populism, religion, Romanticism, Subaltern Studies)

Naipaul, V.S.   227
nationalism   xi, 9, 19, 57, 61, 66ff., 73, 78ff., 90–91, 106, 113, 129, 154 *passim*, 166ff., 170 *passim*, 185, 189, 195, 199–200, 220–21, 240, 250, 259, 261
  patriotism and   190, 236
Nature   7, 30, 59, 102, 116, 185, 186, 198, 227ff., 232ff., 238ff., 242–3
  birth/death   229, 230, 232, 237, 238, 242

God as 59, 102
neo-liberalism 18, 96, 157, 169
  deregulation xii, 84, 88, 91
  monetarism 84
  privatization 28, 84
  (*See also laissez-faire* capitalism, liberalism, the market)
NGOS 8, 34, 145

Orwell, George 116, 128, 183–4

Pan-Slavism 73, 262
patronage xi, 18, 116 *passim*, 125 *passim*, 193, 213, 252, 259
  as 'subsistence guarantee' 12, 18, 46, 47, 117–18, 120ff., 125, 153, 231, 247
  clients 120ff.
  (*See also* conservatism, landlordism, resistance, revisionism, the state)
peasant
  differentiation 17, 62, 165, 216
  disappearance/persistence 40, 41, 228, 246
  familism 58
  family farm 17, 20, 41 *passim*, 62, 213, 214, 227 *passim*, 239, 241, 246, 248ff., 258
  fatalism/passivity 58, 168, 230–31, 245
  fictive kinship 212–13, 222
  kinship 121, 140, 164, 185, 212–13, 214, 222, 224 *passim*
  livestock 2, 229, 232, 233, 234, 238
  localiteness 58
  middle 17, 41, 43, 44, 50, 53, 62, 131, 144, 169, 200, 245, 246, 251
  poor 4, 16, 17, 31, 39, 40–41, 43, 45, 48, 53, 62, 87, 144, 189, 200, 209, 213, 214, 219, 223, 245, 246, 248, 251, 257, 261, 262
  rich/*kulak* 4, 17, 20, 35, 41 *passim*, 53, 62, 131, 136, 144, 166, 188, 189, 200, 202, 204, 211, 213, 214, 218, 223, 240, 245, 248, 251, 256, 258, 261
peasant economy xi, 5, 17, 42–3, 46ff., 80, 95, 99, 134, 144, 169, 186, 189, 194, 201, 206, 214, 227, 232, 244, 245, 249, 250, 263
  as limited good 245
  money and 48, 213, 215, 228, 230 *passim*, 242, 244, 246
  technology and 47, 228, 231, 234, 235, 236
peasant movements 134, 154, 203, 204, 206, 207, 216, 218, 219
  Cristeros (Mexico) 246
  La Convención (Peru) 134, 204 *passim*, 216 *passim*
  Sinarquistas (Mexico) 246
  Vendée (France) 246
permanent revolution 4, 41, 62, 109, 130ff., 253
  (*See also* Marxism, socialist transition, Trotsky)
Peru 20, 124, 134, 142, 204 *passim*, 248
  FIR (*Frente de la Izquierza Revolucionaria*) 218–19
  La Convención 204–23
  PCP (*Partido Comunista Peruano*) 219
petty commodity production
  (*See* depeasantisation/ repeasantization, development, identity, land tenure, nationalism, peasant economy, peasant movements, resistance)
  crafts/handicrafts 67, 68, 228, 241
  jurandes 101–2
Philippines 134
Plekhanov, Georgi 27
Poland 68, 225
populism 11, 16, 19, 25, 27, 29, 30, 34, 38, 41, 42, 52, 58, 62, 63, 79, 80, 87, 155, 157, 169, 170, 173, 199, 200, 201, 222, 224, 225, 227, 232, 241, 244, 250, 251, 252, 254, 255, 261
  Farage, Nigel 182, 261
  Land and Freedom (*Zemlya i Volya*) 24, 25, 27, 38, 185
  Le Pen, Marine 182, 261
  popular sovereignty and 16, 29, 30
  Trump, Donald 182, 261
  Will of the People (*Narodnya Volya*) 24, 25 *passim*, 38–9, 251, 252, 253, 255, 263
  (*See also* agency, capitalism, conservatism, counter-revolution, 'new' populist postmodernism)
postmodernism, 'new' populist xii, 7, 8, 11, 15, 17, 18, 19, 20, 30, 33, 35, 38, 39, 40, 41, 53, 59, 60, 63, 85, 144, 147, 152, 153, 170, 171, 175, 182, 186, 190, 198, 199, 200, 201, 202, 221, 222, 224, 225, 231, 247 *passim*, 255, 259, 260ff.
  aporia xii, 200, 247
  'coolitude' 148–9
  'difference' xi, 8, 10, 67, 68, 70, 82, 85, 87,

129, 144, 163, 167ff., 177, 184, 185, 191, 195, 199, 200, 201, 248, 262
moral economy 169, 174
post-colonialism xii, 28, 142, 147, 155, 191, 225, 251
post-development 225, 248
post-structuralism 159, 168, 169, 225
(*See also* academia, conservatism, counter-revolution, democracy, development, ethnicity, historiography, identity, intellectuals, multitude, myth, nationalism, neo-liberalism, peasant, populism, religion, resistance, Romanticism, Subaltern Studies)
poverty 25, 27, 34, 84, 118, 127, 128, 129, 130, 132, 209, 226, 242, 259
as moral issue xi, 10, 34, 35, 36, 79, 98, 102, 103, 113, 116, 124, 128, 130, 132, 219, 224, 236, 253, 255, 262
precariat 10
Preobrazhensky, E.V. 43
Primo de Rivera, Miguel 4
proletariat 3, 4, 5, 8, 9, 32, 43, 44, 51, 52, 53, 54, 55, 61, 69, 71, 72, 73, 74, 75, 77, 104, 106, 111, 114, 130, 131, 144, 145, 185, 197, 200, 217, 226, 251, 253, 254, 262
(*See also* agency, class consciousness, class formation, class struggle, labour, labour-power, Marxism, Lenin, socialism, Trotsky)

reformism xii, 17, 41, 62, 65, 66, 69, 71, 74, 90, 196, 250, 251, 255
religion 3, 23, 40, 60, 78, 79, 98, 103, 148, 159, 165, 169, 172, 174, 185, 212, 228, 229, 261
anti-semitism 79, 81, 263
clergy 23, 96, 100, 102, 107
Evangelical Protestantism 212
fiesta system 212, 222
Katholische Volkspartei 78, 79, 80
(*See also* Austria, conservatism, counter-revolution, France, Karl Lueger)
Renner, Karl 70, 74, 90
reserve army of labour xi, 10, 17, 61, 63, 66, 83 *passim*, 109, 113, 127, 129, 193, 250, 252, 256, 261ff.
(*See also* agency, capitalism, class consciousness, class formation, class struggle, depeasantisation,

deproletarianisation, development, ethnicity, full employment, identity, labour-power, market, migration, nationalism, neo-liberalism, populism,)
resistance 2, 3, 7, 9, 18, 30, 33, 35, 36, 37, 38, 39, 41, 46, 106, 154, 156, 157, 159, 160, 168, 169, 170, 174, 198, 200, 201, 218, 225, 235, 247, 250ff., 259ff.
banditry as 220–21
quotidian 7, 9, 30, 35, 36, 38, 41, 154, 156, 157, 168, 200, 252, 253, 259, 260, 262
(*See also* agency, Austro-Marxism, colonialism, culture, democracy, development, ethnicity, human rights, identity, land tenure, modernisation, multitude, nationalism, peasant movements, populism, postmodernism, postmodernism, poverty, religion, revisionism, Subaltern Studies)
revisionism 32, 41, 45, 62, 63, 72, 96, 182, 183, 188, 189, 201, 250, 259
revolution xi, xii, xiii, 1 *passim*, 23 *passim*, 40 *passim*, 65 *passim*, 95 *passim*, 116 *passim*, 135, 136, 152, 154, 156, 181 *passim*, 203, 205, 217, 223, 225, 233, 246, 250ff.
aesthetics and 19, 189ff., 194, 201, 250
Cuban 1959 182
French 1789 7, 18, 23, 95, 96, 98, 107, 181, 182, 184, 185, 186
Green 86
Russian 1905 9, 31, 197
Russian 1917 1, 2, 5, 16, 19, 31, 42, 50, 52, 72, 181 *passim*, 194, 201, 202, 250, 251
(*See also* agency, Bolsheviks, capitalism, class, counter-revolution, development, Enlightenment, historiography, intellectuals, labour, Lenin, Marxism, peasant movements, permanent revolution, proletariat, socialism, Trotsky)
Romanticism 7, 184, 185
(*See also* counter-revolution, culture, Enlightenment, Germany, Johann Gottfried von Herder, historiography, identity, intellectuals, Justus Möser, nationalism, Nature, peasant, populism, postmodernism, religion,

SUBJECT INDEX

resistance)
Rome 2
Rostow, W.W. 7, 10, 58, 61, 255
royalty 4, 30, 48, 51, 103, 108, 185
Louis XVI 96
Russia 1, 2, 3, 5, 7, 9, 11, 16, 19, 24 passim,
  34ff., 40ff., 52, 71–2, 90, 109, 131, 181
  passim, 194ff., 200ff., 250ff., 263
autocracy 16, 24, 27, 29, 30
Emperor Alexander II 24
mir (village) 9, 16, 25ff., 30ff., 38, 43, 192
New Economic Policy 46

Saint-Simon, Henri 96 passim, 114, 256, 257
Sartre, Jean-Paul 226
Schönerer, Georg Ritter von 24, 67, 80–81, 90, 262
semi-feudalism 6, 8, 18, 20, 63, 75, 76, 95ff., 105 passim, 118, 119, 135ff., 144, 166, 167, 210, 211, 215, 254, 256ff.
(See also feudalism)
serfdom 101, 109, 210, 215
servants 24, 49, 120, 121, 122, 124, 125
Shanin, Teodor 226, 244–5
slavery, chattel 4, 55, 56, 100, 101, 103, 105, 108, 122, 123, 140, 141, 146, 150
 'modern' 140
 'new' 140
 'new coolies' 140
Social Darwinism 121, 122
social science 8, 18, 117, 133, 134, 144, 151, 200, 204, 205, 209, 261
(See also anthropology)
Social-Democracy 17, 34, 35, 47, 50, 62, 69, 70, 72, 73, 76, 77, 78, 89, 90
(See also Austro-Marxism, Bolsheviks)
socialism xi, xii, xiii, 3, 6, 8, 10, 11, 12, 14, 17, 18, 19, 20, 26, 31, 32, 35, 36, 39, 41, 42, 44, 45, 46, 47, 51, 54, 55, 56, 57, 63, 64, 66, 67, 71, 72, 77, 78, 80, 85, 87, 90, 95, 97, 98, 107, 109, 110, 114, 116, 117, 130ff., 136, 144, 154, 174, 181ff., 187, 190, 193 passim, 205, 209, 211, 215, 217, 220 passim, 248, 250, 251ff., 257ff.
(See also capitalism, class, communism, feudalism, intellectuals, labour, Marxism, permanent revolution, proletariat, revolution, transition)
Sombart, Werner 5, 44–5, 50, 53, 130, 196

South Africa 142
Spain 4, 53, 109
State xi, 1, 2, 3, 7, 9, 10, 12, 16, 17, 18, 20, 27, 28, 30, 31, 34, 36, 38, 41, 43, 44, 46, 49, 51 passim, 70 passim, 81 passim, 98, 100, 101ff., 114, 116, 119, 123, 124, 126 passim, 141ff., 165, 166, 182, 188, 190, 193, 195, 199, 200, 201, 209, 214, 217, 235, 236, 241, 246, 248, 250ff., 256, 257, 259, 262, 263
parasitical 101
welfare 10, 52, 83
strikes 6, 69, 111, 136, 218, 220, 223
Subaltern Studies 19, 39, 144, 148, 153 passim, 164 passim, 175ff., 191, 198–99, 225, 259ff.
(See also academia, citizenship, colonialism, culture, democracy, ethnicity, Ranajit Guha, historiography, imperialism, India, nationalism, new Cambridge School, peasant movements, populism, postmodernism, resistance)
'subaltern worker' 144, 145, 152
Switzerland 52

taxation xi, 27, 44, 48, 55, 88, 99, 107, 150, 188, 202, 230, 235–6, 245
taille 97, 99, 101, 106
television
  Civilization: A Personal View (1969) 191
  Tunes for Tyrants: Music and Power (2017) 194
  Ways of Seeing (1972) 239–40
Thompson, E.P. 160, 162–3, 173–4, 193
Tocqueville, Alexis de 128
trade unions 9, 16, 33, 34, 35, 38, 39, 50, 61, 73, 78, 83, 90, 112, 114, 197, 252, 261
  Provincial Federation of Peasant Unions
  (Federación Provincial de Campesinos de La Convención y Lares) 218
transition
  capitalist 6, 74, 95, 97, 98, 103, 104, 106, 107, 109, 110, 114, 167, 202, 208–9, 215, 218, 223, 254, 256
  socialist xi, xii, 2, 3, 6, 12, 16, 20, 32, 36, 41, 45, 51, 57, 62, 64, 65, 66, 67, 76ff., 80, 95, 97, 98, 109–10, 114, 127, 130, 132, 133, 136, 152, 156, 181, 183, 195, 202, 203, 205, 211,

251, 252, 256
Trotsky, Leon   4, 9, 30, 40, 41ff., 45ff., 50
  passim, 62, 103ff., 130–31, 136, 157, 182,
  187ff., 192, 195ff., 202, 226, 241, 253, 254
Turgot, Anne-Robert-Jacques   96 passim, 114,
  256, 257

United States   14, 45, 48, 49, 52, 135, 142, 225
  antebellum South   4, 105, 122–3, 140
Utley, T.E.   52, 187

Venezuela   206
Venice   243–44
von Bülow, Prince Bernard   185
von Schlegel, Frederick   185
von Vollmar, Georg   5, 44

wages   6, 10, 16, 34, 49, 50, 55, 56, 61, 63,
  67ff., 83, 86, 88–89, 91, 112, 118, 125,
  127, 129–30, 139, 145–6, 211, 248, 252,
253, 255
war
  1914–18   48, 50, 129, 185
  1939–45   5, 49, 57, 83, 135, 188, 208, 222,
    255
  Cold   188
Williams, Raymond   193
Wittgenstein, Ludwig   181
workers
  agricultural   43, 142, 199, 213, 214, 251, 261
  (See agency, capitalism, class
    consciousness, class formation, class
    struggle, development, Marxism,
    modernisation, proletariat, revolution,
    socialism)
World Bank   118, 123

Yugoslavia   221